Opening Dialogue: Understanding the
Dynamics of Language and Learning in
the English Classroom
MARTIN NYSTRAND with ADAM
GAMORAN, ROBERT KACHUR, and
CATHERINE PRENDERGAST

Reading Across Cultures: Teaching
Literature in a Diverse Society
THERESA ROGERS and
ANNA O. SOTER, Editors

"You Gotta Be the Book": Teaching
Engaged and Reflective Reading
with Adolescents
JEFFREY D. WILHELM

Just Girls: Hidden Literacies and
Life in Junior High
MARGARET J. FINDERS

The First R: Every Child's Right to Read
MICHAEL F. GRAVES, PAUL VAN DEN
BROEK, and BARBARA M. TAYLOR, Editors

Exploring Blue Highways:
Literacy Reform, School Change, and
the Creation of Learning Communities
JOBETH ALLEN, MARILYNN CARY, and
LISA DELGADO, Coordinators

Envisioning Literature:
Literary Understanding
and Literature Instruction
JUDITH A. LANGER

Teaching Writing as Reflective Practice
GEORGE HILLOCKS, JR.

Talking Their Way into Science:
Hearing Children's Questions and
Theories, Responding with Curricula
KAREN GALLAS

Whole Language Across the
Curriculum: Grades 1, 2, 3
SHIRLEY C. RAINES, Editor

The Administration and Supervision of
Reading Programs, SECOND EDITION
SHELLEY B. WEPNER, JOAN T. FEELEY,
and DOROTHY S. STRICKLAND, Editors

No Quick Fix: Rethinking
Literacy Programs in America's
Elementary Schools
RICHARD L. ALLINGTON and
SEAN A. WALMSLEY, Editors

Unequal Opportunity:
Learning to Read in the U.S.A.
JILL SUNDAY BARTOLI

Nonfiction for the Classroom:
Milton Meltzer on Writing, History,
and Social Responsibility
Edited and with an Introduction by
E. WENDY SAUL

When Children Write: Critical
Re-Visions of the Writing Workshop
TIMOTHY LENSMIRE

Dramatizing Literature in Whole
Language Classrooms, SECOND EDITION
JOHN WARREN STEWIG and
CAROL BUEGE

The Languages of Learning:
How Children Talk, Write,
Dance, Draw, and Sing Their
Understanding of the World
KAREN GALLAS

Partners in Learning: Teachers and
Children in Reading Recovery
CAROL A. LYONS, GAY SU PINNELL,
and DIANE E. DEFORD

Social Worlds of Children
Learning to Write in an
Urban Primary School
ANNE HAAS DYSON

D0208282

(Continued)

LANGUAGE AND LITERACY SERIES (*continued*)

The Politics of Workplace Literacy:
A Case Study
  SHERYL GREENWOOD GOWEN

Inside/Outside:
Teacher Research and Knowledge
  MARILYN COCHRAN-SMITH
  and SUSAN L. LYTLE

Literacy Events in a
Community of Young Writers
  YETTA M. GOODMAN
  and SANDRA WILDE, Editors

Whole Language Plus:
Essays on Literacy in the
United States and New Zealand
  COURTNEY B. CAZDEN

Process Reading and Writing:
A Literature-Based Approach
  JOAN T. FEELEY,
  DOROTHY S. STRICKLAND,
  and SHELLEY B. WEPNER, Editors

The Child as Critic:
Teaching Literature in Elementary
and Middle Schools, THIRD EDITION
  GLENNA DAVIS SLOAN

The Triumph of Literature/
The Fate of Literacy: English in the
Secondary School Curriculum
  JOHN WILLINSKY

The Child's Developing Sense of Theme:
Responses to Literature
  SUSAN S. LEHR

Literacy for a Diverse Society:
Perspectives, Practices, and Policies
  ELFRIEDA H. HIEBERT, Editor

The Complete Theory-to-Practice
Handbook of Adult Literacy:
Curriculum Design and
Teaching Approaches
  RENA SOIFER, MARTHA IRWIN,
  BARBARA CRUMRINE, EMO HONZAKI,
  BLAIR SIMMONS, and DEBORAH YOUNG

# THE FIRST R

*Every Child's Right to Read*

## MICHAEL F. GRAVES
## PAUL VAN DEN BROEK
## BARBARA M. TAYLOR

### EDITORS

**TEACHERS COLLEGE PRESS**

Teachers College, Columbia University
New York and London

Published by Teachers College Press, 1234 Amsterdam Avenue, New York, NY 10027

*Library of Congress Cataloging-in-Publication Data*

The first R : every child's right to read / Michael F. Graves, Paul
van den Broek, Barbara M. Taylor, editors.
    p. cm. — (Language and literacy series)
    Includes bibliographical references and index.
    ISBN 0-8077-3533-7 (cloth). — ISBN 0-8077-3580-9 (pbk.)
    1. Reading (Elementary)  2. Children—Language.  3. Reading
comprehension.  I. Graves, Michael F.  II. Broek, Paul van den.
III. Taylor, Barbara (Barbara M.)  IV. Series: Language and literacy
series (New York, N.Y.)
LB 1573.F526   1996
372.41—dc20                                                96-15093

ISBN 0-8077-3580-9 (paper)
ISBN 0-8077-3533-7 (cloth)

Printed on acid-free paper
Manufactured in the United States of America

03  02  01  00  99  98  97  96    8  7  6  5  4  3  2  1

# Contents

**Acknowledgment**                                                                vii

**Introduction**   The Continuing Quest Toward Literacy
                   for All Children                                                 ix
                   *Michael F. Graves*

**Chapter 1**   Literacy and Learning                                                1
                *Ernest L. Boyer*

### PART I   THE ROOTS OF LITERACY

**Chapter 2**   Creating and Sustaining a Love of Literature . . . And
                the Ability to Read It                                              15
                *Elfrieda H. Hiebert*

**Chapter 3**   What It Means to Learn to Read                                      37
                *Charles A. Perfetti and Sulan Zhang*

**Response**   Looking Beyond Ourselves to Help All Children
               Learn to Read                                                        62
               *Barbara M. Taylor*

### PART II   CHANGING CURRICULUM AND
             CLASSROOM DISCOURSE

**Chapter 4**   Literature-Based Curricula in High-Poverty Schools                  73
                *Richard Allington, Sherry Guice, Nancy Michelson,*
                *Kim Baker, and Shouming Li*

**Chapter 5**   Questioning the Author: An Approach to Developing
                Meaningful Classroom Discourse                                      97
                *Margaret G. McKeown, Isabel L. Beck, and*
                *Cheryl A. Sandora*

**Response**    Howling in the Wind: Academics Try to Change
                Classroom Reading Instruction                        120
                *S. Jay Samuels*

                **PART III   PHONOLOGICAL PROCESSES
                AND CONSTRUCTION OF MEANING**

**Chapter 6**   Preventing and Remediating Reading Disabilities:
                Instructional Variables That Make a Difference for
                Special Students                                     133
                *Joseph K. Torgesen and Steven A. Hecht*

**Chapter 7**   How Do Children Understand What They Read and
                What Can We Do to Help Them?                         160
                *Tom Trabasso and Joseph P. Magliano*

**Response**    On Becoming Literate: The Many Sources of Success
                and Failure in Reading                               189
                *Paul van den Broek*

                **PART IV   TEACHER DEVELOPMENT AND
                CLASSROOM ASSESSMENT**

**Chapter 8**   Improving the Literacy Achievement of Low-Income
                Students of Diverse Backgrounds                      199
                *Kathryn H. Au and Claire L. Asam*

**Chapter 9**   Assessing Critical Literacy: Tools and Techniques    224
                *Robert Calfee*

**Response**    Improving Literacy Instruction and Assessment
                for All Children                                     250
                *Susan M. Watts*

**Conclusion**  Reclaiming the Center                                259
                *P. David Pearson*

**About the Contributors**                                           275

**Index**                                                            285

# Acknowledgment

For 29 years, from 1937 to 1966, Guy Bond served the University of Minnesota and children and teachers throughout the nation as one of the foremost reading educators of his time. He authored a host of articles on reading instruction and diagnosis of reading problems, co-authored the leading reading diagnosis text of the time — *Reading Difficulties* — and served as the principal author of a major basal reading series. He also served as principal investigator of the largest investigation of beginning reading instruction ever conducted — the First Grade Studies — and as the advisor and mentor of a group of students who themselves became national leaders in reading education.

Guy Bond died in 1980, but his contributions to the field of reading continue to be felt. In 1994, through the generosity of Fredericka Bond, The University of Minnesota College of Education and Human Development established the Guy Bond Chair in Reading, a perpetual endowment to promote the cause of literacy and literacy instruction. The Guy Bond Memorial Reading Conference, which served as the impetus for this volume, was one of the first activities of the endowment. We are very thankful to Dr. Bond for being who he was and doing what he did for children, and we are very thankful to Fredericka Bond for giving us the opportunity to continue to pursue Dr. Bond's goal of literacy for all children.

INTRODUCTION

# The Continuing Quest
# Toward Literacy for All Children

## MICHAEL F. GRAVES
*University of Minnesota*

In 1979, several years before the publication of *A Place Called School* and while he was in the process of gathering data for that widely read report on the malaise of American high schools, John Goodlad wrote a slim volume titled *What Schools Are For*. In this book, Goodlad speculated on three broad questions: What are schools asked to do? What do schools actually do? And what should schools do? Although the book provides some answers to all three questions, its focus is on the discrepancy—Goodlad might well say the *chasm*—between what schools do, on the one hand, and what schools should do, on the other. Goodlad saw this chasm as broad and deep, a condition that clearly called for massive changes in schools. And this realization led him to write with a good deal of passion about the desperate need for change.

In 1994, *What Schools Are For* was reissued—without change. That a book arguing for massive change could be re-released without updating 15 years after it was first published suggests strongly that very few changes— at least very few changes of the sort Goodlad saw as essential—actually had taken place. And in the preface of the new edition, Goodlad says this: "The question arises as to whether the passage of these 15 years has revised my thinking, whether I would like to revise or retract what I wrote then. I would not. In the [original] preface, dated precisely 15 years ago, I referred to some stridency in my writing driven by the urgency of the issues raised. Were I to rewrite today, I would do so with even more urgency and even more passion" (p. 9). Quite obviously, the changes that Goodlad saw, and still sees, as necessary to move schools toward doing what they should be doing, have yet to take place.

The problem of learning how schools can effectively teach all children to read would appear to be markedly less complex than that of agreeing on what schools ought to do, and one would expect it to be more readily solved. Yet, as I consider the status of reading instruction and students' achievement in reading today and look back over those same 15 years that Goodlad speaks of, or back over the 4 decades since the first edition of Bond and Tinker's *Reading Difficulties* (1951) was published, Goodlad's feelings of urgency and passion seem appropriately applied to the field of reading education.

On the one hand, the past several decades have produced some truly remarkable insights into the reading process. Concepts such as the schema-theoretic model of reading (one of a number of concepts that chapter author P. David Pearson has illuminated), the role of prior knowledge, the interactive nature of reading, the importance of efficient decoding (a position that chapter authors Charles Perfetti and Joseph Torgesen have long maintained), the function of automaticity (a concept first described by chapter author Jay Samuels), the sorts of mental processing a reader engages in as he or she reads (something chapter authors Tom Trabasso and Paul van den Broek have investigated throughout much of their careers), the sorts of texts that foster learning and those that do not (one of many practical matters chapter authors Margaret McKeown and Isabel Beck have researched), the importance of readers' being strategic as they grapple with text, the centrality of metacognition to effective reading, the critical role of affective factors, the influence of context on learning, and the active, constructive nature of learning in general—all of these are centrally important concepts that have both obvious and not-so-obvious instructional implications.

Many of these implications have been investigated. We have substantial data supporting the efficacy of repeated reading to increase automaticity. We have validated procedures for teaching full and deep word meanings (a topic chapter author Susan Watts continues to pursue). Several early intervention programs (including programs developed by chapter authors Elfrieda Hiebert and Barbara Taylor) have been shown to be successful when used with first-grade students who appear destined for failure in learning to read. Specific approaches to working with children from non-mainstream cultures have been developed and tested (by chapter author Kathryn Au, among others). Sustained silent reading has been shown to be more effective than worksheets in fostering reading proficiency. Ways of actively engaging students with texts have been developed and validated. Also, in my judgment at least, appropriate comprehension strategies to teach to children have been identified, and effective approaches to teaching comprehension strategies have been documented.

Over this same period, we also have discovered or rediscovered a good deal of common sense. We now recognize, but did not always, that having beginning readers read nonsense is nonsense, that it is better for students to read quality literature than poorly written texts, that filling out worksheets is excellent practice for filling out worksheets, that (as chapter author Richard Allington has so memorably argued) one gets good at reading by doing a lot of reading and one gets even better at reading by doing a lot more reading, that being banished forever to the dumb group leaves a child banished forever to the dumb group, that (as chapter author Robert Calfee has stressed repeatedly) a machine-scored, multiple-choice test is a far-from-adequate and perhaps even misleading gauge of children's reading proficiency, that reading and writing reinforce each other and can profitably be taught together, and that leading students to love reading—to choose reading now and in the future as a road to information, pleasure, and self-discovery—is as important as teaching them how to read.

Paralleling our increased understanding of the reading process, our growing ability to design effective instruction, and our rediscovery of common sense, there appears to have been a significant shift in reading education practices in schools—a shift toward more open, more holistic, and more student-centered practices. Instructionally oriented journals such as *The Reading Teacher* and *Journal of Adolescent and Adult Literacy* regularly include articles and columns on whole language, literature-based reading, process writing, and performance assessment. And the 1992 NAEP study, which included questions to fourth-grade teachers about their instructional practices, indicated that 82% of the fourth-grade teachers surveyed reported at least moderate emphasis on whole language, 88% reported at least moderate emphasis on literature-based reading, and 98% reported at least moderate emphasis on integrating reading and writing activities (Mullis, Campbell, & Farstrup, 1993).

All this—the theoretical discoveries, the successful instructional interventions, the spreading fidelity to common sense, and the changes in school practices—seems very much worth celebrating. Yet despite these positive efforts and outcomes, significant problems remain. Increasingly frequently, I hear comments from teachers about primary-grade students who are not learning to read, who simply are not getting it and are being left behind. Turning to the national scene, I would note that the same NAEP report that indicates that the vast majority of teachers embrace contemporary and widely recommended approaches to instruction, also indicates that only 25% of the fourth graders tested demonstrated solid academic achievement and only 2% of the twelfth graders tested demonstrated superior performance. A comparison of NAEP reading data over the 25 years in which NAEP has assessed reading indicates that—except for the fact that Black and Hispanic youngsters have made some substantial gains, gains that still leave them scoring well below their White counterparts—American students' reading performance over the past 25 years has remained very nearly constant (Mullis et al., 1993; Williams, Reese, Campbell, Mazzeo, & Phillips, 1995). Additionally, recent data on students' habits and attitudes toward reading are discomforting. To quote from one recent report, "Students appear to be infrequent readers, and the few changes that have occurred over time reflect decreases in propensity to read" (National Center for Educational Statistics, 1992).

It is our failure to improve the reading proficiency of American students, despite what appear to be a lot of good things that have happened, that engenders the sense of urgency I described earlier. That sense of urgency becomes even stronger when I consider two well-known social factors that are now and will continue to influence literacy instruction—the increasing number of students entering schools for whom learning to read is likely to prove difficult and the increasing literacy demands of our evolving society.

The percentage of students likely to experience difficulties in learning to read—the percentage of poor students, minority students, and students for whom English is not a first language—is already very large and continues to grow. Commerce Department statistics indicate that 38.1 million Americans, 14.5% of the population, live below the poverty line (U.S. Department of Commerce, 1995). Commerce Department projections indicate that by the turn of the century approximately 35% of school-age children will be minorities (U.S. Department of Commerce, 1992). And a recent report by the American Council on Education indicates that the foreign-born population of the United States—over a fourth of whom live in households where very little or no English is spoken—is growing at a rate four times faster than the population as a whole (Otuya, 1994).

The changing expectations of schooling represent still another factor influencing the urgency of the matter. Literacy demands have, of course, increased dramatically over the past two centuries—from signing one's name and "reading" essentially memorized portions of the Bible to reading complex texts and formulating equally complex responses. Lauren Resnick (1987) has noted that the skills and abilities that employers demand today are at least those demanded for college entrance just a few years ago, and she has argued that in the near future entry level jobs will require skills equivalent to those of today's college sophomores. As David Perkins (1992), John Bruer (1994), and nearly every national report on the status of education have pointed out, full participation in the American society, indeed the continuance and prosperity of the American society itself, will require much higher levels of literacy than have ever been demanded before, and it will require these higher levels from a large percentage of the population. As Bruer notes, these "rising expectations represent an unprecedented challenge to public education" (p. 7), a challenge that no previous educational system has even attempted to meet.

This, then, is the context in which the present chapters were written—a context in which there have been huge gains in our understanding of the reading process, a context in which we appear to have made great progress in understanding how to teach reading, and a context in which a number of changes appear to have been implemented in schools—and yet a context in which substantial numbers of students fail to gain adequate reading skills and only a handful gain higher-level skills, a context in which schools can expect increasing numbers of students for whom learning to read traditionally has proven difficult, and a context in which society as a whole is demanding and will continue to demand substantially more sophisticated reading skills than any past society has even considered.

Not all of the chapter authors, of course, take precisely this view of the present-day context of reading instruction. The contributors to this volume represent a wide range of viewpoints and an even wider range of interests. Some, I believe, view the shift toward more open, more holistic, and more student-centered practices as incomplete and advocate more movement in the same direction. Others, I believe, view important elements of literacy instruction as having been displaced or at least inappropriately minimized in recent years and call for the reinstatement of some of the goals and values of more traditional approaches. Some take more theoretical stances; and, at least in the short run, their work is indeed more theoretical than practical. Others are intensely practical and describe classroom practices that are already in place in some schools and could be implemented in others tomorrow. Some focus primarily on phonological processing and the centrality of basic decoding skills. Others focus primarily on comprehension and critical thinking.

However, all of the authors share several characteristics that make their research and theorizing particularly worth consideration if we are to solve the conundrum of why we have not moved further in ensuring literacy for all students. For one thing, although each author would acknowledge the place of insight and intuition in solving educational problems, each also believes in the role of empirical observation in arriving at conclusions on important educational matters. For another, although each author has pursued a number of topics over the course of his or her career, each also has pursued a particular theme, a specific line of inquiry, over a lengthy period of time, decades in most cases. For still another, although each author has definite ideas about reading and reading instruction, each also recognizes that his or her ideas — the topic that he or she investigates — are only one of a number of important facets of reading. That is to say, each recognizes that the argument that metacognition, or affective factors, or authentic assessment is particularly important simply does not imply that some other facet of reading — phonemic awareness, or word recognition, or vocabulary knowledge — is unimportant. This realization leads them to attend to the reasoned arguments of others, to consider carefully data that challenge their position, and to learn from others. As David Pearson notes in the concluding chapter of the book, such civility and good sense often have been in short supply in recent years.

## INTRODUCTION TO THE CHAPTERS

At the Bond Conference itself, Ernest Boyer served as the keynote speaker, energizing the participants and reminding all of us of the centrality of language to learning and to life itself. His chapter here can serve a similar purpose, reminding us, for example, that the vast majority of teachers see teaching children to read as their number one priority, that reading is not just another subject but the means through which other subjects are pursued, that all children can learn to read, that we need to hold high expectations for all children, and that we need to instill in all children the confidence and motivation that will enable them to become successful readers. "Clearly," Boyer concludes, "the most urgent task our generation now confronts is to ensure literacy, not just for the most advantaged, but . . . for all children."

In the two chapters that follow Boyer's, Elfrieda Hiebert considers the all-too-unanswered question of what to do with children who have reached third or fourth grade and still struggle with basic literacy, and Charles Perfetti and Sulan Zhang draw some comparisons between learning to read Chinese and learning to read English that illustrate what they see as the fundamental problem in learning to read. Hiebert begins her chapter by pointing out that the theme of remediation is not a popular one in today's literacy community. She then notes that when compensatory literacy programs are increasingly directed at early intervention, as is currently the case, there may be few opportunities within schools and classrooms for solving the problems of middle-elementary-grade students who are still struggling with literacy. Next, she describes a project in which she and two third-grade teachers developed a small-group remedial component for struggling, older readers and integrated that component into the students' existing literature-based classroom programs. Her description focuses on four aspects of the project: identifying the problem, examining the research literature for solutions, transforming the solutions for particular classroom contexts, and evaluating the project and its effects.

Perfetti and Zhang begin their chapter by arguing that the fundamental problem the child faces in learning to read — whether he or she is learning to read a largely ideographic language such as Chinese or an alphabetic language such as English — is to learn how the writing system works, how the marks on the page are used to represent the sounds of the language. They then go on to describe some research-based comparisons between English and Chinese that demonstrate the pervasive role of phonology in learning to read either language. Ultimately, Perfetti and Zhang argue that "we need to understand that the child comes to the reading situation not only with a strong language competence, but with a strong proclivity to use phonology in encoding and representing linguistic messages in memory." By concentrating on teaching the child how the writing system works, beginning reading programs can best build on this language competence and proclivity to use phonology.

Barbara Taylor's comments focus on the way in which both Hiebert and Perfetti and Zhang help us to learn by looking beyond ourselves. Hiebert forces us to look beyond current and popular early intervention and literature-based reading programs to consider what is happening to struggling readers beyond the primary grades. Perfetti and Zhang force us to look beyond the English writing system and reading education in the United States to consider what an understanding of the Chinese writing system and methods of reading education in China can suggest about methods of reading instruction here.

In the next two chapters, Richard Allington and his colleagues describe the implementation of literature-based instruction in six schools, and Margaret McKeown and her colleagues discuss a new approach to encouraging young students to engage deeply with text ideas. Allington and his colleagues begin with a review of existing research on implementing literature-based instruction and then discuss the implementation of literature-based instruction in six schools — two of which used literature-based anthologies, two of which used trade books and basals, and two of which used trade books exclusively. In addition to providing a good deal of information about the positive reading practices that take place in these settings, Allington and his colleagues raise several thought-provoking and troublesome issues. Perhaps the most troublesome issue is that these teachers often were confronted with more diverse groups of students and more lower-achieving students at the same time that they were being pressed to use a single, standard curriculum for all students, a situation that seems unlikely to provide lower-achieving students with the support they need.

After reviewing the background and initial effects of the approach called Questioning the Author, McKeown and her colleagues present a qualitative analysis of the classroom discourse patterns that appeared to result from the approach, an analysis that showed that students were exhibiting greater involvement with text ideas and focusing more on meaning in their interaction with text. Next, using a number of excerpts of student and teacher discussions, the authors illustrate the changes that occurred. Finally, McKeown and her colleagues describe the collaborative interactions that they and their teacher colleagues engaged in to effect these changes and discuss how their future work will include developing resources — specifically, printed material and videotapes — that have the potential to reach much larger numbers of teachers than could they or other resource personnel.

S. Jay Samuels's comments on the chapters by Allington and colleagues and McKeown and colleagues focus on the tradition of controversy and change in reading instruction in the United States, a tradition that has been a part of reading education since the colonial period. Literature-based instruction and approaches such as Questioning the Author are part of this long history of new ideas. Like previous ideas for change in the classroom, Samuels maintains, the success of these ideas will depend on how they fit in with teachers' existing belief systems and the persistence of advocates of the ideas in disseminating them.

In the next set of chapters, Joseph Torgesen and Steven Hecht discuss the nature of phonologically based reading disabilities and their research on instructional approaches to preventing such difficulties, and Tom Trabasso and Joseph Magliano consider what it means to understand what one reads and draw on their research to describe some ways of helping students understand better. Torgesen and Hecht begin by describing the research that led to our current understanding of phonologically based reading disabilities, the nature of such disabilities, and their prevalence. They then outline some of the alternative instructional approaches suggested by the research, discuss some of the variables they are currently investigating in their long-term study of prevention and remediation of phonologically based reading difficulties, and present some preliminary results of their study. Finally, Torgesen and Hecht suggest some remaining questions and future directions for research. As Torgesen and Hecht's research richly illustrates, even when students' reading difficulties are relatively clear and resources are quite substantial, designing and evaluating an effective compensatory program is a major challenge and demands our very best efforts.

Trabasso and Magliano describe and integrate some 15 years of research in which they have carefully analyzed how text is organized and what is required to understand it, how text is actually understood during reading, what sorts of assessment methods can be used to reveal understanding, and how the knowledge that has been gained from their research might be applied in teaching students to better understand what they read. Their research shows that text can be fruitfully analyzed in terms of its episodic structure and the causal relations that hold among sentences, that comprehension requires readers to integrate information and make inferences across sentences, and that both asking questions after reading and asking students to think aloud during reading can reveal important comprehension processes. Trabasso and Magliano conclude their chapter with a discussion of using a think-aloud procedure and questions to promote comprehension.

Paul van den Broek's comments stress that, although Torgesen and Hecht deal with phonological processes of beginning readers with reading difficulties and Trabasso and Magliano deal with comprehension processes of relatively advanced readers with no particular problems in reading, the two chapters do not in fact represent different views of the reading process. Proficiency in both areas is crucial for all readers, van den Broek explains, but different readers will exhibit different strengths and weaknesses in these and other areas and will travel different roads in becoming accomplished readers.

In the final pair of chapters, Kathryn Au and Claire Asam report the results of the most recent 5 years of the Kamehameha Elementary Education Program (KEEP), a long-term program aimed at improving the literacy achievement of students of Native Hawaiian ancestry, and Robert Calfee considers some of the issues involved and the approaches that can be used in assessing *critical literacy*, which he defines as "the capacity to use language as a tool for thinking and communicating." Au and Asam begin by noting the importance of the standards movement for those concerned with the literacy achievement of disadvantaged students and by describing the theoretical perspective of social constructivism, which underlies recent work at KEEP. They then describe the changes in the curriculum, assessment, and teacher development that began in 1989 in response to testing that suggested that KEEP students were not succeeding as hoped. They conclude with a detailed description of the year-to-year successes and failures they experienced as teachers attempted to implement the new whole literacy curriculum. Au and Asam stress the need for simultaneously considering curriculum, assessment, and teacher development when attempting to change schools, particularly the need to support teachers in the change process.

After defining critical literacy, which he sees as vital for success in today's information age, Calfee describes a framework for assessing critical literacy — a framework that considers the purpose of the assessment, what needs to be taken into account in designing the assessment, how evidence will be collected and analyzed, how the evidence will be interpreted and evaluated, and how and to whom reporting should be done. Following this, Calfee uses his experiences with statewide assessment in California and Kentucky to comment on a variety of problems and possibilities of alternative assessments. Next, he returns to his assessment framework and shows how it can guide school faculty as they think about school-based programs for assessing their students' literacy. Calfee concludes by describing a strategy for building a reporting system that highlights and makes public teacher judgments.

Susan Watts's comments focus on the common ground shared by Au and Asam and by Calfee. Watts applauds the fact that both chapters argue for a curriculum based on a developmental model of reading and emphasize the value of teachers being closely involved in assessment. She also recognizes, as do Calfee and Au and Asam, that teacher development is crucial to effecting school change and that long-term collaborative efforts in which teachers are equal partners in the enterprise offer the best chance of success.

In the concluding chapter of the book, P. David Pearson conducts a cost–benefit analysis of recent changes in the field, asking whether the progress that has been made in moving toward more holistic and student-centered approaches has come at too great a cost. After considering curricular, philosophical, and political perspectives underlying whole language and some of the casualties of the movement, Pearson presents his plan for "reclaiming the center" — a set of core principles, many of which are consistent with whole language and many of which are consistent with earlier and more traditional approaches to literacy education. Although Pearson's principles reflect a good deal of common sense, much of what they suggest is, unfortunately, not common practice. They are thus a set of principles well worth serious consideration.

One common feature of many of the chapters deserves special mention. We suggested to the senior author of each chapter that it might be useful to describe the intellectual journey that led him or her to the present research and to suggest where the research is next headed. Many of the chapters reflect this suggestion and thus include some unusually rich context for the work presented. We believe that you will find both the authors' current work and the history that surrounds their work interesting and informative.

Finally, as you examine the research of our contributors and seek to integrate their findings with your own and to consider how their findings might influence your efforts to make "The First R" a reality for all students, the words of Nate Gage (1989) seem worth recalling.

> Educational research is no mere spectator sport, no mere intellectual game, no mere path to academic tenure and higher pay, not just a way to make a good

living or even to become a big shot. It has moral obligations. The society that supports us cries out for better education for its children and youth — especially the poor ones, those at risk, those whose potential for a happy and productive life is all too often going desperately unrealized. (p. 10)


# REFERENCES

Bond, G. L., & Tinker, M. A. (1951). *Reading difficulties: Their diagnosis and correction*. New York: Appleton-Century-Crofts.

Bruer, J. T. (1994). *Schools for thought*. Cambridge, MA: MIT Press.

Gage, N. L. (1989). The paradigm wars and their aftermath: A "historical" sketch of research on teaching since 1989. *Educational Researcher, 4*(7), 4–10.

Goodlad, J. I. (1994). *What schools are for*. Bloomington, IN: Phi Delta Kappa.

Mullis, I. V. S., Campbell, J. R., & Farstrup, A. E. (1993). *NAEP 1992 reading report card for the nation and the states*. Washington, DC: U.S. Department of Education.

National Center for Educational Statistics. (1992). *NAEPfacts: Trends in school and home contexts for learning*. Washington, DC: U.S. Department of Education.

Otuya, E. (1994). *The foreign-born population of the 1990s: A summary*. Washington, DC: American Council on Education.

Perkins, D. (1992). *Smart schools: From training memories to education minds*. New York: Free Press.

Resnick, L. B. (1987). *Education and learning to think*. Washington, DC: National Academy Press.

U.S. Department of Commerce. (1992). *Projections of the population of the United States: 1992 to 2050* (Series P–25). Washington, DC: U.S. Census Bureau.

U.S. Department of Commerce. (1995). *Income, poverty, and valuation of noncash benefits: 1994* (P60–189). Washington, DC: U.S. Census Bureau.

Williams, P. L., Reese, C. M., Campbell, J. R., Mazzeo, J., & Phillips, G. N. (1995). *1994 NAEP reading: A first look*. Washington, DC: Department of Education.

CHAPTER 1

# Literacy and Learning

## ERNEST L. BOYER

*President, The Carnegie Foundation for the Advancement of Teaching*

It is indeed fitting that we are gathered here to share our beliefs and findings on reading as a tribute to the truly remarkable contributions of Professor Guy Bond. For almost 30 years, this outstanding scholar served with great distinction at the University of Minnesota. Even more important, as one of the most outstanding reading educators of his time, he served children and teachers throughout the nation. While Professor Bond's specific focus was on reading, in a larger sense his entire professional career affirmed what I would describe as the "sacredness of language."

Language is our most essential social function. Steven Pinker reminds us of this in his book *The Language Instinct* (1994). "Language," he writes, "is so tightly woven into human experience that it is scarcely possible to imagine life without it." He goes on to say, "If you find two or more people together anywhere on earth, they will soon be exchanging words. When there is no one to talk with, people talk to themselves, to their dogs, even to their plants" (p. 17). We cannot help but talk. First comes life, then language.

In most respects the human species is far less well equipped than other creatures on the planet. We are no match for the lion in strength; we are outstripped by the ostrich when it comes to speed. No human can outswim the dolphin, and we surely see less acutely than the hawk. But in one area, the exquisite use of symbols, we are, in fact, superior. This capacity sets human beings apart from all other forms of life, the porpoise and the bumblebee notwithstanding. It is through language that we define who we are and imagine what we might become, and it is through language that we are connected to each other.

Language begins, of course, long before a child marches off to school. It begins, I'm convinced, even before birth itself, as the unborn infant monitors the mother's voice and listens to the rhythm of her heart. There is a theory that the reason the first words are *mama* and *dada* and *baba* is that they have the rhythm of the heartbeat. It is fascinating, and I believe no accident, that the three middle-ear bones — the hammer, the anvil, and the stirrup — are the only bones that are fully formed at birth. Young children start to listen before they start to speak.

Following birth, a child's language exponentially expands, first with coos, then phonemes, then isolated words, followed by complicated syntax. By the time a child enters school for formal learning, he or she has mastered on average more than 3,000 words and has achieved a remarkable competence in both understanding and using the complexities of grammar. But all of this has occurred without a teacher. The instinct for language is imprinted in the genes, a God-given, gene-driven capacity that emerges with life itself. Lewis Thomas (1983) captured the essence of this miracle when he suggested that childhood is for language.

I am dazzled by the capacity of young children to use words not only for affection or questions or conversation, but also as weapons of assault. When I was growing up in Dayton, Ohio, I used to say to playmates who would tease me, "Sticks and stones will break my bones, but names will never hurt me." What nonsense! I'd usually say that with tears running down my cheeks, thinking all the time, Hit me with a stick, but stop the words that wound so deeply. Isn't it amazing that 2- and 3- and 4-year-olds discover this power, put the words together, and sling them out like arrows, knowing precisely how to hit the mark, and all of that without a formal teacher?

Research reveals that children who fail to develop proficiency in language during the first years of life are up to six times more likely to experience reading problems when they go to school (Clapp, 1988). Parents are, in fact, the child's first and most essential teachers. It is in the home where children must become linguistically empowered. Wouldn't it be wonderful if every child in this country grew up in a language-rich environment, where words were used to encourage what is best in humanity? Wouldn't it be wonderful if children received thoughtful answers to their questions instead of "Shut up" or "Go to bed"? Wouldn't it be wonderful if bookshelves in every home were filled with children's books instead of knick-knacks and plastic flowers? And what if all parents would turn off the television and read to their children at least 30 minutes every night?

Excellence in education means understanding that language begins early and that all children need and deserve an environment that nurtures and enhances the natural intelligence for communication. Hannah Nuba, a librarian at the New York Public Library, has said that one wonderful way parents can promote language is through reading to their children beginning right after birth (Nuba-Scheffler, Sheiman, & Watkins, 1986). She said, "I am often asked by . . . new parents about the best time for introducing books to young children. My answer is always: 'Right now'" (Nuba, 1989, p. 19). This bonding around books can be a great experience for parents and grandparents, too. I must have read Dr. Seuss a hundred times, to my children and my grandchildren, but each time is a joyful journey as we playfully imagine eating green eggs and ham.

Reading expert Bernice E. Cullinan, of New York University, put it well when she wrote: "Children who sit beside a reader and follow the print from an early age learn to read quite 'naturally.' We know that the modeling has a lasting effect; children do what they see others do" (Putnam, 1994, p. 363). Children who are read to by their parents are inclined to become good readers later on.

Children's curiosity about language is stimulated not just by books, but also by the signs, signals, and symbols that surround them in their neighborhoods. Recently I talked with Kristy McDaniel, a wonderfully creative teacher at Jackson-Keller Elementary School in San Antonio, who told me that she began the first day of school last year by asking her new students, "How many in this class know how to read?" All the children dropped their heads in silence. Ms. McDaniel then switched on a slide projector and flashed familiar neighborhood images on the blackboard. First came a stop sign, and she asked, "How many can read this?" Every child shouted out the word, "*Stop!*" Then came the image of a green traffic light, and everyone shouted, "*Go!*" Then came a picture of the "golden arches" and everyone shouted, "*McDonald's!*" She then asked, "How many of you can read?" Every hand enthusiastically went up.

I am not suggesting that preschoolers be forced to learn the alphabet, or to memorize words, or to move methodically through a printed page. I reject absolutely any so-called "reading readiness test" that would keep children out of school or place them arbitrarily in a rigidly restricted group. What I am suggesting is that children, even when they are very young, begin to assign meaning to the symbols and to the objects that surround them, and that the most essential obligation of parents, as the first teachers, is to give love, then language, to their children. Simply stated, reading, as a complex act of interpretation, starts long before school, and the task of formal learning is to build on the symbol system already well in place.

On my own first day of school, walking there with my mother, I asked if I'd learn to read that day. My mother replied quite wisely, "No, you won't learn to read today, but you will before the year is out." Well, I walked into the classroom and there she stood, half human, half divine — Miss Rice, my first-grade teacher. Miss Rice said, "Good morning, class. Today we learn to read." These were quite literally the first words I heard in school.

Fifty years later, when I wrote a book on high school and then another one on college, I placed chapters near the front of each book on the centrality of language. It occurred to me one day that this was no accident. It was, in fact, the influence of an unheralded first-grade teacher at Fairview Avenue Elementary School, who taught me in my first year of formal learning that language is the centerpiece of learning, that it is through words that we're linguistically and intellectually empowered.

Recently, the Carnegie Foundation published a report on elementary education called *The Basic School* (Boyer, 1995). In conducting this study, we asked hundreds of teachers all across the country to name the most important purpose of education. Almost without exception, they said, "Teaching children to read." According to elementary school principals, more than one-third of all instructional time, from kindergarten to grade 5, is devoted to language arts, to the mastery of symbols (Carnegie Foundation for the Advancement of Teaching, 1990).

I'm suggesting that language is not just another subject, but the means by which all other subjects are pursued. The first and most essential goal of formal learning must be to ensure that all children read with comprehension, write with clarity, and effectively speak and listen. If, by the end of the third or fourth grade, all children were linguistically empowered, their successive learning would expand exponentially, and later failure would be diminished dramatically.

Thirty years ago, Guy Bond began the second edition of *Reading Difficulties: Their Diagnosis and Correction* (one of his influential books, of which there were very many) with this paragraph:

> The ability to read well constitutes one of the most valuable skills a person can acquire. Our world is a reading world. It is difficult to discover any activity . . . that does not demand some, and often considerable, reading. And, in many situations, reading constitutes the indispensable channel of communication. (1967, p. 4)

The key issue, of course, and the one that has led to the inspiration of this volume, is *how* this essential goal of literacy is to be accomplished. The data show that, in spite of much effort and new insights, overall reading improvement among the nation's children, for the past 20 or 30 years, has been marginal at best. How then do children learn to read? I think it's correct to say that no one really knows. And further, I suspect that the secret will not be fully revealed until the mysteries of the mind and the brain are themselves understood. This does not mean, however, that teaching reading is all guesswork. We do have brilliant instruction and profoundly successful reading teachers in every school and great progress in literacy all across the country.

Throughout the years, proven procedures have been discovered, beginning with the most basic truth that children learn to read if they are well motivated and if they believe that they can and will succeed. In a beautiful story about her work with children in South Texas, Ann Alejandro writes: "I know my students are geniuses, but I won't tell them that until they show me that they are." Her whole year, she says, "works toward their recognition of genius in themselves and their ability to go out independently, like the people in the Nike commercials, and 'Just do it'" (1994, p. 19).

James Agee wrote, "In every child who is born, under no matter what circumstances, . . . the potentiality of the human race is born again" (Agee & Evans, 1966, p. 263). This inspiration, this absolute confidence in the potentiality of each child, is the conviction that must undergird every successful reading program.

Beyond confidence and positive motivation, success in reading also means being flexible in adjusting the method of instruction to the uniqueness of each student. This is, of course, a touchy subject. Still, progress in language arts has been diminished dramatically in the past precisely because of the inclination of reading specialists to organize into competing camps, driven more by ideology than insight. At the same time, I find it encouraging that today thoughtful voices on all sides recognize what I'd call "the essentialness of balance." For example, a recent report from New Zealand (1985), arguably the most literate country in the world, declared that the best strategy for effective reading is a *comprehensive* strategy, one that is both balanced and eclectic.

Children differ in their approaches to reading, and for some, understanding the phonetic structure, the building blocks of language, may be helpful. My own field was medical audiology. I was professionally engaged in working with children with inner-ear deafness. They couldn't speak because they could not hear. Frequently, I was saddened by the debates of the profession in which the "lip-reader people" and the "sign people" fought their ideological battles — while children were caught in the middle. I remember children who could not communicate, who had no method of reaching out, who became enraged because they could not make connections with each other. I observed that deaf children were led to understanding as they began to grasp the phonetic structure of language. I became convinced that the obligation of those of us in education is to make available *all* of the linguistic tools and pedagogical procedures that, taken together, will be useful to children.

Dorothy Strickland, one of the nation's most influential and insightful reading experts, has it absolutely right. She says that we should treat instruction in phonics as an important part of beginning reading, not as a precursor to it. We should view phonics for what it is, one of several enablers for literacy—nothing more, nothing less (1994/1995). In helping children to read, however, phonics is surely not the ultimate point of focus. Children need a rich vocabulary that is continually expanding. Reading is most successful when sounds and words are placed in larger contexts as children discover meaning and become linguistically empowered.

Children gain meaning from the printed page, but they also must bring their own experience to what they read, and to the observant, sensitive teacher, this vital interaction in reading can provide powerful insights about who the student *is*. As part of my doctoral dissertation, I asked students to read a series of statements, some of which were evocatively loaded, and others not. What I discovered was that the students became far less fluent when reading the emotionally loaded passages, even though the sentences were otherwise the same. The obvious conclusion was that the students weren't just looking at *words*; they were bringing meaning to the message. Their reading fluency was, in fact, controlled by the content of the message. They were wrapping themselves within the words, and the meaning was flowing back and forth.

Clearly, when we say a child cannot read, what we may be observing is a child who, in reality, may be reading "too much." The child may be experiencing nonfluency precisely because of the deep emotional responses that are being stirred by the passages he or she encounters. Consider, for example, a student who is asked to read a story about a father. What if the child, the preceding evening, had a confrontation with his or her own father, or experienced abuse? In the reading class, it's quite possible that such memories could preoccupy the child and interrupt the flow of speech we call reading. The emotional dimensions of reading—the feeling children bring to the printed page—remind us that reading is a dynamic, interactive process between the child and the passage on the page.

When fully successful, reading is discovery—a joyful, exciting process, one that is ultimately an empowering engagement. Diane Stephens (1994) describes that powerful scene in *The Miracle Worker* in which Helen Keller feels the water with her hand and then feels the sign for water with her hand, and, in one magical moment, makes the connection. Oh, that and that connect! The sign means water. Aha! And Helen Keller, having grasped that elegant and empowering insight, rushes around; she leaps and runs, filled not only with comprehension, but also with great joy. This discovery, this sense of exhilaration, is precisely what language instruction is all about.

When all is said and done, reading is not just about sounds, it's not about isolated words, it's about *meaning*—that powerful interaction between the reader and the page. I am sure that most teachers, and many parents, too, have surely felt the excitement when a young child sees a symbol, discovers meaning, and is joyfully empowered.

We also know that students learn to read as they learn to write. Writing is, in fact, the other side of reading. More than any other form of communication, writing holds students responsible for their words. Writing is not copying, writing is not penmanship—writing is a creative act that allows children to be wonderfully self-expressive. Through clear writing, clear thinking can be learned. It's exciting to observe young children as they become authors and then read with pride what they have written.

During the Carnegie Foundation study of the American elementary school, we visited one classroom that had what the teacher called the "Author's Chair," a place where children could go with a friend and read aloud the stories they themselves had written. This was, we were told, one of the most popular exercises of the day, in which a child could make a statement of his or her own that went beyond the familiar. The goal of writing is, in fact, to encourage students to be creative, to express themselves in imaginative new ways.

Recently, I spoke at a commencement exercise at Mount Union College. I thought I'd given an effective speech, but I was upstaged by the valedictorian of the class, who said that the spring before, she was babysitting her 5-year-old niece and to pass the time, brought along a new coloring book and a new box of crayons. The two of them sat down together and immediately the child flipped through the first 30 pages, skipping all the line drawings to be colored in. At the back page, which was completely blank, she took out the crayons, coloring furiously. The young woman asked, "Why did you skip over all those pages and go to the back?" The little girl answered, "Well, on the back page there aren't any lines and you can do anything you want."

In writing and in speech, children should learn about grammar and about syntax, but they also should learn to think creatively, to choose bold, descriptive words, to paint vivid language pictures—to color outside the lines.

Prospects for enriched reading also are enhanced as students read great children's literature, not just bland basal readers. Several years ago, when I was Commissioner of Education, I walked unannounced into a sixth-grade classroom in New Haven. There were nearly 30 children crowding around the teacher's desk. I discovered that, rather than confronting an emergency, I had, in fact, become part of a moment of great discovery. The children had just finished reading Charles Dickens's *Oliver Twist*, and these sixth-graders in inner-city New Haven were vigorously debating whether little Oliver could make it in their city. After much discussion, the children concluded that, although Oliver Twist had survived in far-off London, he could never make it in New Haven.

Apart from the poignancy of their conclusion, the beauty of that moment was that an inspired teacher had related the insights of great literature to the reality of the children's lives. It seems evident that we *can* take nineteenth-century syntax and translate it into twentieth-century understanding. Classic literature *can* speak to children today and *can* empower their desire and ability to read. Years ago, Guy Bond (Bond & Wagner, 1966) put it this way: "A child learns to read well only when what he is asked to do seems both useful and vital, both compelling and authentic" (pp. 72–73).

Thus far, I've suggested that achieving literacy for all children means holding high expectations for students, exercising flexibility in teaching styles, connecting reading to what students write, and introducing children to great literature that relates learning to life. Beyond these essential tools, however, success in reading depends ultimately on helping students to see connections, to discover, through language, relationships and patterns.

In today's fragmented academic world, students complete the separate subjects, they fill in the worksheets, they're handed a diploma; but what they fail to gain is a more coherent view of knowledge and a more integrated, more authentic view of life. I've observed that when young children come to school they are filled with curiosity. They keep asking *why*. They're searching for connections. They are dissatisfied with little fragments that don't present a larger pattern. However, very soon children stop asking *why* and begin to ask, "Will we have this on the test?" Those two questions tell us much about diminished inspiration as children move from their own curiosity to conformity to the system.

More than 50 years ago, Mark Van Doren wrote: "The connectedness of things is what the educator contemplates to the limit of his capacity. . . . The student who can begin early in his life to think of things as connected . . . has begun the life of learning" (1943, p. 115). I'm convinced that what American education urgently needs today is a curriculum with connections. It should begin in the language arts. I think it is really sad that in the world of language we have reading specialists and writing specialists and speech specialists and hearing specialists and literature specialists and linguistics specialists and the list goes on, who do their own research, while we have too few academics engaged in what we called, in a recent Carnegie report, "the scholarship of integration" (Boyer, 1990).

Frank Press, former president of the National Academy of Sciences, sent me a copy of a speech he gave several years ago in which he said that the work of the artist and the work of the scientist are essentially the same (1984). To illustrate his point, he referred to the magnificent double helix that broke the genetic code, suggesting that it was not only rational, but beautiful as well. When I read the speech, I thought of the lift-offs at Cape Kennedy—those spine-tingling moments that many now take for granted. I remember watching the engineers on the TV screen, anxiety pasted on their faces. When the count reached "three, two, one, lift-off," and the space-craft began to rise, the anxiety fell away and there were great smiles of satisfaction. They didn't say, "Well, our formulas worked again." What they said, almost in unison, was *Beautiful!*" They chose an aesthetic term to describe a technological achievement. Where does the world of the scientist or the mathematician and that of the artist begin and end? Is it possible that, fundamentally, we are all searching for relationships and patterns and connections?

When Victor Weisskopf, the renowned physicist, was asked on one occasion, "What gives you hope in troubled times?" he replied, "Mozart and quantum mechanics." Where in our fragmented academic world do students see connections such as these? The good news is that we are beginning to make connections in what Michael Polanyi (1967), of the University of Chicago, called the "overlapping [academic] neighborhoods" (p. 72). Some of the most exciting work going on today is in the hyphenated disciplines—psycho-linguistics, bio-engineering, and the like—and I would like to see more hyphenated disciplines within language arts itself.

Jo Stanchfield, of Claremont College, made this important observation: "For the last fifteen years, I've been convinced that reading cannot be taught in isolation, but rather as a part of the whole," a part of what she called the "gestalt of literacy. . . . Today, most educators stress the word literacy, rather than reading. If we can implement this holistic concept in our curriculum, we will be well on our way to producing better readers and more literate citizens" (Putnam, 1994, p. 365).

I couldn't agree more. The issue is not reading, in its narrow sense; the issue is not even literacy. The issue is *understanding*, in its fullest sense, which means cutting across the narrow specialties and discovering how they reinforce each other. The vision of the wholeness of language is, I believe, absolutely right. Reading and writing and speech and listening belong to-gether; they are all what I'd call "verbal literacy," and they reinforce each other.

What I'm really talking about is bringing together all of the symbol systems we use to communicate with one another. Consider, for example, that language and literacy also must include not just words but mathematics, a universal language by which we communicate about quantity, space, and time, and which, incidentally, also requires words for discussion. At a recent conference in Big Sky, Montana, Leon Lederman, a Nobel laureate in science, said to me: "I wish we would stop saying 'math and science.' I wish we would start saying 'words and science' because learning the word symbols is even more important than the number symbols, since we have to use words to talk about our numbers."

Surely literacy must include the language of *the arts*, another universal symbol system by which we express feelings and ideas. We all understand that words cannot portray sufficiently the joy of a spring morning, or the fruits of a fall harvest, or the grief and loneliness that mark the ending of a love relationship. To express our deepest and most profound feelings, we turn to art. Art is, as a teacher once told me, the "language of the angels." I'm intrigued that very young children, even before they can speak, respond intuitively to color and to music and to rhythm.

The structure for art is within our children in the same way as the structure for words. Yet art often is considered a frill in schools, and by the time students are in the third grade, it is something they do to fill in time. Again, for the most intimate and most profoundly moving human experiences, we need music and dance and the visual arts. Conductor Murry Sidlin put it this way: "When words are no longer adequate, when our passion is greater than we are able to express in a usual manner, people turn to art. Some people go to the canvas and paint; some stand up and dance. But we all go beyond our normal means of communicating, and *this* is the common human experience for all people on this planet" (Sidlin, 1978).

Several years ago, I read an interview with Victor Weisskopf, who was discussing the Big Bang theory. Near the end of this provocative conversation, Weisskopf said, "If you wish to understand the Big Bang theory, you should listen to the works of Haydn." At first I was bemused and bewildered, but this proposition, upon reflection, seemed to be absolutely clear. Weisskopf was reminding us that occasionally human experiences are so profound, so intellectually and emotionally overwhelming, that they call for symbols beyond words or numbers for full expression. The Big Bang theory, he was saying, must be felt as well as thought.

Simply stated, we as humans have *three* elegant symbol systems—the verbal system we call words; the number system, which allows us to think about quantity, space, and time; and the arts, which allow us to deal with profound feelings and ideas and express them in ways that words and numbers cannot convey. These are the tools we use to describe our world and engage intimately with each other. To be truly literate means becoming proficient in *all* the symbol systems and discovering how they are inseparably intertwined. This is literacy at its fullest.

In the end, literacy, like love, knows no limits. It is a lifelong journey. The spirit of this journey was poignantly captured by Carl Sandburg (1964) when he wrote,

> Once having marched
> Over the margins of animal necessity,
> Over the grim line of sheer subsistence,
> Then man came
> To the deeper rituals of his bones,
> To the lights lighter than any bones,
> To the time for thinking things over,
> To the dance, the song, the story,
> Or the hours given over to dreaming,
> Once having so marched. (p. 285)

We have a moral obligation to empower the coming generation with this capacity that makes us truly human. John Gardner (1984) wrote that a nation is never finished. You can't build it and leave it standing as the pharaohs did the pyramids. It has to be rebuilt with each new generation. And so it is with schools and with the education of our children. Clearly, the most urgent task our generation now confronts is to ensure literacy, not just for the most advantaged, but, as the title and theme of this book remind us, for all children.

## REFERENCES

Agee, J., & Evans, W. (1966). *Let us now praise famous men*. New York: Ballantine Books.

Alejandro, A. (1994, January). Like happy dreams — integrating visual arts, writing and reading. *Language Arts, 71*, 12–21.

Bond, G. L., & Tinker, M. A. (1967). *Reading difficulties: Their diagnosis and correction* (2nd ed.). New York: Appleton-Century-Crofts.

Bond, G. L., & Wagner, E. B. (1966). *Teaching the child to read*. New York: Macmillan.

Boyer, E. L. (1990). *Scholarship reconsidered: Priorities of the professoriate*. Princeton, NJ: The Carnegie Foundation for the Advancement of Teaching.

Boyer, E. L. (1995). *The basic school: A community for learning.* Princeton, NJ: The Carnegie Foundation for the Advancement of Teaching.

Carnegie Foundation for the Advancement of Teaching. (1990). *National survey of elementary school principals.* Princeton, NJ: Author.

Clapp, G. (1988). *Child study research: Current perspectives and applications.* Lexington, MA: Lexington Books.

Gardner, J. W. (1984). *Excellence: Can we be equal and excellent too?* (rev. ed.). New York: W. W. Norton.

New Zealand Department of Education. (1985). *Reading in junior classes.* Wellington, New Zealand: Author.

Nuba, H. (1989, Fall). Books and babies. *Day Care and Early Education, 17,* 19.

Nuba-Scheffler, H., Sheiman, D., & Watkins, K. (1986). *Infancy: A guide to research and resources.* New York: Teachers College Press.

Pinker, S. (1994). *The language instinct: How the mind creates language.* New York: William Morrow.

Polanyi, M. (1967). *The tacit dimension.* Garden City, NY: Doubleday.

Press, F. (1984, May 30). Address to the Annual Commencement Convocation, School of Graduate Studies, Case Western Reserve University, Cleveland, Ohio.

Putnam, L. R. (1994, September). Reading instruction: What do we know that we didn't know thirty years ago? *Language Arts, 71,* 362–366.

Sandburg, C. (1964). *The people, yes.* New York: Harcourt Brace and World.

Sidlin, M. (1978, June). *Someone's priority.* Speech given at the Aspen Conference on the Talented and Gifted, sponsored by the U.S. Department of Health, Education, and Welfare, Office of the Gifted and Talented, Aspen, Colorado.

Stephens, D. L. (1994, January). Learning what art means. *Language Arts, 71,* 34–37.

Strickland, D. (1994/1995, December/January). Reinventing our literacy programs: Books, basics, balance. *The Reading Teacher, 48,* 294–302.

Thomas, L. (1983). *Late night thoughts on listening to Mahler's ninth symphony.* New York: Viking Press.

Van Doren, M. (1943). *Liberal education.* Boston: Beacon Press.

# PART I

# THE ROOTS OF LITERACY

CHAPTER 2

# Creating and Sustaining a Love of Literature . . . And the Ability to Read It

## ELFRIEDA H. HIEBERT

*University of Michigan*

From a variety of sources that range from anecdotes of parents to the quantitative reports of large-scale studies (e.g., Mullis, Campbell, & Farstrup, 1993), we can conclude that access to high-quality reading instruction is not guaranteed for all children. This statement is most true for those students who depend on schools for that access: the children of low-income families. My first contribution toward providing this access was as a teacher's aide in the first round of Chapter I programs in Fresno, CA. The year was 1967 — the same year that Guy Bond, with Robert Dykstra, published a seminal work that reflected a particular perspective on early reading (Bond & Dykstra, 1967). The underlying perspective of the U.S. Office of Education (USOE) studies that Bond and Dykstra summarized was that American educators needed to identify and disseminate information on the best possible beginning reading instruction so that children would not establish a syndrome of failure and ill-fitting literacy strategies. Bond's commitment to a strong early start has seen a rejuvenation in the past decade, as a number of projects have returned to the theme of strong beginning literacy instruction as the best prevention (e.g., Hiebert & Taylor, 1994).

Another theme ran through Bond's work as well: the need for remediation or diversified instruction for students who aren't successful at the beginning stages. Even though Bond's identification with the USOE study may be most visible to future generations, his professional energies were directed more to this second theme than to the first. My introduction to Guy Bond occurred early in my educational career through his classic textbook, *Reading Difficulties: Their Diagnosis and Correction* (Bond & Tinker, 1957), in my master's program in reading education at the University of Illinois.

This theme of remediation is not a popular one at present in the literacy community. In many of our university master's programs, the names of courses have been changed from "Remediation and Diagnosis" to "Processes in Literacy" or some variant. The attention of reading educators who work with middle-grade students is almost solely on literature-based instruction regardless of students' proficiency. In some projects and in the teachers' manuals of textbook series, the advice is for teachers or peers to read the text to students who can't read it by themselves. Similarly, perusal of *Reading Research Quarterly* and *Journal of Reading Behavior* shows little attention to remedial instruction in the past 5 years.

This chapter addresses the needs of students who haven't gotten off to a solid early start. As Chapter 1 policies increasingly move away from support for older students to the frontloading of resources in early interventions, there may be more of a need for this attention than ever before. When students don't become independent readers in the first 2 years of school, a perception that the problem lies with the students may be perpetuated. If the first R is to be a right for all children, school- and university-based educators need to attend very carefully to the needs of middle-grade students who are still not proficient readers.

This chapter describes a project of two third-grade teachers in integrating a small-group component of consistent instruction for struggling readers into literature-based programs. This project was an action-based research project in which these teachers engaged as students in a masters-level course that I taught. The progression that these teachers and I followed in conducting this project is mirrored in this chapter: a review of available literature to identify practices that we might model or adapt, the implementation of the project and analysis of its effectiveness, and reflections on the project and future directions.

## REVIEW OF LITERATURE

Since my initiation into elementary reading instruction as a teacher's aide over 25 years ago, I have had various roles as an educator. First, I taught elementary students in a school close to Fresno. Later, after receiving a Ph.D. from the University of Wisconsin, I worked with preservice and inservice teachers at the University of Kentucky and the University of Colorado–Boulder. In all of these roles, I maintained an interest in creating the best possible school literacy programs for low-performing students, many of whom were low-income students. In the late 1980s, this interest was reflected in three studies. I use these three studies as the point of departure in the review of the literature because these projects led directly to the present project. These projects, however, represent the fruition of studying the work of numerous scholars over an educational career that is approaching the 30-year mark. While all of this scholarship cannot be reviewed, I recognize the legacy of these scholars, including many of the contributors to this volume.

In the first project, Charles Fisher and I (Fisher & Hiebert, 1990) examined the nature of tasks in literature-based classrooms relative to those in skills-oriented classrooms. In the literature-based classrooms, extensive amounts of writing were occurring and library books had replaced contrived text. Students were not stigmatized for reading problems. Whereas students in the skills-oriented classrooms spent their time on relatively small, discrete tasks, both second graders and sixth graders in the literature-based classrooms were devoting their time to extended tasks (reading an entire chapter book, writing a book) over which they had some degree of autonomy. For example, they could select the topic and genre of their compositions. The day-to-day experiences in literature-based classrooms were distinctly different from those in skills-oriented classrooms for all students, including low-performing ones. These experiences particularly departed from the typical scenarios that have been described for low-performing students (Johnston & Allington, 1991).

The nature of student accomplishments as a function of literature-based experiences, particularly those of initially low-performing students across grades 1 and 3, was the focus of the second project. Observations and assessments showed that a substantial number of students were struggling with literacy (Hiebert, 1994). Their teachers, even at first grade, were unclear as to how to accommodate to these differences other than through individual conferences. The mechanisms that were assumed to be the basis for literacy growth among literature-based experts at that time (Goodman, 1986)—extensive reading and extensive writing—had not served to bring the students who were struggling most to independent literacy.

In the third project (Hiebert, Colt, Catto, & Gury, 1992), a group of teachers and I designed a small-group instructional program for initially low-performing students within whole language programs. The intervention used the activities that teachers viewed as compatible with whole language—repeated reading of predictable text and extensive writing. However, there were a number of differences from the teachers' typical application of these activities: Activities were consistently applied each day, teachers worked with students who had similar profiles of needs in small-group settings for concentrated periods of time; children were assessed periodically to determine progress toward goals; books were selected to represent particular word patterns and text difficulty; and target word patterns were discussed with the words from the books and were the basis for writing activities on acetate slates or magnetic boards.

This effort with first and second graders proved highly effective. Many of the initially low-performing students became sufficiently fluent by the end of first grade that they did not require the additional instruction in second grade. However, for low-performing newcomers to the school in second grade and for about 25% of the first-grade group, the intervention also was provided in second grade. As a result of these efforts, by the end of second grade 87% of the lowest 40% of students were reading at or above grade level on an informal reading inventory.

As I described the results of the early intervention in graduate courses and at conferences, many middle-grade teachers who were teaching in whole language schools asked for extensions of the intervention to their grades. In the schools where we had successfully implemented the early intervention in grades 1 and 2, our emphasis had changed from one of automatic reading of narrative text with first and second graders to reading and writing of informational text with third graders. This change was appropriate in light of the high levels of fluency that children in the early intervention program showed. However, middle-grade teachers from other districts and states that had not been involved in the early intervention asked about extensions of the automaticity component in the middle grades because they felt that many of their students were not fluent enough as readers and writers to complete grade-level tasks independently. When two third-grade teachers in a course I was teaching described class profiles in which about one-third of their new students in the fall were considerably below grade level, I began an inquiry with them as to how this situation might be ameliorated.

Before we embarked on implementing instruction, we studied the literature for information on modifications or adaptations that had proven effective with older, struggling readers: repeated reading of text, extensive writing, and instruction in patterns and structures of written language.

## REPEATED READING OF TEXT

The idea of repeated reading — also called echoic or assisted reading — is that an expert reader serves as a model for the struggling reader by reading a text aloud. The novice reader then rereads the text until he or she can render an accurate and smooth rendition of it. As Allington (1984) notes, the technique of reading along with others has had a long history in American schools, dating back to colonial times when the scarcity of books made this technique a matter of necessity. It was with LaBerge and Samuels's (1974) description of automaticity that the more recent attention of educators was drawn to repeated reading of text. The opportunity to read a passage over and over until they can give an oral rendition comfortably and quickly allows students who are not facile readers to participate in automatic reading.

Dahl (1979) examined this assumption in a project with the poorest readers among second graders in a suburban elementary school. After an initial reading of a passage to an adult, students read the passage independently. They kept track of these independent readings and stayed with the same passage until they reached the criterion level of 100 words a minute. Students in the repeated reading group made fewer errors and read passages faster than students who had spent a comparable amount of instructional time learning single words or listening to or reading cloze exercises. On a standardized reading test, however, the performance of the cloze group surpassed that of the repeated reading and the word recognition groups, while on tasks that required recognition of words in isolation or in sentences, the repeated reading and cloze groups had comparable performances.

More recently, Dowhower (1987) supplemented Dahl's independent session with a read-along procedure. Second graders who had good decoding ability but below-average reading rates showed gains in reading rate from either independent repeated reading or reading along with an adult. However, the read-along procedure was more advantageous for improving students' ability to read in meaningful phrases.

Chomsky (1976) used tape recordings of selections with five struggling third-grade readers. Students read along with taped versions of their individual selections daily. Once or twice a week, they met with an adult to read the selection and to play language games that drew on words and sentences from students' selections. Students also wrote compositions, extending the material in the text. On several different measures, students averaged approximately 6 months' growth over the 15-week period of the project.

It should be noted that Chomsky believed that the interestingness of text superseded other characteristics of the text. Students were asked to select from a set of books (some apparently quite long). This choice was different than in the Dahl and Dowhower studies, where texts were shorter and were selected by researchers to contain unfamiliar words but still be within students' ranges. The difficulty and length of text may have influenced Chomsky's students' progress. For example, she talks about the children losing their place in the text and spending approximately a month on a passage. In a similar project, Herman (1985) allowed students to choose their own stories, but the choices were limited to a set of stories that were shorter than the book-length passages available to Chomsky's students. Herman found that rate and comprehension scores increased significantly over a 3-month period.

Although repeated reading is recommended frequently, in the literature-based classrooms of the projects that were described earlier (Fisher & Hiebert, 1990; Hiebert, 1994), I saw no evidence of it. While currently there may be much more lip service to this activity than implementation of it, the foundational research holds promise for struggling, middle-grade readers in becoming fluent.

## EXTENSIVE WRITING

Developing independent writing proficiency is important in its own right, but extensive writing also can support students' understandings of the features of written language in a way that extends to reading. As Juel (1991) argues, because of the analysis that is required in writing, writing can be an ideal context in which to attend to sound–letter correspondences. At least for the beginning writer, the process of writing words requires attention to individual units—first letters, then chunks of words. Further, in encoding the written form from knowledge of the spoken form, the student has an opportunity to test hypotheses about sound–letter correspondences.

One aspect of many elementary classrooms that has changed dramatically over the past decade is the quality and quantity of writing. When Connie Bridge and I (Bridge & Hiebert, 1985) observed classrooms in the early 1980s, students wrote infrequently, and much of the writing that did occur involved paraphrasing or copying. In our more recent observational study of literature-based classrooms (Fisher & Hiebert, 1990), we found extensive amounts of writing. Even in skills-oriented classrooms, students were involved in more extended writing than had been the case in the classrooms observed earlier. I was hopeful that the move to writer's workshop and various writing process models would give insights into the effects of extensive writing on the literacy proficiency of struggling, middle-grade readers.

The body of literature on writer's workshop is growing (e.g., McCarthey, 1994), but unlike the literature on repeated reading, there is not a substantial literature on how writing might change the course of struggling, middle-grade readers. There is a more substantial literature on the role of extensive writing on reading acquisition. Precocious readers are described as "pencil-and-paper" kids (Durkin, 1966), and the reading proficiency of precocious writers is similarly noted (Read, 1975). A study by Clarke (1988)

of first graders in two different types of classrooms – traditional and invented spelling classrooms – showed that there is a carryover in school settings as well. While the role of the writing component has not been sepa-
rated from the effects of other activities in early interventions (e.g., Clay,
1985; Hiebert et al., 1992; Juel, 1994; Taylor, Strait, & Medo, 1994), writing components are integral to these early interventions and, presumably,
the reported effects. While the movement to writer's workshop and process
models in many classrooms has not been studied for its influence on initially
low-performing readers, evidence of the role of writing in the development
of young readers (Sulzby, 1992) supports the notion that the retooling of
struggling, middle-grade readers also could be supported through extensive
writing.

## PATTERNS AND STRUCTURES OF WRITTEN LANGUAGE

Because of the alphabetic character of the English written system, it follows
that students learning to read and write English benefit from information
on how the language they already know (spoken English) is manifest in
written form. Reviews of research have shown consistently that instruction
that focuses the attention of beginning readers and writers on the critical
features of these connections is beneficial (Adams, 1990; Bond & Dykstra,
1967; Chall, 1983). However, the differences between young children introduced to school literacy as first graders and middle-grade students who
have struggled with literacy for several years are numerous. Most factors,
such as motivation and ingrained faulty strategies, not in favor of the older
students. Middle-grade students may, however, be at an advantage in one
realm. The notion of metacognition as a means of executive control and
monitoring of word-level strategies has been proposed as an asset in reading
(Gaskins et al., 1988). Because of their several years of school participation, middle-grade students have a grasp of the academic nature of tasks
and language in school as well as the tasks and language of literacy. While
they are not always adept at acting on this academic knowledge, this sophistication in knowing about school, literacy, and language may make middle-
grade students better able to benefit from metacognitive guidance about
written language.

The unit of written language that is the focus of this metacognitive
instruction may be the critical issue. As Henry, Calfee, and LaSalle (1988)
state, "Teachers believe that letter–sound correspondences must be mastered before syllable and morpheme patterns can be introduced. As a consequence, learning disabled students are often limited to letter–sound correspondences as a strategy for analyzing unfamiliar words" (p. 4). Rather
than the individual letter–sound correspondences, such as the sound associ-

ated with the letter *b*, the rime or the word pattern has been suggested as a more important unit of analysis used by proficient readers (Cunningham, 1975–76). Rimes consist of a vowel and subsequent consonant(s) within the syllable, such as *at* in *cat* and *fat*. With awareness of the rimes of written language, students can be taught an analogical decoding process whereby they use this knowledge of rimes to figure out unknown words (Cunningham, 1975–76). The Benchmark program, which is geared to elementary-age poor readers with average or above intelligence, provides students with metacognitive training in analogical decoding (Gaskins et al., 1988). The 120 key words that are used as a corpus for this decoding are taught by sight, but lessons are provided concomitantly with the sight word instruction in which students are taught to use the regular patterns in the sight words to figure out unknown words by analogy.

A second unit of analysis used in the Benchmark program pertains to morphemic and syllabic elements (Gaskins et al., 1988). In the intermediate phase of the program, students learn about the morphemic similarities across groups of words such as the Latin root *puls* (drive, push, or throw) and its relation to *impulsive, pulse, pulsation, repulse, compulsory*, and *propulsion*. Benchmark students have been shown to perform better on a pseudoword test and transfer word test than comparable students who did not receive this training (Gaskins et al., 1988). Within the Benchmark group, the amount of time devoted by teachers to the instruction and the fidelity of the instruction were highly related to students' performances.

The Project READ effort initiated at Stanford University (Calfee & Henry, 1985) shares with the Benchmark program an emphasis on morphemic and syllabic elements but relates these elements to their historical origins. The metacognitive training in Project READ guides students in understanding the structural elements (letter–sound correspondences, syllables, or morpheme patterns) in relation to their historical roots (Anglo-Saxon, Romance, or Greek). Henry (1988) reports on an examination of middle-grade students who received this metacognitive training. On a pretest of words with Anglo-Saxon, Romance, and Greek origins that represented the major structural categories (letter–sound correspondences, syllable patterns, and morpheme patterns), most of the students showed little understanding of common syllable or morpheme patterns. After this pretest, four classes of Project READ teachers provided students with units on word structure and word origin, and another group of four teachers used the same units along with metacognitive instruction. The students who received either form of instruction did better than students who received no instruction, but the instruction with a metacognitive component produced greater gains than the instruction without it.

In a second study, Henry (1988) focused on learning disabled students, who knew little about complex letter–sound correspondences and even less about syllable and morpheme patterns on the pretest. When they were taught structural patterns and strategies, they made marked gains in both word structure knowledge and reading and spelling achievement.

A project with a similar emphasis on rimes and onsets in writing and in reading conducted by Englert, Hiebert, and Stewart (1985) was much shorter in duration than Henry's and did not show a similar effect on students' reading performances. However, even after a short treatment (approximately 12 hours of instruction), the students who received the analogical instruction performed significantly better on spelling tasks. The complementary activity of spelling words that share structural or phonic features, as well as applying the strategy when reading words, may be helpful to struggling, middle-grade readers.

## SUMMARY

While this review is not exhaustive, the primary studies have been included. The scarcity of available literature is troublesome. In examining Garcia, Jimenez, and Pearson's (1989) review of the literature on reading instruction of at-risk students, the lack of research on interventionist projects for middle-grade students who have experienced difficulty with literacy also is evident. However, based on what literature there is, the use of repeated readings of text, extensive writing (including the writing of words that contain target patterns), and metacognitive instruction about word elements definitely seem warranted for struggling, middle-grade readers.

## THE NATURE AND OUTCOMES OF THE PROJECT OF TWO THIRD-GRADE TEACHERS

With these ideas about what works, the teachers and I set about designing activities and an organizational scheme. To contextualize the project, I begin with a brief description of the overall school contexts, follow that with a description of the content of the project, and conclude this section with a summary of the influence of the project on students.

### THE OVERALL SCHOOL CONTEXTS

Literature-based instruction had a considerable history in the school districts and schools in which the two project teachers, Cindy and Cara (pseudonyms), taught. Further, the districts had similar instructional philosophies and views of staff development and of literacy. Instructional materials were chosen by the teachers at a school site, and the teachers chose trade books. Numerous sets of trade books were shared by teachers within a school.

Both schools were relatively stable and middle-class, although about 10% of the students in Cara's school qualified for Chapter 1. There was some support from Chapter 1 and special education specialists in Cara's school, but most of it went toward assisting students on their compositions. In Cindy's school, there were not sufficient students at low-income levels to warrant a Chapter 1 program. When the beginning third graders in these two classes were given informal reading inventories, 7 of 25 students in Cara's class and 7 of 21 in Cindy's class were reading poorly.

## THE NATURE OF INSTRUCTIONAL CHANGES

Prior to the project, the teachers were implementing a form of reader's workshop as well as writer's workshop. Reader's workshop, which was based on Atwell's (1987) descriptions, consisted of an independent reading period during which students read from trade books that they had selected; a period when students read from a shared set of books and discussed their responses to these books in teacher-led discussion groups or in peer-led groups or dyads; whole-class minilessons in which teachers modeled and led discussions on genres and reading strategies; and individual teacher–student conferences on students' literature logs. If students were struggling with reading, these individual conferences might focus to a greater extent on vocabulary than would be the case in teachers' conferences with more proficient readers, but the number of conferences that teachers had with students did not differ as a function of students' reading proficiency. There was also an element of instruction in the teacher-led small groups, with a focus on the quality or content of students' responses to the trade books.

*Changes in the classroom program.* As part of this project, both teachers added two components to their overall classroom program: the weekly reading of magazine or newspaper articles and weekly "Word Wall" lessons based on the Benchmark program. The first activity, increasing weekly reading of magazine or newspaper articles, emanated from the teachers' goal of increasing students' involvement with informational text. Cara and Cindy identified relatively short articles (approximately 350–500 words in length) that related to topics of study in social studies, science, and general interest (e.g., holidays). Articles came from such magazines as *World*, *Ranger Rick*, and *Cricket*, as well as from books. For the weekly reading of the magazine or newspaper article, both teachers ensured that the struggling readers had opportunities to read in the small group. Many inventive adaptations came out of this activity. Cindy had students generate questions to ask peers. Cara used the weekly informational reading as a source of background for the narratives that students were reading during the literacy period. For example, she had her students read articles on the Alaskan flag and animals indigenous to Alaska so that they could better understand the books with settings in Alaska that were part of the literature curriculum.

During their master's program, Cindy and Cara viewed a videotape of the word pattern instruction at Benchmark School (Downer et al., 1990). Additionally, the lessons that had been developed by Benchmark teachers were available to Cindy and Cara. While neither used the lessons verbatim, both used the strategies common to Benchmark classrooms in their weekly minilessons. Cindy's adaptation was to select five words with a common spelling pattern (e.g., *main*, *vain*, *plain*, *stain*, *strain*). Additional words fitting that pattern would be identified in brainstorming sessions as were words that rhymed but used different spelling patterns (e.g., *main*, *mane*). Looking for "chunks" of words (i.e., word patterns) within multisyllabic words was modeled by the teacher as part of these minilessons. The meanings of words also were discussed, with a focus on homonyms. In both classes, Word Walls were created where exemplars for patterns were added as patterns were discovered. Students were encouraged to use the Word Wall when uncertain about spellings or pronunciations of words, particularly during writer's workshop. Both Cara and Cindy increased the amount of attention that they gave to students' use of conventional spellings in the final drafts of compositions during writer's workshop. If patterns were on the Word Wall, students were responsible for carrying over this knowledge into the final drafts of their compositions.

There were other changes in the teachers' instructional program as well. For example, the teachers talked about their increased awareness of the importance of including books of appropriate text difficulty for students' selection in reader's workshop. They also discussed the need to guide struggling readers more in selecting from the books that were available for literature units.

***Changes in instruction for struggling readers and writers.*** Both Cara and Cindy initiated small-group instruction for their struggling readers and writers. The small-group sessions occurred four times a week for 20 to 30 minutes during independent reading time. Both teachers identified this as a time when they were available to work with a small group. They also believed that independent reading opportunities were not jeopardized for students since they were encouraged to select books to take home at the end of the small-group sessions. Further, the teachers reasoned that, without the small-group opportunities, the quality of students' reading was not high during the independent reading periods. Finally, students continued to participate in the class-wide reading program, which consisted of reading shared library books that students selected on a particular theme.

One matter that needed to be resolved prior to instruction was the selection of books. Both schools had extensive collections of class sets of library books, but teachers were faced with the perennial problem of locating books that dealt with appropriate topics for third graders and yet were at an appropriate difficulty level for struggling readers. Since teachers had no additional resources for this project, they worked with their primary-level colleagues to identify books. The books that appeared to engage children's interest the most and also allowed for teachers' instructional aims were easy-to-read chapter books such as the Henry and Mudge series by Cynthia Rylant, the Ronald Morgan series, and Arnold Lobel's Frog and Toad books. The first page of a Henry and Mudge tale, *Henry and Mudge in the Sparkle Days* (Rylant & Stevenson, 1993), illustrates the nature of the text: "It was winter. Winter! Henry and his big dog Mudge loved winter, because Henry and his big dog Mudge loved snow" (p. 6).

The third-grade intervention differed significantly from the first- and second-grade projects in that text with predictable patterns was not the focus. The students gravitated to these short chapter books, which give substantial opportunities to develop automaticity with high-frequency words. Many of these words are also phonetically regular, which meant that the teachers could guide students in the use of word patterns.

To begin the sessions, students reread a selection from a set of familiar books that had been read in previous sessions. Cara frequently had students read from a book independently, followed by dyads of peers sharing with one another. Cara read with students individually during this time, taking running records. The warm-up period ended with students' choral reading of a shared passage. Cindy relied primarily on choral reading for the warm-up phase, with students reading a shared text in unison followed by turn-taking by individuals on sections of the text. Both teachers used the warm-up period to consciously draw students' attention to strategies that they were using proficiently. For example, they might say something like, "I noticed that Darwin reread a sentence when it didn't make sense. Reading always needs to make sense." Teachers also guided students in describing their strategies, with comments and questions such as, "How did you know this word? What did you do when you came to this part of the word?"

The second part of a session was directed toward a discussion of key words and their patterns. Words representing a pattern that had not been studied previously were introduced once or twice a week, with subsequent sessions during the week devoted to integrating this new pattern with others that had been studied. Whenever possible, teachers used a familiar text to draw students' attention to a word pattern, such as the two sounds associated with "ow" in *snow* and *now* or the sound of "udge" in *Mudge* (the manifestation of a short vowel sound despite the presence of the *e* at the end of the word). The example of "udge" as in *Mudge* might be extended to the same pattern with other vowels such as *bridge* or *badge*. Students were encouraged to perform changes on the key words themselves in a notebook or on a chalkboard. In generating rhyming words while writing, the emphasis was on flexibility, since some of the words that students identified as rhyming have different spellings (e.g., *bare* and *bear*) and some words that share spellings have different sounds (e.g., *hear* and *bear*). The writing of words in notebooks or on chalkboards was followed by writing sentences or paragraphs that used one or more of the key words. In Cara's class, the group often created a paragraph together on chart paper. This paragraph then became part of the repertoire of familiar text and was used for warm-ups on following days.

During the third part of a session, students read a new text that included words with the pattern that had been taught or reviewed. Following a short discussion of the text, students read it silently. Students were responsible for identifying any words that were troublesome to them as they read. Following a discussion of what happened in the text, the lesson moved to troublesome words, with students advising one another as to strategies that could be used to solve the problem. Students also engaged in repeated reading of the text. A session ended with students reading at least part of a text rapidly and smoothly.

By April, both teachers modified the procedures of the small groups because of the students' increased proficiency. Cara moved to the reading and writing of informational texts that were related to students' social studies and science curriculum. She continued to meet with the students in the small groups, but the focus was on content, with students working independently on their research reports and Cara working with students individually on reading selections for their reports and on the spellings and content of their written reports.

## THE INFLUENCE OF THE PROJECT ON THE STUDENTS

Data on 2 of the 14 students were not available because one child moved abruptly just before the final assessments and the parents of another child did not give permission to use the data.

***Assessments: Tasks, criteria, and procedures.*** In the fall, Cindy administered the Silver Burdett Ginn Reading Placement Inventory (Baumann et al., 1989), while Cara administered the Analytical Reading Inventory (ARI) (Woods & Moe, 1989). In the spring, a graduate research assistant who was unknown to the children and to the teachers administered the assessments. These assessments consisted of narrative passages from the ARI and expository passages from the Qualitative Reading Inventory (QRI) (Leslie & Caldwell, 1991). Comprehension questions that accompanied the ARI and QRI were asked. Students' answers to these questions and the rate at which they read the text were used to determine the appropriateness of their moving to the next level. The first passage that was administered to students was the second-grade, narrative passage from the ARI. If a student was unable to read 90% of the words fluently, no new texts were given.

Since narrative passages had been the basis for the fall assessments and constituted the only tasks for the comparison groups that will be described shortly, the narrative text reading task was presented first. When students' reading level had been established on the narrative task, the informational text measures were administered. Again, the second-grade passage was administered first, with the criteria for movement up or down to the next passage being the combination of fluency and comprehension.

***Students' mean performances.*** There are three ways in which I have chosen to approach the data: the examination of mean performances on the narrative and informational texts, absolute performances of students, and the profile or distribution of the project group relative to comparable groups.

To maintain agreements with the schools, the focus for the discussion is the performances of the 12 students as a group rather than as separate classroom groups. The distribution of students' scores is presented in Table 2.1.

In the fall, the average for the group was the preprimer level. By the spring assessment, the average for narrative text was the third-grade level. The mean performance for informational text was somewhat lower—an average level of 2.6.

***Students' absolute performances.*** As Table 2.1 indicates, eight of the 12 students were able to read third-grade narrative text fluently. Within this group of eight, three were able to read narratives at third-grade level, three at fourth-grade, one at fifth-grade, and one at sixth-grade. Four students had not attained that level, with three reading at first-grade level and one at second-grade level.

As Table 2.1 further indicates, the profile was less balanced and

**TABLE 2.1.** Performances of students in the project classrooms.

| Text | Narrative text Fall | Narrative text Spring | Informational Spring |
|------|------|------|------|
| below |  |  |  |
| pre-preprimer | 3 |  |  |
| pre-preprimer | 2 |  |  |
| preprimer | 3 |  | 2 |
| primer | 1 |  | 1 |
| Grade 1 | 2 | 3 | 1 |
| Grade 2 | 1 | 1 | 3 |
| Grade 3 |  | 3 | 2 |
| Grade 4 |  | 3 | 1 |
| Grade 5 |  | 1 | 1 |
| Grade 6 |  | 1 | 1 |

weaker for reading of informational text. Fewer than half of the students were able to read the informational text at their grade level, and only 25% of them were able to read at the fourth-grade level or higher, which is likely the level of many tasks in subsequent grades.

*Students' performances relative to comparable groups.* This project was initiated by the teachers for the purpose of increasing the literacy levels of children who had entered third grade as struggling readers. The teachers had no interest in randomly assigning their students to experimental or control group conditions. As I have suggested in a previous teacher-researcher project (Hagerty & Hiebert, 1989), the experimental model that necessitates control groups and random assignment can have a deleterious effect within school districts that are working on change projects. The research community, however, has a need to ascertain whether the growth from a project reflects the targeted instructional changes or is the result of typical development and growth. As a researcher, I agree with this concern, but I believe that researchers need to explore designs other than a control-experiment model to use in school change contexts.

A solution that I explore in this chapter is to compare the performances of students within an intervention with those of students who received a similar intervention or were in the comparison group in another intervention project. As candidates for these comparative groups, I studied data from several projects, including Juel's (1988) longitudinal study of students who had received different first-grade reading programs and Reading Recovery's longitudinal comparison of tutored, nontutored, and regularly achieving students (DeFord, Pinnell, Lyons, & Place, 1990). However, the data set that served as the best source for the present context consisted of the performances of third graders who, as first or second graders, had been in the intervention and nonintervention groups of my earlier first- and second-grade project (Hiebert et al., 1992).

The distributions of students above, at, or below grade level on the text-level reading task are given in Table 2.2 for the present project, and the third-grade performances of students in the intervention and comparison groups of the early intervention project that was described earlier (Hiebert et al., 1992).

When the profile of the students in the present project is compared with that for the comparison group in the early intervention project, participation in the present project as third graders appears to have made a difference. Approximately 66% of the students in the present project were reading at or above grade level, while the figure for the nonintervention students was 45%. When the profile of the present project students is compared with that of the early intervention students, the percentage of students reading at or above grade level is somewhat lower for the students in the present project than for the early intervention students (66% vs. 77%).

## FUTURE DIRECTIONS

Daily involvement in repeated reading of text, writing, and metacognitive guidance in the structure of written language changed the direction of reading participation for at least two-thirds of the children in this project. If their teachers had not attended more carefully to the instruction, a portion of this group (between 33 and 50% of the group) would have been expected to perform below grade level. For those students who had been viewed by their parents and by the school as candidates for special education, this is a big change.

Of course, the results of a single, action-based study should not be

TABLE 2.2. Percentage of third graders above, at, or below grade level for the present project and the early intervention.

| Text Level | Present Project | Early Intervention | |
|---|---|---|---|
| | | Intervention | Control |
| Above | 41 | 71 | 25 |
| At | 25 | 62 | 0 |
| Below | 33 | 23 | 55 |

overgeneralized. However, its results do corroborate consistent findings of projects that provide focused instruction with high expectations (Anderson, Hiebert, Scott, & Wilkinson, 1985). That is, most children learn to read and write in schools with a focused literacy program and expectations that all children can learn to read and write. A percentage of a cohort may not attain the highest levels of literacy, but all indicators point to a percentage in the vicinity of 6–10% rather than the 28–33% within Cara's and Cindy's classrooms prior to the project or the 30–40% found in national assessments (Mullis et al., 1993).

To be sure, high expectations need to be accompanied by strong instructional practice. This information, too, is available. From the work of Bond and his predecessors to the work of social constructivists, we find a rich knowledge base for designing literacy environments for struggling readers. In revisiting the first edition of Bond and Tinker's (1957) textbook that I used in my diagnosis and remediation course at the University of Illinois in 1970, I found the fundamental stance toward remediation to be similar to that of this project: increasing the amount of reading that students are doing, connecting writing experiences to students' reading, and filling in the gaps of knowledge about the critical elements of words that students missed or misunderstood. Since Bond's time, perspectives from cognitive psychology and social constructivism have given even stronger theoretical substantiation to these activities. The constructs from cognitive psychology of automaticity and metacognition argue for activities such as repeated readings of text and talk between teacher and students that increases reflection on strategies and their applications. Social constructivism has brought into focus the need for grounding instruction in meaningful reading and writing tasks and in peer interaction.

The knowledge is available that shows that the vast majority of students can become proficient readers. The knowledge also is available on the nature of the hard work that is required for this to happen with struggling, middle-grade readers. High-quality instruction for initially low-performing students is a philosophical and ethical choice for educators, parents, policy makers, and citizens. There is a set of critical roles that university-based educators can play in ensuring that a choice for high-quality instruction is made in more communities. In the remainder of this chapter, I will discuss directions that need to be taken within the university-based reading community to provide this support.

The first role is one of communicating the potential of children in becoming literate. I have yet to read a study that indicates that 40% of our population is incapable of learning to read. Yet, this figure describes the percentage of fourth-grade students who are unable to read a grade-level passage automatically (Campbell & Kapinus, 1993). There is research to be mustered, such as evidence from contexts where students have learned to read and write well, that needs to be communicated to shift the national conversation about the potential of children to learn to read. As teachers in preservice and inservice university courses, as writers of articles in professional journals, as speakers at national conferences, and as leaders of workshops in local schools, university-based educators can focus the attention of school-based educators and community members on the effects of high expectations on literacy learning.

A second role for university-based educators lies in their participation with schools and classrooms. What many teachers have lacked are exemplary models of instruction and classroom organization. For many beginning teachers, their models have been the teachers who served as their supervisors for student teaching and the scripted lessons in teachers' manuals that accompany textbook programs. The problems with both of these sources as models of exemplary instruction have been elaborated at length in many places. In the past decade, an alternative format has surfaced in the form of teacher-researcher networks. In projects that encourage literature-based instruction, such as the Book Club project (Raphael et al., 1992) and the Language to Literacy project (Hoffman, Roser, Battle, Farest, Myers, & Labbo, 1991), and in early interventions such as those of Goldenberg (1994), Juel (1994), Hiebert (1994), and Taylor and colleagues (1994), school- and university-based educators are collaborating to create models of good instruction. These networks of teacher-researchers and researcher-teachers are only at the initial stages, and many questions remain to be answered. One particularly pressing question is the relationship of these collaborative efforts to other classroom sites. Presumably, the aim of these networks is not an "each one teach one" model. How the processes and outcomes of an inquiry process can be extended beyond the target classrooms remains to be seen.

University-based educators are important in establishing a core group of such projects because of the perspective of disciplined inquiry that they bring. There are clearly many teachers who have applied the strategies that have been described in this chapter. For Cara and Cindy, the involvement of a university-based educator allowed for continual reflection and questioning—a commodity that is a basic in the university community but a luxury in a school community. Clusters of school- and university-based educators need to work together to tell the stories of students' literacy learning.

A third role is for university-based educators to study particular elements of literacy projects. There are numerous questions about literacy instruction and learning that would benefit from the lenses of observant university-based educators studying classrooms. For example, the types of text that foster automaticity among middle-grade readers are unclear. Chomsky (1976) assumed that the interestingness of the text was the primary criterion, with length and difficulty of the text a far second. The balance between these factors and the role of student autonomy in selecting text would benefit from study. This role of studying particular dimensions of learning or instruction is one that researchers typically have taken, but I see a transformation in the context in which they execute this role. The embedding of focused research projects within already existing collaborative instructional projects has the benefit of clarifying what happens in the best possible contexts. Further, such projects can provide the reader with the larger context into which a particular technique or process fits. Henry's (1988) project on the effects of metacognitive guidance in word elements and origins within Project READ classrooms illustrates the embedding of a focused research project within a larger collaborative instructional/research effort.

I conclude with the directions that I intend to take for the next phase of my career. I intend to build on my beginnings as a researcher-teacher with networks of teachers who are working hard to transform the trajectories of struggling readers. Through collaborative efforts with teachers such as Cara, Cindy, and others (e.g., Hiebert et al., 1992), I have seen what is possible when school- and university-based educators work together to give low-income children access to the best possible instruction. But there are many questions that remain. Our thrust in these projects has been on establishing automaticity in reading by the end of the primary grades. Once students have been brought to automaticity, a foundation has been laid. But it is the literacies related to content areas such as science and social studies that have been most difficult for low-income children to access (Chall, Jacobs, & Baldwin, 1990). Without automaticity, students have hardly a chance. With automaticity, they at least have an opportunity to gain high-level literacy. But to ensure access to the higher literacies, the efforts of teachers in the middle grades as well as the middle school will need to be marshalled. I anticipate that this phase of collaborative projects will be as challenging as, if not more so, engaging with primary-level teachers in the redesign of initial literacy instruction.

The goal of making the higher literacies accessible to low-income children motivated the initiation of programs like Chapter 1 and the instructional and research efforts of previous generations of literacy educators such as Guy Bond and his colleagues. It is time that we build on the foundation that Bond and others have left us and increase the access of low-income students to the higher literacies.

## REFERENCES

Adams, M. J. (1990). *Beginning to read: Thinking and learning about print*. Cambridge, MA: MIT Press.

Allington, R. L. (1984). Oral reading. In P. D. Pearson, R. Barr, M. L. Kamil, & P. Mosenthal (Eds.), *Handbook of reading research* (Vol. 1, pp. 829–864). New York: Longman.

Anderson, R. C., Hiebert, E. H., Scott, J. A., & Wilkinson, I. A. G. (1985). *Becoming a nation of readers*. University of Illinois at Urbana–Champaign: Center for the Study of Reading.

Atwell, N. (1987). *In the middle: Writing, reading, and learning with adolescents*. Portsmouth, NH: Heinemann.

Baumann, J. et al. (1989). *Informal reading inventory*. Needham Heights, MA: Silver Burdett Ginn.

Bond, G., & Dykstra, R. (1967). The Cooperative Research Program in first-grade reading instruction. *Reading Research Quarterly, 2*, 5–141.

Bond, G. L., & Tinker, M. A. (1957). *Reading difficulties: Their diagnosis and correction*. New York: Appleton-Century-Crofts.

Bridge, C. A., & Hiebert, E. H. (1985). A comparison of classroom writing practices, teachers' perceptions of their writing instruction, and textbook recommendations on writing practices. *The Elementary School Teacher, 86*, 155–172.

Calfee, R. C., & Henry, M. K. (1985). Project READ: An inservice model for training classroom teachers in effective reading instruction. In J. V. Hoffman (Ed.), *Effective teaching of reading: Research and practice* (pp. 199–229). Newark, DE: International Reading Association.

Campbell, J., & Kapinus, B. (December, 1993). *Special studies: The integrated reading performance record*. Paper presented at the annual meeting of the National Reading Conference, Charleston, SC.

Chall, J. S. (1983). *Learning to read: The great debate* (2nd ed.). New York: McGraw-Hill.

Chall, J. S., Jacobs, V. A., & Baldwin, L. E. (1990). *The reading crisis: Why poor children fall behind*. Cambridge, MA: Harvard University Press.

Chomsky, C. (1976). When you still can't read in the third grade: After decoding, what? *Language Arts, 53*, 288–296.

Clarke, L. S. (1988). Invented versus traditional spelling in first graders' writings: Effects on learning to spell and read. *Research in the Teaching of English, 22*, 281–309.

Clay, M. M. (1985). *The early detection of reading difficulties* (3rd ed.). Portsmouth, NH: Heinemann.

Cunningham, P. M. (1975–76). Investigating a synthesized theory of mediated word identification. *Reading Research Quarterly, 11*, 127–143.

Dahl, P.R. (1979). An experimental program for teaching high-speed word recognition and comprehension skills. In J. E. Button, T. Lovitt, & T. Rowland (Eds.), *Communications research in learning disabilities and mental retardation* (pp. 33–65). Baltimore: University Park Press.

DeFord, D. E., Pinnell, G., Lyons, C., & Place, A. W. (1990). *The Reading Recovery follow-up study* (Vol. 11). Columbus: Ohio State University.

Dowhower, S. S. (1987). Effects of repeated reading on second-grade transitional readers' fluency and comprehension. *Reading Research Quarterly, 22*, 389–406.

Downer, M. et al. (1990). *Viewers' guide: Teaching word identification. A videotape series: Teaching reading—strategies from successful classrooms.* Urbana–Champaign: University of Illinois at Urbana–Champaign, Center for the Study of Reading.

Durkin, D. D. (1966). *Children who read early.* New York: Teachers College Press.

Englert, C. S., Hiebert, E. H., & Stewart, S. (1985). Spelling unfamiliar words by an analogy strategy. *Journal of Special Education, 19*, 291–306.

Fisher, C. W., & Hiebert, E. H. (1990). Characteristics of tasks in two approaches to literacy instruction. *Elementary School Journal, 91*, 3–18.

Garcia, G. E., Jimenez, R. T., & Pearson, P. D. (1989). *Annotated bibliography of research related to the reading of at-risk children* (Tech. Rep. No. 482). Urbana–Champaign: University of Illinois at Urbana–Champaign, Center for the Study of Reading.

Gaskins, I. W., Downer, M. A., Anderson, R. C., Cunningham, P. M., & others. (1988). A metacognitive approach to phonics: Using what you know to decode what you don't know. *Remedial and Special Education, 9*, 36–41, 66.

Goldenberg, C. (1994). Promoting early literacy development among Spanish-speaking children: Lessons from two studies. In E. H. Hiebert & B. M. Taylor (Eds.), *Getting reading right from the start: Effective early literacy interventions* (pp. 171–200). Boston: Allyn & Bacon.

Goodman, K. S. (1986). *What's whole in whole language?* Portsmouth, NH: Heinemann.

Hagerty, P., & Hiebert, E. H. (1989). Students' comprehension, writing, and perceptions in two approaches to literacy instruction. In S. McCormick & J. Zutell (Eds.), *Cognitive and social perspectives for literacy research and instruction* (38th Yearbook of the National Reading Conference, pp. 453–460). Chicago: NRC.

Henry, M. K. (1988). Beyond phonics: Integrated decoding and spelling instruction based on word origin and structure. *Annuals of Dyslexia, 38*, 258–275.

Henry, M. K., Calfee, R. C., & LaSalle, R. A. (1988, November). *A structural approach to decoding and spelling curriculum and instruction: A design for transfer.* Symposium presented at the annual meeting of the National Reading Conference. Tucson, AZ.

Herman, P. A. (1985). The effect of repeated readings on reading rate, speech pauses, and word recognition accuracy. *Reading Research Quarterly, 20*, 553–564.

Hiebert, E. H. (1994). Becoming literate through authentic tasks: Evidence and adaptations. In R. B. Ruddell, M. R. Ruddell, & H. Singer (Eds.), *Theoretical models and processes of reading* (4th ed., pp. 391–413). Newark, DE: International Reading Association.

Hiebert, E. H., Colt, J. M., Catto, S. L., & Gury, E. C. (1992). Reading and writing of first-grade students in a restructured Chapter 1 program. *American Educational Research Journal, 29*, 545–572.

Hiebert, E. H., & Taylor, B. M. (Eds.). (1994). *Getting reading right from the start: Effective early literacy interventions*. Boston: Allyn & Bacon.

Hoffman, J. V., Roser, N. L., Battle, J., Farest, C., Myers, P., & Labbo, L. (1991). Evaluating the effects of a read aloud/response program. In J. Zutell & S. McCormick (Eds.), *Learner factors/teacher factors: Issues in literacy research and instruction* (pp. 277–284). Chicago: National Reading Conference.

Johnston, P., & Allington, R. L. (1991). Remediation. In R. Barr, M. Kamil, P. Mosenthal, & P. D. Pearson (Eds.), *Handbook of reading research* (pp. 984–1012). New York: Longman.

Juel, C. (1988). Learning to read and write: A longitudinal study of fifty-four children from first through fourth grades. *Journal of Educational Psychology, 80*, 437–447.

Juel, C. (1991). Beginning reading. In R. Barr, M. L. Kamil, P. B. Mosenthal, & P. D. Pearson (Eds.), *Handbook of reading research* (Vol. 2, pp. 759–788). New York: Longman.

Juel, C. (1994). At-risk university students tutoring at-risk elementary school children: What factors make it effective? In E. H. Hiebert & B. M. Taylor (Eds.), *Getting reading right from the start: Effective early literacy interventions* (pp. 39–61). Boston: Allyn & Bacon.

LaBerge, D., & Samuels, S. (1974). Toward a theory of automatic information processing in reading. *Cognitive Psychology, 6*, 293–323.

Leslie, L., & Caldwell, J. (1991). *Qualitative reading inventory*. New York: Harper Collins.

McCarthey, S. (1994). Opportunities and risks of writing from personal experience. *Language Arts, 71*, 182–191.

Mullis, I. V. S., Campbell, J. R., & Farstrup, A. E. (1993). *NAEP 1992 reading report card for the nation and the states*. Washington, DC: U.S. Department of Education.

Raphael, T. E., McMahon, S. I., Goatley, V. J., Bentley, J. L., Boyd, F. B., Pardo, L. S., & Woodman, D. A. (1992). Literature and discussion in the reading program. *Language Arts, 69*, 54–61.

Read, C. (1975). *Children's categorization of speech sounds in English*. Urbana, IL: National Council of Teachers of English.

Rylant, C., & Stevenson, S. (Il.). (1993). *Henry and Mudge in the sparkle days*. New York: Aladdin Books.

Sulzby, E. (1992). Research directions: Transitions from emergent to conventional writing. *Language Arts, 69*, 290–297.

Taylor, B. M., Strait, J., & Medo, M. (1994). Early intervention in reading: Supplemental instruction for groups of low-achieving students provided by first-grade teachers. In E. H. Hiebert & B. M. Taylor (Eds.), *Getting reading right from the start: Effective early literacy interventions* (pp. 107–121). Boston: Allyn & Bacon.

Woods, M. J., & Moe, A. J. (1989). *Analytical Reading Inventory* (2nd ed.). Columbus, OH: Charles E. Merrill.

CHAPTER 3

# What It Means to Learn to Read

## CHARLES A. PERFETTI
## SULAN ZHANG
*University of Pittsburgh*

Occasionally, students who are teachers, or are on their way to becoming teachers, enroll in a class that I teach on psycholinguistics and reading. I always welcome the opportunity to explain what research has to say about how reading and learning to read work, but what I want to explain is not always what students and teachers want to hear. They often seem eager for me to dispense with discussions of the importance of phonology in reading, the alphabetic principle, phonemic awareness, and other such presemantic concepts. When do we get to the part about meaning?

My impression is that many such aspiring and practicing teachers have had such concepts as phonology, phonics, phonemic awareness, and the like explained to them in a way that doesn't connect with what they intuitively understand to be the goal of reading. My approach to these aversive topics is to try to make clear the question of what learning to read is about, and it has met with some success. When some agreement can be reached on the fundamental task of learning to read, the role of critical concepts having nothing to do with meaning becomes more clear.

As the senior author in this chapter, my goal springs from the kinds of experiences I've just mentioned: to explain a way of thinking about learning to read that makes more central the basic task faced by the learner. My proposal brings a perspective slightly different from what appears to be the typical view of reading instruction. It is a way of thinking that illuminates the critical role that nonsemantic concepts play in learning to read. However, before returning to this main issue (and joint authorship as well), I follow the format of other chapters by first providing an autobiographical story about why I have come to think that this perspective on learning how to read is useful.

## READING AND LANGUAGE: AN AUTOBIOGRAPHICAL PRELUDE

I came to questions of reading from a psycholinguistics background, the field of my Ph.D. specialization at the University of Michigan. My early research was concerned with the bread and butter of language processes — syntax and semantics. I was interested in the representation of word meanings, the role of syntactic structures in language memory and understanding, and the interface of syntax and semantics, topics I continue to pursue (see, for example, Perfetti, 1990, and Perfetti & Britt, 1995). When I began to turn my attention to the processes of reading comprehension, I was occupied with the cognitive implications of structural meanings and grammar, what I called at the time "psychosemantics" (Perfetti, 1972). My first pass at thinking about reading ability — what makes some people better at reading comprehension than others — reflected my theoretical dispositions. Perhaps, I thought, the important factor in reading ability is that some people have "better" semantic and syntactic processes than others.

Before pursuing these aspects of reading, however, I asked myself what I assumed was a more basic question: Could it be that some children with low skill in reading comprehension have problems in word identification that might lead to their comprehension limitations? Only for children for whom the answer to this question is "no," I reasoned, does it make sense to ask about syntactic, semantic, and other aspects of reading. Comprehension could go nowhere without a process that yielded words as the fuel for further comprehension.

This was the right reasoning, but following it led to an unintended consequence: What I found caused me to put aside my study of higher-level comprehension processes. I learned quickly that when 8- to 11-year-old students were divided on comprehension measures, they showed corresponding differences in word identification ability. Furthermore, the differences were magnified for less frequent words, more complex words, and, especially, pseudowords; and, contrary to prevailing views, they actually were reduced with context. It was clear that a basic problem with decoding was strongly associated with problems in comprehension. Context-free word identification ability, I concluded, is the hallmark of skilled readers. In other studies, my students and I found that a second major factor, memory for immediately processed words, was part of the picture. Poor comprehenders had reduced working memories (functional capacity) for both spoken and written language. Importantly, the processing difficulties so visible in decoding were accompanied by a general language processing problem not specific to reading. Some of what we learned about these problems was discussed in *Reading Ability* (Perfetti, 1985).

The conclusion that decoding ability is important to reading comprehension ability seems beyond controversy now. Our additional conclusion was that a level of "automatic" word identification was necessary for skilled comprehension—a level that went beyond accuracy to include facile, resource-cheap word identification. But all this had to do with *comprehension*, and, although it seems a mild claim, it engendered some objections. I appeared to be ignoring other important things in comprehension. Of course, my point was that most other processes in reading used the output of word identification and decoding processes, so these latter processes were important for readers to develop. It did not follow, nor was it ever implied, that a learner somehow had to improve first at lexical processing before developing comprehension skill. I assumed that the best way to practice word reading was to read.

Prompted by these conclusions about the importance of word-level skills, my work on reading began to extend downward from comprehension along two related lines. One line concerned the nature of lexical skill acquired by children who learn to read. Although I carried out relatively little experimental work on this question, I did examine how learning to read words was related to the child's explicit knowledge of phonological structure. I concluded that, in some specific sense, knowledge of phonological forms was both a cause and an effect of learning to read (Perfetti, Beck, Bell, & Hughes, 1987). Later, I addressed the theoretical question of what kinds of word representations children develop, suggesting that the acquisition of word-specific forms, critically boosted by knowledge of phonology, was the central achievement in the development of word representations and hence reading skill (Perfetti, 1992).

The second line of research reflected my long-standing assumption about phonological processes: that both the inner voice referred to by Huey (1968) and the arousal of phonological forms of words as part of word identification were a natural part of reading. Their occurrence is a fundamental derivative of the fact that writing systems are invented on speech systems, which in turn may derive from a human cognitive system that is predisposed to encode linguistic inputs in phonological forms (Perfetti & McCutchen, 1982). The strong evidence I saw for the role of phonology even in skilled reading, in combination with evidence on the orthographic-phonological foundations of children's word reading (e.g., Ehri, 1980; Gough & Hillinger, 1980; Liberman & Shankweiler, 1979), has led me to the issue I address in this chapter: What it means to learn to read.

There is one final important part of this prelude. I became increasingly persuaded that alternative writing systems must be considered in understanding reading. The basic processes discovered in research on English and other alphabetic writing systems need to be evaluated from the perspective of nonalphabetic writing systems. Only cross-system comparisons allow the discovery of the universal and highly general principles that guide reading and learning to read, as well as the distinctive properties of writing systems that modify the details of their use. Pursuing this goal was made possible by the interest of Sulan Zhang, who came to Pittsburgh from Beijing Normal University to work with me on reading. Our joint research has focused on adult skilled readers, comparing Chinese and English word identification and, to a limited extent, text reading (see Perfetti & Zhang, 1995a). What we have learned so far has implications for how to conceptualize basic reading instruction. These implications, along with those arising from previous research on reading, constitute the main message of this chapter.

Once again, we are forced to ignore many interesting higher-level aspects of reading in order to make priorities clear, and the things ignored include some that are important in reading pedagogy. However, a clear and focused account of what it means to learn to read sharpens the image of the central problems of reading acquisition. In what follows, we first develop our general argument that learning to read is learning how a writing system works; we then discuss research on Chinese that supports this argument and consider children's acquisition of word representations in English and Chinese. Finally, we point out some of the practices of Chinese reading instruction that have implications for teaching reading generally.

## LEARNING HOW A WRITING SYSTEM WORKS

The title of this section, we suggest, identifies the fundamental problem of learning how to read. Notice that this framing of the problem is different from the more common construal of learning to read as learning to get meaning from print. It is not that the idea of "getting meaning from print" is incorrect. Rather, framing the problem this way fails to specify a precise learning problem. Learning to read, whatever else it is, is a question of *learning*. And what is learned is the workings of a writing system and a specific orthography.

To say a child learns a writing system is to say that he comes to know how that writing system works—the principles on which it is based and the controlling details of its orthography. These are two interrelated learning tasks, equally important for successful reading. A child born in Italy, Hungary, Russia, or Korea, as well as in the United States, must learn the principles of an alphabetic writing system, although each learns a different orthography. In an alphabetic writing system, basic, meaningless graphic units (letters) associate with basic meaningless speech units (phonemes). A child born in Iran, Egypt, or Israel learns a modified alphabetic system in which consonants are more reliably represented than vowels. A child born in China or Taiwan learns what is usually, and perhaps misleadingly, called a "logographic" system, in which graphic units are assumed to associate primarily with morphemes. (In fact, the graphic units also associate with syllables to some extent.) A child born in Japan learns a syllabary system in which graphic units correspond to syllables, as well as a second morpheme-based system based on Chinese characters.

How are the children in any of these locations supposed to discover the principles of writing system design (and the critical orthographic details) that they must master? For a point of departure, consider how this discovery works in the case of language. A large component of prior implicit knowledge about the possible forms of language appears to guide the acquisition process. A child knows — biologically — the principles of language design prior to acquiring spoken language (Pinker, 1984). Thus, language acquisition is rapid for the first few years of life regardless of the particular language and with modest impact of opportunities to learn.

In contrast to the biological foundation of language, writing systems result from human invention; they are altered, refined, and culturally transmitted across generations. At first glance, there is little in the child's native language endowment to provide any constraints on the learning of the writing system. The form of the system appears to be unpredictable. Nevertheless, a more careful examination suggests one important constraint: Writing systems are based on speech. We return to this argument later.

## THE ALPHABETIC PRINCIPLE

The story of alphabetic writing systems is reasonably well understood, and perhaps not in need of recounting. One point worthy of attention, however, is that the Phoenician-Greek invention of the alphabetic principle appears to have been a much-delayed achievement, one that followed far behind the use of visual symbols for objects and meanings (Gelb, 1952). As Gleitman and Rozin (1977) observed, an idea so slow in coming to the species might not spring easily to the mind of a child. Fortunately, although difficult to discover, the alphabetic principle is quite learnable. The basic idea of reading instruction in an alphabetic system is that children can be taught the alphabetic principle, either directly or indirectly.

At the risk of repeating the obvious, it is important to keep in mind what the alphabetic principle is. The principle is that the elementary unit in the writing system corresponds to a phoneme, a meaningless speech segment. It is the meaninglessness of both the writing unit and the speech unit that is at the heart of the alphabetic principle. This is what allows the tremendous productivity of an alphabetic writing system — its limitless representation of the words of a language from its small inventory of graphic symbols.

A major obstacle to learning the alphabetic principle is that prior to schooling, children have only dim awareness of the phonological structure of their language. Because phonemes are abstractions over highly variable acoustic events, it is not easy to appreciate their status as discrete speech segments that exist outside of ordinary word perception. Obviously, children perceive speech and recognize words, but there is nothing in that ability that makes visible the composition of the speech in terms of phoneme constituents. Furthermore, the child's preschool use of language is communicative and contextualized, seldom directing attention to spoken word forms.

Moreover, how the writing system might map onto the phonological properties or even acoustic properties of spoken language is not transparent to the child. Rozin, Bressman, and Taft (1974) found that many preschool children could not perform their *mow-motorcycle* test, in which children need merely to point to which of two printed words corresponds to each of the spoken words. Associating the longer of two written words with the longer of two spoken words would solve the task. Nevertheless, preschool children found this task difficult and in Sweden, where reading instruction is delayed until the age of 8, even older children find the task difficult (Lundberg & Torneus, 1978). If there is any preliterate knowledge concerning the correspondence principles of speech-based writing systems, it appears to be relatively inaccessible. Indeed, where would such knowledge arise in the absence of learning?

Although accessible knowledge of phonemes as abstract speech segments does not come easily, such knowledge is important for discovering and using the alphabetic principle. Some phonemic awareness is required for children to be successful in reading in an alphabetic writing system (Bradley & Bryant, 1983; Mann, 1991; Tunmer, Herriman, & Nesdale, 1988; Vellutino & Scanlon, 1991). In addition, evidence suggests that phonemic awareness develops as a consequence of reading instruction in an alphabetic system (Morais, Bertelson, Cary, & Alegria, 1986; Perfetti et al., 1987). Thus, in an alphabetic orthography, the relationship between awareness of phonology and progress in reading acquisition is reciprocal and mutually facilitative.

## THE CHINESE WRITING SYSTEM

Southeast Asian scripts span the full range of writing systems — from the putatively logographic Chinese, through the syllabic Japanese Kana, to the alphabetic Korean. We focus on the Chinese case, because it is the system that provides the highest contrast with alphabetic systems.

Chinese writing usually is considered a logography, a system in which the basic unit in writing associates with a unit of meaning (morpheme) in the spoken language. Lacking any components (e.g., letters) that represent subword speech units, a pure logography would be controlled by a morphological (meaning) principle. One would learn the meaning of each character without any reference to phoneme constituents. Such a writing system, in principle, is very different from both alphabetic and syllabaric systems. Each symbol would associate uniquely with a unit of meaning, a morpheme, and would be limited in productivity to families of morphemes.

A pure logography would present a formidable learning task to a child. The learning essentially would be one of associating each character with a meaning. Such economy as could be gained would come from symbols that have meaning relations in common. For example, the character referring to "sun" is used as part of the compound character that refers to "sunshine," as shown in Figure 3.1. (The character for "sun" is actually a radical, one of the 214 elementary morphemic units of the writing system that are used independently as words and as components of compounds of various kinds. We use "character" in general terms to include any free-standing morpheme, including radicals.) A reader who knows the character for "sun" may be able to infer that the compound character that contains "sun" has something to do with sun. But the reader will have to learn the rest of the compound and connect the whole specifically with "sunshine," rather than,

**FIGURE 3.1.** The compound character for "sunshine."

|  |  | Pin Yin/Spelling | Translation |
|---|---|---|---|
| Semantic Radical | 日 | [ri] | sun |
| Phonetic Component | 青 | [qing] | green |
| Compound Character (with valid phonetic information) | 晴 | [qing] | sunshine |

say, "bright" or some other word that has the character for sun as a component.

This description of Chinese morphological composition often is brought to the attention of English-language readers. Less noticed, however, is another feature of character composition revealed in Figure 3.1. The compound character "sunshine" contains a second character, the word *qing*, meaning "green." In using the character for *qing* as part of the character for "sunshine," Chinese produces a phonetic compound: The word meaning "sunshine" is also *qing*. Only the tones differ between the word meaning "green" (*qing1*) and the word meaning "sunshine" (*qing2*). Compounds consisting of two single characters constitute a substantial portion of Chinese characters (82%, according to Zhou, 1978). Zhou (1978) estimates that 39% of these compounds contain a component with a pronunciation similar or identical to that of the compound. Perfetti and Zhang (1995a) provide further examples, illustrating both compounds whose names are the same as a phonetic component and compounds whose names deviate from their component.

Given that the composition of Chinese compounds appears to be based on more than morphology, the characterization of Chinese as a logography can be challenged, and some scholars, including DeFrancis (1989), have done so. DeFrancis joins an earlier Chinese writing scholar (Boudberg, 1937) in arguing that the phonetic component in Chinese writing has been underestimated by a misleading logographic analysis. There are many compound characters that combine a semantic and phonological component in Chinese. From its ancient origins as a system based on pictographic and then semantic symbols, Chinese writing, according to DeFrancis, has evolved into a system dominated by symbols that carry both semantic and phonetic information: a morpho-phonological system rather than an exclusively morphological one.

Although Chinese has phonological information, it is far from reliable. By Zhou's estimate, 61% of the compounds fail to share pronunciation similarity with one of their components. Thus, the odds of encountering an invalid phonetic component (i.e., an invalid cue to pronunciation) in a compound are considerably higher than the odds of encountering a valid phonetic component. In ordinary reading, unless a phonetic component is identical in pronunciation to the compound, it is of limited value; in fact, such nonidentity produces a condition of interference. Nevertheless, that there is a significant phonological component for the Chinese writing system is beyond dispute. Although the details of how this component contributes to reading remain to be worked out, the mere existence of this phonological potential provides an important fact concerning writing systems. It appears, as DeFrancis (1989) argues, that all human writing systems have evolved toward reliance on speech, even those logographic systems assumed to be strictly meaning-based.

## HOW READING CHINESE WORKS

Because Chinese is at least partly a meaning-based script, some researchers and educators have been led to suggest a correlated nonsequitur: Reading Chinese is strictly a visual-semantic process, one in which phonology plays no role. For example, Smith (1985) observed that fluent readers of English "recognize words in the same way that fluent Chinese readers [do]" (p. 103). The claim here is that in both English and Chinese, skilled reading is a direct mapping of the script to meaning. Others also have made this suggestion about Chinese reading. Baron and Strawson (1976), for example, referred to one category of English-language readers as "Chinese" by way of suggesting that they read by strictly visual-to-semantic processes.

Recent evidence suggests a rather different view of reading Chinese. Rather than ignoring phonology in a direct script-to-meaning process, skilled Chinese readers appear to activate phonology as part of the reading process. We illustrate this evidence by summarizing results from our research program (Perfetti & Zhang, 1995b; see also Perfetti & Zhang, 1991; Zhang & Perfetti, 1993).

One form of evidence comes from experiments in which subjects name a target word that is preceded by a prime related to it visually, semantically, or phonologically (as a homophone). For example, in Experiment 4 of Perfetti and Zhang (1991), native Mandarin-speaking subjects named a Chinese character that was preceded by a prime exposed for 180 ms (.18 second). To illustrate a homophone case, the character to be named was *shi*, meaning "to look at" and the homophone prime was *shi*, meaning "matter." The two characters had neither visual nor semantic similarity. If meaning is the only output of word identification in Chinese, there is no basis for expecting a priming effect from a briefly presented character on the basis of its pronunciation. Instead, one would expect priming on the basis of meaning. So naming *shi* ("to look at") would be primed only by its near synonym, *kan*, "to see." The results, however, clearly confirmed a large phonological priming effect. Subjects were faster to name a word if they had viewed a semantically unrelated homophone. There was additionally a somewhat smaller but significant semantic priming effect. Interestingly, there was no effect of a visually similar character.

Other experiments, using brief presentations, suggest that phonological effects occur at least as quickly as semantic effects. At 20 ms of word exposure, we found no effect of either semantic or phonological similarity,

**TABLE 3.1.** Examples of materials from Perfetti and Zhang, 1995b.

| | Pronunciation | Translation | Correct response | |
|---|---|---|---|---|
| | | | Synonym Judgment | Homophone Judgment |
| Homophone | 事 [shi] | matter | No | Yes |
| | 视 [shi] | see | | |
| Control | 清 [qing] | clear | No | No |
| | 视 [shi] | see | | |
| Synonym | 看 [kan] | look at | Yes | No |
| | 视 [shi] | see | | |

whereas at 50 ms both semantic and phonological primes produced greater target identification accuracy. Such results suggest a character reading process that produces both phonological and semantic codes very rapidly, within the first 50 ms of processing (Perfetti & Zhang, 1991, Experiment 3).

To demonstrate that phonological activation is general in Chinese reading, however, we need to observe it in conditions other than naming or explicit identification. Perfetti and Zhang (1995b) created such conditions by having subjects make a decision about whether two characters presented quickly one after the other had similar meanings. In a parallel task, the subjects had to decide whether the two characters had the same pronunciation. Table 3.1 illustrates the materials from these experiments.

The critical data come from "foil trials," trials on which the pair of characters did not have the relationship defined by the task. When subjects were judging meaning similarity, the key foil trials occurred when the two characters had the same pronunciation but not the same meaning. If phonological activation is difficult to suppress, as we believe, then reading two characters having the same name could interfere with the subject's attempt to decide whether they had the same meaning. Notice that this could occur only if the phonological information was activated as the subject read each character. It is of absolutely no value in this task to have the name of the character activated if the subject can perform the task without it. If ever there were a case of reading directly from script to meaning, this should be it.

The results clearly confirm that phonological information was activated during the identification of the characters. When readers had to make a judgment of meaning, their decisions were impaired (slower and less accurate) if the two characters had the same pronunciation. When subjects had to make a judgment of pronunciation similarity, their judgments were impaired if the two characters had meaning similarity. As with the naming studies, this is evidence for phonological and semantic information activated together.

The question of the time course of activation—whether semantic activation precedes phonological activation—was addressed in a second experiment by Perfetti and Zhang (1995b). This study varied the delay (or Stimulus Onset Asynchrony [SOA]) between the onset of the first character and the onset of the second character. At very short SOAs, the subject has little time to encode information in the first character. The script-to-meaning view of Chinese reading predicts the following: The subject can selectively encode semantic information to help perform the meaning judgment task; thus we should observe a delay in phonological interference (the decision time difference between a homophone and control foil for a meaning judgment) compared with semantic interference (the decision time difference between a synonym and control foil for a pronunciation judgment). Instead, it was semantic interference that was delayed, while phonological interference was very rapid.

The interference functions over SOAs can be considered estimates of the time course of semantic and phonological activation. Figure 3.2 shows these functions in a way that eliminates the differences in the amount of interference found in the two cases, which was greater for phonological interference at every point. Instead, the amount of interference at each point is relative to the maximum amount (100%) observed for each task, which occurred at 310 ms. As Figure 3.2 illustrates, phonological activation shows a fast rise time; semantic activation, a somewhat slower one.

Within the first 90 ms, (the shortest SOA tested) phonological activation was sufficient to interfere with a semantic judgment. This is evidence for very early phonological activation in character reading in a task in which it is of no use. Chinese readers appear to have difficulty suppressing phonological information, despite the potential of the writing system for allowing direct script-to-meaning reading.

What causes phonological processing to occur in a writing system that is supposed to be meaning-based? We must conclude, first, that our Chinese readers were demonstrating what usually is called "postlexical" phonology, the activation of word pronunciations following the access of the word

**FIGURE 3.2.** The time course of phonological and semantic activation based on interference data replotted from Perfetti & Zhang (1995b). The percent activation is based on difference scores (phonological interference and semantic interference relative to controls) plotted as a function of the maximum amount of interference obtained in each condition. Thus, although phonological activation was greater than semantic activation, both reach 100% by definition.

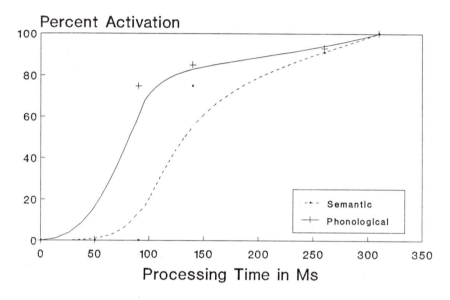

from its printed form. We prefer to characterize this phonology as *atlexical*, that is, occurring at the moment of access, to capture the assumption that the identification of a word consists, in part, of the retrieval of its phonological form. (See Perfetti & Zhang, 1995a, for a fuller argument on this point.) On this account, as the reader identifies a character, the name of that character is accessed and phonologically represented just as its meaning is. This is the most straightforward explanation and it is consistent with our data.

Ruled out is the possibility that our Chinese readers were using sublexical phonological information within the character. Although Chinese compounds can contain phonological components (recall the sunshine example of Figure 3.1), the materials of Perfetti and Zhang were not of this type. Generally, the phonological foils (homophones), like those of Table 3.1, did not share a phonetic component with the target character.

Phonological components might well play a role in other circum-stances, as evidence on naming low-frequency words suggests (Peng, Young, & Chen, 1994; Seidenberg, 1985). (We've already noted the overall limited reliability of phonetic components. They are more reliable as cues to pronunciation for low-frequency words.) Furthermore, we think phonetic compounds can help organize learning of characters. However, there is no reason so far to conclude that phonetic components routinely mediate character identification. Instead, we suggest that the identification of a character brings about an automatic phonological representation as part of the identification process.

Finally, we note that phonological processing has an important func-tion in reading beyond word identification. Phonological representations serve to secure reference (Perfetti & McCutchen, 1982) and to maintain recently read information in memory. These functions in turn serve com-prehension in reading in any writing system, including Chinese. Zhang and Perfetti (1993) found that Chinese readers show a phonological interference in the reading of texts (the tongue-twister effect) just as readers of English do. Furthermore, the source of this phonological interference is in working memory (Zhang & Perfetti, 1993, Experiment 2). Combined with the results of other memory and reading comprehension tasks in Chinese reading (Tzeng & Hung, 1980; Tzeng, Hung, & Wang, 1977), such results suggest that Chinese reading, once words are recognized, is similar to reading in English. The Chinese reader holds words in phonological forms for the purposes of memory and comprehension. What we have emphasized here goes beyond this conclusion. In Chinese reading, the process of word identi-fication is what produces these phonological forms.

## LEARNING TO READ ENGLISH, LEARNING TO READ CHINESE

There are implications of our analysis of Chinese reading, in combination with what we know about reading in English, for issues of reading acquisi-tion and instruction. In considering these implications, we are guided by the Universal Phonological Principle (Perfetti, Zhang, & Berent, 1992) and also by a model of lexical representation in English (Perfetti, 1992).

### THE UNIVERSAL PHONOLOGICAL PRINCIPLE

The Universal Phonological Principle (UPP) is actually a set of three princi-ples that guide reading across different writing systems. The central princi-ple is that, in any writing system, skilled readers' encounters with most printed words automatically lead to phonological activation. This activation includes the word's phoneme constituents and its pronunciation. A second, corollary principle is that writing systems constrain the extent to which this phonological activation includes sublexical phonology, but not whether phonological activation occurs. A third principle, again a corollary one, is that activated phonology serves memory and comprehension, with phonological rehearsal, but not the activation itself, under reader control.

The research summarized here on skilled Chinese reading is consistent with the UPP. We already know that reading English involves phonology. The debate has been whether such phonological activation is "prelexical" or "postlexical." Some evidence points to automatic phonological activation in English as a process that occurs prior to word identification (Ferrand & Grainger, 1992; Lukatela & Turvey, 1990; Perfetti, Bell, & Delaney, 1988; Van Orden, 1987). Other evidence suggests an optional use of phonology within the context of a dual route model (Besner, 1990; Coltheart, 1978; Paap & Noel, 1991). However, even with such variation in the details, there is consensus for a significant role played by phonology in English word identification.

One view on the relationship between writing systems and the use of phonology is provided by the orthographic depth hypothesis of Frost, Katz, and Bentin (1987). According to this hypothesis, the writing system determines the extent to which phonology will be used in identifying a word. Alphabetic writing systems promote prelexical use of phonology; logographic systems would discourage use of prelexical phonology. The orthographic depth hypothesis is consistent with an assumption that the reader will acquire a writing system and adapt his or her reading strategies to the fundamental principles of the writing system. Coupled with the UPP, it suggests a set of constraints on the way writing can influence the reading process.

It is important to emphasize that phonological processes in reading are natural products of human cognition, and that is why they are universal. The adaptation that a reader might make to a writing system does not arise from the conscious selection of some strategy, but rather is a natural result of learning the writing system. As the writing system is learned, the phonological processes naturally accommodate the properties of the learned system. According to the UPP, all readers use phonological processes, if they are able. Speech is ontogenetically prior to print. All children learn a native language; not all children learn to read. Such considerations compel the conclusion that speech processes are privileged as a child begins to learn to read. Furthermore, skilled reading continues to make use of phonological information well beyond the time at which one might suppose that it could be discarded. The reason, again, is simple and fundamental. Human language processing and human memory systems are structured to rely on speech-based coding. Thus, the UPP is grounded in observations about fundamental human cognition and language.

## LEXICAL REPRESENTATIONS IN ALPHABETIC WRITING

The importance of phonology in reading, as captured by the UPP, also must be part of any specific model of learning to read. Such a model must link explicitly the child's knowledge of the writing system and knowledge of the language. According to the Restricted Interactive Model of lexical representation (Perfetti, 1991, 1992), learning to read increases the numbers of orthographically addressable words and modifies individual word representations. What a child knows about words is represented by specified strings of letters, phonemes, and whole words in an interconnected network consistent with the kinds of representations proposed by McClelland and Rumelhart (1981). Thus, for a skilled reader, there is representation of the word with its position-correct letters, the phonemic values of those letters, and the pronunciation of the word as a whole. The representations of words develop in two ways with increased reading competence. First, the representations increase in *specificity*: the number of position-correct specific letters in a lexical representation. The second quality modification involves *redundancy*: an increase in the number of redundant phonemic representations contained in a lexical entry. The redundancy idea rests on the assumption that word names (pronunciations) are part of the child's earliest lexical representations and that, with learning, phonemes are added to this representation in connection to individual letters. Thus, learning is a question of the child's acquisition of increased specificity and increased redundancy in lexical representations.

Together, increasing specificity and redundancy allow high-quality word representations to be reliably activated by orthographic inputs. As individual words become fully specified and redundant, they move from a functional lexicon that allows reading, to the autonomous lexicon that allows efficient resource-cheap reading (Perfetti, 1992). It is the words in the autonomous lexicon that produce the kind of automatic phonological activation we see in highly skilled reading.

## LEXICAL REPRESENTATIONS IN CHINESE

How would a model of written Chinese compare with the model of representation for English? As in English, specificity and redundancy are important in characterizing a quality word representation. A word is identified to the extent that the reader has a precise representation of its specific components. Thus, a compound is represented as a graphic object comprising two components, and a multicharacter word as a string of characters with these components. The composition process itself, the sequence of strokes, also may be a part of the word representation (Flores D'Arcais, Saito, & Kawakami, 1995). Importantly, phonological as well as semantic information is represented in the form of connections among compounds sharing components.

Thus, a word representation for a skilled Chinese reader contains information about visual form, pronunciation, and meaning. Figure 3.3 illustrates a fragment of a network of lexical entries of Chinese compounds interconnected on the basis of character components.

The idea expressed in Figure 3.3 is that the Chinese reader has an interconnected representation of character constituents (appearance), pronunciation, and semantic values. Some of the phonetic information represented in a compound is valid and some is not. Thus, the character pronounced *yang* ("sheep") appears in several compounds, including the word meaning "ocean," which has the same (except for tone) pronunciation, *yang*. However, this same component also links sheep semantically to the word for antelope, pronounced *ling*. Thus, a single component brings about both semantic and phonological links to different words. Finally, we see additional words pronounced *yang* that do not share this "sheep" component.

**FIGURE 3.3.** A network of interconnected lexical entries for compound Chinese characters.

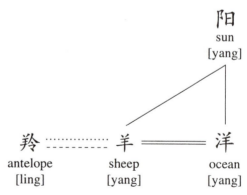

Phonological Links ————
Phonological Plus Graphic Links ══════
Phonological Inhibition ················
Semantic Links ─ ─ ─ ─ ─

As shown, the information in Figure 3.3 is not a model of reading, but rather a representation of information from a small fragment of the lexicon. However, if we assume the representation corresponds to a network of information activated during word identification, there are some implications for reading processes. One is that, during word identification, there may be partial activation of relevant phonology from a phonetic component; there may be activation of irrelevant, misleading phonology, again from a phonetic component; and there may be activation of both relevant and irrelevant semantic information from a character component. There is, as in a restricted interactive model of the type we propose for English, the idea that multiple levels of activation occur, only some of which are decisive in the final product of identification.

In connection with such representations, we argue that word identification is not the access of meaning, but the retrieval of phonological form (pronunciation) and the activation of meaning. Neither in English nor in Chinese does a reader identify a word by accessing its meaning. Word identification has to entail the potential ability to name the word that is being accessed, and this requires consulting its phonological representation. Whether phonological activation precedes or follows semantic activation is a detail, important only for certain purposes. If we can agree that identifying a word is about getting what the word is, then we have to include the word's pronunciation in Chinese as well as in English.

### LEARNING TO READ CHINESE

How does a Chinese child come to acquire these kinds of representations? The central fact of learning is clear: Children spend a lot of time reading and writing characters, both in school and out of school. Estimates suggest that Chinese children learn more than 600 characters each year over 6 years of schooling (Leong, 1973), an accumulation of 3,600 characters, which is sufficient to read a newspaper. A second important feature of Chinese literacy instruction may be the closer connection between reading and writing. Instruction at first is focused more on reading than writing, as in most Western reading instruction. However, Chinese children, by the second half of the first year, are spending a lot of time writing characters. The approach to writing is systematic, and the composition process itself, which is based on a strict spatial ordering of strokes, undoubtedly strengthens the lexical representations that the child acquires. Chinese children acquire a lexical representation of very high quality because they both write the character and read it, the two activities mutually reinforcing each other.

In English, increases in reading skill reflect increases in the number and quality of word representations — specificity and redundancy. In Chinese, we assume there is a corresponding increase in the number and quality of word representations. Clearly, specificity of representation is part of the picture — the precise representation of the character components, their connection with phonology, and their connection with appropriate meanings. Indeed, compared with the development of lexical representations in English, the young Chinese reader's functional lexicon may have a more fully specified lexical representation — one free of "variables" and containing mainly "constants" (Perfetti, 1992). Less clear in Chinese is whether there is a redundancy principle, similar to that in alphabetic systems, operating on the components of the characters. That is, does the child learn that the simple character for sheep (*yang*) provides the name for the compound character for ocean? Of course, the child does learn that the first is a constituent of the second in some sense. Whether this is a piece of "redundant" information similar to that in our model of English reading is not clear. However, evidence from Chen, Lau, and Yung (1993), showing a strong link between second- and third-grade reading and knowledge of component character pronunciation, is consistent with this possibility.

Chinese children acquire their reading skill, of course, through a level of homework much greater than is seen in the United States. Lacking documented information on China itself, we cite Stevenson and Lee's (1990) comparison showing superior reading achievement in Taiwan compared with the United States. First-grade children, according to parent interviews, spent seven times as much time on homework as did American first-grade children. Interestingly, they spent less time being read to and came to school with less knowledge of reading. Of course, cross-cultural comparisons are misleading unless they are part of a broader culturally referenced study. This isolated Chinese–U.S. comparison cannot be used legitimately to fuel a more-homework doctrine in the United States. Still, one does not have to abandon the idea of first grader as child to imagine that homework is helpful to learning to read and write.

The teaching of reading in China appears to have undergone its share of pushes and pulls over the years, just as reading instruction has in the United States. A major push came with the introduction of Pin Yin instruction, which provided alphabetic letters as part of word representations. Pin Yin, literally "spell-sound," has provided Romanized alphabetic spellings since 1958. Chinese children, in fact, learn to read with this alphabetic writing system before they learn characters. The child first gets Pin Yin instruction, then characters appear with Pin Yin, and finally the Pin Yin is taken away and the characters can be read. Pin Yin is most helpful for new words that the child encounters, because it provides a pronunciation for an unfamiliar word.

In the typical sequence of instruction (summarized in Table 3.2), the

TABLE 3.2. Summary of Chinese reading instruction.

I. Alphabetic (Pin Yin) learning: 8 weeks.
    A. 26 letters; instruction in phonological awareness.
    B. Simple syllable decoding:
        *ba, pa, fa; ban, pan, man, fan.*
    C. Pin Yin sentences.

II. Pin Yin and characters for remainder of first year.
    A. 202 characters learned over 20--43 days.
    B. Gradual removal of Pin Yin for familiar characters.
    C. Pin Yin for introduction of character only.

III. By end of second year: 2500 characters learned.

child first learns a 26-letter alphabet along with some instruction in phonological awareness. The first 8 weeks of instruction present the child with simple and compound vowels (in isolation), followed by an introduction to simple syllables in a pattern that repeats syllable endings (e.g., *ba, pa, ma, fa; ban, pan, man, fan*). Instruction soon includes reading sentences written in Pin Yin. The goal is that after 8 weeks, the child should know Pin Yin very well. The success of this instruction suggests that 8 weeks is sufficient to learn to read in an alphabetic system.

Following mastery of Pin Yin, characters are introduced, written above Pin Yin, for the remainder of the first school year. Pin Yin is removed gradually, first for familiar characters, and later for all characters, except when they are first introduced. Over 43 days of instruction (only 20 days in the newest methods of instruction), the child learns 202 characters, on the way to 2,500 after the first 2 years (Zhang, 1993).

A current issue in teaching reading in China concerns the role of phonetic components. The fact that Chinese compounds can share phonetic components has led to different approaches concerning these components. The traditional way has been largely to ignore phonetic components and teach the characters in what is called a "distributed" method. In this method, the fact that two components happen to share the same pronunciation, for example, *yang*, would not cause them to be taught together. A move in the opposite direction, an experimental approach called the "concentrated" method, instead introduces compounds containing the same phonetic component at the same time in instruction. Essentially, in the concentrated method, children learn families of characters that share the same phonetic component.

Clearly, this concentrated method reflects a belief that children can and should take advantage of phonological information in forming their lexical representations. Thus, connections among the lexical representations for the many words that have the phonetic component *yang* would be strengthened in learning, as would the many words sharing the pronunciation *mao*, and so on. Such a procedure would highlight the usefulness of phonology in the reading system and perhaps make it a more important part of the representation system. On the other hand, the fact that the child will face more invalid than valid phonetic components implies some caution in the use of such a method.

The issue of concentrated versus distributed methods seems surprisingly similar to debates in America about the teaching of reading. At one level, it is a technical issue about how to order materials in a decoding-based system. At another level, it may be approximately a contrast between "sight learning" and "code-based learning," including some of the side issues typical of such debates. Thus, one of the criticisms of the concentrated method is that it relies too much on reading of characters out of context. Although this debate may sound familiar, it is very different in one important respect: The differences in these two methods are trivial compared with their shared commitment to Pin Yin instruction. Children in China learn the alphabetic principle through what must be considered direct decoding instruction. Obviously, the corresponding debate in the West about teaching reading lacks that fundamental consensus.

Whether the distributed or concentrated method is better, is beyond our purpose. We wish merely to demonstrate that there are issues in Chinese reading about how to take advantage of the phonological similarity that exists in the writing system. Such observations bring Chinese closer to alphabetic systems in some respects. Teaching every character as a unique association is a possibility in Chinese, whereas the analogous practice in English or in any other alphabetic writing system clearly would be counterproductive. Thus, it is of interest that there is any movement in the other direction, that is, to teach Chinese as a partly phonetically productive system. This implies not only that there is a principle organizing the Chinese writing system other than meaning and morphology, but that this principle can be applied to instruction. The Chinese example adds irony to the resistance to the application of this phonological principle in countries with alphabetic writing systems. For such systems, in contrast to Chinese, its application is essential rather than merely convenient.


## LEARNING A WRITING SYSTEM: CONCLUSIONS

We return to the main question: What does it mean for a child to learn his writing system? Our central claim is that this is the right question to ask about the acquisition of reading skill. It is misleading to focus, instead, on such side issues as context, comprehension, or even getting meaning from print, important as all of these components are. These commonly cited goals are not the heart of what learning to read is all about. A child learns to read only by acquiring the knowledge about how her writing system works, that is, how the writing system encodes the language. This learning has to be the center of attention in defining the goals of beginning reading instruction.

The case of Chinese is interesting for several reasons. First, superficial considerations of Chinese have promoted the misconception that writing systems not only can be completely meaning-based, but can be read by strictly visual-to-semantic processes. The consequences of this misleading analysis have been to reinforce a mistaken belief that English could be read as Chinese. We conclude that not even Chinese is read in exactly this way.

This conclusion follows from the research suggesting the pervasive use of phonology in Chinese. We think this reflects a universal principle of reading. We need to understand that the child comes to the reading situation not only with a strong language competence, but with a strong proclivity to use phonology in encoding and representing linguistic messages in memory. This phonological tendency does not diminish merely because the child gets better at reading.

Another implication from a consideration of Chinese is what it takes to become good at reading. The differences between what Chinese parents and educators expect children to do and what American parents and educators expect children to do in the way of learning are profound. With expectations comparable to those in China and commitments to meeting them, it is hard to imagine that educators (in the United States) would still be debating the "best method." All details about teaching methods would be swamped by a massive increase in the amount of time children spent learning their writing system. Furthermore, an alphabetic system is significantly easier to learn than a nonalphabetic system, so an English-speaking child has a big advantage. The writing system is productive: A handful of letters and phonemic elements combine to generate an indefinitely large set of words. The system is there to be acquired as a system, despite its irregularities.

Such irregularities are the source of far too much lamenting and too many superficial excuses for not teaching the alphabetic principle. The fact of the matter is that nearly all of English is reflective of the alphabetic principle. It just happens not to be a one-to-one mapping of graphemes to phonemes; but one-to-one mappings are not what the alphabetic principle is about. The vast majority of words, in fact, have pronunciations that are predictable from their spelling. Moreover, the acquisition of context-sensitive decoding links would account for the ability to identify virtually all English words. "Context-sensitive" is a key qualifier in the preceding claim. What the child has to learn about the English writing system is that there are context dependencies beyond single letters. Learning the most regular and predictable, that is, the least context-dependent, parts of the system first is the reasonable course.

Beyond these specific implications of Chinese for reading English, we want to make a more general suggestion concerning writing systems and the learning of them. If writing systems were based on associations between visual objects and meaning, then there would be a problem in learning. The learner would not be able to interpose his knowledge of the structure of spoken language between the visual objects and the meaning. In fact, it appears that there is no writing system in current use that is like that. It is becoming increasingly clear that writing systems cannot be seen as fundamentally arbitrary in their design. Of course, they are quite variable in the mix of principles that underlie their design. But there are no systems of writing based only on meaning and not on speech, not even Chinese.

One would suppose there is a reason for this, some function being served by the similarities of writing systems as well as their differences. We think that function is fairly clear: It allows users of the writing system to take advantage of their pre-existing linguistic knowledge, especially their knowledge of speech. The goal of the learner is to figure out how her writing system works. This varies with writing systems, but there is a principle that links language, reading, and writing systems: This principle is that writing systems build on speech. Thus, language is encoded in writing systems. Reading decodes these systems.

ACKNOWLEDGMENT. The research that is the basis for this chapter was funded by a grant to the first author from the National Science Foundation, SBR 9293125. The authors also wish to thank Mara Georgi for her assistance in the preparation of the chapter.

## REFERENCES

Baron, J., & Strawson, C. (1976). Use of orthographic and word specific knowledge in reading words aloud. *Journal of Experimental Psychology: Human Perception and Performance, 2*, 386–393.

Besner, D. (1990). Does the reading system need a lexicon? In D. A. Balota, G. B. Flores d'Arcais, & K. Rayner (Eds.), *Comprehension processes in reading* (pp. 73–99). Hillsdale, NJ: Erlbaum.

Boudberg, P. A. (1937). Some proleptic remarks on the evolution of archaic Chinese. *Harvard Journal of Asiatic Studies, 2*, 329–372.

Bradley, L., & Bryant, P. E. (1983). Categorizing sounds and learning to read—a causal connection. *Nature, 301*, 419–421.

Chen, M. J., Lau, L. L., & Yung, Y. F. (1993). Development of component skills in reading Chinese. *International Journal of Psychology*, *28*, 481–507.

Coltheart, M. (1978). Lexical access in simple reading tasks. In G. Underwood (Ed.), *Strategies of information processing* (pp. 151–216). New York: Academic Press.

DeFrancis, J. (1989). *Visible speech: The diverse oneness of writing systems*. Honolulu: University of Hawaii Press.

Ehri, L. C. (1980). The development in orthographic images. In U. Frith (Ed.), *Cognitive processes in spelling* (pp. 311–388). London: Academic Press.

Ferrand, L., & Grainger, J. (1992). Phonology and orthography in visual word recognition: Evidence from masked non-word priming. *Quarterly Journal of Experimental Psychology: Human Experimental Psychology*, *45A*, 353–372.

Flores D'Arcais, G. B., Saito, H., & Kawakami, M. (1995). Phonological and semantic activation in reading Kanji characters. *Journal of Experimental Psychology: Learning, Memory, and Cognition*, *21*, 34–42.

Frost, R., Katz, L., & Bentin, S. (1987). Strategies for visual word recognition and orthographical depth: A multilingual comparison. *Journal of Experimental Psychology: Human Perception and Performance*, *13*, 104–115.

Gelb, I. J. (1952). *A study of writing*. Chicago: University of Chicago Press.

Gleitman, L. R., & Rozin, P. (1977). The structure and acquisition of reading I: Relations between orthographies and the structure of language. In A. S. Reber & D. L. Scarborough (Eds.), *Toward a psychology of reading: The proceedings of the CUNY conferences* (pp. 1–54). Hillsdale, NJ: Erlbaum.

Gough, P. B., & Hillinger, M. L. (1980). Learning to read: An unnatural act. *Bulletin of the Orton Society*, *20*, 179–196.

Huey, E. B. (1968). *The psychology and pedagogy of reading; with a review of the history of reading and writing and of methods, texts, and hygiene in reading*. Cambridge, MA: MIT Press.

Leong, C. K. (1973). Reading in Chinese with reference to reading practices in Hong Kong. In J. Downing (Ed.), *Comparative reading: Cross-national studies of behavior and processes in reading and writing* (pp. 383–402). New York: Macmillan.

Liberman, I. Y., & Shankweiler, D. (1979). Speech, the alphabet, and teaching to read. In L. B. Resnick & P. A. Weaver (Eds.), *Theory and practice of early reading* (Vol. 2, pp. 109–132). Hillsdale, NJ: Erlbaum.

Lukatela, G., & Turvey, M. T. (1990). Automatic and pre-lexical computation of phonology in visual word identification. *European Journal of Cognitive Psychology*, *2*, 325–344.

Lundberg, I., & Torneus, M. (1978). Nonreaders' awareness of the basic relationship between spoken and written words. *Journal of Experimental Child Psychology*, *25*, 404–412.

Mann, V. A. (1991). Phonological abilities: Effective predictors of future reading ability. In L. Rieben & C. A. Perfetti (Eds.), *Learning to read: Basic research and its implications* (pp. 121–133). Hillsdale, NJ: Erlbaum.

McClelland, J. L., & Rumelhart, D. E. (1981). Interactive activation model of context effects in letter perception: 1. Account of basic findings. *Psychological Review*, *88*, 357–407.

Morais, J., Bertelson, P., Cary, L., & Alegria, J. (1986). Literacy training and speech segmentation. *Cognition, 24,* 45–64.

Paap, K. R., & Noel, R. W. (1991). Dual-route models of print and sound: Still a good horse race. *Psychological Research, 53,* 13–24.

Peng, D. L., Young, H., & Chen, Y. (1994, September). *Consistency effect in naming of Chinese phonograms.* Paper presented at the sixth international symposium on cognitive aspects of the Chinese language, National Taiwan University, Taipei.

Perfetti, C. A. (1972). Psychosemantics: Some cognitive aspects of structural meaning. *Psychological Bulletin, 78,* 241–259.

Perfetti, C. A. (1985). *Reading ability.* New York: Oxford University Press.

Perfetti, C. A. (1990). The cooperative language processors: Semantic influences in an autonomous syntax. In D. A. Balota, G. B. Flores d'Arcais, & K. Rayner (Eds.), *Comprehension processes in reading* (pp. 205–230). Hillsdale, NJ: Erlbaum.

Perfetti, C. A. (1991). Representations and awareness in the acquisition of reading competence. In L. Rieben & C. A. Perfetti (Eds.), *Learning to read: Basic research and its implications* (pp. 33–44). Hillsdale, NJ: Erlbaum.

Perfetti, C. A. (1992). The representation problem in reading acquisition. In P. B. Gough, L. C. Ehri, & R. Treiman (Eds.), *Reading acquisition* (pp. 145–174). Hillsdale, NJ: Erlbaum.

Perfetti, C. A., Beck, I., Bell, L., & Hughes, C. (1987). Phonemic knowledge and learning to read are reciprocal: A longitudinal study of first grade children. *Merrill-Palmer Quarterly, 33,* 283–319.

Perfetti, C. A., Bell, L., & Delaney, S. (1988). Automatic phonetic activation in silent word reading: Evidence from backward masking. *Journal of Memory and Language, 27,* 59–70.

Perfetti, C. A., & Britt, M. A. (1995). Where do propositions come from? In C. A. Weaver III, S. Mannes, & C. R. Fletcher (Eds.), *Discourse comprehension: Essays in honor of Walter Kintsch* (pp. 11–34). Hillsdale, NJ: Erlbaum.

Perfetti, C. A., & McCutchen, D. (1982). Speech processes in reading. In N. Lass (Ed.), *Speech and language: Advances in basic research and practice* (pp. 237–269). New York: Academic Press.

Perfetti, C. A., & Zhang, S. (1991). Phonological processes in reading Chinese characters. *Journal of Experimental Psychology: Learning, Memory, and Cognition, 17,* 633–643.

Perfetti, C. A., & Zhang, S. (1995a). The universal word identification reflex. In D. L. Medin (Ed.), *The psychology of learning and motivation* (Vol. 33, pp. 159–189). San Diego: Academic Press.

Perfetti, C. A., & Zhang, S. (1995b). Very early phonological activation in Chinese reading. *Journal of Experimental Psychology: Learning, Memory, and Cognition, 21,* 24–33.

Perfetti, C. A., Zhang, S., & Berent, I. (1992). Reading in English and Chinese: Evidence for a "universal" phonological principle. In R. Frost & L. Katz (Eds.), *Orthography, phonology, morphology, and meaning* (pp. 227–248). Amsterdam: North-Holland.

Pinker, S. (1984). *Language learnability and language development*. Cambridge, MA: Harvard University Press.

Rozin, P., Bressman, B., & Taft, M. (1974). Do children understand the basic relationship between speech and writing? The Mow–Motorcycle test. *Journal of Reading Behavior, 6*, 327–334.

Seidenberg, M. S. (1985). The time course of phonological code activation in two writing systems. *Cognition, 19*, 1–30.

Smith, F. (1985). *Reading without nonsense* (2nd ed.). New York: Teachers College Press.

Stevenson, H. W., & Lee, S-Y. (1990). *Contexts of achievement: A study of American, Chinese, and Japanese children*. Chicago: University of Chicago Press.

Tunmer, W. E., Herriman, M. L., & Neesdale, A. R. (1988). Metalinguistic abilities and beginning reading. *Reading Research Quarterly, 23*, 134–158.

Tzeng, O. J. L., & Hung, D. L. (1980). Reading in a nonalphabetic writing system: Some experimental studies. In J. F. Kavanagh & R. L. Venezky (Eds.), *Orthography, reading and dyslexia*. Baltimore: University Park Press.

Tzeng, O. J. L., Hung, D. L., & Wang, W. S-Y. (1977). Speech recoding in reading Chinese characters. *Journal of Experimental Psychology: Human Learning and Memory, 3*, 621–630.

Van Orden, G. C. (1987). A ROWS is a ROSE: Spelling, sound, and reading. *Memory & Cognition, 15*, 181–198.

Vellutino, F. R., & Scanlon, D. M. (1991). The effects of instructional bias on word identification. In L. Rieben & C. A. Perfetti (Eds.), *Learning to read: Basic research and its implications* (pp. 189–203). Hillsdale, NJ: Erlbaum.

Zhang, C. F. (1993). Introducing the method of direct reading into the teaching of concentrated literacy. *Chinese Language Construction, 3*, 24–26.

Zhang, S., & Perfetti, C. A. (1993). The tongue-twister effect in reading Chinese. *Journal of Experimental Psychology: Learning, Memory, and Cognition, 19*, 1082–1093.

Zhou, Y. G. (1978). To what degree are the "phonetics" of present-day Chinese characters still phonetic? *Zhongguo Yuwen, 146*, 172–177.

RESPONSE

# Looking Beyond Ourselves to Help All Children Learn to Read

BARBARA M. TAYLOR

*University of Minnesota*

By looking beyond ourselves, outside of our own culture and what is familiar to us, we often can see things more clearly and understand ourselves better. The chapters by Charles Perfetti and Sulan Zhang and by Elfrieda Hiebert both help us look beyond ourselves, but in different ways. Perfetti and Zhang help us look beyond our own culture. Hiebert helps us work beyond what is familiar to us in terms of current reading practices in the United States.

In their chapter, Perfetti and Zhang reveal some valuable insights by examining how the writing system and learning to read work in Chinese. They also remind us that to be most effective in teaching children to read, it is essential for teachers to have a good understanding of the fundamental task of learning to read.

Perfetti and Zhang explain that children need to learn how their writing system works. They need to learn the principles on which their writing system is based. I think this is an essential concept for teachers to keep in mind as they are helping beginning readers. Teachers help children learn how letters associate with phonemes. Teachers will be most effective, particularly with struggling readers, if they see their role as one of helping children discover the writing system as opposed to simply teaching children about the writing system. Children must be actively involved in this process of discovery.

In explaining writing systems, Perfetti and Zhang contrast Chinese and

English. In Chinese, graphic units are associated with morphemes, as well as having a phonological component. In English, graphic units are associated with phonemes. A potential problem for English-speaking children is that they may not have a good conceptualization or awareness of phonemes as they enter first grade. They may not be aware that "sun" has three phonemes or that these phonemes are /s/ /u/ /n/. Given the isolated phonemes /s/ /u/ /n/, they may not be able to blend these into the word "sun."

We have learned a number of things from Perfetti and Zhang's research that will help us do a better job of teaching children to read. Perfetti and Zhang convincingly argue that learning to read English is simpler than learning to read Chinese, yet comparisons have indicated that English-speaking children are not better readers earlier. As educators in the United States, it is important for us to keep in mind that English, comparatively speaking, is not that difficult a writing system to learn and that many of our children can and should do better when it comes to learning to read.

Perfetti and Zhang make the point that there is a vast difference between the expectations of Chinese parents and educators and those of American parents and educators. They note that Chinese children complete more homework than American students. Chinese first graders learn to read in Pin Yin, an alphabetic writing system with 26 letters, in 8 weeks, before they learn characters. They learn 600 characters a year during each of their first 6 years of school. In spite of this complexity, Chinese-speaking Taiwanese children (a population for whom documentation is available) exhibit superior reading achievement compared with children in the United States.

Teachers in our country need to operate from the perspective that all of their students, including less successful first- and second-grade students, can be reading at an acceptable level by the end of the school year. Teachers need to maintain high expectations for their lower-achieving students and encourage parents to work as partners in supporting their children's literacy development at home. Teachers should send home reading activities in which parents are expected to assist and participate.

Perfetti and Zhang's chapter provides us with valuable food for thought and inspiration. Additionally, this work has important practice implications for first- and second-grade teachers. I offer a few suggestions based on my interpretations of points Perfetti and Zhang have raised.

Perfetti and Zhang stress the importance of phonemic awareness, as have many others in recent years (e.g., Adams, 1990; Juel, 1988; Stanovich, 1986). Phonemic awareness is the ability to recognize and blend together the individual phonemes in words. I believe the importance of phonemic awareness in learning to read has been underestimated or poorly understood in this country. Considerable data make it quite clear that phonemic awareness is an essential, but not sufficient, ability that children must have to learn to read (Adams, 1990). The data also suggest that it is worthwhile for teachers to help children develop their phonemic awareness in kindergarten and first grade.

How do teachers help children develop their phonemic awareness? In kindergarten, this might be done in an entertaining, game-like manner. For example, it is useful for children to hear nursery rhymes and rhyming poems frequently. They also can be asked to generate rhyming words. "Who can think of a word that rhymes with fun?" Children can play rhyming games; for instance, a board game involving answering questions such as, "Do these words rhyme, fun/sun?" and "What about cat/dog?"

In first grade, teachers need to help children develop the ability to hear the phonemes in words and to represent these phonemes with letters. Sound boxes often are used to highlight the phonemes in words. For example, from the story *Where the Wild Things Are*, the teacher may ask children to write the following words: "Max," "wild," "bed," "boat," and "back." The teacher can ask children what they hear at the beginning of "Max," in the middle, and at the end. Children then can represent these sounds in a string of boxes $\boxed{\text{M}|\text{a}|\text{x}}$. Representing one phoneme per box, children would write "boat" as $\boxed{\text{b}|\text{oa}|\text{t}}$. Through an activity like this, children develop their phonemic awareness and ability to make phoneme–grapheme associations. Most important, perhaps, this activity helps children discover how the English writing system works.

Word manipulation is another activity that can help focus children's attention on phonemes. Using manipulative letters, children can start by spelling "Max." By changing the *x* to a *d* they can turn "Max" into "mad." "Mad" can be changed into "bad," "bad" into "bed," "bed" into "bad," and "bad" into "back." This type of word generation activity is further explained in Cunningham and Allington (1994).

Perfetti and Zhang point out that writing is also an important activity for children who are learning to read. As children try to write words in sentences, they are learning how their writing system works. Just as I believe the importance of phonemic awareness has been poorly understood in the United States, I believe the value of writing in learning to read has been underestimated. Writing in English helps children understand phonemes and their relationship to graphemes. It helps them to form grapheme–phoneme associations needed to decode unknown words.

Guided writing in response to a story is one type of writing activity that is useful in developing children's reading ability. A group of children can generate sentences in response to a story they have heard or read. For example, a common sentence is agreed upon, and each child attempts to write it with teacher guidance. Given a sentence such as, "Max was a good king of the wild things," the teacher can move through the sentence word by word, asking, "What do you hear at the beginning, in the middle (or next), and at the end of each word?" Children write the letters for as many of the phonemes as they can. The teacher tells them the letters in instances where there is phonetic irregularity. For example, she might tell them the letters for the middle and end sounds of "was," or the letters for the middle sound of "good."

Independent writing and invented spelling are also important for the development of children's reading ability in first and second grade. In this instance, children are encouraged to represent the sounds they hear in words as best they can, with the understanding that not all words will be spelled correctly. The primary goal is to get as many ideas on paper as possible. In the process, children gain a great deal of practice in listening for phonemes in words they wish to write and in representing these phonemes with letters.

Another insight for teachers of emergent readers, which comes indirectly from Perfetti and Zhang's work, is the notion that children need to *discover* how our writing system works. They will need to develop independence to do this. In this process of discovery, they must learn to depend on themselves as they are learning to decode. The teacher needs to coach and hint but not tell children words too readily in instances where children can and should try to figure out words for themselves.

I found the closing remarks in Perfetti and Zhang's chapter particularly memorable. They close with the reminder that the English writing system is not that difficult a system to learn to read compared with Chinese. They describe English as a "handful of letters and phonemic elements [that] combine to generate an indefinitely large set of words. The system is there to be acquired as a system, despite its irregularities." They also have highlighted the point that a primary focus for teachers of emergent readers should be to help children learn how the English writing system works. Children will need guidance from their teachers, but they also will need to make the discovery themselves.

In her chapter, Hiebert forces us to look beyond current trends in American reading instruction and consider the implications for struggling readers. Literature-based reading programs and early intervention programs have been received with great enthusiasm in recent years. In spite of the popularity of literature-based reading and the success of early intervention programs, however, Hiebert is not afraid to say what we need to hear. Often, an "emperor's new clothes" observation is healthy. Hiebert points out that many students beyond first and second grade need remediation, or special help, in reading. Literature-based reading programs are not meeting the needs of all students. Furthermore, early intervention programs are not a magical cure-all.

Part of the problem is that, in literature-based reading programs, the reading problems of individual students often have been ignored. Today, typically, we have moved away from ability groups, with all children in a grade receiving the same reading instruction. At the same time, Chapter 1 dollars have been shifting to early prevention programs. Consequently, children in third grade and up are receiving less specialized help from the classroom teacher and less Chapter 1 help than in the past.

Hiebert has been a strong advocate of the concept that there are many students, especially many low-income children, who depend on schools to become literate. We must do a better job of meeting their needs. As children reach the third or fourth grade, they have shifted from reading easy readers to reading longer novels. Also, the reading demands have moved, increasingly, to reading to learn from informational text. By third or fourth grade, and on up through the school years, there are many students who are struggling with reading. These children need help overcoming the reading difficulties that emerge as they encounter these more difficult tasks. These children depend on schools to become literate, and yet we are failing many of them.

It does not require detailed analyses of NAEP data to see that many students are reading less well than we would like. The 1992 NAEP data (Mullis, Campbell, & Farstrup, 1993) show that reading scores of 9-year-olds went up in the 1970s but are now back to their 1971 level. At grades 4, 8, and 12, 48, 43, and 52%, respectively, of advantaged urban children were reading at a proficient level in 1992. This means that about 50% of these students are not at a reading level that teachers would consider proficient. The gaps between advantaged and disadvantaged urban students at grades 4, 8, and 12 remain large. In contrast to the above data, 12, 9, and 20% of disadvantaged urban children were reading at a proficient level in grades 4, 8, and 12, respectively (Mullis, Campbell, & Farstrup, 1993). Furthermore, NAEP trend data show that this gap has not been closing in recent years (Mullis & Jenkins, 1990). This is the same time period during which literature-based reading and early intervention programs have been thriving.

Hiebert (1994) has suggested caution when looking at Reading Recovery as a way to wipe out reading failure in our schools. She presents data suggesting that only 4 of 72 students, or 5.5% of an age cohort, will be reading on grade level by grade 4 because of their involvement in Reading Recovery in first grade. Reading Recovery is an important, valuable program, but it alone cannot achieve the goal of having all students reading well enough to keep up with the reading demands of schooling throughout their school years.

Unfortunately, as Hiebert points out, we have few successful programs or models to guide us in helping older struggling readers. Remediation with middle-grade students generally has been unsuccessful. We will need much more commitment, research, and development in this area before we will see major improvements in the NAEP data reporting on the reading abilities of fourth-, eighth-, and twelfth-grade students.

I was impressed with the pilot project Hiebert developed with two colleagues who are elementary teachers. The 20- to 30-minute period of supplemental instruction four times a week with the classroom teacher is an excellent foundation for an effective model of support for older struggling readers. Allington and McGill-Franzen (1989) have been arguing for years that extra, quality instruction with the classroom teacher is needed, irrespective of other special services children receive, to maximally help struggling readers. We cannot depend on specialists alone to help struggling readers become proficient readers at their grade placement. Classroom teachers must see themselves as part of the effort.

In Hiebert's program, I particularly liked the focus on discussion among children of the strategies they used to figure out difficult words they encountered in their reading. Teachers need to help children not yet fluent in word recognition to develop a metacognitive awareness of what they are doing when they attempt to decode. The discussion approach used by Hiebert and her colleagues is one reasonable way to do this.

I also liked the shift to reading and writing informational text related to the students' science and social studies curriculum as the year progressed. NAEP data have documented that elementary children have more difficulty comprehending informational texts than narratives (Langer, Campbell, Neuman, Mullis, Persky, & Donahue, 1995). Elementary teachers must take responsibility for helping all students, particularly struggling readers, learn how to learn from reading informational material.

Hiebert and her colleagues obtained impressive results with their pilot project, but I agree with the advice that their project be viewed with caution at the present time because of its small scope. Nevertheless, I found the study particularly impressive for two reasons. First, the project inspires us as educators to become more hopeful about the possibilities of success for older struggling readers. Second, it inspires us to devote more energy to the thoughtful design of instruction and related research focusing on strategies that work to improve the reading of struggling readers beyond the primary grades.

Hiebert boldly, but aptly, makes the point in her chapter that older struggling readers are very much in need of our attention. Perhaps inadvertently, we have been ignoring many of them in recent years as we have focused on literature-based reading and early intervention. Educators need to assume that most struggling readers do not need to remain struggling readers, and teachers must actively work to help these students improve. In particular, educators, researchers, policy makers, and policy implementors must focus greater energy on closing the gap in reading ability during the school years.

This volume is written in memory of Guy Bond. Therefore, I would like to close by citing from the Preface and Introduction to the original (1951) edition of *Reading Difficulties: Their Diagnosis and Correction* by Guy Bond and Miles Tinker. These excerpts support many of the points that Hiebert makes in her chapter. They also provide us with inspiration:

> This book was written because the authors firmly believe that the children who get into difficulty with reading need immediate help. Such children need to have their reading problems diagnosed and corrected if they are to gain the reading ability needed today. (p. v)
>
> In the well-organized instructional program, there will be a natural emphasis upon prevention of reading disability. If it were possible in day-to-day teaching to provide for each pupil's progress in terms of his capabilities, less occasion for remedial work would arise. Such an ideal educational environment cannot be achieved yet. Even with the best of teaching and the best organized systematic program, certain children will be in difficulty serious enough to require remedial instruction. . . . There will be found in our present-day schools an appreciable number of pupils who are in serious difficulty with their reading. A remedial program must be provided to correct these difficulties. (pp. 11–12)
>
> The writers hold to the view that remedial instruction in reading is essentially the same as good classroom teaching that is individualized. . . . The writers are convinced that well-conceived remedial instruction will result in improvement of reading ability. . . . It is a rare case where a skilled teacher is not able to bring about significant improvement in reading ability. (p. 13)

I think Dr. Bond would be pleased with the progress we have made in recent years in understanding how the reading process works and in the prevention of reading difficulties in first and second grade based on early intervention programs. I expect he would approve of the movement toward literature-based instruction and natural, enjoyable reading and writing activities. I would hope that his optimism about what skilled teachers can accomplish remains with us as we make use of our understanding of the writing system, as Perfetti and Zhang recommend, and direct our attention to older struggling readers, as Hiebert recommends.

## REFERENCES

Adams, M. J. (1990). *Beginning to read: Thinking and learning about print*. Cambridge, MA: MIT Press.

Allington, R. L., & McGill-Franzen, A. (1989). School response to reading failure: Chapter 1 and special education students in grades 2, 4, & 8. *Elementary School Journal, 89*, 529–542.

Bond, G., & Tinker, M. (1951). *Reading difficulties: Their diagnosis and correction*. New York: Appleton-Century-Crofts.

Cunningham, P., & Allington, R. (1994). *Classrooms that work: They can all read and write*. New York: Harper Collins.

Hiebert, E. H. (1994). Reading recovery in the United States: What difference does it make to an age cohort? *Educational Researcher, 23*(9), 15–25.

Juel, C. (1988). Learning to read and write: A longitudinal study of fifty-four children from first through fourth grades. *Journal of Educational Psychology, 80*, 437–447.

Langer, J., Campbell, J., Neuman, S., Mullis, I., Persky, H., & Donahue, P. (1995). *Reading assessment redesigned*. Washington, DC: U.S. Department of Education, Office of Educational Research and Improvement.

Mullis, I. V. S., Campbell, J. R., & Farstrup, A. E. (1993). *NAEP 1992 reading report card for the nation and the states*. Washington, DC: U.S. Department of Education.

Mullis, I., & Jenkins, L. (1990). *The reading report card, 1971–88*. Washington, DC: U.S. Department of Education.

Stanovich, K. (1986). Matthew-effects in reading: Some consequences of individual differences in the acquisition of literacy. *Reading Research Quarterly, 19*, 278–303.

# PART II

# CHANGING CURRICULUM AND CLASSROOM DISCOURSE

CHAPTER 4

# Literature-Based Curricula in High-Poverty Schools

RICHARD ALLINGTON
SHERRY GUICE
NANCY MICHELSON
KIM BAKER
SHOUMING LI
*The State University of New York at Albany (SUNY)*
*National Research Center on Literature Teaching and Learning*

There has been a recent rapid shift away from the skills-mastery models of reading and language arts curriculum in American elementary schools (Pearson, 1993). After nearly a quarter-century as the dominant curriculum model, skills-mastery approaches to reading and language arts instruction are being replaced with more holistic curriculum plans.

Several themes seem to characterize the curriculum plans found in schools today: (1) an emphasis on greater integration of reading and writing instruction; (2) increased use of unedited, authentic children's literature as the base of the curricular planning; (3) developing reading and writing skills and strategies in the context of actual reading and writing activity; and (4) attempting to provide all learners with access to the same high-quality curriculum. Each of these themes differs from the central tenets of traditional skills-mastery curriculum planning, where reading and writing were taught through different curricula, usually using specially constructed texts and tasks that focused on practicing skills in isolation from actual reading and writing, and where differential curriculum goals and experiences were deemed appropriate for learners of presumed different aptitudes.

Our interest in the impact of curricular plans and experiences on children's literacy learning emerged about 20 years ago with a report of substantial differences in the reading lessons experienced by higher- and lower-achieving readers (Allington, 1977). In subsequent reports, we further documented these differences and explored the impact of differential curriculum experiences on children's literacy development (e.g., Allington, 1983; Allington & McGill-Franzen, 1989; Guice, Allington, Johnston, Baker, & Michaelson, 1994; Johnston, Allington, & Afflerbach, 1985). Many of the shifts in instructional practices that now can be observed in reading and language arts instruction seem generally consistent with recommendations we, along with many others, made for enhancing literacy instruction in elementary schools.

However, there seem to be many aspects of the reforms in literacy curriculum and instruction that are not well understood. A central issue, for instance, is that little agreement exists as to what constitutes a literature-based curriculum other than providing children with the opportunity to read original children's literature (Giddings, 1992). Likewise, the nature of curriculum integration is not well defined; and descriptions of effective instructional practice, especially for economically disadvantaged children, remain generally elusive.

Because reading and language arts curriculum and instruction have shifted so dramatically, so quickly, it is, perhaps, not surprising that the research literature on literature-based instruction provides less than optimal information on the nature of such curricula and their impact on student literacy development. We found, in our review of the available research, two distinct limitations. First, many reports document changes that occurred in a single classroom or school. Also, while we located several multiple-classroom studies (e.g., Mervar & Hiebert, 1989; Morrow, 1992; Reutzel & Cooter, 1990; Scharer, 1992; Walmsley, Fielding, & Walp, 1991; Zarillo, 1989), we found none that reported a study of literature-based instruction in a number of classrooms in several elementary schools in multiple school districts. Second, little of the available research reports on literature-based instruction in schools serving large numbers of children from low-income families — historically, the children most often at risk of experiencing difficulty in learning to read and write. In this chapter, we review the knowledge base on implementation of literature-based instruction, describe the literature-based instruction we observed in six schools serving large percentages of low-income students, discuss several concerns stemming from this study, and present our conclusions and some of our plans for future research.

## WHAT WE KNOW ABOUT THE IMPLEMENTATION
## OF LITERATURE-BASED CURRICULA

Probably the most compelling finding of several large-scale studies is the widespread implementation of literature-based instruction. The data from the 1992 National Assessment of Educational Progress (Mullis, Campbell, & Farstrup, 1993) indicate that half of all fourth-grade teachers report a "heavy emphasis" on literature-based reading. The NAEP data also show that the students of teachers reporting heavier emphases on literature-based reading instruction achieved higher levels of proficiency on the assessments. Just over half of the fourth-grade students reported that they were provided daily time to read a book of their choice. Teachers also report widespread use of children's literature. Hoffman, Roser, and Battle (1993) reported that three-quarters of the teachers in their 24-state survey read aloud to children from literature. Fractor, Woodruff, Martinez, and Teale (1993) indicated that almost 90% of the 183 Texas teachers in their study had children's trade book collections available in their classrooms. Thus, the case seems well made for the current popularity of literature-based approaches.

However, there are the five-state teacher survey data from Canney (1993), which indicate that 80% of the teachers responding reported using a basal anthology to teach reading (less than one-third reported that their districts required basal use). Only 10% reported using trade books exclusively during reading and language arts lessons. Additionally, 80% of the respondents reported that they felt that a "scope and sequence" of reading development was important. Closer inspection of the data reported by Fractor and colleagues (1993) indicates that, while virtually all teachers reported having trade book collections, less than a third of the teachers had classroom library centers. Similarly, the Strickland, Walmsley, Bronk, and Weiss (1994) data from teachers interviewed in eight states indicate that 18% of the respondents used children's literature exclusively, while over 80% used both basals and books. Additionally, the data reported by Hoffman and colleagues (1993) indicate that while most teachers do read aloud from literature, few select trade books linked to the curriculum under study and few follow the read-aloud event with any sort of student response activity. Thus, while it does seem that children's literature has made inroads in American classrooms, few teachers seem to actually use children's books in many of their lessons. Literature is more likely to be used in either read-aloud events or independent reading activities than to be used as part of an instructional episode or integrated curriculum.

Nonetheless, there are indications that the very presence of literature in classrooms has altered some aspects of traditional reading and language arts lessons. First of all, most children, it seems, have the opportunity to choose the literature read for independent reading activities. Second, children at least are exposed to a variety of authors and classic stories during read-aloud events. Third, as the basal anthologies have changed, children are gaining increased exposure to a wider variety of award-winning children's literature, although often the selections are excerpted from longer works.

There are other shifts linked to the wider use of literature in elementary schools. Walmsley, Fielding, and Walp (1991) and Mervar and Hiebert (1989) report that children read and wrote more in classrooms using literature. Hiebert and Colt (1989) note that the talk in classrooms using literature was different from that in traditional skills-mastery classrooms. Teachers and children talked with each other about what had been read or written, about content and their response to it. In contrast, talk in the skills-mastery classrooms was more often procedural and direction giving, than focused on content or response to texts read or written.

However, Walmsley and Walp (1989) also note some areas of concern. Few teachers in their study had begun to articulate a philosophy of literature instruction, even though many created a book list curriculum. Few teachers had resolved the intended relationship between reading skills and literary strategies, between reading achievement and literary knowledge. Walmsley and Walp end their paper noting that

> It appears that reading skills instruction is still the primary mission of the elementary school, and literature still is regarded as something to be done after the reading skills have been sufficiently developed. (p. 37)

They also note that poorer readers rarely participated in the guided reading of full-length literature, and that when they did participate, the lessons were more slowly paced, offered more teacher direction, and focused more on literal understandings than did lessons offered to better readers.

Fisher and Hiebert (1990) note an emphasis on narrative texts in literature-based classrooms, with far less focus on informational texts and, relatedly, the limited linkage between the literature used in the reading and language arts periods and other subjects studied. Similarly, Walmsley and Walp (1989) suggest that literature has been added to the school day but not yet integrated into the curriculum.

The final aspect of literature-based instruction that has been studied in several situations is the transitions that teachers must make in adding literature to the curriculum. There is some agreement concerning the limited awareness most teachers have of the substantial scope of children's literature. However, as Walmsley and Walp (1989) note, most of the teachers currently employed in schools were offered little preservice preparation in this area.

Shanklin (1990) found that even after a 3-year staff development project, a number of teachers found it difficult to select books of appropriate difficulty for their students. Some teachers relied almost exclusively on narrative texts and often failed to provide students with either strategy lessons or opportunities to talk about the books being read. The transition is also difficult for children. Purcell-Gates and Dahl (1991) noted that for the successful acquisition of literacy in literature-based classrooms, "self-directed cognitive activity seems to be one of the keys" (p. 27). In their study, some children did not easily engage in such activity, expecting instead knowledge to be delivered to them. This should not be surprising. Children differ in their enthusiasm for literacy activities just as adults do (Solsken, 1993). Often, children of economically disadvantaged and less well-educated parents arrive at school with far fewer experiences with print, stories, and books and thus have developed few of the ways of thinking about literate activity so valued in schools. These "inexperienced" children often are the children who fail to thrive in the schools we have (Allington, 1994b).

We also know that many, if not most, teachers find change difficult and anxiety producing. Scharer (1992) and Pace (1992), for instance, document the transitions that teachers attempted to make and how the organizational and social contexts of their schools fostered or impeded these transitions. It matters whether the change process is more generally self-initiated or part of a larger mandate from the institution. Pace (1992) found that substantial tensions existed between the teacher-initiators and other teachers and within initiators themselves when their innovations ran afoul of school mandates. Teachers responded to these tensions in different ways: Some returned to traditional teaching methods, others became isolated, and some made the transition successfully.

Likewise, Scharer (1992) found that collegial support was critical, as were opportunities to develop necessary expertise (e.g., familiarity with children's literature). She noted steadily but slowly changing classroom environments as teachers shifted their teaching practices, but these shifts were gradual and were often difficult for reasons other than lack of collegial support or limited expertise in needed areas. For instance, Walmsley and colleagues (1991) and Afflerbach and Johnston (1992) note the difficulty teachers had applying traditional assessment strategies to literature lessons. As long as assessment practices (including report cards) remained unchanged, teachers literally felt compelled to maintain some of traditional activities that fit traditional grading schemes. As long as student development was assessed with high-stakes standardized tests, there remained a

press to perpetuate traditional teaching practices that were thought to produce higher scores on those instruments.

There can be little argument that children's literature has emerged as a
popular vehicle for fostering literacy development in our elementary
schools. However, it seems that few schools have well-developed literature
curricula, few have yet evolved different sorts of assessments of literacy
development, few seem to have yet developed an articulated curriculum
that differentiates between reading skill and literary understanding, and few
teachers yet seem comfortable without some sort of commercial curriculum
material as a framework for their instruction, perhaps because few teachers
have been adequately prepared to create their own lessons (Graves &
Graves, 1994).

Thus, while the research points to increasing use of children's literature
in schools, the available studies also report a substantial variation in how
literature is used. At least some of the observed variation seems to stem
from the fact that "literature-based" instruction means different things to
different people. One obvious question, then, is, How are literature-based
curricula defined in schools?

## LITERATURE-BASED INSTRUCTION IN SIX SCHOOLS

In an attempt to begin to answer this question, we set as our task a broad
exploration of literature-based literacy instruction. We studied the implementation of literature-based reading and language arts instruction in 54
classrooms in six elementary schools serving large numbers of economically
disadvantaged children (30–90% of the student population) in five school
districts. (Full details of our methodology can be found in Allington,
Guice, Li, Michelson, & Baker, 1995.)

We selected these schools after surveying a larger number of district
administrators about their reading and language arts curriculum. We found
different interpretations of literature-based literacy curricula in these
schools. The six schools represented three broadly different plans for the
organization and delivery of literature-based instruction (Allington,
1994a). Two schools had purchased a literature-based basal anthology for
each student (we called these *basal* schools); two had plans for incorporating the use of both a basal anthology and trade books (we called these
*basal-and-books* schools); and two had plans for relying on trade books as
the literacy curriculum (we called these *books* schools).

We next set out to explore whether these different curriculum plans
resulted in different literacy experiences for children and posed different
challenges for classroom teachers. To do this we observed instruction in

classrooms and interviewed teachers and administrators in each school on several occasions. More specifically, we completed approximately 300 hours of classroom observations and nearly 100 interviews. During our observations we recorded individual student time by activity categories and curriculum materials. Our interviews were conducted largely in classrooms, using both a structured interview protocol and coding guide and, with some teachers and administrators, a semistructured interview that was audiotape recorded for later transcription and analysis. These data provided a portrait of the curriculum and instruction offered in each classroom. Below, we report on the sorts of instructional materials teachers use in these literature-based classrooms, the amounts of time allocated for reading and language arts, the sorts of activities that occupy students' time, students' access to books in classroom and school libraries, and teachers' familiarity with children's literature.

## WHAT MATERIALS TEACHERS USE

We found that instructional material use was related to the three different curriculum plans. For instance, in the two literature-based basal schools, virtually all of the teachers we studied reported normally using commercial basal anthologies in their daily lessons, compared with half of the teachers in the basal-and-books schools and only 10% of the teachers in the books schools.

All teachers in the books schools reported using children's trade books in their classrooms, but so did 80% of the teachers in basal-and-books and basal schools. We found some differences in children's opportunities to read complete trade books in these schools, with children in the books schools, of course, spending more time reading complete full-length books than in the other curriculum schemes.

However, reading children's books was a quite common experience for virtually all children in the schools studied. This finding seems remarkably similar to that of two other recent large-scale studies, which have reported that nearly all elementary teachers now use trade books in their reading and language arts programs (Canney, 1993; Strickland, Walmsley, Bronk, & Weiss, 1994). In both of these studies, the basal-and-books curriculum plan dominated in popularity, with few teachers reporting use of either basals alone or books alone.

## TIME SCHEDULED FOR READING AND LANGUAGE ARTS

We found no substantial differences in the average amount of time allocated daily to reading and language arts instruction in these schools with different curriculum plans. At the same time, we did find a fair amount of variation among classrooms, a finding consistent with other large-scale studies of classroom instruction (Allington & McGill-Franzen, 1989; Leinhardt, Zigmond, & Cooley, 1981; Taylor, Frye, & Maruyama, 1990). Some classrooms allocated about 1 hour, and others allocated nearly 3 hours, each day to teaching reading and language arts. Across all classrooms in the six elementary schools we studied, students averaged 117 minutes of reading and language arts instruction daily, accounting for over a third of the school day.

This average time allocation is substantially larger than the average amount of time reported in other studies of schools with many students from low-income families (Birman et al., 1987; Knapp, 1991), but generally comparable to recent national reports of time allocations in American elementary schools (NCES, 1993). While comparable allocations of instructional time for reading and language arts may not be sufficient to accelerate the literacy development of the traditionally lower-achieving poor children in these schools, time allocations that are comparable to those found in the average American elementary school represent an improvement over what was found in earlier studies (Birman et al., 1987).

Perhaps the most surprising finding here was the lack of substantial differences in the time allocated for reading and language arts instruction in the schools with differing curriculum plans. This may have more to do with the total time available being a relatively fixed feature of the school day. The 2 hours of daily time allocated for reading and language arts instruction in these schools represents more than half the time allocated for all academic study. While the scheduled school day provides between 5 and 5-1/2 hours for instructional time, nearly an hour each day is allocated to areas such as art, music, physical education, computer labs, and library visits, and almost another hour is lost to organizational and transitional activities. Thus, the time allocations we found would seem to indicate a strong commitment to developing literacy proficiencies in students.

## How Children Spend Time

While teachers in these schools offered roughly comparable amounts of reading instruction, there were differences in how that time was used. Three activities—teacher-guided reading, silent reading, and being read to by the teacher—dominated the lesson periods in all schools, but wide variations existed from classroom to classroom in the extent to which these activities were used. In addition, different activities dominated time, depending on the curriculum plan in place at the school. For instance, teacher-guided reading, wherein teachers literally led reading and writing activities, was more common in basal schools than in books schools. Silent reading was the dominant activity in a basal-and-books school. Reading to children, conferencing with the teacher, and sharing responses to a book with other children were regular activities in the books schools.

In our interviews with teachers, we found that those with books classrooms were more likely to provide students with daily opportunities to read independently (basal = 75%, basal and books = 80%, books = 85%), although most classroom teachers set aside some time for children to read each day. All teachers in the books schools reported reading aloud to children regularly, while about three-quarters of the teachers in the basal schools and basal-and-books schools said they did so. While precise comparisons are difficult, it seems that the children attending these schools had substantially more exposure to children's literature than was reported in studies conducted during the heyday of the skills-mastery curriculum plans (Allington, 1977; Leinhardt, Zigmond, & Cooley, 1981).

However, children did not spend all their time reading in any of these classrooms. They spent more or less time engaged in seatwork activities, depending on the curriculum plan. In the basal schools, worksheet activities occupied larger amounts of children's time than did listening to the teacher read from children's books. Just the opposite was true of children in the books schools. In the basal schools, worksheet activity accounted for between 15 and 25 minutes a day. In none of the other sites did students spend more than 10 minutes a day on worksheet activities. Compared with the results of earlier studies of classroom reading instruction, these time allocations suggest a substantial decrease in time spent on worksheet activity (Anderson, 1984; Leinhardt, Zigmond, & Cooley, 1981).

During the interviews with teachers, we also found that while two-thirds indicated that the role of literature was to add enjoyment to the reading and language arts program, nearly 60% indicated that the role of literature also was to teach reading skills and to provide children an opportunity to practice reading skills. Only about a third of the teachers reported that literature served to develop content knowledge or to develop students' writing skills. This may explain, in part, why on most observation days students spent relatively little time composing.

In only one of the books schools did composing rank among the most common reading and language arts tasks. Generally, students in all schools wrote briefly on some days, but not all. Roughly three of every four composing activities were allocated 9 minutes or less, and half were allocated 4 minutes or less. The majority of the classrooms were rated as having very weak linkages between reading and writing activities, with no clear pattern between schools with different curriculum plans. Thus, while these different literature-based curriculum plans generally provided substantial opportunities for children to read or listen to literature, rather few offered any sustained writing opportunities and few had integrated the reading and writing processes, regardless of the curriculum plan in place.

We observed hardly any art or drama activities linked to the reading children were doing in any of the classrooms, but then fewer than 10% of all the teachers observed and interviewed indicated that such activities were regular features of any of the instruction they provided. Fewer than 20% of these teachers reported that they regularly incorporated oral response or sharing activities (e.g., author's chair) into classroom activities. On the other hand, nearly half of the teachers indicated that vocabulary and comprehension worksheet and response journal activities were common, although such worksheets were least common in the books schools, where only about a third of the teachers used these materials.

In most classrooms, there were few extended periods for either reading or writing. Instead, the more common daily scheme produced a number of relatively brief reading, and to a lesser extent, writing episodes. Usually, classrooms seemed organized around 10–20-minute blocks of time, although many activities were much briefer.

Across all classrooms, teachers overwhelmingly (82%) controlled the daily choice of available reading materials for guided-reading activities. However, in three-quarters of the classrooms, students were allowed to choose the books they read independently. Nearly half of the teachers indicated that they planned for all children to read the same literature, while nearly a third indicated that literature was differentiated by children's reading ability. No teacher indicated differentiating literature by children's interests, although a few (15%) reported differentiation by individual needs. In these classrooms, then, we found literature selection to be largely adult-controlled regardless of the curricular organization.

Overall, we found few classrooms that fit Huck's (1992) description of the *comprehensive literature program* — classrooms where children more often chose the books to read, and where discussion, drama, art, and writing dominated responses to the literature read. Creating such classrooms requires substantial shifts in perspectives on children and learning, as well as shifts in the curriculum.

## WHAT CHILDREN HAVE AVAILABLE TO READ

It would seem almost axiomatic that schools moving to literature-based instruction would need to ensure that all children have easy access to appropriate books. Thus, we also studied the availability of children's books in school and classroom libraries.

*School libraries.* We found that children's access to library books varied as a result of the curriculum plan of the school. However, only two of the schools, both basal-and-books schools, met the American Library Association's standards for the number of library books per child (approximately 20 volumes). Two of the school libraries, in one basal school and one books school, had only about half the number of recommended volumes per child.

Evaluating the adequacy of school libraries is tricky because there are important factors other than the sheer number of volumes available. For instance, different schools had different policies controlling children's access to the library, and different teachers had different patterns of book display and different procedures for student access to classroom libraries. By and large, though, children's access to the school library was restricted to a weekly visit. Only in one school, a books-and-basal school, did children have regular library access outside of scheduled weekly visits.

Earlier, we (Guice et al., 1994) reported comparative data for the libraries in six elementary schools that generally enrolled economically advantaged children and for the six schools reported on here. Our analyses indicated that in the schools serving more-advantaged children the libraries contained roughly 50% more books than were found in the schools that enroll many poor children. We noted a similar disparity in magazines subscriptions available in these schools. In other words, children from economically disadvantaged communities had a restricted selection of books and magazines available in their school libraries.

*Classroom libraries.* Classroom libraries are another way in which schools can enhance children's access to books, especially if access to the school library is restricted to a single weekly visit. In tallying the size of classroom libraries, we found that these collections varied more by individual teacher than by curriculum plan, although on average the classroom libraries were smaller in the two basal schools and larger in the two books schools. However, the largest collections were located in classrooms where teachers reported purchasing most of the books themselves. Disturbingly, 40% of all teachers reported that their classroom libraries consisted primarily of books they had purchased themselves or acquired through book club incentive programs; these teachers were found in schools using each of the curriculum plans.

Our counts revealed that roughly a third of the classroom libraries had fewer than 100 books, another third had between 100 and 200 books, and a third had over 200 titles, with a few collections having more than 500 books. Examining just the number of books available in classroom collections can be misleading. Classroom collections also differed in the variety of books, with some collections having multiple copies of a few books (often whole-class sets) and others having one or two copies of 100 or more books. There was a particular problem in the basal schools and in "core book list" classrooms in books schools, where the classroom libraries often consisted of multiple copies of a few titles that largely constituted the curriculum plan. Throughout the school year, individual trade books from the collection were to be read by all students, with the reading of the titles restricted to the schedule established in the teacher's resource book accompanying the anthology-based curriculum or the teacher's lesson plans. These collections were less like classroom libraries and more like curriculum collections.

We found that most classroom collections of trade books offered a fairly restricted range of selections in terms of both genre and complexity. Most collections were dominated by modern narrative fiction, with far fewer titles representing other genres. Often, the classroom trade book collections had rather few "easy" books, instead offering mostly books considered to be of appropriate complexity for the grade level. This, of course, often meant that children experiencing difficulty acquiring literacy had access to the fewest appropriate books.

In only a few classrooms did we locate libraries that met the adequacy standards set by Fractor and colleagues (1993). But even in some of these classrooms the collections contained few books that most at-risk children could read independently. Generally, classrooms had some children's books available, but often these titles were not well displayed or organized in any particular fashion. Most classrooms did not have a reading area or library corner set aside. Most did not have special seating in the book area or special decorations marking that area as a library.

In summary, we found that only a few classrooms had what we felt was an adequate supply of children's books. The problem seemed especially acute in primary-grade classrooms, where we observed teachers using photocopied versions of children's books. While there were funds for photocopying, there were none to purchase books! In addition, children experiencing delays in developing literacy proficiency were the children least likely to have access to books of appropriate difficulty. Most often classroom collections simply contained few books that such children could read independently.

TEACHERS AND CHILDREN'S LITERATURE

During our interviews with the teachers, we discussed their familiarity with children's books and developed an estimate of each teacher's familiarity.

Few teachers in any of the schools exhibited what we considered to be extensive knowledge of children's books. Most teachers knew a few books quite well, but most were unable to engage in extended discussions of children's books generally. However, *none* of these schools offered any sort of professional development opportunities focused on familiarizing teachers with children's books. No school had developed a formal mechanism for introducing teachers to new books available in the school library or for enhancing the awareness of recently published children's books. Even so, 9 of 10 teachers across all schools reported positive attitudes toward the use of literature in the reading and language arts program.

Unfortunately, a favorable attitude simply is not enough. These schools were implementing literature-based instruction without working to enhance teachers' knowledge of the rich supply of children's books that might be used. Thus, teachers often opted for commercial collections of books, sets of books organized and leveled by outside experts. In some cases, teachers opted for commercial collections that included teaching guides and student practice materials (e.g., chapter questions and vocabulary worksheets). However, without a good working knowledge of children's literature that is regularly updated, it is difficult to maintain a responsive literature-based curriculum plan.

## ISSUES OF CONCERN

As we have just reported, we found that the three different school plans for literature-based curriculum had different effects on the opportunities children had to experience full-length children's literature and on the type of instructional activities they were likely to be engaged in. However, in each of these schools substantial blocks of time were allocated to listening to literature read by the teacher and for reading independently, compared with earlier studies. Rather little time was spent on traditional seatwork activities in any of these schools. All this suggests that an instructional day in all of these classrooms looked quite different than it did just a few short years ago (Allington, 1977; Leinhardt, Zigmond, & Cooley, 1981).

The good news reinforced by these data is that more children seem to be doing more reading and writing and less isolated skills work than was the case just a decade ago. We found, for instance, hardly a classroom where full-length children's literature was not part of the curriculum plan, and there were only a few classrooms where children were not expected to compose something at least once each week. But many readers will be disappointed, we suppose, in the data we report here. While our study suggests that literacy instruction in American elementary school classrooms is changing, the change is likely to be viewed as too little and too slowly arriving for many.

We found many forces that seemed to constrain school and teacher change in these schools and, we expect, most other schools as well. Unfortunately, these constraining forces have been little discussed in the research on literacy instruction, perhaps because so much of the research is largely decontextualized — in the sense that classroom-based research rarely extends beyond the classroom walls. We found the most significant constraints were situated largely outside the classroom, in federal, state, and school district offices. In this section of the chapter, we discuss these constraints, the press for standardization in schools, the influence of teacher conversation groups, and the challenge of dealing with the increasing diversity in student achievement found in many schools.

## INSTITUTIONAL CONSTRAINTS

Educational reform generally, and implementing literature-based instruction specifically, requires an enormous amount of institutional and individual learning. Institutional learning involves developing more appropriate organizational plans for attempting an equitable distribution of resources, for creating curriculum, and for supporting professional staff. In the schools we observed, we concluded that teachers often were expected to change even though the institutions — the schools, the school districts, the state and federal education agencies — often resisted change. In too many cases, it seemed that the lack of institutional learning and the slow pace of institutional change inhibited the possibility that teachers would or could change.

In all schools, teachers were expected to make substantial changes in the organization and delivery of instruction, usually without any substantial support from federal, state, or district offices. For instance, in many cases professional development opportunities were available on a voluntary (unpaid) basis, but only some of the basal teachers had the benefit of substantial (30 hours) paid training in the initial year of implementation. We are not sure that 30 hours (or 50, or 100) is an essential minimum. However, given the paid retraining provided by industry when major reorganizations take place this would seem a very modest amount, and it was offered in only a single district.

Our experience with other schools suggests that this situation is common. No state or federal education agency has provided any substantial fiscal support for the individual learning that must occur if schools are to change. While President Clinton has called for businesses and corporations to invest 1.5% of their annual budgets in upgrading their workforces (Clin-

ton & Gore, 1992), there have been few calls for such investments to enhance the professional development of classroom teachers, the mainstay of
the educational workforce.

In many cases, individual learning substantially outstripped institutional learning in these schools. That is, teachers were ready to implement
changes that were unacceptable to the institutional forces that constrained
teachers' decision making. As we have noted, teachers wanted to order
more books for their classrooms, but the district budget allocated substantial funds only for photocopying. Thus, teachers purchased single copies of
books and photocopied them for reading material. Teachers were ready to
rethink traditional remedial and special education services but were unable
to effect many of the desired changes because either district administrators
were unwilling to revamp these programs or state education agency direc-
tives constrained even consideration of such options (Allington, 1994c).

In most classrooms, we found few extended periods of time allocated
for sustained reading or writing activities. Instead, the more common daily
schemes produced a number of relatively brief reading and writing episodes. Many children in these schools participated in instructional support
programs funded by state and federal agencies. These support programs
regularly interrupted classroom activities and contributed to some of the
frequent activity shifting we observed. More often than not, the various
special programs, usually state or federal initiatives, interfered with the
organization and delivery of classroom lessons. In addition, state-mandated
special subjects such as physical education, art, and music were interjected
into the daily schedule seemingly at random. As a result of institutional
mandates, classroom teachers had few extended and uninterrupted blocks
of time in which they could schedule extended reading and writing activity.

There are abundant similar examples of institutional delay that we
could discuss. However, it seems important to point out that teachers not
only bore the brunt of the effort in the accomplished changes, but also
that teachers often were frustrated in their efforts to change practice by
institutional resistance or delays in institutional changes.

## THE PRESS FOR STANDARDIZATION OF SCHOOL EXPERIENCES

In each school, we found substantial pressures supporting a relatively standardized school experience for children. Although the press for standardization is another little discussed feature of schooling, in these schools it
seemed to be a major barrier to implementing either teacher- or child-
centered curricular approaches. In none of these schools were teachers
given the authority actually to create their own curriculum. In each district,
we found a strong interest in establishing curriculum standards that could

create some sort of comparability among different classrooms at the same grade level.

In all of these schools, there existed multiple views about how to organize instruction, how to design the curriculum, and what roles children's literature should play. There were differences among key administrators in each district, although these differences varied in degree between sites. There were differences among teachers in the same schools, although again these differences varied in degree. In three of the schools, the nature of the curriculum and classroom organization were decided more often by district administrators than by teachers. In the other three schools, teachers seemed more influential in shaping these decisions, which then were supported by district administrators. Regardless of who seemed more influential on these issues, in each school only some members of the professional staff were wholly supportive of decisions about curriculum and instructional organization.

In each school some sort of curricular compromise was expected from teachers. Compromise was expected in one basal school when district administrators mandated a single basal series and set a curricular pacing schedule for teachers. Compromise was expected in the other basal school, where a majority of, but not all, teachers had elected a basal plan and the particular series used. We also found compromise expected in books and basal-and-books schools, where teachers created for each grade level core book lists and thematic units that "protected" certain titles from all but designated teachers, and where teachers were expected to use the themes and the core books as their curriculum.

We further found a press for standardization that came from administrators, school boards, and parents. As one school board member wondered aloud, "What is so hard about figuring out what book second graders will be reading on any given day?" Thus, while teachers often attempted to respond to children's interests and needs, they continued to feel pressure to standardize lessons and book lists from child to child and from classroom to classroom. After the prominent recent discussions of the debilitating effects of tracking and grouping children by achievement, teachers, administrators, and members of the community seemed concerned that all children receive similar treatment — which often meant reading the same books.

This press for standardization would seem an important influence in terms of the ability of teachers to respond to individual children's interests and needs. It represents an example of Fraatz's (1987) paradox of collective instruction. The paradox is that classrooms represent collective social enterprises in which teachers must constantly consider what is in the best interest of the collective whole. At the same time, teachers recognize that children differ and they must attempt to address those differences in a nondiscriminatory way. The dilemma for teachers, administrators, and communities is how to provide instruction that offers similar opportunity for everyone, thus exhibiting nondiscrimination, while also responding to individual preferences and needs. Historically, equity often has been defined as some sort of uniformity (same state curriculum, same number of school days, same outcome standards, etc.); in these schools the press for standardization influenced, among other things, how literature-based curriculum was conceived and delivered.

Unlike in most other industrialized nations, in the United States the state or local board of education is ultimately empowered to make most curricular decisions (Cohen & Spillane, 1992). That is, decisions about what to teach, how to teach it, and what materials are to be used, are left to the school board — that group of citizens elected by the community to oversee the schools.

In the schools we studied, there were differences in how willingly these boards approved decisions made by administrators or teachers. Some boards seemed to approve such recommendations routinely without much comment or discussions, while other boards requested much more detail and substantially greater documentation for such decisions. Such differences also shaped the nature of literature-based curriculum in these schools.

## THE INFLUENCE OF PROFESSIONAL CONVERSATION GROUPS

In those schools where we saw changes occurring most readily, teachers supported each other and administrators supported teachers. Peer support seems absolutely critical because teaching, like learning, should be a collective social activity (Scharer, 1992). Too often in these schools, though, teaching remained an individual activity, and schools had few structures available to support collaboration and conversation among teachers.

We noted that teachers involved in professional conversation groups found change less threatening and more attainable than did other teachers. These conversation groups were located in every school, but in some schools only very few teachers participated. These were not institutionally sanctioned groups and, in fact, were likely to be "underground" groups that masked their very presence. Their activity consisted of private, professional conversations, usually held in classrooms at the end of the school day. There was no schedule, no calendar of topics, no leader, and no support for these events. However, the teachers involved told us that it was these conversations that provided the support, incentive, and shared wisdom that was needed to sustain change efforts.

ADDRESSING INCREASING DIVERSITY IN STUDENT ACHIEVEMENT

In each of the schools, the diversity of students was increasing as a result of wide-ranging educational reform initiatives developed from afar. All of the school districts recently had eliminated transitional-grade (e.g., pre-first-grade) primary classrooms. Thus, first-grade teachers now had larger numbers of children who historically had been considered unready for first-grade work. In each of the schools, there was administrative pressure to reduce retention in grade. All schools were becoming more "inclusive," with more extensive mainstreaming of handicapped children. Each of these initiatives seemed designed to respond better to the needs of at-risk children, and each could be well supported by available research. However, each initiative also increased the range of student diversity that teachers faced in their classrooms. Unfortunately, the federal, state, and school district offices provided little in the way of professional development opportunities to support teachers in dealing with this increased diversity.

At the same time, in each school, we found an administrative press to move away from more homogeneous achievement grouping of students during reading and language arts lessons. These teachers were, then, confronted with a more diverse student population, usually with increased numbers of lower-achieving students, and a press to use a single, standard curriculum with all children. This was to be accomplished without much professional development support in classrooms with few books generally and with very few books appropriate for lower-achieving students. Given these circumstances, we found it surprising that such an overwhelming majority of the teachers responded positively to literature-based curriculum plans.

Unfortunately, standard lessons usually do not have an equally supportive impact on the literacy development of children with a wide range of achievement — regardless of whether the curriculum is literature-based. The teachers in these schools struggled with the difficulty of providing appropriate instruction for their students, especially the lowest-achieving ones. Too often, though, we observed classrooms where some students were never presented with texts they could read, with or without support. The traditional nature of most instructional support programs (e.g., remedial reading, resource room, paraprofessionals) did not often offer solutions to the classroom dilemmas that lower-achieving students encountered.

The most effective strategies we observed for dealing with such problems were for classroom teachers to (1) ignore the mandates for a common curriculum for all students, (2) purchase appropriate alternative curriculum materials (trade books) themselves, and (3) attempt to co-opt the instructional support program personnel into assisting in providing adapted instruction. Once again, teachers worked around the institutional constraints. Once again, teacher learning and change were simply out in front of institutional learning and change.

## CONCLUSIONS AND FUTURE RESEARCH

At the heart of these findings is our realization of the enormity of the task confronting educators if we hope to accomplish the changes that have been called for in our elementary schools. We began this study expecting simply to look at the implementation of different approaches to literature-based reading and language arts curriculum, and were stunned when we finally realized that this was but a small piece of a wide-ranging transformation of elementary schools that was underway. In retrospect, it seems we should have been able to discern the larger issues before we started, but we did not. It is simply the case that implementing a literature-based curriculum is but one component of the effort to literally reformulate elementary schools.

Studying the implementation of literature-based curriculum is messy, especially if our inquiry leads us beyond the classroom in an attempt to explore the forces that foster or impede change. We noted that different curriculum plans resulted in different patterns of experiences for children, even though we observed wide variation in practices in classrooms in the same schools. This variation points to the problem of attempting to define the "average" literature-based classroom. Perhaps it is time to move beyond such attempts and begin, instead, to attempt to better understand why comprehensive literature programs (Huck, 1992) seem so difficult to create in the schools we have.

The classrooms we observed have changed and are, in fact, continuing to change (we are continuing to observe and interview these teachers and administrators). The teachers in these classrooms are being called upon to learn new ways of teaching, new ways of organizing and evaluating instruction, and new ways of looking at curriculum, children, and learning. In most cases, these teachers are inadequately supported in this learning. In most cases, teachers are bearing the burden of the efforts to change, while all around them pressures exist that subvert change.

We spent a year-and-a-half listening to and observing teachers in the process of changing the way they teach reading and language arts. All of these teachers could document and detail changes they had made in their teaching. Yet there is a real impatience evident in the literature, lectures, and legislation concerning the schools we have and the schools we need. The "thoughtful schools" that have been called for (Brown, 1991) will not emerge in full bloom overnight, although that often seems the desired end.

Change is incremental and, even with support and nurturing, it will take time (Allington & Walmsley, 1995).

Often, change has no constituency because it is simply easier to maintain the status quo. In contrast, there seems to be an emerging consensus about the need for change in literacy instruction offered in our elementary schools but, as of yet, no clear consensus on the nature of the changes that are needed nor any clear plan on how best to facilitate the change. Thus, change proceeds — neither neatly nor easily — with retaining the status quo always a potentially attractive option to at least some of the constituents involved.

We have a wealth of opinion that schools, generally, must change to meet the changing demands of American society. Many have argued that our elementary schools are not producing "thoughtful" readers and writers (Langer, 1990; Ravitch, 1985); that criticism of our schools has a long tradition. Others argue that our schools work better for some children (usually children of the middle class) than for others (Kozol, 1991; Levin, 1987; McGill-Franzen & Allington, 1991), and that too is a long-standing grievance. There is no shortage of those who would reform our schools in one way or another, and because of the central role of elementary schools in developing literacy, most of the reformers would change the way literacy lessons are taught.

We, too, believe that elementary schools must change and that they must become places where thoughtful learning predominates, places where *all* children learn to read and write alongside their peers, places where books are central to literacy learning and where writing assumes a natural role as part of that learning. As a research team, however, we are a divergent lot and have no grand scheme for precisely how schools might best undertake the changes that are viewed as necessary. Instead, we set as our task to try to better understand how schools are changing and the nature of literacy lessons in schools implementing literature-based approaches and serving large numbers of children from poor families. At this time we are continuing to interview and observe; we hope to be better able to describe both the effects of different curriculum plans and the nature of effective literature-based instruction. However, it is time-consuming work — not well suited to the impatient reformer.

Still, we would urge readers to view our findings as reflecting half-full glasses, not half-empty ones. One common feature in the schools implementing literature-based instruction is teacher change. While we were able to document the influences that different curriculum plans had on children's experiences, we also heard teachers describe the changes in their instruction and classroom organization. As we have noted, change is difficult; the status quo is always safer and easier. Our deepest concerns are that the changes underway may be stymied or stagnate if the pattern of minimal support for teacher learning is not soon altered, and that children who are experiencing difficulty will not be well served without some fundamental rethinking of curricular and instructional support.

There needs to be a re-emphasis on supporting the professional development of classroom teachers if the implementation of literature-based instruction is to provide the basis for a new, thoughtful literacy in our schools. Effective schools are but collections of effective classrooms (Allington & Cunningham, 1996). Until classroom teachers become the focus of improvement efforts, change will proceed only ever so slowly.

We noted the seemingly critical role that involvement in a professional conversation group played for the teachers we studied. We have attempted to devise ways to support such conversations and to expand the membership in such groups. To date, unfortunately, we cannot report any substantial successes in this regard. While organizing focus groups, establishing teachers-as-readers groups, and attempting on-line network communications all seemed to have potential, none of these activities have been sustained after our initial efforts. Still, the professional conversations continue among some teachers in all of the school sites. Deducing how such activity might be expanded and the precise roles such conversations play in teachers' professional development seems an important goal.

At the same time, the changes we documented across programs seem to represent real improvements in the literacy lessons that children experience daily in these schools. The implementation of literature-based curriculum plans seems to have increased the opportunities that children, especially children from low-income families, have to read in school, and to have enhanced the access they have to full-length children's literature. These are positive steps, but for continued progress, the larger institutional players must become more supportive.

ACKNOWLEDGMENT. Preparation of this report was supported under the Educational Research and Development Center program (Grant No. R117G10015) as administered by the Office of Educational Research and Improvement, U.S. Department of Education. The findings and opinions expressed here do not necessarily reflect the position or policies of the sponsoring agency.

## REFERENCES

Afflerbach, P., & Johnston, P. (1992). *Writing language arts report cards: Eleven teachers' conflicts of knowing and communicating* (Rep. No. 3.6). Albany:

State University of New York, National Research Center on Literature Teaching and Learning.

Allington, R. L. (1977). If they don't read much, how they ever gonna get good? *Journal of Reading, 21*, 57–61.

Allington, R. L. (1983). The reading instruction provided readers of differing abilities. *Elementary School Journal, 83*, 548–559.

Allington, R. L. (1994a). Reducing the risk: Integrated language arts in restructured elementary schools. In L. M. Morrow, J. K. Smith, & L. C. Wilkinson (Eds.), *Integrated language arts: From controversy to consensus* (pp. 193–213). Boston: Allyn & Bacon.

Allington, R. L. (1994b). The schools we have. The schools we need. *The Reading Teacher, 48*, 14–28.

Allington, R. L. (1994c). What's special about special programs for children who find learning to read difficult? *Journal of Reading Behavior, 26*, 1–21.

Allington, R. L., & Cunningham, P. (1996). *Schools that work: All children readers and writers*. New York: Harper Collins.

Allington, R. L., Guice, S., Li, S., Michelson, N., & Baker, K. (1995). *The implementation of literature-based instruction in schools serving low-income children* (Rep. No. 1.15). Albany: State University of New York, National Research Center on Literature Teaching and Learning.

Allington, R. L., & McGill-Franzen, A. (1989). School response to reading failure: Chapter 1 and special education students in grades 2, 4, & 8. *Elementary School Journal, 89*, 529–542.

Allington, R. L., & Walmsley, S. A. (Eds.). (1995). *No quick fix: Rethinking literacy programs in America's elementary schools*. New York: Teachers College Press.

Anderson, L. M. (1984). The environment of instruction: The function of seatwork in a commercially developed curriculum. In G. G. Duffy, L. R. Roehler, & J. Mason (Eds.), *Comprehension instruction: Perspectives and suggestions* (pp. 93–103). New York: Longman.

Birman, B. F., Orland, M. E., Jung, R. K., Amon, R. J., Garcia, G. N., Moore, M. T., Funkhouser, J. E., Morrison, D. R., Turnbull, B. J., & Reisner, E. R. (1987). *The current operation of the Chapter 1 program: Final report from the National Assessment of Chapter 1*. Washington, DC: U.S. Government Printing Office.

Brown, R. G. (1991). *Schools of thought: How the politics of literacy shape thinking in the classroom*. San Francisco: Jossey-Bass.

Canney, G. (1993). Teachers' preferences for reading materials. *Reading Improvement, 30*, 238–245.

Clinton, B., & Gore, A. (1992). *Putting people first: A national economic strategy for America*. Little Rock, AK: National Campaign Headquarters.

Cohen, D. K., & Spillane, J. P. (1992). Policy and practice: The relations between governance and instruction. In G. Grant (Ed.), *Review of research in education* (Vol. 18, pp. 3–49). Washington, DC: American Educational Research Association.

Fisher, C. W., & Hiebert, E. H. (1990). Characteristics of tasks in two approaches to literacy instruction. *Elementary School Journal, 91*, 3–18.

Fraatz, J. M. B. (1987). *The politics of reading: Power, opportunity, and prospects for change in America's public schools.* New York: Teachers College Press.

Fractor, J. S., Woodruff, M., Martinez, M., & Teale, W. (1993). Let's not miss opportunities to promote voluntary reading: Classroom libraries in the elementary school. *The Reading Teacher, 46,* 476–485.

Giddings, L. R. (1992). Literature-based reading instruction: An analysis. *Reading Research and Instruction, 31,* 18–30.

Graves, M., & Graves, B. (1994). *Scaffolding reading experiences: Designs for student success.* Norwood, MA: Christopher-Gordon.

Guice, S., Allington, R., Johnston, P., Baker, K., & Michaelson, N. (1994). *Access? Books, children, and literature-based curriculum in schools* (Rep. No. 1.13). Albany: State University of New York, National Research Center on Literature Teaching and Learning.

Hiebert, E. H., & Colt, J. (1989). Patterns of literature-based reading instruction. *The Reading Teacher, 43,* 14–20.

Hoffman, J. V., Roser, N. L., & Battle, J. (1993). Reading aloud in classrooms: From the modal to a "model." *The Reading Teacher, 46,* 496–505.

Huck, C. S. (1992). Literacy and literature. *Language Arts, 69,* 520–526.

Johnston, P. A., Allington, R. L., & Afflerbach, P. (1985). The congruence of classroom and remedial reading instruction. *Elementary School Journal, 85,* 465–478.

Knapp, M. S. (1991). *What is taught, and how, to the children of poverty: Interim report from a two-year investigation.* Menlo Park, CA: SRI.

Kozol, J. (1991). *Savage inequalities: Children in America's schools.* New York: Crown.

Langer, J. A. (1990). Understanding literature. *Language Arts, 67,* 812–823.

Leinhardt, G., Zigmond, N., & Cooley, W. (1981). Reading instruction and its effects. *American Educational Research Journal, 18,* 343–361.

Levin, H. M. (1987). Accelerated schools for disadvantaged students. *Educational Leadership, 44,* 19–21.

McGill-Franzen, A. M., & Allington, R. L. (1991). The gridlock of low-achievement: Perspectives on policy and practice. *Remedial and Special Education, 12,* 20–30.

Mervar, K., & Hiebert, E. H. (1989). Literature-selection strategies and amount of reading in two literacy approaches. In S. McCormick & J. Zutell (Eds.), *Cognitive and social perspectives for literacy research and instruction* (38th yearbook of the National Reading Conference) (pp. 529–535). Chicago: National Reading Conference.

Morrow, L. M. (1992). The impact of a literature-based program on literacy achievement, use of literature, and attitudes of children from minority backgrounds. *Reading Research Quarterly, 27,* 250–276.

Mullis, I. V. S., Campbell, J. R., & Farstrup, A. E. (1993). *NAEP 1992 reading report card for the nation and states.* Washington, DC: U.S. Department of Education.

National Center for Educational Statistics. (1993). *Schools and staffing in the United States: A statistical profile, 1990–91* (Rep. No. 93–146). Washington, DC: U.S. Department of Education, Office of Educational Research and Improvement.

Pace, G. (1992). Stories of teacher-initiated change from traditional to whole language literacy instruction. *Elementary School Journal, 92*, 461–476.

Pearson, P. D. (1993). Teaching and learning reading: A research perspective. *Language Arts, 70*, 502–511.

Purcell-Gates, V., & Dahl, K. (1991). Low-SES children's success and failure at early literacy learning in skills-based classrooms. *Journal of Reading Behavior, 23*, 1–34.

Ravitch, D. (1985). *The schools we deserve: Reflections on the educational crises of our time*. New York: Basic Books.

Reutzel, D. R., & Cooter, R. B. (1990). Whole language: Comparative effects on first-grade reading achievement. *Journal of Educational Research, 83*, 252–257.

Scharer, P. L. (1992). Teachers in transition: An exploration of changes in teachers and classrooms during implementation of literature-based reading instruction. *Research in the Teaching of English, 20*, 408–443.

Shanklin, N. (1990). Improving the comprehension of at-risk readers: An ethnographic study of four Chapter 1 teachers, grades 4–6. *International Journal of Reading, Writing, and Learning Disabilities, 6*, 137–148.

Solsken, J. W. (1993). *Literacy, gender, and work in families and schools*. Norwood, NJ: Ablex.

Strickland, D., Walmsley, S., Bronk, G., & Weiss, K. (1994). *School book clubs and literacy development: A descriptive study* (Rep. No. 2.22). Albany: State University of New York, National Research Center on Literature Teaching and Learning.

Taylor, B. M., Frye, B., & Maruyama, G. (1990). Time spent reading and reading growth. *American Educational Research Journal, 27*, 351–362.

Walmsley, S. A., Fielding, L. F., & Walp, T. P. (1991). *A study of second graders' home and school literary experiences* (Rep. No. 1.6). Albany: State University of New York, Center on Learning and Teaching of Literature.

Walmsley, S. A., & Walp, T. P. (1989). *Teaching literature in elementary school* (Rep. No. 1.6). Albany: State University of New York, Center on Learning and Teaching of Literature.

Zarillo, J. (1989). Teachers' interpretations of literature-based reading. *The Reading Teacher, 43*, 22–28.

CHAPTER 5

# Questioning the Author:
# An Approach to Developing
# Meaningful Classroom Discourse

MARGARET G. McKEOWN
ISABEL L. BECK
CHERYL A. SANDORA
*University of Pittsburgh*

A study that we conducted in 1991 on students' history learning included interviewing eighth graders as they finished their study of early American history. A question about what happened in the Revolutionary War prompted the following response from Jennifer, one of the students:

> I don't really remember this too well; I don't know why. We always learn about this and I always forget. It's so important, too. Something like one of the colonies was too strong and something happened and they got into a war over it, and it was going on for a while and that's just one of the things. I don't know why I don't remember this. It's pretty embarrassing. (Beck & McKeown, 1994, p. 249)

Jennifer's remarks illustrate two themes that have pervaded the program of research in which we have been involved over the past decade. The first is that textbooks, which are customarily the basis of students' history knowledge at this level, are not serving students well. The second is that students often react to inadequate text presentations by developing a view of themselves as inadequate readers.

In this chapter, we begin with a brief chronology of our research on students and texts and how it has moved from a focus on the qualities of textbooks to a focus on developing students' abilities to deal with text. In the second section of the chapter, we present a detailed look at how Questioning the Author, the approach we designed to help students deal with texts, influenced their thinking about what they read. In the final section, we describe a new shift in our research focus, this time toward developing ways to support teachers in helping students interact productively with the texts they read.

## OUR WORK IN EXAMINING TEXTBOOKS
## AND HOW STUDENTS UNDERSTAND THEM

In the mid-1980s we initiated our program of research on students' understanding and learning from textbooks, with an analysis of the extent to which learning and understanding were promoted by the content as presented in four elementary social studies programs (Beck, McKeown, & Gromoll, 1989). Our approach to analyzing text was based on theory and research from a cognitive perspective. The cognitive orientation to reading research had brought much progress in understanding the ways that readers interact with texts. In investigations of the reading process, emphasis turned to trying to understand the mental activities involved in reading, that is, what the reader does while reading, rather than being confined to the products of reading, that is, what the reader remembers from reading. Insights gained from the cognitive perspective also yielded understanding of how the reader's execution and coordination of the processes involved during reading affect the products of reading (Just & Carpenter, 1987; Perfetti, 1985; Trabasso & Magliano, Chapter 7, this volume).

We saw the understandings gained from cognitive reading research as having much to offer textbook analysis work. Particularly fruitful is the inherent focus on learning, which could open the way for understanding how characteristics of texts affect the way textbooks function in a learning environment. Two specific areas of research particularly influenced our text analysis work: understandings about the nature of the reading process, with emphasis on the interaction of a reader's background knowledge and a text's content (Chiesi, Spilich, & Voss, 1979; Pearson, Hansen, & Gordon, 1979), and characteristics of texts that promote or impede comprehension (Black & Bern, 1981; Frederiksen, 1981; Trabasso, Secco, & van den Broek, 1984).

Drawing from cognitive theory and research, we developed an approach to analysis of text in which we examined extensive topic sequences.

Examination of sequences of text content enabled us to consider the learning that might develop as students move through a sequence and to communicate a sense of the raw material from which young students are expected to build understanding of a topic. In our analyses we gave particular attention to the explanatory material used to develop specific concepts within general topics and themes.

A major focus of our analyses was content about the American Revolutionary period, specifically the time frame from colonial development through the events at Lexington and Concord, from the fifth-grade texts in each of the four programs we examined. It was our judgment that the presentation of content in the programs was not likely to promote the development of understanding of the chain of events that led to the Revolution. We saw two major problems. The first was that the texts seemed to assume an unrealistic variety and depth of background knowledge on the part of young students. For example, although the issue of "no taxation without representation" is a critical element for understanding the causes of the Revolution, the texts, in presenting that issue, merely stated that the colonists had no representation in Parliament. None of the texts we analyzed attempted to explain the basic issue of what it means to be represented in a governmental body or how strong the motivation to acquire or protect that form of government can be. Rather, the text presentations seemed to assume that students already had a full grasp of the concept of representative government.

The second major problem identified in our text analyses was that the presentations lacked the coherence needed to enable students to draw connections between events and ideas. For example, the actions involved in the Boston Tea Party were portrayed quite clearly. But the cause of the event, which was rooted in the colonists' ongoing protest over Britain's taxes, was not explained. Thus, the event was not linked to the causal chain of events leading to the Revolution.

Following the analyses of textbook sequences, we engaged in a study to examine the kind of understandings that students were able to develop from reading these texts (McKeown & Beck, 1990). In this work we presented fifth graders with a sequence of passages about events leading to the Revolution from one of the textbooks that we had analyzed. The sequence covered the French and Indian War, the dispute over taxation without representation, the Boston Tea Party, and the Intolerable Acts. We asked students to read each passage and then recall what they had read and respond to some open-ended questions. The study occurred just before the students were slated to read the same material in their regular classrooms, and so they had already covered all the background material.

Examination of the students' recalls and answers to questions showed that the understanding that students were able to develop was rather shallow, suggesting that their interactions with the text were on a very surface level. As an illustration of why that might have been the case, consider a paragraph from the text that is meant to convey the harshness of the regulations that the British imposed on the colonists after the Boston Tea Party.

> The British were very angry! Within a few months, they passed what the colonists called the Intolerable Acts. Intolerable means "unbearable." These acts were meant to punish the people of Boston. The port of Boston was closed. No self-government was allowed in Massachusetts. British troops had to be housed by the Massachusetts colonists. (Silver Burdett, 1984, p. 109)

Many students' recalls of this terse text suggested that they did not engage with the material, but only picked up some isolated pieces of information. Matthew's response is an example. When asked to tell what the passage was about, Matthew simply said:

> It's about people from Great Britain [who] were very angry. . . . There was this new thing called the intolerable act, and they didn't like it. Then people from Massachusetts put them in houses for something.

Based on students' accounts of what they read, we concluded that the problems we had identified in our text analyses did indeed create obstacles to comprehension. Students did lack assumed background knowledge and often were unable to draw appropriate inferences.

Our research next turned to examining the extent to which more coherent text presentations would facilitate students' understanding. In this work we created revised versions of the four textbook passages about events leading to the Revolutionary War (Beck et al., 1989). Our revisions were intended to establish textual coherence by clarifying, elaborating, explaining, and motivating important information and by making relationships explicit.

The goal of our revisions was to create a text based on a causal sequence of events, with the information presented in a way that explained the connections from a cause to an event and from an event to a consequence. The basis for the revisions was our mental simulation of how a typical target-aged reader would respond to the information in the text. Thus, the original texts were evaluated by considering how each new piece of text information might be handled, what kind of knowledge the reader would need to bring to bear, and how the developing text representation would be influenced. Points where the process might break down, such as where an explanation seemed inadequate, were hypothesized, and ways in which an ideal reader might repair such breaks were generated. These potential repairs were used as the basis for the revised version of the text. As we considered what might happen as a young reader processed the text, we switched back and forth among hypothesizing what the student might be thinking, inducing what seemed to be intended by the text, and constructing text statements that might promote a coherent representation.

When the revised passages were presented to the students, they recalled significantly more of the text and answered more questions correctly (Beck, McKeown, Sinatra, & Loxterman, 1991). Even more important, the additional recall produced by the students reading the revised text represented exactly the concepts needed to explain the actions and connect them with the major chain of events. For example, in the "no taxation without representation" segment, the students reading revised text were more likely to understand that the colonists' objection to the taxes arose from their desire for representation in government rather than a squabble over money.

Despite the advantages shown for readers of the revised passages, the results of our study indicated that readers in both groups still had considerable difficulty understanding the texts. The recalls of many students from both groups pointed to surface-level treatments of text information. Reading the recalls gave us the impression that students took what they could get in one swift pass through the words on a page, and then formed that into a shallow representation of the text. This kind of cursory use of the text suggests that students resist digging in and grappling with unfamiliar or difficult content.

## PROMOTING YOUNG READERS' ENGAGEMENT
## WITH TEXT: QUESTIONING THE AUTHOR

At this point, our research interests shifted to exploring ways to get readers to engage with texts and to consider ideas deeply. In cognitive terms, engagement with text means active processing of what is read, and research suggests that little meaningful interaction with text can take place unless a reader is active. Considering what it means for a reader to be active made us realize that the kind of processing we did in revising textbook passages was the kind of experience we wanted to create for students. One must become actively engaged with the content of a text in order to transform it into a comprehensible form. We reasoned that giving students a "reviser's eye" might create a subtle but important shift in their goal when interacting with a text — from trying to understand it to making it understandable.

The shift to trying to make a text understandable also embodies a change in attitude toward the status of the text. Textbooks carry weighty authority in the classroom. This authority arises both from the traditional role of the text as the center of the classroom curriculum and from the impersonal, objective tone of textbook language (Luke, DeCastell, & Luke, 1983; Olson, 1980). Having difficulty with a text, then, can give students the notion that they are to blame, as illustrated in Jennifer's interview excerpt at the beginning of the chapter. Students often respond by applying the principle of least effort; they seem to resist digging in and dealing with difficult text, because "not to try is not to fail."

As we developed our ideas into an approach to use with students—an approach that we have come to call Questioning the Author—three principles became key.

- Depose the authority of the text by letting students know that texts are just someone's ideas written down, and they need to be worked on if understanding is to develop.
- Focus attention directly on grappling with the meaning of what is written in the text.
- Have students take part in meaning-getting interactions on-line as text is read initially.

Based on these principles, we began pilot work with individual students, introducing our ideas to the students by telling them that "different people write things in different ways, and sometimes what someone has in their mind to say just doesn't come through clearly in their writing of it."

The purpose of this introduction was to create the expectation that figuring out the ideas behind an author's words requires work, and thus needing to work to understand was not an indication that their abilities were inadequate. We then modeled for students how a reader might think through a text in order to build understanding. The modeling involved our reading a brief text aloud and commenting on and evaluating text statements. For example, the text we used states, "Russia has used rockets to put a new moon in the sky," to which we responded, "Hmmm, I don't know what the author means. How can you put up another moon?"

Following the introduction, we worked with students by having them think aloud as they read a text, sometimes prompting them with questions such as, "What's that all about?" or "What's the author trying to say there?". We used these general probes in order to focus students on constructing meaning rather than on locating and retrieving specific information. Based on those questions that seemed most effectively to encourage students' construction of meaning, we developed a set of "Engagement Queries." The queries include questions to initiate meaning-building such as, "What is the author trying to say?" or "What is the author talking about?" and follow-ups such as, "What could the author mean by that?" and "Why is the author telling us that?" to prompt students to go beyond words to the ideas being communicated.

## BRINGING QUESTIONING THE AUTHOR TO THE CLASSROOM

Our next step, after work with individual students, was to take our approach to the classroom. After testing the classroom dynamics of Questioning the Author by working with groups of about a dozen students, we were able to set up a collaborative relationship with two teachers and work toward implementing Questioning the Author in their fourth-grade classrooms.

From observations of the collaborating teachers, we learned that they both taught in a traditional manner, with lessons that focused on a text section or story, which was read in round robin style, followed by a teacher-led question and answer session directed toward retrieving text information. Students provided brief responses, and the teachers evaluated the correctness of each response and moved to the next question.

Questioning the Author was introduced to teachers during the summer. When the school year began, the teachers implemented the new approach, conducting their lessons with text by reading or asking students to read a portion of text, and then posing Engagement Queries from the set we developed to initiate and focus discussion. As the teachers worked with Questioning the Author, it was clear that the approach "upset the apple cart" of the traditional lesson in the way text was handled and in the way teachers needed to interact with students. In terms of the text, the Questioning the Author framework meant that lessons no longer consisted of reading straight through a text, followed by questions aimed at literal text information and direct student responses. Rather, the teachers needed to develop techniques for probing ideas as they were encountered in text, monitoring students' understanding, and prompting students to grapple with text ideas.

Questioning the Author required the teachers to deal with students in new ways. Teachers no longer got brief, predictable responses from students, but rather longer, elaborated accounts of what students understood or did not understand from the text, and student-initiated questions that could take the discussion in unpredictable directions. Also, teachers no longer were dealing with an individual student's isolated response; rather, students were reacting to each other's contributions by challenging each other's ideas, elaborating on comments, agreeing, disagreeing, and competing for opportunities to comment on issues that arose. Frequent and extensive interactions with the teachers over the year were directed toward supporting them in handling the changes that Questioning the Author required and using the changes to bring about a more productive learning environment.

## OUTCOMES FROM TWO YEAR—LONG IMPLEMENTATIONS

As the implementation progressed, we began to observe changes in the discourse environments in the classrooms. We noticed that the pattern of questions requiring students to locate information followed by brief responses seemed to be giving way to a focus on meaning and a more collaborative atmosphere. We then developed indices to examine these changes systematically. These indices examine four aspects of the discourse environment: (1) types of questions teachers ask, (2) ways teachers respond to student comments, (3) proportion of teacher talk to student talk, and (4) frequency of student-initiated comments and questions.

We used these indices to analyze lessons of our two initial collaborating teachers (Beck, McKeown, Worthy, Sandora, & Kucan, 1996) and from two additional teachers who implemented Questioning the Author in their fourth-grade classrooms the following year. The set of lessons that was analyzed included at least one baseline lesson of each teacher and a sample of Questioning the Author lessons. The sample was selected to include lessons from across the school year and to represent both language arts and social studies classes. A total of 29 lessons was analyzed. The following brief description of the findings from our analyses highlights the changes that occurred in the four classrooms as a result of Questioning the Author.

Our examination of the discourse environment in the collaborating classrooms began with the kinds of questions teachers ask of students as they read, because teacher questions are a driving force behind the lesson. We identified four types of questions based on the type of information the teacher was seeking from students. Teachers appeared to ask students questions in order to:

(1) retrieve information from the text, such as, "Who are the characters in this story?"
(2) construct the message of the text, such as, "What is the author trying to tell us about these characters?"
(3) extend the construction of meaning, such as, "How did the author give you the idea that the characters weren't getting along?"
(4) check students' knowledge of a particular piece of information, such as, "Who remembers what *conceited* means?"

Examination of the questions according to these four categories showed that the types of questions teachers asked students as a result of Questioning the Author represented a shift from retrieving information to constructing meaning, particularly in extending the construction of meaning. The analysis showed that when teachers used Questioning the Author they no longer focused on factual questions, asking students to take information directly from the text, but rather on questions that asked students to think about and build ideas from what they were reading.

The changing nature of teachers' questions set in motion a change in classroom discourse patterns. In the Questioning the Author environment, rather than a student's response to a teacher's question being followed by a simple evaluation and then another teacher question, connections were drawn from the content of a student's response to the teacher's next move. Thus, our second analysis examined teachers' rejoinders to students' responses.

In a preliminary examination of lesson transcripts, we noted that teachers seemed to respond to student comments using one of three moves:

(1) repeating the comment;
(2) paraphrasing the comment, sometimes substantially changing the wording but leaving the meaning intact;
(3) refining the comment, shaping the ideas by clarifying or focusing them, or lifting them to more general language.

Analysis of the sample transcripts revealed differences between baseline and Questioning the Author lesson transcripts with regard to teacher rejoinders. In the baseline lessons, the most common way of making students' comments public was repetition; paraphrases and refinements of students' contributions were relatively rare. In Questioning the Author lessons, however, teachers increased their tendency to refine students' comments, indicating that teachers no longer were simply repeating students' comments, but were using students' comments as a means to move the discussion in a productive manner.

The two indices described so far suggest that Questioning the Author promotes constructive discourse, which begs the question of who is doing the constructing. Typically, one consequence of the traditional lesson pattern of teacher question, student response, and teacher evaluation is that teachers dominate the talk that occurs in a lesson and students are given very few opportunities to respond at any length (Alvermann, O'Brien, & Dillon, 1990; Cazden, 1986; Goodlad, 1984).

The changing pattern of discourse observed within Questioning the Author lessons included a shift away from teachers' domination of discussion. In order to examine the extent to which this shift occurred, we computed the amount of teacher talk and the amount of student talk in the sample set of transcripts. Results showed that the amount of student talk during Questioning the Author lessons increased significantly; student talk more than doubled in a typical lesson. This analysis of the proportion of talk in the classroom makes it evident that, in addition to affecting teacher behavior, Questioning the Author also influenced students' behavior.

The fourth analysis examined the extent to which students initiated their own questions and comments in addition to responding to teacher questions. In baseline lessons students rarely asked questions, but a substantial increase in student-initiated comments and questions in Questioning the Author lessons indicated that such contributions were an important part of those lessons.

The results of the four indices indicated that the discourse pattern had changed substantially under Questioning the Author. However, these indices shed somewhat more light on changes in teachers' actions in the classroom than on what students were doing. Although we knew that students were talking more and initiating more comments, the nature of their contributions had not been examined. In the next section of this chapter, we turn the focus to the students, to explore the kinds of thinking about and responding to text that were prompted by Questioning the Author.

## CHANGES IN STUDENTS' THINKING
## ABOUT AND RESPONDING TO TEXT

Our observations of students' contributions during Questioning the Author lessons indicated that not only were students' comments longer than those in traditional lessons but the ideas expressed were more complex and the focus was more on meaning than on literal wording.

### THE NATURE OF STUDENTS' RESPONSES

To examine these changes systematically, we developed a categorization scheme describing the responses students gave during discussions. Four categories were developed that encompassed the kinds of student responses found in the lessons. One category included responses that were verbatim or near verbatim repetitions of text. Both the concepts and the language of these responses stayed close to the text.

A second category included responses in which students constructed local meaning. These responses represented students' attempts to manipulate text ideas, explaining them and recasting them in their own language and sometimes adding simple elaborations. These responses stayed fairly close to the text in concept, although the language was transformed and movement toward meaning was evident. An example would be responding to the text sentence, "Reindeer herders depended on reindeer to fill all their needs," by saying, "They're hunters that go out and that depend on reindeer for their food and their fur and places to live." Some transformation and elaboration of the wording occurs; for example, the instantiation of *needs* as "food, fur, places to live."

A third category included responses in which students integrated information. These responses indicated dealing with text ideas or ideas in the discussion by integrating prior knowledge or previously learned text information, hypothesizing solutions to conflicts or problems that arose from the reading, or extrapolating consequences of text events and ideas. An example would be responding to the concept of reindeer herders by comparing their lifestyle with that of a group of people that the class had read about earlier: "The people who we learned about, Eskimos, they do like that, but they make their houses and clothes and stuff out of, well, caribou."

A fourth category included responses in which students introduced their own questions or comments into the discussion, and responses in which peers directly addressed those comments, either by answering a question, expressing agreement or disagreement, or adding to a comment made by a peer. For example, a student responded to the discussion of reindeer herders by adding: "Like Shanelle said, I think they get their food and stuff out of the reindeer, but they don't go out and hunt them, because they raise them and just herd them together."

The same set of sample transcripts analyzed for the four indices described earlier—teacher questions, teacher rejoinders, proportion of student/teacher talk, and student-initiated comments—was used for the analysis of student responses. A separate analysis was done for each teacher by subject area taught. Although we examined four teachers' classrooms, this resulted in five analyses because one collaborating teacher used Questioning the Author in both language arts and social studies, while two teachers taught only language arts, and one taught only social studies.

## RESULTS OF THE ANALYSES

Because the same pattern emerged for the two analyses of social studies and for the three analyses of language arts, we present the results according to content area. Table 5.1 shows the patterns for both the language arts classes and the social studies classes.

Although the patterns for the two subject areas differed slightly, the table indicates that a similar shift occurred for both areas in the kinds of student responses. That is, in Questioning the Author, student responses were much more likely than in the baseline lessons to focus on meaning and

**TABLE 5.1.** Mean percent (and frequency per lesson) of student responses across four categories in baseline and questioning the author language arts and social studies lessons.

| | Verbatim | Local meaning | Integration | Student comments |
|---|---|---|---|---|
| Baseline language arts | 40(11) | 49(14) | 9(3) | 2(1) |
| Q & A language arts | 10(6) | 49(28) | 26(15) | 15(10) |
| Baseline social studies | 88(19) | 12(2) | 0(0) | 0(0) |
| Q & A social studies | 17(6) | 51(21) | 23(9) | 9(4) |

integration. The table also shows the increase in number of student responses during Questioning the Author lessons. Of note is that although the overall number of student responses increased substantially compared with baseline lessons, the number of verbatim responses dropped. Thus, the change in student response pattern was not simply an increase in more sophisticated responses, but also a decrease in verbatim responses.

Table 5.1 suggests that in the baseline language arts lessons, the majority of student comments fell into the first two levels, with 40% of the comments staying very close to the text, and 49% moving to construction of local meaning. There were very few comments in which students integrated outside information or interacted with their peers. During Questioning the Author lessons, the proportion of comments that were considered to be construction of local meaning remained the same. However, the proportion of verbatim responses dropped to 10%, with concomitant increases in the integration and student comments categories.

The table indicates that in the social studies baseline lessons, 88% of student comments were verbatim accounts of the information in the text, with 12% representing construction of local meaning. There were no responses that involved integration of information or student-initiated comments. The analysis of the Questioning the Author lessons reveals a different picture: The proportion of verbatim responses decreased to 17%, with a significant increase in comments in the other three levels.

SAMPLING THE QUESTIONING THE AUTHOR ENVIRONMENT

The analysis of the categories of student responses characterizes the nature of children's thinking about text ideas within Questioning the Author. In this section, we present excerpts from classroom lessons that illustrate the nature of the discourse environments that the student responses helped to create.

*A context for contrast.* To set up a context in which to consider the discourse environment, we first present an excerpt from a baseline lesson taught by one of our collaborating teachers prior to implementation of Questioning the Author. The class in this excerpt has been reading Beverly Cleary's *Ralph S. Mouse* (1982). In the part of the text that the class has just read, Ralph, the motorcycle riding mouse, had a spat with Ryan, the boy who keeps him. Ryan had taken away his motorcycle, so Ralph decided to stay at school alone over the weekend, and now he's been contemplating that decision, feeling lonely and thinking about his home. The teacher tried to engage students in a discussion of Ralph's feelings, but she did so by focusing on individual words to describe those feelings. The students responded in kind, offering individual words; little attempt was made to connect the words to create a picture of the scene or what it means in terms of the story.

TEACHER: Okay, I want some words now from you that would describe Ralph. All right? How does Ralph feel right now? Eric?

ERIC: He feels lonely.

TEACHER: Lonely. All right, we have a lot of adjectives to describe his feelings.

NICOLE: Cold.

TEACHER: Cold. How else?

LUKE: A little scared.

TEACHER: Scared.

STACEY: Disappointed.

TEACHER: Disappointed.

STACEY: That his motorcycle is broken.

TEACHER: All right, he's disappointed.

JUSTIN: He misses the hotel.

TEACHER: All right, he misses the hotel. Anything else he misses besides the hotel?

CHAD: His motorcycle.

TEACHER: His motorcycle.

MELISSA: His relatives.

At this point, the teacher did ask students to make a connection, but the student who responded simply hooked together two words with "and," making no further elaboration.

TEACHER: Okay. Can we put "misses" with something else? Can we connect some of these? Are there two words that we can connect here? Anthony?

ANTHONY: Misses and lonely.

This list-like treatment of the story continued, and little was done to explore ideas; the focus was on naming feelings and states. This excerpt very much typified what we saw in baseline lessons, both in language arts and in social studies.

**Working to understand ideas.** A very different kind of interaction characterized Questioning the Author lessons. Discussions focused much more on exploring and building meaning, with the students and teacher connecting and reacting to each other's responses. In the excerpt below from a Questioning the Author lesson, the class was reading the story *Ben and Me* (Lawson, 1939), which is about Benjamin Franklin and his mouse companion, whom he sends up in a kite to examine lightning. At the point in the lesson at which the excerpt begins, the class just read a portion of text early in the story and was grappling with this sentence: "This question of the nature of lightning so preyed upon his mind that he was finally driven to an act of deceit that caused the first and only rift in our long friendship." The teacher asked, "What's the author trying to tell us about Ben and Amos?"

TEMIKA: That their friendship was breaking up.

TEACHER: Their friendship was breaking up? OK, let's hang on to that. What do you think, April?

APRIL: I agree with the part that their friendship did break up, but um, I think that they got back together because when you were reading um, further, it said that he was enjoying the mouse.

TEACHER: OK, so let me make sure. You say that he knows that they're friends, and something happened that made them almost not be friends? But they're still friends?

ALVIS: I think that um, Amos is just, I think Amos is just lying because in the story it said if they weren't good friends, why would um, um, Ben build a um, kite for, build a kite for him so he could have fun?

TEACHER: OK, so Alvis is telling us that, why would Ben go to all that trouble and build that beautiful kite if they weren't friends? A lot of people agreed that their friendship was broken up. Alvis doesn't think their friendship is broken up. Can somebody help me out? What's the author want us to figure out here?

In their responses, April and Alvis were working to make sense of the text sentence by bringing in support from other parts of the text. The teacher responded by rephrasing their ideas in a way that defined the issue of whether the two story characters remained friends.

As the dialogue below shows, the discussion continued with two more students grappling with the meaning of the sentence. First, Tammy worked with the words of the text, manipulating them in an effort to make the ideas understandable to herself.

TAMMY: Um, um, deceit was an act of lying so that means, that means um, sometimes a lie broke up a friendship and, because it made a rift and um, so, and deceit was an act of lying, so their friendship must've broke up because of somebody told um, some kind of lie.

TEACHER: Oh, that's interesting. Tammy said that if there were some lying going on, something to break up their friendship, because that's what Amos said, "the first and only rift in our friendship," something must've happened. How many of you agree that something had to happen?

Next, Jamal's comments suggested a distinction between "a break" in the friendship and dissolving the friendship, which the teacher then acknowledged before reading resumed.

JAMAL: I disagree, 'cause a break in their friendship don't mean they gotta break their friendship.

TEACHER: OK, so Jamal thinks that they might still be friends, even though something happened. OK? We're gonna continue 'cause the only way we're gonna find out is if we read some more.

This excerpt showed students trying to come to terms with the meaning of one key sentence. In trying to figure out its meaning, the students spontaneously applied strategies such as rephrasing it, explaining parts of it, and bringing in other text information to interpret it. The teacher guided this process by rephrasing or clarifying comments, by keeping the focus on the issue being discussed, and by trying to draw other students into the discussion.

***Developing ownership of ideas.*** An excerpt that provides a somewhat different flavor of the kinds of dialogue patterns that emerged during Questioning the Author discussions is presented below. In this example, students played off each other's comments to an even greater extent than in the foregoing discussion. The conversation focused on one idea, which the students seemed to have grasped from the beginning. Here, they worked to take ownership of the idea, creating an interpretation of it and expressing it in their own ways.

The excerpt is from a social studies class about Pennsylvania history. The class just read a text segment about the presidency of James Buchanan, a Pennsylvania native, which stated that many people believed that Buchanan liked the South better than the North because he held that it was a person's choice whether to have slaves. As an example of the problems that this position caused the President, the text states that settlers from Kansas wrote a proslavery constitution, which Buchanan supported but Congress rejected.

The teacher began the discussion by posing a general query about the paragraph. A student responded with a paraphrase of the main issue of Buchanan's position, and the teacher then asked a follow-up question that prompted the interpretation that the students then worked with.

TEACHER: All right. This paragraph that Tracy just read is really full of important information. What has the author told us in this important paragraph?

LAURA: Um, they um, think that Buchanan liked the South better because they, he said that it is a person's choice if they want to have slaves or not, so they thought um, that he liked the South better than the North.

TEACHER: Okay. And what kind of problem then did this cause President Buchanan when they thought that he liked the South better? What kind of problem did that cause?

In the next exchange, Janet generated an interpretation of how Buchanan's developing position on slavery might have affected the voters in his home state:

JANET: Well, maybe um, like less people would vote for him because like if he ran for President again, maybe less people would vote for him because like in Pennsylvania we were against slavery and we might have voted for him because he was in Pennsylvania, because he was from Pennsylvania. That may be why they voted for him, but now since we knew that he was for the South, we might not vote for him again.

The teacher and another student then took up and elaborated Janet's comment in their own ways. First, the teacher offered a capsulization of the idea:

TEACHER: Okay, a little bit of knowledge, then, might change people's minds.

Then another student, Jamie, acknowledged her peer's idea. She then went on to make explicit Janet's implication that Pennsylvania voters originally might have thought that Buchanan was himself against slavery because he was from Pennsylvania:

JAMIE: I have something to add on to Janet's 'cause I completely agree with her, but I just want to add something on. Um, we might have voted for him because he was from Pennsylvania so we might have thought that since he was from Pennsylvania and Pennsylvania was an antislavery state, that he was also against slavery. But it turns out he wasn't.

A third student, Angelica, weighed in with her spin on the developing interpretation. She turned the focus to another part of Janet's earlier comment, that Buchanan was "for the South":

ANGELICA: I agree with the rest of them, except for one that um, like all of a sudden, like someone who would be in Pennsylvania you want to vote for them but then they wouldn't, they be going for the South and then you wouldn't want to vote for them after that.

The teacher followed with another capsulization of the developing ideas:

TEACHER: Yeah. Just like, someone whom you think is your best friend, and then all of a sudden you find out, ooh, they're not.

Then, seemingly sensing that the notion under consideration had run its course, Rachel turned the discussion to a new part of the paragraph:

RACHEL: Um, as you said um, this paragraph is full of like a lot of stuff, well, the settlers wrote a constitution that the Wizard of Oz state would be a slave state and then they jump to 4 years later, and it's a free state.

The example suggests that the students have taken charge, even to moving on to a new topic. The degree to which students attended to and reacted to each other's comments was far beyond what typically is reported about traditional discussions of text in classrooms.

The analyses of student responses and excerpts from lessons presented in this chapter show students engaging in complex, meaning-focused, interactive thinking. The work that we have done with Questioning the Author suggests that this kind of thinking can emerge, given an environment in which the text is addressed as a product of a fallible author and discussions are based on general probes for the meaning of what has been written.

*Teachers' roles in discussion.* The kind of thinking and responding that students were doing in Questioning the Author lessons had much to do with the teachers' shaping of the environment. Teachers asked questions that encouraged students to focus on meaning rather than on locating text information; for example, asking, "What did Tony mean when he said that to his brother?" rather than simply, "What did Tony say to his brother?" The rejoinders that teachers gave to students' responses showed attention to the content of student responses and consideration of how they could fit into the discussion, as in this example: "Shanelle said that the reindeer herders moved to follow the reindeer. How does that fit in with what the author has already told us about these people?"

Teachers also encouraged student contributions to discussion by making it clear that students' responses were valued and that a range of responses was appropriate. Teacher comments such as the following were typical: "That's an interesting way to look at it, Amy, I never thought of it that way." Additionally, teachers shared their own reactions to the texts being read, with comments such as, "When I read this I was really confused," or "How can the author say it's cold when he just told us the sun shines 24 hours a day?" Such comments may have played a role in exposing the kinds of thinking that mature readers undertake when reading, also helping to reinforce the notion that reading takes effort and a "figuring it out" attitude.

## LOOKING TO THE FUTURE

Developing and sustaining an environment that encourages students to share their thinking about text ideas and to work toward building meaning is a highly complex task. Discourse that leads to meaning-building needs direction, focus, and movement toward a goal. To foster such discourse effectively, a teacher must not only attend to the content of what is being read and the ideas important for building meaning from that content, but must also monitor where students are in that construction process and then pull from that combination of factors ways of directing the dialogue to promote understanding. As Cazden (1988) says, "It is easy to imagine talk in which ideas are explored rather than answers to teachers' test questions provided and evaluated. . . . Easy to imagine, but not easy to do" (p. 54).

We addressed the difficulties our collaborating teachers had in developing discourse environments in which ideas are constructed by providing extensive, ongoing, firsthand support. We observed and videotaped lessons and met with the teachers weekly. At those meetings we provided teachers with feedback about their lessons, and together we analyzed transcripts, identifying successful and less successful aspects, and worked to develop solutions to problematic issues. We also held collaborative planning sessions with the teachers to map out ways of dealing with specific texts or topics, and provided occasional demonstration lessons for the teachers to observe and critique.

Thus, our face-to-face interactions with the teachers were the major agent for the change that took place in the classroom discourse environment. This is a situation common to current research that is aimed at revamping instructional practices toward guiding students to build their own knowledge and understanding rather than transmitting information to them. This trend in pedagogical practice is referred to as "teaching for understanding" (Cohen, McLaughlin, & Talbert, 1993). In the current zeitgeist, researchers work closely with teachers, collaborating on developing and refining approaches to instruction and even taking turns in the classroom.

The current collaborative orientation arises from researchers' cognizance of the failure of older ways of working toward instructional change in which teachers were given an innovation to perform. Rather, the collaborative interactive approach recognizes that enacting new instructional strategies is a learning process, and that change needs to include teachers' understanding of the rationale for the change as well as their ownership of the new practices (see Au & Asam, Chapter 8, this volume, for a discussion of related issues). This research focus has produced some broad outlines of what seems to be needed for teachers to develop teaching-for-understanding orientations: fundamental change in teachers' beliefs about what learning is (Prawat, 1992; Richardson, 1990), development of practices that put those beliefs into action (Blumenfeld, Krajcik, Marx, & Soloway, 1994; Wood & Cobb, 1991), and ability to reflect on how classroom actions match beliefs (Colton & Sparks-Langer, 1993; Russell, 1993).

The details of how to produce changes in beliefs, practices, and reflection are quite sketchy, however. For example, in the area of pedagogical practices, constructs such as modeling, scaffolding, assisted performance, and coaching are pervasive (Duffy & Roehler, 1987; Duffy et al., 1989; Palincsar & Brown, 1984; Tharp & Gallimore, 1991). Yet, it is difficult to move from general constructs such as modeling and coaching to the kind of details that would bring those constructs to life, because the details are embedded in anecdotal accounts of face-to-face collaborations between researchers and teachers.

With the predominance of collaborative interactions, the focus in current instructional research has been on making change occur. Less attention has gone into what gives changed practice a life of its own after the research intervention is over, in particular when researchers can no longer sit face-to-face with teachers. Even when teacher–researcher interactions are carefully documented, the knowledge gained cannot be transported readily to new environments. In our work with Questioning the Author, we are confronted with the situation that is emblematic of current collaborative research on instruction; that is, the knowledge gained from 2 years of work with teachers and their classrooms produced a rich, extensive, anecdotal database, but that knowledge needs to be transformed in order to be applicable to new settings.

Various approaches exist to addressing the problem of transforming knowledge. Most commonly, they involve support personnel, either in the form of special implementors or teacher consultants who are more experienced with the innovative approach than their peers. Having access to "live" support and assistance can be very advantageous for teachers trying out a new instructional approach. There are drawbacks as well, however, to transforming knowledge through support staff. One issue is the quality of the personnel—their understanding of the approach and their ability to transform their understanding into productive assistance for others may exhibit wide individual differences. Another drawback is that support personnel may not be present when a problem arises and needs to be addressed. These potential drawbacks can be mitigated by extensive training of personnel and by having adequate numbers of support staff available. However, these solutions make this approach cost-intensive.

An alternative approach to supporting teachers in instructional innovation involves resources that teachers can use on their own. Probably the major issue with this approach is having the information, usually in the form of print materials, come to life in a powerful way. In the next phase of our work, we plan to design ways to transform the detailed and exquisite content of our face-to-face interactions with teachers into forms that are available and accessible to teachers broadly.

Our approach to transforming the knowledge will be to develop tangible resources that teachers can access in the course of acquiring a teaching-for-understanding orientation. The resources, in the form of printed materials and videotape segments, will be based on actual classroom interactions and issues that concerned teachers during our Questioning the Author implementations. We view the resources to be developed as vehicles for fostering principled understanding of the rationale underlying Questioning the Author and how the approach functions. Although developing principled understanding is key, providing teachers only with principles is insufficient. Principles and guidelines are merely abstract statements of what should be done. Experiences with instantiations of principles that clearly portray how the principles are put into action are called for if deep understanding is to develop.

The resources we develop will present a classroom problem or instructional issue accompanied by explanatory annotations addressed to teachers. The purpose of the annotations will be to set up the problem or issue, draw attention to how it was manifested, and show how it was dealt with in the classroom or in teachers' preparations for lessons. In our view, the interaction of textual and videotape examples and annotations has strong communicative potential because it operates at the intersection of understanding and actions. That is, it avoids both the Scylla of cookbook-type lesson plans that put words into teachers' mouths and connect only with actions, and the Charybdis of general principles that have only vague connections to useful pedagogical actions. We believe that the interaction of authentic examples from classrooms and explanatory annotations will encourage principled understanding by giving life to the principle that meaning is constructed through actively grappling with information.

The current focus of instructional research on collaborative classroom efforts between researchers and teachers has yielded rich and detailed information about what it takes to get new instructional approaches working in classrooms. The information provides great opportunity for enhancing classroom instruction. Attention now needs to be given to putting the richness and detail of what has been learned into generative forms.

ACKNOWLEDGMENT. The research described in this chapter was supported by the National Research Center on Student Learning of the Learning Research and Development Center, University of Pittsburgh, supported by funds from the Office of Educational Research and Improvement (OERI), United States Department of Education. The opinions expressed do not necessarily reflect the position or policy of OERI, and no official endorsement should be inferred.

# REFERENCES

Alvermann, D. E., O'Brien, D. G., & Dillon, D. R. (1990). What teachers do when they say they're having discussions of content area reading assignments: A qualitative analysis. *Reading Research Quarterly*, *24*(4), 296–322.

Beck, I. L., & McKeown, M. G. (1994). Outcomes of history instruction: Paste-up accounts. In J. F. Voss & M. Carretero (Eds.), *Cognitive and instructional processes in history and the social sciences* (pp. 237–256). Hillsdale, NJ: Erlbaum.

Beck, I. L., McKeown, M. G., & Gromoll, E. W. (1989). Learning from social studies texts. *Cognition and Instruction, 6*(2), 99–158.

Beck, I. L., McKeown, M. G., Sinatra, G. M., & Loxterman, J. A. (1991). Revising social studies text from a text-processing perspective: Evidence of improved comprehensibility. *Reading Research Quarterly, 26,* 251–276.

Beck, I. L., McKeown, M. G., Worthy, J., Sandora, C. A., & Kucan, L. (1996). Questioning the Author: A year-long implementation to engage students with text. *The Elementary School Journal, 94*(4), 358–414.

Black, J. B., & Bern, H. (1981). Causal coherence and memory for events in narratives. *Journal of Verbal Learning and Verbal Behavior, 20,* 267–275.

Blumenfeld, P. C., Krajcik, J. S., Marx, R. W., & Soloway, E. (1994). Lessons learned: How collaboration helped middle grade science teachers learn project-based instruction. *The Elementary School Journal, 94*(5), 539–551.

Cazden, C. (1986). Classroom discourse. In M. C. Wittrock (Ed.), *Handbook of research on teaching* (3rd ed.) (pp. 432–462). New York: Macmillan.

Cazden, C. (1988). *Classroom discourse: The language of teaching and learning.* Portsmouth, NH: Heinemann.

Chiesi, H. L., Spilich, G. J., & Voss, J. F. (1979). Acquisition of domain-related information in relation to high and low domain knowledge. *Journal of Verbal Learning and Verbal Behavior, 18,* 275–290.

Cleary, B. (1982). *Ralph S. Mouse.* New York: Dell.

Cohen, D. K., McLaughlin, M. W., & Talbert, J. E. (Eds.). (1993). *Teaching for understanding: Challenges for policy and practice.* San Francisco: Jossey-Bass.

Colton, A. M., & Sparks-Langer, G. M. (1993). A conceptual framework to guide the development of teacher reflection and decision making. *Journal of Teacher Education, 44*(1), 45–54.

Duffy, G. G., & Roehler, L. R. (1987). Teaching reading skills as strategies. *The Reading Teacher, 40*(4), 414–418.

Duffy, T. M., Higgins, L., Mehlenbacher, B., Cochran, C., Wallace, D., Hill, C., Haugen, D., McCaffrey, M., Burnett, R., Sloane, S., & Smith, S. (1989). Models for the design of instructional text. *Reading Research Quarterly, 24,* 434–457.

Frederiksen, J. R. (1981). Understanding anaphora: Rules used by readers in assigning pronominal referents. *Discourse Processes, 4,* 323–348.

Goodlad, J. L. (1984). *A place called school: Prospects for the future.* New York: McGraw-Hill.

Just, M. A., & Carpenter, P. A. (1987). *The psychology of reading and language comprehension.* Rockleigh, NJ: Allyn & Bacon.

Lawson, R. (1939). *Ben and me.* Boston: Little, Brown.

Luke, C., DeCastell, S., & Luke, A. (1983). Beyond criticism: The authority of the school text. *Curriculum Inquiry, 13*(2), 111–127.

McKeown, M. G., & Beck, I. L. (1990, April). What young students understand from their textbooks about the American Revolution. In *Subject specificity in social studies: How does the nature of the subject matter affect curriculum theory and practice?* Symposium conducted at the annual meeting of the American Educational Research Association, Boston.

Olson, D. R. (1980). On the language and authority of textbooks. *Journal of Communication, 30*(1), 186–196.

Palincsar, A. S., & Brown, A. L. (1984). Reciprocal teaching of comprehension-fostering and monitoring activities. *Cognition and Instruction, 1*(2), 117–175.

Pearson, P. D., Hansen, J., & Gordon, C. (1979). The effect of background knowledge on young children's comprehension of explicit and implicit information. *Journal of Reading Behavior, 11*, 201–209.

Perfetti, C. A. (1985). *Reading ability.* New York: Oxford University Press.

Prawat, R. S. (1992). Teachers' beliefs about teaching and learning: A constructivist perspective. *American Journal of Education, 100*, 354–395.

Richardson, V. (1990). Significant and worthwhile change in teaching practice. *Educational Researcher, 19*(7), 10–18.

Russell, T. (1993). Critical attributes of a reflective teacher. In J. Calderhead & P. Gates (Eds.), *Conceptualizing reflection in teacher development* (pp. 144–153). London: Falmer.

Silver Burdett. (1984). *The United States and its neighbors.* Morristown, NJ: Author.

Tharp, R. G., & Gallimore, R. (1991). *Rousing minds to life: Teaching, learning, and schooling in social context.* Cambridge: Cambridge University Press.

Trabasso, T., Secco, T., & van den Broek, P. (1984). Causal cohesion and story coherence. In H. Mandl, N. L. Stein, & T. Trabasso (Eds.), *Learning and comprehension of text* (pp. 83–111). Hillsdale, NJ: Erlbaum.

Wood, T. W., & Cobb, P. (1991). Change in teaching mathematics: A case study. *American Educational Research Journal, 28*(3), 587–616.

# Howling in the Wind: Academics Try to Change Classroom Reading Instruction

## S. JAY SAMUELS
### *University of Minnesota*

My task is to comment on the chapter by Margaret McKeown and her colleagues and that by Richard Allington and his colleagues. However, to explain how their work fits into the "big reading picture," I will place their work in a historical context. Consequently, my chapter begins with a brief journey through the history of reading in the United States. In this section, I will describe how reading methods and school reading books have appeared and disappeared, and the impact that psychology has had on reading. Then, I will discuss the McKeown and Allington chapters and place them within the larger context of what is happening in schools.

### CONTEMPORARY READING RESEARCH
### IN A HISTORICAL CONTEXT

Since the early colonists who arrived in this country came to find religious freedom, it is not at all surprising that they emphasized religious reading. In fact, one of the major purposes for schooling during the colonial period was to educate children so that they could read their Bibles, Psalms, and catechisms. In 1647, the first compulsory education law, titled "The Old Deluder Act," was passed. This law stated that Satan deluded people into believing they did not need to read their Bibles, and one of the major reasons for teaching children to read was to defeat his evil intent. By reading the Bible, the colonists would be able to achieve salvation.

Most of the reading done during the colonial period was oral. Family prayers and Bible reading were done orally to instruct, but oral reading was also a form of entertainment, and heavy emphasis was placed on reading with expression.

Instructional texts used during the colonial period were different from those we are used to today. During the 1600s, there were no basal readers or primers. The books used for instruction came from home, books such as *The Bay Psalm Book* or the family Bible. Learning to read was done by orally repeating memorized prayers while looking at the printed words on the page. Older skilled readers repeatedly read the same passage aloud to the less skilled until the beginning readers had learned the words. This technique of repeating the oral reading of the text until the words were learned is reminiscent of what I described as "The Method of Repeated Reading" in the 1970s (LaBerge & Samuels, 1974).

Does the similarity between what was done in the name of reading instruction 3 centuries ago and what is done today mean that teachers during the colonial era were using modern techniques of reading instruction? Not at all. There was a serious flaw in the instruction of the colonial period, namely, that the alphabet-spelling method was used almost universally to teach reading. In the alphabet-spelling method, before reading a word orally the student first had to name each letter. It was assumed that there was a necessary connection between letter naming and word recognition. No other approach to the pronunciation of the printed symbols was imagined by the great majority of teachers.

For 200 years, from the early colonial period to shortly after the Civil War, the alphabet-spelling method remained the dominant approach to reading instruction. There were, however, teachers who were critical of the alphabet-spelling method and they initiated change. They found strong support in Horace Mann, Superintendent of Schools for Massachusetts, who believed that spelling a word before pronouncing it interfered with comprehension. What he advocated instead was the look-say/whole-word method. The pedagogical battle lines of the mid-1800s were not centered around skills- versus meaning-based reading as they are today, but on the alphabet-spelling method versus the look-say/whole-word method. By 1905, Edmund Huey, in his classic text on the psychology and pedagogy of reading, noted that the alphabet method was no longer used and the whole-word method had become the way of the land.

In addition to changes in the method of reading instruction, there were many changes in the texts used for instruction. By 1683, *The New England*

*Primer* had become the first book specifically meant to be used to teach reading. Like its predecessor, the horn book, *The New England Primer* contained letters of the alphabet, syllables, and short illustrated verses such as, "The moon gives light, In time of night"; "Job feels the rod, Yet blesses God"; and "As sand runs through the hour glass, Man's life doth pass." So popular was *The New England Primer* that it was used for 150 years and sold more than 3 million copies.

While *The New England Primer* was the first "best seller" among the early school books, Noah Webster's Blue-back Speller, as it was called, replaced it and eventually far outsold it. Between 1783 and 1843, 47 million copies were sold. Webster's book constituted an alphabet book, primer, speller, and reader, all in one. Current twentieth-century literacy methodology, which combines writing, spelling, and reading, was presaged by Webster's speller. Previously, spelling in America was highly variable, reflecting the dialect spoken in a particular part of the country. Webster's dictionary and spelling books established a single spelling standard for the entire country, and the ability to spell words as they were found in Webster's books became the hallmark of an educated person. His legacy of standardized spelling left an indelible mark which time can not turn back.

Another popular reading series was the McGuffey readers, first published 1857, with the last edition appearing in 1920. The story content of these famous texts conveyed religious and moral lessons. Some of the unique aspects of the series were the graded difficulty of lessons, the combination of reading and spelling, and superb art.

### THE IMPACT OF PSYCHOLOGY

Toward the end of the 1800s, important psychological discoveries were made on eye movements, the function of the brain in reading, and word recognition. In France, Emile Javal had observed that in reading, the eye appears to take in information only when it is fixated and not when it is moving, contrary to what previously had been thought. Joseph Dejerine, a French physician, did an autopsy on an adult who died after experiencing several strokes. The stroke victim had lost his ability to read words but maintained his ability to write and read music. Dejerine was the first to postulate that different parts of the brain had specific cognitive functions relating to literacy.

At about the same time, James Cattell, an American working in Germany, developed a tachistoscope, which allowed him to expose a word for a brief period of time in order to study the word recognition process. Using graduate students as experimental subjects, Cattell found that they could recognize a whole word as easily as they could recognize a single letter. In

America, teachers who were looking for scientific support for their shift to the whole-word method of beginning reading instruction used Cattell's findings. However, since Cattell's work was done with skilled adults rather than beginning readers, there was no scientific justification for using his work for this purpose.

## BEHAVIORISM AND READING

Behaviorism got its start in the early 1900s when psychologists, in attempting to improve the status of psychology as a respected science, decided to abandon studies that probed the internal workings of the mind because data derived from the mind were thought to be unreliable. Consequently, studies of comprehension as an inside-the-head process were not done. But test development was ideally suited to the goals of behaviorism, and two important measurement discoveries occurred that had an impact on reading. An educational crusader by the name of Joseph Rice was convinced that schools had no way to make sound educational decisions because there were no standardized tests available to allow comparisons. His standardized spelling test marked the beginning of the proficiency testing movement, which then moved rapidly into the realm of reading. Standardized reading tests were developed and provided a yardstick to compare individuals and methods.

The second event of importance during this period was Alfred Binet and Theodore Simon's 1905 discovery of a way to measure intelligence. Intelligence tests in combination with reading achievement tests became diagnostic tools for determining reading disability.

Another project that had an enormous impact on reading took place in the 1920s at Teachers College with the publication of Edward L. Thorndike's *The Teacher's Word Book*, which showed the frequency of occurrence of the 10,000 most frequent words. Thorndike reasoned that words should be introduced into reading books based on their frequency of occurrence in printed English, because words that appeared frequently in print would be the most useful to learn. As students advanced to higher grade levels, less common words would appear. Thorndike's word frequency counts were widely used in the development of basal readers, which were used by a majority of children in school. The word-frequency data also were used in developing readability estimates.

For about 85 years the whole-word method reigned supreme. By the 1950s, almost 90% of the school districts were using basal readers and the whole-word method. But change was in the wind. In 1955, Rudolph Flesch's *Why Johnny Can't Read* took the nation by storm and remained on the best seller lists for over 30 weeks. Then, in 1967 Jeanne Chall's blockbuster

*Learning to Read: The Great Debate* was published. Both Flesch and Chall attacked the whole-word method. They concluded that American students were having trouble with word recognition because from 1912 to 1967 not much emphasis was given to phonics instruction. The great pedagogical reading wars of the early 1800s were being staged once again, but this time in the guise of whole-word versus phonics methods. And the controversies continue today.

What seems most ironic is that during the period when the whole-word/meaning-emphasis method reigned supreme, little was known about how to teach comprehension skills. For example, when Dolores Durkin (1979) asked teachers if they included comprehension instruction as a regular part of their reading lessons, a large majority said they did. However, observations of their teaching revealed that little comprehension instruction was actually taking place. What was occurring was that the teachers routinely asked literal comprehension questions to test for understanding. Durkin's argument was that testing for understanding and teaching children how to construct meaning are two different things. One explanation for the lack of comprehension instruction was that during the period of behaviorism, psychology had little to offer that teachers could use.

## COGNITIVE PSYCHOLOGY AND READING

What broke the back of behaviorism was Noam Chomsky's 1959 critique of B. F. Skinner's 1957 book on language acquisition. Skinner's book presented an outside-the-head environmental explanation of language development. Chomsky's critique showed that human language was a genetically driven behavior and that outside-the-head factors such as learning conditions played only a minor role. Psychologists, realizing that for too long they had been ignoring what took place within the human head, began studying internal processes such as comprehension.

The paradigm shift that Chomsky began in the late 1950s led psychology into a new period known as that of cognitive psychology. Reading researchers began to explore how inside-the-head factors, such as the reader's knowledge of text structures and vocabulary, influenced understanding. They also examined how outside-the-head variables, such as text revisions and causal connections between concepts in a text, influenced comprehension. From a pedagogical viewpoint, educators and publishers listened to the Flesch and Chall messages by introducing more phonics. But the curriculum was still primarily a basal-reading/whole-word program, and educators referred to their methods as eclectic, since they tried to take the best of the meaning and decoding methodologies.

Then, starting in about 1965, two beginning professors, Kenneth

Goodman at Wayne State University and Frank Smith at the Ontario Institutes for Studies in Education, began criticizing the eclectic approach to reading instruction with arguments such as these:

* The scope and sequence charts that detailed the sequencing of skills from grade level to grade level lack validity and a scientific basis.
* The use of a controlled vocabulary based on word frequency led to stilted texts such as, "Look, Dick, Look, Oh, look, Oh, Look."
* Phonics instruction is of no use. In fact, teaching phonics is one way to make learning to read difficult.
* Standardized achievement tests fail to assess important skills.

The approach fostered by Goodman and Smith is, of course, known as whole language, and numerous teachers today have embraced the whole language philosophy. What is ironic is that while whole language empowers teachers to cast off an eclectic, skills-based program of reading, it apparently fails to empower whole language teachers to feel comfortable enough to teach phonics and other word recognition skills, even when they feel such skills are needed. Many whole language teachers would like to include decoding skills but are fearful to do so. The issue has led Susan Glazer, President of International Reading Association, to write an article titled "Do I Have to Give up Phonics to Be a Whole Language Teacher?" (1995). Glazer writes, "We need to stop breaking into camps that support phonics or no phonics, basals or real books, standardized testing or alternative assessment" (p. 3).

This brief review indicates that there has been a long history of conflict over the methods used in reading instruction. The conflict continues today in the guise of skills-based versus whole language programs.

## A DISCUSSION OF THE McKEOWN AND ALLINGTON CHAPTERS

McKeown and her colleagues describe the efforts that went into helping teachers learn how to get students to interact deeply with texts so as to improve text comprehension, while Allington and his research group describe the characteristics and problems encountered in literature-based reading programs.

I will start with McKeown's chapter. There are three different ways to improve text comprehension: (1) through text revisions to improve its readability, (2) by getting students to process text deeply through the kinds of questions that are asked, and (3) by training students so they know how to process the text deeply on their own. In the mid-1980s, the work of McKeown and her co-author Isabel Beck focused on text revisions, while the present work focuses on depth of processing, a research endeavor central to the concerns of cognitive psychology.

McKeown and Beck's current depth-of-processing research had its beginning in the mid-1980s. At that time they and their group examined how social studies texts dealt with the American Revolutionary period in order to determine whether the texts presented information in such a way that students would be able to develop coherent understandings of the information. Their analysis revealed a number of problems. For one thing, the texts assumed more background knowledge than students actually had. For example, one text stated that one reason the revolution started was there was "taxation without representation." In order to understand this phrase, however, the students had to understand representative government, taxation, and the relationship between the two abstract concepts — a level of understanding that many students lacked. Another problem was a lack of text cohesion; that is, events and episodes were presented in the texts in such a way that students had difficulty understanding the causal chain connecting them.

To overcome these problems, McKeown and Beck and their colleagues revised the passages, adding more explanations and more examples, and providing the missing causal elements. Their revisions paid off by improving comprehension, but not enough for the researchers to feel totally satisfied. Although students were better at recalling events, there was evidence that they did not understand the significance of the events. What they recalled of the events were surface characteristics, with little evidence that there was depth of understanding. For students to consider the ideas deeply, either they would have to become active readers and learn how to question and analyze text themselves, or they would need the help of a skilled teacher to guide them in interacting with the text in a manner that could lead to greater depth of processing.

McKeown and her colleagues describe their current depth-of-processing work as helping teachers and their students learn how to ask questions that force students to engage in higher-order thinking, construct new interpretations, and extend the information contained in the text. For example, when teachers ask questions such as the following — "Is there anything in the text which is not clear?" "How might this have been said better?" "What is the author trying to say?" "Why do you think the author said this?" — students are compelled to increase their level of engagement with the text. Over a period of time, the researchers observed two things. First, teachers were learning better ways to get students to interact deeply with text; second, the students were learning some of the questioning skills the teachers were modeling, and they were learning better text comprehension strategies.

McKeown and her colleagues' current project, in which questions encourage students to interact deeply with text, is an outgrowth of the depth-of-processing research, which has been widely studied by cognitive psychologists. With the shift away from behaviorism starting in the late 1950s, psychologists began to explore the depth-of-processing strategy, which had the potential to enhance learning, comprehension, and recall. To understand depth of processing, assume that students had to learn a long list of paired associates such as hat–chair. A depth-of-processing approach might give students instructions such as, "Create a mental image of a hat on a chair," or, "Construct a sentence using the two words, something like, 'The hat was placed on the chair.'" This strategy improves learning by changing a rote memory task into one in which students create a meaningful context for the two words in the pair.

The same principles can be applied to reading. When students are asked simply to read a text for later recall, the assignment is essentially a rote memory task, which frequently leads to poor comprehension. But when students take the text information and relate it to other information they have, or when they go beyond the literal interpretation of the text and try to interact with the text in a meaningful manner, the students are creating additional meaning and employing a depth-of-processing strategy.

The approach used by McKeown and her colleagues to get students to interact deeply with text is very much what Harry Singer and Dan Donlan (1988) advocated in a procedure they called "active comprehension." As Singer and Donlan put it,

> Active comprehension teaches students a process of comprehension by having them formulate and read to answer their own questions. The knowledge that students bring to their reading task provides a basis for asking questions. For example, knowledge of story schemata can be used to generate such questions as "What is the setting? Who are the characters and what do they do in the story?" (p. 83)

According to Singer and Donlan, in many classrooms the teacher is the one who formulates the questions and the students answer them. What Singer and Donlan advocated instead is for students to learn how to formulate their own questions. When this occurs, learning is increased (Nolte & Singer, 1985; Yopp, 1987). McKeown and her colleagues are showing teachers how to make use of the advice offered by Singer and Donlan.

Are depth-of-processing techniques effective? The rule of thumb is that when students construct their own meaning as they read, learning, comprehension, and recall are increased. A variety of techniques are available to accomplish this end. For example, using mental imagery, elaborating, summarizing, cognitive mapping, and answering inferential, analytical, and application questions are effective techniques for enhancing comprehension. In fact, if Durkin were to replicate her famous 1979 study of teacher comprehension instruction in the classrooms in which McKeown and her group have worked, she would be impressed with the way students were learning comprehension strategies through the questions teachers were modeling for them.

Let me turn now to Allington and his colleagues' chapter. Allington and his research group have investigated literature-based reading programs in elementary schools with large populations of at-risk students. One of the problems with studying literature-based reading is that different programs tend to be so individualistic that their only shared characteristic is the use of authentic literature. For example, the literature-based classrooms studied by Allington's group used basals and a literature-based anthology, basals and trade books, and trade books alone. What their research revealed was that, regardless of how the literature-based program was implemented, in all the schools over a third of the day (2 hours) was spent on reading and language arts. However, despite the availability of these extended periods of time for literacy instruction, the instructional periods were chopped up into tiny segments because half the children were constantly being pulled out of the regular programs for remedial work. Not surprisingly, classroom teachers often complain about the many pull-out interruptions that prevent them from having an intact group for instruction.

Some of the most interesting findings of Allington and his group pertained to the increase in student diversity and the schools' failure to provide appropriate instruction for these heterogeneously grouped students. The increase in student diversity is the product of factors such as lack of school readiness resulting from cutbacks in pre-first-grade education, and full inclusion into the regular classroom of children who used to be in special education classes. The literature-based classrooms contained students with wide ranges of intelligence, knowledge, and motivation, as well as students with special learning problems. It was not uncommon to find a single trade book and whole-class instruction used for all students, regardless of their reading abilities, a "one size fits all" approach. When increased student heterogeneity is combined with use of a book that is too difficult for many of the students, and there is "a press to use a single, standard curriculum with all children," the conditions leading to reading failure have been established.

Despite all the rhetoric about empowerment, institutional pressures to standardize the curriculum in terms of method, pacing of instruction, and text used, prevented teachers from exercising their professional autonomy and judgment. Faced with these conditions, desperate teachers did what they have always done. Those teachers who tried to meet individual student needs did so by working in secrecy. They ignored the misguided philosophies and did what made sense — they grouped, differentiated instruction, taught needed skills, and tried to supply books that were appropriate for their students.

One wonders by what magical method these students who were most at risk were going to learn how to read? Often, when students from middle-class homes fail to learn how to read because of a poor method, their parents instruct them, so the end result is that the children learn, despite the school. But children from lower-class homes who encounter poor instruction have a more difficult time mastering reading because their parents may lack the time or knowledge to help them. Small wonder that evaluations of whole language programs are showing that lower-ability students are not faring too well (Stahl & Miller, 1989).

## CHANGING CLASSROOM PRACTICE

During the 1800s, important changes in reading methods were initiated by classroom teachers. However, since the 1920s, changes in methods and materials have been driven primarily by academic scholars such as Thorndike, Chall, Goodman, and Smith. This trend in initiating classroom change through the efforts of academics continues with the efforts of McKeown and Allington and their co-workers. While it has always been difficult to influence classroom practice, it is unusually hard at present because reading methods are linked with philosophies and belief systems. How will McKeown's and Allington's ideas fare in this environment? McKeown and her colleagues probably will have an easier time of it, since their approach does not tread on cherished beliefs; teachers have only to learn how to get students to interact deeply with text.

Allington's group probably will have a more difficult time, since their exposé of counterproductive practices in the name of literature-based reading flies in the face of current belief systems. When instructional methods are closely tied to a teacher's personal philosophy of education and some inadequacy is shown, it is difficult to introduce change, as we have seen with many reading practices from colonial times to the present.

However, as difficult as the task of introducing change in the classroom is, we know it can be done. What it takes to produce needed change is a good idea, dissemination on a broad scale, and the persistence of the long-distance runner.

# REFERENCES

Durkin, D. (1979). What classroom observations reveal about reading comprehension instruction. *Reading Research Quarterly, 15,* 481–533.

Glazer, S. (1995). Do I have to give up phonics to be a whole language teacher? *Reading Today, 12*(4), 3.

LaBerge, D., & Samuels, S. (1974). Toward a theory of automatic information processing in reading. *Cognitive Psychology, 6,* 293–323.

Nolte, H., & Singer, H. (1985). Active comprehension: Teaching a process of reading comprehension and its effects on comprehension. *The Reading Teacher, 38,* 24–31.

Singer, H., & Donlan, D. (1988). *Reading and learning from text* (2nd ed.). Hillsdale, NJ: Erlbaum.

Stahl, S., & Miller, P. (1989). Whole language and language experience approaches for beginning reading: A quantitative research synthesis. *Review of Educational Research, 59,* 87–116.

Yopp, R. (1987). Active comprehension: Declarative knowledge for generating questions and procedural knowledge for answering them. Unpublished doctoral dissertation, University of California, Riverside.

# PART III

# PHONOLOGICAL PROCESSES AND CONSTRUCTION OF MEANING

CHAPTER 6

# Preventing and Remediating Reading Disabilities: Instructional Variables That Make a Difference for Special Students

JOSEPH K. TORGESEN
STEVEN A. HECHT
*Florida State University*

The purpose of this chapter is to discuss instructional variables that may make an important difference for children who have special difficulties learning to read. Instructional variables are defined narrowly to include the content and method of reading instruction. In the past, such variables as classroom organization and management, and home and community support, usually have been shown to make a larger contribution to learning progress than specific instructional methods (Spreen, 1988; Wang, Haertel, & Walberg, 1993). However, recent developments in our knowledge about the reading acquisition process, as well as our knowledge about the specific cognitive weaknesses of children with reading disabilities, suggest that we may soon be able to achieve significant instructional effects through reading curricula that are adapted specifically to the needs of reading disabled children.

This chapter is divided into four sections. We first will outline the work of the senior author that led to the current intervention research reported in this chapter. This section focuses on advances since the early 1980s in our knowledge about the cognitive weaknesses that cause difficulties in learning to read for many children. In the next section, we will establish a context for our current research on the prevention of reading disabilities, by briefly considering both previous intervention research and recently acquired knowledge about the reading acquisition process. The third section of the chapter will provide a discussion of instructional methods and preliminary results from our present intervention research. In the concluding section, we will discuss the future of our own research program as well as interesting questions for others to pursue.

## THE NATURE OF READING DISABILITIES

Since this section focuses on the work of the senior author that led him to ask many of the central questions discussed in the chapter, it is written in the first person singular. We will return to joint authorship in the next section. I will begin with an account of my early research on the short-term memory problems of learning disabled children, and then will describe how my interests expanded to include a broader range of phonological difficulties in children with reading disabilities. Finally, this section will show how my work is linked to the current widely accepted theory of phonologically based reading disabilities.

### INITIAL DISCOVERIES OF PHONOLOGICAL DISORDERS IN CHILDREN WITH LEARNING DISABILITIES

After some preliminary research and writing about learning disabled children's use of inefficient strategies on learning and memory tasks (Torgesen, 1980), I decided to focus my research on a subgroup of learning disabled children who had extreme short-term memory problems. These children were severely retarded in the development of their ability to remember brief sequences of verbal information like strings of words or digit names. My hope was that, if we could understand why these children had such severe problems on simple memory tests, this might contribute to a more complete understanding of their problems learning in school.

In a series of experiments in which we contrasted the performance of children with severe short-term memory problems with that of other learning disabled children and of normal children (Torgesen & Houck, 1980), we reached the conclusion that the short-term memory problems were not the result of inefficient memory strategies or lack of attention or motivation, but rather were caused by the use of degraded, or indistinct, memory codes for verbal material.

When confronted with the task of storing short sequences of verbal information for brief periods of time, both children and adults depend primarily on memory codes that represent the phonological, or acoustic, features of the stimuli to be remembered. These memory codes reside in long-term memory and are activated either directly in the case of auditory input, or indirectly through articulatory processes, if the input is visual (Baddeley, 1986). Since the short-term memory problems of the children we were studying were restricted to verbal material and were more severe for familiar than unfamiliar stimuli, we proposed that these children did not have distinct phonological representations of words (Torgesen, 1988).

This hypothesis allowed us to link the memory problems of these children to specific difficulties they showed in acquiring basic reading skills. The children with severe memory span problems were more impaired in their word reading skills than other children identified as learning disabled, but they showed no such disparity in math skills (Torgesen, Rashotte, Greenstein, Houck, & Portes, 1987). Their most striking reading problem was manifest on a task requiring them to read phonetically regular nonwords: They were substantially slower and less accurate than other learning disabled children on this task.

Although we had not really shown that the phonological representation problems of the children we studied were the primary cause of their reading difficulties, such a causal relationship was plausible in theory. For example, inadequate representations of phonological units in long-term memory should affect all learning tasks that involve pairing a visual stimulus with a verbal response, such as learning letter–sound correspondences or learning "sight" words. Further, children who perform poorly on verbal short-term memory tasks should find it difficult to perform the simultaneous or rapidly sequential identification, comparison, and blending processes that are required to identify words by phonological/analytical strategies.

Although I was now able to tell an interesting and theoretically important story about the cognitive disabilities of a significant subgroup of children with learning disabilities, I was confronted continually by questions from teachers about the instructional implications of this work. The only implication that I could think of was that these children would find it particularly difficult to acquire alphabetic, or phonetic, reading skills, and so would require many more practice or instructional opportunities than other children. I became interested in the possibility that computers might be used to provide this extra practice, and we experimented with various computer-based interventions to increase the reading skills of children with learning disabilities (Jones, Torgesen, & Sexton, 1987; Torgesen, 1986; Torgesen, Waters, Cohen, & Torgesen, 1988). We were able to show that computers could be used to increase both the sight vocabulary and phonetic reading skills of children with learning disabilities, but these studies examined only a limited range of reading skill, and they did not address the question of how best to provide initial reading instruction.

## CONVERGING EVIDENCE ABOUT PHONOLOGICALLY BASED READING DISABILITIES

During the early to mid-1980s, evidence about the linguistic/phonological basis of reading disabilities in many children was beginning to accumulate. Three separate lines of research were converging on the fact that a significant proportion of children with reading disabilities showed substantial impairments in the ability to process phonological information, when compared with normal readers. One area of research, begun by Martha Denckla and her colleagues (Denckla & Rudel, 1976) and continued by Marianne Wolf and others (Wolf, Bally, & Morris, 1986), indicated that many children with reading disabilities were significantly impaired in the ability to rapidly name sequences of familiar items like colors, digits, letters, and objects. Difficulties on rapid automatic naming tasks can be conceptualized to represent, at least in part, problems in retrieval of phonological information from the lexicon.

In the meantime, another group of researchers led by Isabelle Liberman at the Haskins Laboratories in New Haven, Connecticut was reporting their seminal studies of a range of phonological problems in disabled readers, including delays in the development of phonological awareness, problems in phonological representation in short-term memory, and subtle problems in speech perception (Liberman, Shankweiler, & Liberman, 1989). Perhaps the greatest contribution of this group was to demonstrate, and bring to the attention of the reading research community, the particular importance of phonological awareness to the acquisition of early reading skills (Liberman & Shankweiler, 1991). Phonological awareness can be defined as one's sensitivity to, or explicit awareness of, the phonological structure of words in one's language. In other words, it involves the ability to notice, think about, and manipulate the individual sounds in words.

It occurred to my colleague Richard Wagner and me that the separate lines of research on phonological awareness, phonological memory, and rapid automatic naming should be brought together in a single longitudinal study (Wagner & Torgesen, 1987). Such a study could address not only questions about the causal relationships between these phonological skills and reading, but could also answer questions about relationships among the phonological abilities themselves. In 1989, we received funding from the National Institute of Child Health and Human Development to conduct a 5-year longitudinal study (subsequently extended to 6 years) that would follow approximately 250 children from kindergarten through fifth grade.

## Our Longitudinal Study of Reading-Related Phonological Processes

In this study, we measured phonological awareness in several different ways, including (1) matching words on the basis of whether or not they contain the same first phoneme, (2) telling what word remains after a given phoneme is deleted from a word, and (3) blending separately presented phonemes together to make words. As measures of phonological memory, we used digit and word span tests in which children had to repeat short strings of items verbatim. We assessed children's ability to rapidly access phonological information from long-term memory by asking them to name sequences of letters and digits as rapidly and accurately as they could.

One of the questions we were interested in was whether these phonological skills are best conceptualized as different expressions of some unitary underlying ability, or whether they are best thought of as unique abilities. In both a preliminary examination of a large group of kindergarten and second-grade children (Wagner, Torgesen, Laughon, Simmons, & Rashotte, 1993) and in our longitudinal study itself (Torgesen, Wagner, & Rashotte, 1994; Wagner, Torgesen, & Rashotte, 1994), it was clear that these phonological abilities are best conceptualized as separate, though highly correlated, abilities.

When we examined the causal relationships of each of these abilities to individual differences in early reading growth, it was apparent that they each have a significant causal relationship, but their causal contributions are somewhat redundant with one another. In our first report of causal relationships from kindergarten to first grade and from first to second grade (Wagner et al., 1994), only phonological awareness emerged as a unique causal agent of growth in word reading skills. However, in more recent analyses of growth extending over longer time periods (Wagner, Torgesen, & Rashotte, 1995), both phonological awareness and rapid naming ability make unique causal contributions to the early growth of word reading skills. In another recent analysis of the data from a subset of our longitudinal sample (Hecht, Burgess, Torgesen, & Wagner, 1995), we have obtained evidence that phonological awareness remains a powerful cause of growth in word reading skills in first grade, even when differences in home literacy environment, letter and print concept knowledge, and kindergarten teacher ratings of instructional readiness are allowed to be simultaneous causes.

To summarize, there is now overwhelming evidence that a primary cause of variability among children in growth of early word reading skills involves individual differences in the ability to process the phonological features of language. At present, the most important of these phonological skills appears to be phonological awareness and rapid automatic naming ability.

## THE THEORY OF PHONOLOGICALLY BASED READING DISABILITIES

We have focused our work on trying to understand individual differences in the development of word reading skills because of the compelling evidence that difficulties in this area lie at the heart of reading problems for most dyslexic, or reading disabled, children (Morrison, 1987; Stanovich, 1988). More specifically, most reading disabled children have great difficulty learning to apply the "alphabetic principle" to take advantage of grapheme–phoneme regularities in reading unfamiliar words (Rack, Snowling, & Olson, 1992). These children often are unable to attain fully alphabetic, or phonological, reading skills. Not only does this limit their ability to read independently, but it most likely interferes with subsequent development of the orthographic word reading strategies that support fluent text processing (Adams, 1990; Share & Stanovich, 1995).

When we combine information about the central role of text-based word reading difficulties in dyslexia with our understanding of the way that phonological processing abilities affect the acquisition of these skills, we have the beginnings of the theory of phonologically based reading disabilities. This theory is the most coherent and most completely developed current explanation for dyslexia in children and adults (Stanovich, 1988; Torgesen, 1993). Although there may be more than one subtype of specific developmental dyslexia, the best described, most common, and perhaps most difficult-to-treat subtype (Lovett, Ransby, Hardwick, Johns, & Donaldson, 1989; Snowling & Hulme, 1989) is phonologically based reading disability. The core cognitive disability in children with this type of reading problem involves limitations in their ability to process phonological information.

## A CONTEXT FOR INTERVENTION RESEARCH IN READING

Although there is a strong consensus about the nature and importance of phonologically based reading disabilities, before strong instructional implications can be derived from this information, the role of phonology, or phonological processes, in learning to read also must be well understood. This section of the chapter develops a context for intervention research with reading disabled children by first describing a model that details the role of phonological processes in the growth of word reading skills. Following this, we will discuss briefly previous intervention research to illustrate important instructional contrasts that should be studied in the future.

## The Self-Teaching Model of Word Reading Acquisition

Current knowledge about reading acquisition provides strong support for the central role of alphabetic reading skills, and the phonological processing abilities that support them, in the general development of reading. The self-teaching model of reading acquisition developed by David Share and his colleagues (Share & Jorm, 1987; Share & Stanovich, 1995) provides an account of the role of phonological skills in reading growth that integrates the research on early reading development with the literature on individual differences in reading acquisition that was discussed in the previous section.

The self-teaching hypothesis begins with a recognition that skilled readers identify most of the words in text on the basis of visual/orthographic representations that code the essential letter patterns of the word as a visual unit and do not require phonological analysis for activation. Another important background proposition for the self-teaching model is that the alphabetic nature of the English writing system (its orthography) requires that fluent reading involve the complete, or near complete, processing of orthographic detail (Rayner & Pollatsek, 1989). That is, the orthographic representations by which words are identified represent the complete, or near complete, spelling of the word. Skilled readers do not simply sample a few letters in a word in order to identify it; they process information about the word's complete spelling. The self-teaching model seeks to explain how these orthographic representations, which are so important in skilled reading, are developed as children learn to read.

The model proposes that emergent skills in phonological decoding, which consist of letter–sound knowledge and a basic level of phonological awareness, provide the basis for acquiring accurate orthographic representations of words from the very beginning of the learning process. If children use partial or complete phonological cues to derive an approximate pronunciation for a word in text, and then identify the fully correct pronunciation of the word from context, the prior attention to individual letters that is involved in alphabetic decoding provides a solid basis for the acquisition or refinement of an orthographic representation for the word.

Since there is evidence that word-specific orthographic information may be learned from relatively few correct exposures to a word (Manis, 1985; Reitsma, 1990), children may begin acquiring words for their "sight vocabulary" from the very beginning of the reading acquisition period. As their increasingly developed alphabetic reading skills lead to more detailed analysis of the internal structure of words in print, they begin to acquire increasingly explicit and more fully specified orthographic representations. However, according to the self-teaching model, if children's alphabetic reading skills do not develop, their orthographic representations are likely to remain incompletely specified, and they will be inaccurate readers and poor spellers.

The self-teaching model asserts that even English words that do not follow normal patterns of letter–phoneme correspondence contain sufficient regularities, particularly in their consonant construction, to allow alphabetic reading skills an important role in the identification of words in text. That is, even an approximate phonological decoding of such words can provide a base for their correct identification in text, and the analysis involved in this partial decoding will contribute to the formation of a more completely specified orthographic representation. The role of alphabetic reading skills in acquiring orthographic representations of irregular English words is supported by the strong and consistent correlations between the ability to read pseudowords and exception words (Gough & Walsh, 1991; Stanovich & West, 1989).

This very brief overview of the self-teaching model of reading acquisition does not begin to do justice to the volume of research that it successfully integrates (see Share & Stanovich, 1995). It simultaneously encompasses most of the general research on reading development, and it is entirely consistent with the research on individual differences in early reading development that has identified such a strong role for phonological processing skills. When the self-teaching model is combined with the information reviewed earlier on the nature of specific reading disabilities, several important implications for instruction of children with reading disabilities emerge:

1. *If preventive and remedial approaches to reading instruction with reading disabled children are to be successful, they* must *lead to the development of accurate and fluent text-based word reading skills.*

These children also may need special instruction in comprehension skills, but the first goal of instruction should be to ensure that they can read words fluently and accurately.

2. *As the basis for early independence in word identification, and gradual development of efficient visual codes for words, the early growth of alphabetic reading skills* must *be fostered.*

These are precisely the reading skills that most reading disabled children have difficulty with.

3. *As a basis for the acquisition of the alphabetic principle, instructional interactions* must *stimulate the growth of phonological awareness.*

Phonological awareness provides the basis for understanding and utilizing the alphabetic principle in reading.

4. *In order to receive the maximum number of opportunities to acquire accurate orthographic representations for words, children* must *be taught explicitly to integrate the use of phonological cues and context in order to arrive at accurate pronunciations of words in text.*

Because of the role of print exposure in the development of orthographic reading skills (Barker, Torgesen, & Wagner, 1992; Stanovich & West, 1989), it also seems important to involve reading disabled children in manageable and meaningful reading experiences from as early in the instructional process as possible.

Although these instructional goals are relatively clear, a number of interesting and important questions remain regarding the implementation of instruction to achieve them. As we shall see in the next section, many instructional programs currently exist that place varying emphases on each of these goals. However, because of a lack of systematic and well-controlled research, there is little evidence available to help determine which pattern of instructional emphasis or timing will be most effective for children with phonologically based reading disabilities. The following section illustrates from previous intervention research several of the major questions about instructional emphasis that remain to be decided in future research.

## RESEARCH ON READING INSTRUCTION FOR CHILDREN WITH READING DISABILITIES

Historically, the dominant approaches to reading instruction for dyslexic children have utilized the multisensory, synthetic phonics techniques originally developed by Samual Orton, Anna Gillingham, and Bessie Stillman (Clark, 1988). These approaches are characterized by the use of multisensory feedback to teach individual grapheme–phoneme correspondences, along with explicit instruction and practice in "sound blending" as a technique to approximate the pronunciation of words by combining individual phonemic units. These approaches place a heavy emphasis on direct instruction and development of alphabetic reading skills. Support for these methods has come largely from case studies and clinically based testimonials, although there is some systematic research evidence to support their utility (Ogden, Hindman, & Turner, 1989; Frankiewicz, 1985). Other approaches employing a primarily synthetic phonics approach, but with less emphasis on multisensory experiences, also have been evaluated positively with groups of children identified as learning disabled (Brown & Felton, 1990; Epstein & Cullinan, 1981; Gittelman & Feingold, 1983).

The study by Brown and Felton (1990) is particularly noteworthy because these researchers identified children for their study who obtained low scores on measures of phonological processing in kindergarten. Thus, the researchers focused on a group of children at risk for reading disability because of poorly developed phonological skills. Their study contrasted a primarily meaning-based, whole-word approach to reading instruction (extending over first and second grades) with a code-emphasis program utilizing a synthetic approach to phonics instruction. Although differences between the groups at the end of second grade favored the code-emphasis group (particularly on measures of alphabetic reading skills), differences were not large and those on measures of real word reading and comprehension were not significant. While more children from the meaning-emphasis than the code-emphasis group were recommended for retention in first grade (52% vs. 5%), about the same number of children from each treatment group met criteria for placement in learning disabilities classes at the end of second grade.

The relatively weak treatment results from this latter study are interesting in light of the earlier work of Lyon (1985), who found that children with phonologically based reading disabilities showed no measurable gains in word reading skill following 26 hours of individual tutoring using a synthetic phonics approach. In another series of studies, Lovett and her colleagues (Lovett, Ransby, Hardwick, Johns, & Donaldson, 1989; Lovett, Warren-Chaplin, Ransby, & Borden, 1990) found that a group of "accuracy disabled" reading disabled children showed significant gains in word reading skill following 35 hours of instruction using a combination of whole-word and synthetic phonics instruction. However, all of the growth in word identification facility resulted from the acquisition of knowledge about specific words; the dyslexic children showed no improvements in their ability to apply alphabetic reading skills to identify words they had not been taught previously. Based on the results of their research, both Lyon (1985) and Lovett and colleagues (1990) speculated that synthetic phonics approaches may place inordinate demands on the weak phonological system of dyslexic children, and that these children might be better served by reading instruction that does not require as much storage, manipulation, and blending of individual phonic elements in words.

Lovett and colleagues (1990) also suggested, however, that their accuracy disabled children (who were the more impaired of their two subtypes of reading disability) may have required special instruction in phonological awareness in order to profit from the explicit instruction in phonics they provided. In fact, Williams (1980) demonstrated that combining prereading oral language instruction in phonological segmentation and blending with later instruction and practice applying synthetic phonics skills produced significant word reading improvements in a large sample of young heterogeneous reading disabled children. Furthermore, Williams reported convincing evidence that the children made significant gains in generalized alphabetic reading skills. That is, they were better able to read groups of unfamiliar, untaught items (both real words and nonwords) than were children in a control group that had not received the same instructional program.

In another study that employed phonological awareness training as a precursor to synthetic phonics instruction, we (Alexander, Andersen, Heilman, Voeller, & Torgesen, 1991) reported relatively dramatic effects on the alphabetic reading skills of a group of dyslexic children with an average age of 10 years, 9 months. Following an average of 65 hours of individual instruction with the Auditory Discrimination in Depth program (Lindamood & Lindamood, 1984), this group of 10 children improved from an average standard score of 77 on a measure of alphabetic reading skills to an average of 98.4 (standard score mean = 100). The poorest reader in the group improved from a score of 62 to 92, which placed him in the average range. This group of children had begun treatment with an average score on a measure of phonological awareness of 57.9, and improved to an average score of 99.9 (maximum possible = 100) following treatment.

These latter studies indicate that incorporating effective instruction in phonological awareness prior to the use of synthetic phonics instruction may be especially effective in ameliorating the alphabetic decoding difficulties of dyslexic readers. However, there is an enormous amount still to learn about ways of combining these approaches. For example, the elements of effective training in phonological awareness for children with phonologically based reading disabilities are not fully understood. Although Williams reported significant group effects for phonological awareness training with a heterogeneous sample of learning disabled children, other investigators (Lundberg, 1988; Torgesen & Davis, in press) found that a significant number of young lower-ability children did not profit from traditional phonological awareness training exercises. With children who are phonologically impaired, more extensive procedures, such as those used in the Auditory Discrimination in Depth program, may be required. Furthermore, no long-term, follow-up data are available to determine whether reading growth, specifically the acquisition of fluent orthographic reading skills, continues after remediation of alphabetic reading problems. It also is not clear whether successful intensive remediation of alphabetic reading skills eventually leads to normalization of reading comprehension in dyslexic children without additional instruction specifically devoted to reading comprehension skills. In fact, one of the frequent criticisms of synthetic phonics approaches is that they do not begin activities to enhance comprehension skills early enough in the instructional sequence (Brown, Palincsar, & Purcell, 1986; Clark, 1988; Williams, 1987).

One approach that has sought to combine explicit instruction in alphabetic reading skills with more, and earlier, opportunities to read, write about, and discuss meaningful text is the Reading Recovery program developed by Marie Clay (1985). Although phonics skills are explicitly taught in this program, they are taught only as one of a set of tools to aid in discovering the meaning of text. Children's knowledge of grapheme–phoneme correspondences, as well as their phonological awareness, also is stimulated by writing activities in the program. The approach has proven quite successful in aiding children in the bottom 20% of readers in first grade to increase their reading skills to average levels. Pinnell (1989), for example, reports that 70–80% of treated children achieved these standards during the course of instruction.

There is, however, relatively little evidence concerning the effectiveness of the Reading Recovery program when compared with other possible instructional approaches. It has rarely been contrasted directly with an alternative remedial program that similarly involves one-on-one tutoring. For example, one recent, and well-controlled, study (Iversen & Tunmer, 1993) did show that Reading Recovery was much more effective than the normal small-group remediation provided in a school district. However, this study also showed that the effectiveness of the Reading Recovery method was increased by about 25% by using part of the time normally devoted to text reading to provide more explicit and systematic instruction in phonics than is normally done.

The Reading Recovery program employs an individual tutorial model in order to be maximally sensitive to the individual instructional needs of each child. Hiebert, Colt, Catto, and Gury (1992) formalized many of the principles of this program and adapted them for small-group instruction. Their program, which was evaluated with children from low socioeconomic status (SES) homes who fell at the bottom of their beginning first-grade class in reading skills, was administered daily in 30-minute sessions to groups of three children. The instruction involved three basic activities: (1) reading and rereading interesting, predictable books, (2) writing rhyming words and word families and journal writing, and (3) strategic guidance about letter–sound patterns in words. The attempt was made to embed explicit instruction in phonics within a context of meaningful reading and writing experiences.

At the end of the year, children in this program were compared with similar children who had received special help within a more typical whole language framework. Children in the embedded phonics program were significantly better readers in all areas of reading and writing that were measured. Approximately 18% of children in the traditional program could fluently read primer level text or higher, while 77% of those in the experimental treatment could read at this level. Although phonological awareness was not explicitly taught prior to reading instruction, the program's emphasis on writing and spelling activities may have increased awareness sufficiently to aid acquisition of word reading skills. For example, Ehri (1989) has reported evidence that spelling instruction has a significant effect on the development of phonological awareness in young children.

While clearly inconclusive at this point, the knowledge gained from the evaluation studies just reviewed provides a useful starting point for additional research in three ways. First, it is clear that programs likely to be successful with children who have phonological processing problems must provide some form of explicit and direct instruction in "phonics" to help these children acquire better alphabetic reading skills. However, whether this instruction should follow traditional synthetic methods that provide much decontextualized practice in sounding out both words and nonwords, or whether the phonics instruction should be embedded within the context of whole-word reading, is a question of instructional emphasis that remains open for research. Second, the recent discovery of the utility of training in phonological awareness prior to reading instruction suggests that this may be an important element in reading instruction for children with phonologically based reading disabilities. However, there are important instructional options here as well. Phonological awareness can be stimulated directly through specific oral language activities that do not involve letters, or it can be stimulated through writing and spelling activities that are embedded within the context of reading instruction. Which of these approaches will prove more effective for children with phonological reading disabilities is an unresolved question. Finally, it is clear that children must be taught to use whatever alphabetic reading skills they have in the service of getting meaning from text. Whether to focus relatively more time on building autonomous alphabetic decoding skills or to work toward earlier integration of phonics and context-based skills in decoding new words is an important question that also remains open.

In the research to be described in the next section, we hope to provide beginning answers to some of these questions through contrasting the effectiveness of instructional programs that vary along the dimensions outlined above.

## OUR CURRENT STUDY OF PREVENTIVE INSTRUCTION FOR CHILDREN WITH PHONOLOGICALLY BASED READING DISABILITIES

At the time of this writing, we are engaged in a 5-year project funded by the National Institute of Child Health and Human Development to conduct both prevention and remediation studies with children who have phonologically based reading disabilities. Each of these studies has two major goals: (1) to determine which type of instructional program has the greatest immediate impact on word-level reading skills and long-term impact on fluency and comprehension skills, and (2) to determine the individual characteristics (cognitive, family background, behavioral) that are most strongly predictive of individual differences in both immediate and long-term response to the instructional programs examined. Although a total of four studies will be conducted, we will focus in this section on only the first prevention study, which is in progress during this writing.

We were particularly well prepared to identify a sample of children at risk for reading failure on the basis of phonological impairments because of our longitudinal study of phonological processes and reading, mentioned earlier (Wagner et al., 1994). Data from this study showed that we could accurately identify children at risk for phonologically based reading disabilities using a combination of three tests: phoneme elision, serial naming rate for digits, and letter-name knowledge.

In selecting the sample for our prevention study, we first screened 1,436 kindergarten children from 13 elementary schools in the first month of school using a test of letter-name knowledge. The sample screened was 51% male, with racial composition being 71.9% Caucasian, 26% African American, 1.5% Asian, and .6% Hispanic. From this initial sample, 382 children were selected for further screening using a phoneme elision task (deletion of a phoneme in a word), serial naming for numbers (naming a series of 36 single digits as rapidly as possible), and the Stanford–Binet vocabulary subtest (Thorndike, Hagen, & Sattler, 1986). Because so few of these children were able to identify number names correctly, this task was not used in the final selection criteria. Two hundred children were selected because of extremely low scores on the letter naming and phoneme elision tasks, along with performance on the vocabulary subtest indicating an estimated verbal IQ above 75.

Subjects in the final sample were randomly assigned to four treatment conditions: (1) a group receiving implicit phonological awareness training plus phonics instruction embedded within real word reading and spelling activities (EP), (2) a group receiving explicit oral and phonological awareness training plus synthetic phonics instruction (PASP), (3) a regular classroom support group receiving individual instruction to support the goals of the regular classroom reading program (RCS), and (4) a no treatment control group.

Although the subjects in our study were selected to be relatively homogeneous with regard to their level of phonological development in kindergarten, they were allowed to be heterogeneous on a number of other important variables. For example, estimated verbal intelligence ranged from 78 to 126, and the children varied broadly in SES and home literacy environment. We also expect children in the sample to vary in the extent to which they show attentional problems, because the results of recent epidemiological studies (Wood, Felton, Flowers, & Naylor, 1992) suggest extensive co-morbidity of phonologically based reading disabilities and attention deficit disorder (ADD).

We will analyze the effects of varying levels of verbal intelligence, SES, ADD, sex, and race on children's responses to our interventions through the use of techniques involving the calculation of growth curves in reading for each child. Whereas in traditional methods of analysis for treatment effects it is possible to test hypotheses about change in groups, methods that involve the estimation of individual growth curves for each subject allow the examination of factors associated with change in individual children (Francis, Fletcher, Stuebing, Davidson, & Thompson, 1991).

Children in each treatment condition are provided with 80 minutes of one-on-one supplemental instruction in reading each week for 2-1/2 years. Two 20-minute instructional sessions are led by certified teachers, and two sessions are led by instructional aides who reinforce what the children learned in the previous teacher-led session. We are assessing regular classroom reading instruction through the use of teacher surveys and direct observation in each classroom in which our subjects receive the bulk of their reading instruction.

This study contrasts the effectiveness of three different approaches to providing supplemental reading instruction for the at-risk children in our sample. The two experimental approaches contain relatively explicit instruction in "phonics" provided in two different ways. One of these approaches (PASP) is a multisensory synthetic phonics program containing intensive training in phonological awareness, while the other approach (EP) provides less intensive, but still systematic, phonics training in the context of early, and meaningful, experiences in reading and writing text. Both approaches recognize that the children being treated have special difficulties processing phonological information. However, the PASP program attempts to ameliorate these difficulties through an intensive program of oral and phonological awareness training, while the EP program seeks to reduce the demands on these skills by using an approach to phonics instruction that does not require full phonological decoding, but rather emphasizes the early integration of partial phonological decodings with context clues to identify unknown words. The progress of children in these groups will be contrasted with each other and with a third regular classroom support group (RCS) that receives individual tutoring in the activities and skills being taught in the regular classroom reading program. Although this condition does not involve an experimental curriculum per se, a potential advantage of this group over the other two is that its instructional activities will be closely coordinated with the instructional activities taking place in the children's regular classroom. It also serves as a control against the possibility that the effectiveness of the experimental curricula is primarily the result of intensity (one-on-one) of instruction rather than content or method.

The curriculum in each of the three treatment conditions is described briefly below.

### THE EMBEDDED PHONICS PROGRAM

In its early phases, the instructional periods in this program consist of four main activities: (1) learning to recognize small groups of whole words by using word-level drill and word games, (2) instruction in letter–sound correspondences in the context of the sight words being learned, (3) writing the words in sentences, and (4) reading the sentences that are written. Some letter sounds (short vowel, r-controlled vowels) are taught through memorization of picture-word cards, but most grapheme–phoneme correspondences are taught in the context of writing activities. The children also receive direct instruction in a small number of highly useful phonics generalizations.

The words the children learn are taken from a basal series that contains short stories. The stories are read orally after the words in them have been learned, and the primary emphasis during the entire "basal" phase is on acquiring word-level reading skills (sight vocabulary and supportive alphabetic decoding skills). After the children finish the first-grade reader in the basal series, the emphasis of the program shifts from learning to read by writing to learning to read by reading. Less time is spent on individual word drills, and more time is spent on reading stories from trade book series. Discussion focuses more on constructing the meaning of the stories that are read. Writing activities during this phase of instruction continue to include generation of sentences containing specific words, but more free writing and writing summaries of stories that are read also are included. During this later period, which will continue to the end of second grade, specific spelling instruction and practice are provided not only on lists of words from the regular class, but also on a larger corpus of commonly occurring words.

### THE PHONOLOGICAL AWARENESS PLUS SYNTHETIC PHONICS PROGRAM

This group is using the Auditory Discrimination in Depth program as outlined by Lindamood and Lindamood (1984) through kindergarten, first grade, and perhaps some of second grade. It will be followed by reading instruction and practice designed to consolidate and build on the phonological reading skills imparted by the early part of the program.

The program begins with instruction designed to make children aware of the specific mouth movements required to produce each phoneme. As part of this instruction, the children also learn labels for each phoneme that are descriptive of these mouth movements and positions (i.e., "lip popper," "tip tapper," "scraper"). Once the children attain a high level of knowledge in oral awareness, they engage in an extensive series of problem-solving exercises that involve representing sequences of phonemes with either mouth-form pictures or colored blocks. This training focuses on helping them acquire sensitivity to the sequences of sounds in syllables, and it also teaches them to represent these sequences with concrete visual objects. Throughout the program, instructional interactions consist primarily of questions that the teacher asks in order to help the children "discover" that they can "think about" the sounds in words by both feeling what happens in the mouth and hearing the sounds with the ear. The object of the teacher's questions is to help the children learn to verify the nature and order of the phonemes in words from their own sensory experience. As they learn to label each phoneme with a descriptive name, they also are taught to associate specific letters with each phoneme. So, once they become facile at representing sequences of sound with concrete objects, it is a natural transition to begin to represent them with letters.

All work in spelling and reading begins with nonword syllables in order to reinforce the habit of feeling and hearing the individual sounds in words. As students begin to experience success in spelling simple-syllable (CVC) patterns, they are introduced to reading similar patterns. Once a child can accurately decode simple CVC words, they are introduced explicitly to the way some words deviate from regular pronunciation patterns. They are encouraged to notice the parts of irregular words that "do not play fair," and they are taught to rapidly recognize lists of high-frequency words, some of which are regular and others irregular. During this period in which alphabetic reading skills are being firmly established, the children also read short books in which the vocabulary is phonetically consistent with their decoding skills. After they have had some beginning practice reading multisyllabic words, they begin to read stories from trade books, and they engage in the same activities with these books as the students in the EP program. During oral reading activities, they are encouraged to rely on their skills in phonological decoding, but also are encouraged to ask whether the pronunciation of an unfamiliar word "makes sense" in the context of the story. During second grade, most of the students also will write summaries of the stories they read, as well as engage in free writing activities. Spelling instruction also will be given in a manner similar to the EP program.

## THE REGULAR CLASSROOM SUPPORT GROUP

The goal of the instruction and practice activities provided to this group is to support the reading instruction being provided in the regular classroom. The instruction provided to children in this group necessarily varies somewhat across the different schools in the study, but we expect it to contain a preponderance of activities consistent with the whole language approach to reading instruction.

The three most common instructional activities designated by the regular classroom teachers during the second semester of kindergarten involved: (1) learning the names of letters, (2) learning to print letters, and (3) child dictation of sentences followed by teacher-supported reading of the sentences. Although the classrooms from which our sample was taken employ primarily a whole language approach to reading instruction, the regular classroom teachers apparently recognize the word reading difficulties of the children in our project. Thus, in first grade, they have tended consistently to ask our teachers to engage in a variety of activities to strengthen alphabetic reading skills and sight word vocabulary. This has tended to make the RCS condition more similar to the EP condition than we had anticipated when we began the study.

## INTERIM RESULTS

Throughout the instructional period, and for 2 years afterward, we will monitor the growth of children in the study on a variety of reading and other cognitive skills. Thus far, we have conducted five assessments of their word-level reading skills and phonological awareness. Although we have not conducted analyses of individual growth patterns, we can provide some group comparisons derived from the end-of-first-grade assessment. Table 6.1 provides data on several reading and phonological awareness measures for the three treatment groups as well as children in the no treatment control group. Where available, we also have included data from a comparison group of 100 randomly selected children from the same schools as the children in the prevention project.

As can be seen from Table 6.1, the most striking difference between the groups occurred for alphabetic reading skills, as measured by the Word Attack test. On this measure, the PASP group performed substantially better than the other treatment groups, and was not distinguishable from the average score of a larger group of randomly selected readers tested at the same time of the year (the average group was not included in the formal data analysis because it is not strictly a control group, but only an informal comparison group).

**TABLE 6.1.** Reading and phonological awareness scores for children in the three treatment groups, the control group, and a comparison group of average readers.

| Measure | Control (N=29) X S.D. | Group RCS (N=34) X S.D. | PASP (N=35) X S.D. | EP (N=33) X S.D. | Average (N=100) X S.D. |
|---------|------|------|------|------|------|
| Blend Phonemes[1] | 11.4  5.4 | 13.0  5.5 | 14.9  3.6 | 13.1  4.0 | 14.8  6.1 |
| Phoneme Ellison[2] | 8.8  2.9 | 10.2  4.8 | 11.6  4.1 | 9.5  4.0 | 12.3  5.0 |
| Word Attack[3] | 2.6  3.5 | 5.8  6.7 | 9.6  7.8 | 5.4  5.1 | 10.0  9.1 |
| Word Iden.[4] | 17.7  13.4 | 25.3  13.9 | 25.5  15.5 | 23.0  11.9 | 32.6  16.8 |
| Passage Comp.[5] | 7.3  6.7 | 11.4  7.1 | 10.7  7.5 | 9.6  6.5 | ---  --- |

[*] Note—This table contains raw score data for children in the study who were promoted to first grade from kindergarten.

[1] *Blending Phonemes test*—a measure of phonological awareness that requires children to recognize words from separately presented phonemes (i.e. /k/-/a/-/t/=*cat*).

[2] *Phoneme Ellison*—a measure of phonological awareness that require children to form a new word by deleting a specific sound from a target word (i.e. delete /d/ from *card = car*).

[3] *Word Attack* subtest from the *Woodcock Reading Mastery Test-Revised* (Woodcock, 1987).

[4] *Word Identification* subtest from the *Woodcock Reading Mastery Test-Revised.*

[5] *Passage Comprehension* subtest from the *Woodcock Reading Mastery Test-Revised.*

Overall group differences on the phonological awareness measures also were significant, but the only group comparisons that were significant were between the PASP and no treatment control groups. Overall group differences on the Word Identification and Passage Comprehension tests were not significant, although when the treatment groups were compared as a group with the no treatment control group, the differences were statistically reliable.

At this point, we are encouraged by the fact that we have a strong manipulation of alphabetic reading skills among our groups. We are not surprised that this difference is not yet reflected in greater real word reading skill on measures like the Word Identification test. There are both psychometric and experiential reasons why the PASP group's newly acquired alphabetic reading skills are not reflected in a more generalized reading advantage. However, if differential growth in alphabetic reading skills continues to characterize the groups through second grade, we would expect differences in this skill to have a more generalized impact on reading as the children progress through the early elementary grades. We want to stress at this time, however, that these results are far too preliminary to draw conclusions about the relative effectiveness of the different methods. Not only are there no reliable differences among treatment groups in reading vocabulary or reading comprehension, but also it is very possible that the other groups may catch up in alphabetic reading skill during second grade.

## IMMEDIATE NEXT QUESTIONS AND FUTURE DIRECTIONS

It is a fact of life for those of us who conduct research that there are always many more interesting questions than we have time and resources to answer. In this section, we will outline the immediate next questions we intend to pursue in our own research and suggest some important questions that we would like to see addressed by others.

One common objection to our current program of research is that it is not realistic in terms of the current service delivery capacity of most school systems in the United States. One-on-one instruction is a very rare luxury within the public schools. It was our original plan to apply what we learn from our first studies of one-on-one instruction, using specially trained staff, to more "realistic" classroom ecologies. The questions in this next set of studies would involve issues of implementation, and potential loss of effectiveness, if techniques that are successful in carefully controlled one-on-one situations are exported to ongoing classrooms. One of the central questions for this research would revolve around the level of intensity of instruction required to be effective with children who have phonologically based reading disabilities.

We originally judged the level of intensity of our current instruction to be sufficient to provide a fair trial of whether our current methods could effectively prevent the emergence of reading disabilities in highly at-risk children. However, half of the 80 minutes of weekly instruction is provided by instructional aides, who are necessarily less competent instructionally than the teachers. One thing we have been struck with is the wide range of individual differences in our children's response to the instruction they have received so far. Some children are reading substantially above grade level with generalized alphabetic reading skills, while others are still struggling to learn letter sounds, have a very limited sight vocabulary, and have very little understanding and ability to apply the alphabetic principle in deciphering new words. It seems clear to us that almost all of the children in our prevention study require at least the level of intensity of one-on-one instruction in reading that we are currently providing in order not to fall far behind their classmates during this critical early phase of reading skill development. For a significant number of the children, more intensive instruction than we are currently providing may be required.

Our initial experience suggests that we need to ask very serious questions about the level of intensity of instruction that may be required for children with serious impairments, if we are to teach all children to read. James Kauffman (1994) makes the excellent point that at least part of the current loss of faith in special education is the result of special educators' frequent willingness to simply "do their best" with children in the face of inadequate instructional resources. It may indeed be the case that the only way to provide opportunities for some children to acquire normal reading skills is to provide one-on-one instruction over a significant period of time. We do not know of any regular classroom program, even exemplary ones like those reported on by Kathryn Au and Claire Asam in this volume, that has shown it is capable of teaching all children to read well in the context of the whole class. Since we know that there are real costs to the child of removing him or her from the regular classroom environment for special instruction (Vaughn, 1994), we need to be sure that the time away is as effective as we can possibly make it. Providing one-on-one instruction is one way to maximize effectiveness during this time. Daily sessions that last longer than 20 minutes, but can be discontinued sooner, may be another way to reduce the total amount of disruption of the child's school schedule. The increasing acceptance of the Reading Recovery model, which involves one-on-one instruction by highly trained teachers, shows that schools can provide this resource if they are convinced it will make a real difference for children.

The question of intensity of instruction applies not only to preventive instruction, but also to remedial efforts. For example, one of our consultants, Patricia Lindamood, has successfully pioneered an intensive intervention approach in which children are seen for 4 hours a day, 5 days a week, for 80 or more hours of instruction. She feels there are special advantages of such intensive instruction in stimulating phonological awareness and the growth of alphabetic reading skills. Our other consultant, Elaine Rose, who guided the development of our embedded phonics curriculum, reports equivalent success using a very different instructional model involving one-hour, one-on-one sessions twice a week combined with daily reading homework administered by parents.

Mention of our two consultants and their successful clinical teaching programs raises another question we would like to see answered, but probably will not have time to address ourselves. This question has special relevance for us because most formal studies like our current ones are as much a test of implementation as of the effectiveness of the instructional programs themselves. One fundamental problem in studies like ours is that the teachers we recruit to implement the methods usually are not highly experienced in their use. Although our teachers are highly motivated, and were selected because they have good phonological skills themselves, one of our methods, the Auditory Discrimination in Depth program, has been particularly difficult for them to master. A better test of the relative effectiveness of different approaches might involve a direct examination of the outcomes of instruction at clinical sites in which the quality of implementation of whatever instructional method is being used, is consistently high. Such research would have to be well funded in order to allow proper sampling procedures and objective measurement of outcomes, but it could provide a much needed benchmark concerning expected remedial outcomes under the best possible conditions.

Another question that has arisen from our present research, and that we may be able to address, concerns the optimal time for preventive instruction to begin. The usual assumption is "the earlier the better." However, if one is delivering expensive one-on-one instruction, its cost effectiveness actually might be improved by waiting until instruction in reading begins in first grade, rather than starting in kindergarten. Many of the children in our project were extremely difficult to teach and showed very little progress during the second semester of kindergarten. However, almost from the beginning of first grade, many of these children have been much more responsive to instruction than they were as kindergartners. Although it simply may reflect our teachers' improving skills in relating to the children, it has appeared as though problems in behavioral control, and the lack of development of language abilities themselves, presented special obstacles to instruction in kindergarten. In addition, the children were not receiving any systematic instruction in reading in the regular classroom, so the total amount of reading instruction was much less in kindergarten than in first grade. All of these factors lead us to wonder if identifying children as at risk at the beginning of first grade (which also can be done more accurately than in kindergarten) and beginning preventive instruction at that point ultimately may be more cost effective than beginning intensive instruction in kindergarten.

Speculating about the best starting point for intensive preventive work does not mean that we question the general truth of the "earlier the better" philosophy. Our reasoning applies only to the cost effectiveness of one-on-one instruction. Certainly, we would be strongly supportive of alterations to the general kindergarten curriculum that provided more opportunities for children to be accelerated in the development of phonological awareness as an oral language skill. There are, of course, interesting questions about how this might be accomplished most effectively. On the one hand, research has shown (Lundberg, Frost, & Peterson, 1988) that growth of phonological awareness can be directly stimulated by oral language activities. On the other hand, phonological awareness also can be stimulated by teaching children to spell and having them engage in invented spelling activities (Ehri, 1989). Since invented spelling tasks may be relatively easier than oral language phonological awareness tasks once a few letter–sound correspondences have been learned (Stahl & Murray, 1994), it may be more efficient to stimulate phonological awareness through early writing activities than by oral language activities.

A final set of questions that are very important, but that we are unlikely to address, were raised at an intervention conference held in August 1994 and sponsored by the National Institute of Mental Health in conjunction with several associations and private agencies concerned with learning disabilities. Much of the discussion at this conference focused on issues of implementation in the public school setting. Most participants agreed that, although we may not know all we want to know about intervention with reading disabled children, we certainly know more than is currently being implemented effectively. Some of the thorniest questions in this area are essentially political, or social-psychological, rather than cognitive or instructional. How do we convince society at large, and individual elementary schools in particular, to devote the resources necessary to teach all children to read? How do we maintain the motivation of teachers to consistently deliver the difficult, edge-of-the-seat type of instruction that is necessary to help children who learn slowly to stick with the task long enough, and intensively enough, to experience real progress? How do we implement the type of teacher training that will produce individuals who understand the reading process thoroughly and are well practiced (and supervised) in the delivery of specific instructional techniques? Unfortunately, answers to the kind of questions we deal with in our research will be relatively meaningless unless we make progress on these broader issues.

ACKNOWLEDGMENT. The research reported in this chapter was supported by grants numbered HD23340 and HD30988 from the National Institute of Child Health and Human Development, and by grants from the National Center for Learning Disabilities and the Donald D. Hammill Foundation.

# REFERENCES

Adams, M. J. (1990). *Beginning to read: Thinking and learning about print*. Cambridge, MA: MIT Press.

Alexander, A., Andersen, H., Heilman, P. C., Voeller, K. S., & Torgesen, J. K. (1991). Phonological awareness training and remediation of analytic decoding deficits in a group of severe dyslexics. *Annals of Dyslexia, 41*, 193–206.

Baddeley, A. D. (1986). *Working memory.* New York: Oxford University Press.

Barker, T. A., Torgesen, J. K., & Wagner, R. K. (1992). The role of orthographic processing skills on five different reading tasks. *Reading Research Quarterly, 27*, 334–345.

Brown, A. L., Palincsar, A. S., & Purcell, L. (1986). Poor readers: Teach, don't label. In U. Neisser (Ed.), *The school achievement of minority children: New perspectives* (pp. 105–143). Hillsdale, NJ: Erlbaum.

Brown, I. S., & Felton, R. H. (1990). Effects of instruction on beginning reading skills in children at risk for reading disability. *Reading and Writing: An Interdisciplinary Journal, 2*, 223–241.

Clark, D. B. (1988). *Dyslexia: Theory and practice of remedial instruction.* Parkton, MD: York Press.

Clay, M. M. (1985). *The early detection of reading difficulties.* Portsmouth, NH: Heinemann.

Denckla, M. B., & Rudel, R. (1976). Rapid automatized naming (R.A.N.): Dyslexia differentiated from other learning disabilities. *Neuropsychologia, 14*, 471–479.

Ehri, L. C. (1989). The development of spelling knowledge and its role in reading acquisition and reading disability. *Journal of Learning Disabilities, 22*, 356–365.

Epstein, M. H., & Cullinan, D. (1981). Project EXCEL: A behaviorally-oriented educational program for learning disabled pupils. *Education and Treatment of Children, 4,* 357–373.

Francis, D. J., Fletcher, J. M., Stuebing, K. K., Davidson, K. C., & Thompson, N. M. (1991). Analysis of change: Modeling individual growth. *Journal of Consulting and Clinical Psychology, 59*, 27–37.

Frankiewicz, R. G. (1985). *An evaluation of the Alphabetic Phonics Program offered in the one-to-one mode.* Houston: Neuhaus Education Center.

Gittelman, R., & Feingold, I. (1983). Children with reading disorders: I. Efficacy of reading remediation. *Journal of Childhood Psychology and Psychiatry, 24*, 167–191.

Gough, P., & Walsh, M. A. (1991). Chinese, Phoenicians, and the orthographic cipher of English. In S. Brady & D. Shankweiler (Eds.), *Phonological processes in literacy.* Hillsdale, NJ: Erlbaum.

Hecht, S., Burgess, S., Torgesen, J. K., & Wagner, R. K. (1995). *Causal relationships of phonological awareness, reading related knowledge, and home background factors with word reading skills in young children.* Unpublished manuscript, Florida State University.

Hiebert, E. H., Colt, J. M., Catto, S. L., & Gury, E. C. (1992). Reading and writing of first-grade students in a restructured Chapter 1 program. *American Educational Research Journal, 29*, 545–572.

Iversen, S., & Tunmer, W. E. (1993). Phonological processing skills and the Reading Recovery program. *Journal of Educational Psychology, 85*, 112–126.

Jones, K., Torgesen, J. K., & Sexton, M. A. (1987). Using computer guided practice to increase decoding fluency in learning disabled children: A study using the Hint & Hunt I Program. *Journal of Learning Disabilities, 20*, 122–128.

Kauffman, J. M. (1994). Places of change: Special education's power and identity in an era of educational reform. *Journal of Learning Disabilities, 27*, 610–618.

Liberman, I. Y., & Shankweiler, D. (1991). Phonology and beginning reading: A tutorial. In L. Rieben & C. A. Perfetti (Eds.), *Learning to read: Basic research and its implications* (pp. 3–17). Hillsdale, NJ: Erlbaum.

Liberman, I. Y., Shankweiler, D., & Liberman, A. M. (1989). The alphabetic principle and learning to read. In D. Shankweiler & I. P. Liberman (Eds.), *Phonology and reading disability: Solving the reading puzzle* (pp. 1–33). Ann Arbor: University of Michigan Press.

Lindamood, C. H., & Lindamood, P. C. (1984). *Auditory Discrimination in Depth.* Austin, TX: PRO-ED.

Lovett, M. W., Ransby, M. J., Hardwick, N., Johns, M. S., & Donaldson, S. A. (1989). Can dyslexia be treated? Treatment-specific and generalized treatment effects in dyslexic children's response to remediation. *Brain and Language, 37*, 90–121.

Lovett, M. W., Warren-Chaplin, P. M., Ransby, M. J., & Borden, S. L. (1990). Training the word recognition skills of reading disabled children: Treatment and transfer effects. *Journal of Educational Psychology, 82*, 769–780.

Lundberg, I. (1988). Preschool prevention of reading failure: Does training in phonological awareness work? In R. L. Masland & M. W. Masland (Eds.), *Prevention of reading failure* (pp. 163–176). Parkton, MD: York Press.

Lundberg, I., Frost, J., & Peterson, O. (1988). Effects of an extensive program for stimulating phonological awareness in pre-school children. *Reading Research Quarterly, 23*, 263–284.

Lyon, G. R. (1985). Educational validation studies. In B. P. Rourke (Ed.), *Neuropsychology of learning disabilities* (pp. 228–253). New York: Guilford.

Manis, F. R. (1985). Acquisition of word identification skills in normal and disabled readers. *Journal of Educational Psychology, 77*, 78–90.

Morrison, F. J. (1987). The nature of reading disability: Toward an integrative framework. In S. Ceci (Ed.), *Handbook of cognitive, social, and neuropsychological aspects of learning disabilities* (pp. 33–63). Hillsdale, NJ: Erlbaum.

Ogden, S., Hindman, S., & Turner, S. D. (1989). Multisensory programs in the public schools: A brighter future for LD children. *Annals of Dyslexia, 39*, 247–267.

Pinnell, G. S. (1989). Reading Recovery: Helping at-risk children learn to read. *The Elementary School Journal, 90*, 161–183.

Rack, J. P., Snowling, M. J., & Olson, R. K. (1992). The nonword reading deficit in developmental dyslexia: A review. *Reading Research Quarterly, 27*, 29–53.

Rayner, K., & Pollatsek, A. (1989). *The psychology of reading.* Englewood Cliffs, NJ: Prentice-Hall.

Reitsma, P. (1990). Development of orthographic knowledge. In P. Reitsma & L. Verhoeven (Eds.), *Acquisition of reading in Dutch* (pp. 43–64). Dordrecht: Foris.

Share, D. L., & Jorm, A. F. (1987). Segmental analysis: Co-requisite to reading, vital for self-teaching, requiring phonological memory. *European Bulletin of Cognitive Psychology, 7,* 509–513.

Share, D. L., & Stanovich, K. E. (1995). Cognitive processes in early reading development: A model of acquisition and individual differences. *Issues in Education: Contributions from Educational Psychology, 1,* 1–35.

Snowling, M., & Hulme, C. (1989). A longitudinal case study of developmental phonological dyslexia. *Cognitive Neuropsychology, 6,* 379–401.

Spreen, O. (1988). Prognosis of learning disability. *Journal of Consulting and Clinical Psychology, 56,* 836–842.

Stahl, S. A., & Murray, B. A. (1994). Defining phonological awareness and its relationship to early reading. *Journal of Educational Psychology, 86,* 221–234.

Stanovich, K. E. (1988). Explaining the differences between the dyslexic and the garden-variety poor reader: The phonological-core variable-difference model. *Journal of Learning Disabilities, 21,* 590–604.

Stanovich, K. E., & West, R. F. (1989). Exposure to print and orthographic processing. *Reading Research Quarterly, 24,* 402–433.

Thorndike, R. L., Hagen, E. P., & Sattler, J. M. (1986). *Guide for administering and scoring the Stanford–Binet Intelligence Scale: Fourth Edition.* Chicago: Riverside.

Torgesen, J. K. (1980). The use of efficient task strategies by learning disabled children: Conceptual and educational implications. *Journal of Learning Disabilities, 13,* 364–371.

Torgesen, J. K. (1986). Practicing reading on computers: A research based perspective. *Learning Disabilities Focus, 1,* 72–81.

Torgesen, J. K. (1988). Studies of children with learning disabilities who perform poorly on memory span tasks. *Journal of Learning Disabilities, 21,* 605–612.

Torgesen, J. K. (1993). Variations on theory in learning disabilities. In G. R. Lyon, D. B. Gray, J. F. Kavanagh, & N. A. Krasnegor (Eds.), *Better understanding learning disabilities: New views from research and their implications for education and public policies* (pp. 153–170). Baltimore: Brooks.

Torgesen, J. K., & Davis, C (in press). Individual difference variables that predict response to training in phonological awareness. *Journal of Experimental Child Psychology.*

Torgesen, J. K., & Houck, G. (1980). Processing deficiencies in learning disabled children who perform poorly on the digit span task. *Journal of Educational Psychology, 72,* 141–160.

Torgesen, J. K., Rashotte, C. A., Greenstein, J., Houck, G., & Portes, P. (1987). Academic difficulties of learning disabled children who perform poorly on memory span tasks. In H. L. Swanson (Ed.), *Memory and learning disabilities: Advances in learning and behavioral disabilities* (pp. 305–333). Greenwich, CT: JAI Press.

Torgesen, J. K., Wagner, R. K., & Rashotte, C. A. (1994). Longitudinal studies of phonological processing and reading. *Journal of Learning Disabilities, 27,* 276–286.

Torgesen, J. K., Waters, M. D., Cohen, A. L., & Torgesen, J. L. (1988). Improving sight word recognition skills in learning disabled children: An evaluation of three computer program variations. *Learning Disabilities Quarterly, 11*, 125–133.

Vaughn, S. (1994, October). *Classroom interaction.* Address presented at conference titled, "Research on classroom ecologies: Implications for inclusion of children with learning disabilities" sponsored by the Division for Learning Disabilities, Council of Exceptional Children, Bandera, TX.

Wagner, R. K., & Torgesen, J. K. (1987). The nature of phonological processing and its causal role in the acquisition of reading skills. *Psychological Bulletin, 101*, 192–212.

Wagner, R. K., Torgesen, J. K., Laughon, P., Simmons, K., & Rashotte, C. A. (1993). The development of young readers' phonological processing abilities. *Journal of Educational Psychology, 85*, 83–103.

Wagner, R. K., Torgesen, J. K., & Rashotte, C. A. (1994). The development of reading-related phonological processing abilities: New evidence of bi-directional causality from a latent variable longitudinal study. *Developmental Psychology, 30,* 73–87.

Wagner, R. K., Torgesen, J. K., & Rashotte, C. A. (1995, April). *Changing causal relations between phonological processing abilities and word-level reading as children develop from beginning to fluent readers: A five-year longitudinal study.* Paper presented at the meeting of the Society for Research in Child Development, Indianapolis.

Wang, M. C., Haertel, G. D., & Walberg, H. J. (1993). Toward a knowledge base for school learning. *Review of Educational Research, 63*, 249–294.

Williams, J. P. (1980). Teaching decoding with an emphasis on phoneme analysis and phoneme blending. *Journal of Educational Psychology, 72*, 1–15.

Williams, J. P. (1987). Educational treatments for dyslexia at the elementary and secondary levels. In W. Ellis (Ed.), *Intimacy with language: A forgotten basic in teacher education.* Baltimore: The Orton Dyslexia Society.

Wolf, M., Bally, H., & Morris, R. (1986). Automaticity, retrieval processes, and reading: A longitudinal study in average and impaired readers. *Child Development, 57,* 988–1000.

Wood, F., Felton, R., Flowers, L., & Naylor, C. (1992). Neurobehavioral definition of dyslexia. In D. Duane (Ed.), *The reading brain: The biological basis of dyslexia* (pp. 1–25). New York: York Press.

Woodcock, R. W. (1987). *Woodcock Reading Mastery Tests — Revised.* Circle Pines, MN: American Guidance Service.

CHAPTER 7

# How Do Children Understand What They Read and What Can We Do to Help Them?

TOM TRABASSO
JOSEPH P. MAGLIANO
*The University of Chicago*

This chapter addresses two questions: What does a reader do when she tries to understand a text? and What are the consequences of what the reader does when she reads? The first question is concerned with strategies and processes that occur during reading comprehension and result in a mental representation of what has been understood. The second question is concerned with what the reader learns, remembers, and uses from what was read and understood.

The reader relies on the text and what she knows to construct the meanings of sentences. This construction requires word recognition, accessing stored word meanings, and integrating these meanings within the sentence. Evidence that a reader has constructed a meaning for a sentence occurs if the reader can paraphrase a sentence, that is, render its content in her own words while preserving its meaning for a listener.

Understanding also entails the construction and integration of information across sentences. The reader must infer relations between the interpretations of each sentence. The inferences should connect the meanings of the sentences and are often causal in nature. The inferences may involve discovering antecedent conditions or providing reasons for the occurrence of the event, state, or activity referenced in the current sentence; or they may be future-oriented and involve the generation of causal consequences or predictions about future actions or outcomes. Alternatively, they may enrich the interpretation of the current sentence by adding information to what is stated.

In our view, then, understanding results in an integrated and enriched interpretation of the content of a text. The reader strives for coherence in understanding (Graesser, Singer, & Trabasso, 1994). Coherence is achieved when the reader is able to relate the information in the text to what is known, find or construct relations or connections between ideas, and create a holistic interpretation of what is read. Coherent understanding is achieved by integrating story sentences in a connected memory representation. The more coherent the interpretation, the more the reader has learned. The more coherent the interpretation, the more likely the reader is to remember what was learned. Finally, the more coherent the interpretation, the wider the range of application of what was read.

This chapter is divided into three parts. In the first part, we provide an overview of our approach to the study of comprehension. Here we show how a story can be analyzed in terms of the episodic structure and in terms of inferences about causal relations among the sentences. Methods for studying on-line comprehension are reviewed with a particular emphasis on thinking-aloud procedures. In the second part, a study of comprehension during reading by third-grade children is reported. The study reveals that understanding is explanation-based, and a questioning intervention is described that both assesses and promotes comprehension. In the third part, implications of the think-aloud method for instruction in reading comprehension are discussed.

## OUR APPROACH

In our initial studies on comprehension (Trabasso, Secco, & van den Broek, 1984), we began with an analysis of the text, which is written and connected, making it amenable to discourse analysis. In our analysis, we identified possible causal, temporal, and logical inferences that could be made by the reader. The *a priori* identification of potential inferences enables assessment of text coherence and predicts ease in understanding, remembering, summarizing, evaluating, or using the text's information. *A priori* discourse analysis continues to guide our research.

Our research focuses on narrative texts. Our approach is applicable to expository texts, especially those that contain causal relations such as those found in physics, biological, biographical, historical, social studies, and newspaper texts. We regard the narrative form as particularly important and central to a person's understanding of personal and social problems, conflict, conflict resolution, emotions, and everyday experience (Trabasso, 1993). The narrative is a powerful form for interpreting, organizing, communicating, and understanding a variety of human experiences. Through the lives of others, real or fictional, we can learn about and evaluate human experience. Narrative is also the most common form of text that young people encounter in and outside of school in many different forms: film, books, and accounts of one's own and others' experiences. Once formulated, narratives are vehicles that allow reflection upon and understanding of these experiences.

The ability to produce and understand narratives begins at an early age and continues to play a central role throughout our lives. We have found that children as young as 2-1/2 to 3 years of age use narratives to recount the causes and consequences of real-life emotional experiences (Stein, Trabasso, & Liwag, 1994; Trabasso, Stein, & Johnson, 1981). Between the ages of 3 and 5, children become sophisticated storytellers, infer goals and plans of characters, and use their knowledge of goal plans to interpret, describe, narrate, and explain sequences of events they witness in an increasingly coherent manner (Trabasso & Nickels, 1992; Trabasso & Rodkin, 1994; Trabasso & Stein, 1994; Trabasso, Stein, Rodkin, Munger, & Baughn, 1992).

## How Do We Analyze and Represent a Narrative?

In this section, we analyze a story and demonstrate how its content may be interpreted and organized causally.

The organization of a narrative is accomplished by the function that the content plays within an episode and the causal relations between the episodic categories of the content. Figure 7.1 shows a story called the King John Story. This story contains a fundamental plot involving a goal of attaining power and a plan of murder to achieve it. Figure 7.2 shows the causal network representation of the King John Story based on Trabasso, van den Broek, and Suh's (1989) model.

We suggest that you read the story in Figure 7.1, one sentence at a time, try to understand each sentence in the context of the story, and imagine that you are communicating your understanding to another person. Think about what you do as you read and understand the story. This exercise will help you to appreciate what we have discovered by our investigations of understanding using the think-aloud method.

In the King John Story, we use a setting to introduce the main protagonist and to tell the reader something about him. The fact is established that he is the *second* son of the king. Settings also enable the episodes and their

**FIGURE 7.1.** Causal network for the King John Story.

*John Story*

1. John was the second son of a king in a country.

2. John wanted to be the king.

3. John worked hard to make his father happy.

4. But his father gave the throne to the first son, William, instead of John.

5. John could not accept his father's decision.

6. John did not like William.

7. John decided to poison William.

8. John invited William to his place.

9. John gave William a poisoned drink.

10. William died several days later.

11. John got his father's attention.

12. John showed his talents.

13. John was crowned the king.

events to occur in space and time. Settings frequently provide information on the circumstances that are important to understanding future motivations and actions of the characters.

Following the setting in the King John Story, the protagonist's goal is introduced. Here, John wants to become king. This goal motivates John's actions as attempts in a plan to achieve the goal of becoming king. Here, John works to please his father. This plan, however, fails and results in an outcome where William, the first son, becomes king instead of John. John's goal and its failure cause a psychological reaction in John. He cannot accept his father's decision to award the throne to William.

Let us stop for a moment and ask ourselves some questions in order to understand what the analysis captures. Consider the following question: Why did John work to please his father? One answer is that John wanted to become king. When we identify a causal connection between a goal and its attempt, we do so on the basis of counterfactual criteria (Trabasso et al.,

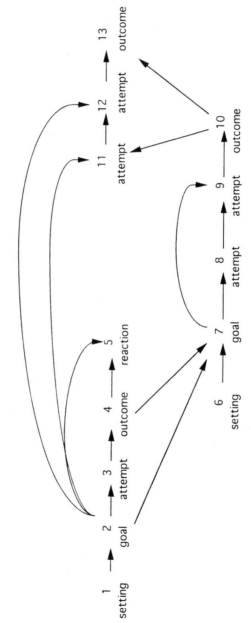

**FIGURE 7.2.** Think-aloud network for Reader 1: First seven sentences of the King John Story.

1984). The reasoning is that if John had not wanted to become king, he would not have worked hard for his father in the circumstances of the story. To identify a causal relationship between clauses in the story, then, we first identify the category of the sentence (e.g., a goal and an attempt). Then we identify a causal relationship between the attempt and the goal. If the goal explains why the attempt occurs, it should serve as an answer to a *why* question on the attempt and satisfy the counterfactual test. These criteria give us confidence about our judgment of a causal relationship between two categorized clauses.

A causal analysis of the King John Story is depicted in Figure 7.2. The arrows in the figure are the causal relations identified between the clauses. In general, settings enable events, states, and actions to occur. In some cases, they provide a basis for inferring goals. Events open a story and begin the plot. Events have effects on the protagonist's well-being. Psychologically, they cause internal reactions (cognitions, perceptions, and emotions), which, in turn, cause goals to be formed. Goals are desired or undesired states, activities, or objects, such as to maintain, attain, avoid, or escape from various states of being. They motivate the formulation of other goals, goal plans, and actions. Actions that are carried out according to a goal plan attempt to achieve goals. Attempts enable other attempts and enable or physically cause outcomes of goal success or failure. Outcomes function like events. They enable future actions and outcomes, and psychologically they can cause internal reactions (particularly emotions and belief revisions). Outcomes can cause goal strategies to be formulated, such as reinstating a goal, abandoning a goal, or replacing a goal with another, often subordinate, goal. The relations between the sentences depicted as arrows in Figure 7.2 summarize the kinds of causal or enabling relations that can be inferred in trying to understand the meaning of events, states, or activities in a narrative.

Returning to the story, try to answer the following question: Why did John decide to poison William? According to the analysis in Figure 7.2, the second goal (sentence 7) is caused by the failure of the first goal (sentence 4) and the first goal itself (sentence 2). That is, John decided to poison William because his father made William the king, instead of John, and John wanted to become king. The decision to poison William could be understood as a subordinate goal generated in a plan to obtain the crown. John's subsequent actions of inviting William (sentence 8) and giving him a drink (sentence 9) then can be understood in terms of John's subordinate goal of wanting to poison William. John's goal succeeds (sentence 10). The renewed attempts by John to impress his father, which are enabled by the removal of William in (sentence 10), can be interpreted as consistent with the goal of wanting to become king (sentence 2).

REVEALING UNDERSTANDING AFTER READING

In our earlier research on comprehension, we carried out discourse analyses similar to that in Figures 7.1 and 7.2. To evaluate the psychological validity of the causal analysis, we predicted readers' performance on various post-reading or comprehension measures. We assumed that retaining what was read and being able to answer questions about what was read would be influenced strongly by the reader's making of causal inferences during reading and comprehension of the text.

We evaluated whether a sentence being on a causal chain or its number of causal connections predicted how much and which information would be recalled. Events, states, and activities on a causal chain each have causes and consequences that move the story along, give it continuity, and allow retrieval of one event by the recall of another. We found (Trabasso et al., 1984; Trabasso & van den Broek, 1985) that causal chain events were indeed recalled twice as well as those that were not on the chain. Another powerful predictor was the number of causal antecedents and consequences (connections) that an event had with other events. Recall increased as the number of connections increased. Causal chains and connections accounted for substantial variance in importance judgments (Trabasso & Sperry, 1985; van den Broek, 1988), retention over time (Trabasso et al., 1984; Trabasso & van den Broek, 1985), and the likelihood of information being included in a summary of the story (Trabasso & van den Broek, 1985; van den Broek, 1988). Finally, readers also gave more attention to certain categories of information than to others. Events and outcomes are recalled better than actions and internal responses such as emotions (Stein & Glenn, 1979; Mandler & Johnson, 1977; Trabasso & van den Broek, 1985).

The kind of information communicated by a sentence is thus very important. The categories of sentences in a story tell us about how information in different kinds of sentences is functional and informative. Goals tell what a person wants to do and indicate in a general way what he might do. Goals help the reader understand a great deal during reading, particularly about actions, outcomes, and emotions. However, if one is telling someone else "what happened," outcomes are more informative than goals. They inform the reader what the goal was and whether or not it was successful (Trabasso & Magliano, 1994). Readers, in recalling events, prefer to state things in terms of external, observable events and outcomes (Nezworski, Stein, & Trabasso, 1982). Identification of the categories of the sentences (Stein & Glenn, 1979) helps us to determine the important content from the perspective of the reader.

Categories that often are not well recalled, for example, emotions, frequently do not have consequences or may only enable things to happen, for example, minor settings or actions. These categories often are not on a causal chain. When these categories have both causes and consequences (Omanson, 1982), the likelihood of their being recalled, retained over time, summarized, and judged to be important is increased. When one controls for the content of the categories so that they are equally informative, the differences in recall disappear (Nezworski et al., 1982). In short, the importance of different categories lies in the information they communicate and the function they perform within the story.

To test the psychological validity of our judgments of causal relations, Trabasso and colleagues (1989) carried out a causal network analysis of stories used by Stein and Glenn (1979) in a recall study involving elementary school children and by Omanson (1982), who studied various measures of the postreading comprehension of college students. College students were asked to judge whether pairs of sentences were causally related. Those pairs of sentences that were identified *a priori* as causally related by the formal analysis also were judged as causally related by the students; those pairs not judged to be causally related by the discourse methods were not judged so by the students. The students gave physical, motivational, and psychological causes the three highest ratings, in that order. They rated enabling conditions (e.g., walking to the door enables one to open it) as low on causality but high on necessity. The study by Trabasso and colleagues (1989) is the most complete summary of our approach.

Another method of revealing what is understood from reading a text is to ask questions. Graesser and his colleagues (Graesser, 1981; Graesser & Black, 1985; Graesser & Clark, 1985) have used questions both during and after comprehension to reveal inferences made from a text. *Why* and *how* questions reveal the causes or conditions necessary to an occurrence. They serve integrative functions since they require the reader to explain or describe events over distances in the text. Trabasso, van den Broek, and Suh (1989) outlined how *how* and *why* questions could be used to assess and promote comprehension in stories during reading. *Why* questions on actions, outcomes, and reactions could be answered in terms of the goals that motivated them. *How* questions on outcomes could be answered in terms of the goals and plans of action that caused them. Liu (1985) found that *why* questions during listening to or reading stories lead to better recall, presumably because the listener or reader was more likely to integrate different parts of the story by answering the questions and because the questions themselves focused attention on the content of a given sentence.

Other kinds of questions (Lehnert, 1978) focus on the constituents within a sentence. *Who, when,* and *where* questions about a sentence ask for information that involves agents who act upon patients using instruments in some location at some time. These questions assess integration within but not between sentences. In our studies, these questions are used as controls since they do not require inferences that go across sentences.

## REVEALING UNDERSTANDING DURING READING

In our more recent work, we have turned to the study of what readers do *while* they are trying to comprehend a text rather than what they do *after* they have read and understood the entire text. There are a variety of "verbal protocol" methods to find out what readers understand "on-line" versus "off-line" (cf. Magliano & Graesser, 1991). Three such methods are summarized that involve communication of understanding between the reader and another person.

Readers can be asked to answer *why* and *how* questions during, rather than after, reading and comprehension (Graesser, 1981; Graesser & Clark, 1985; Trabasso et al., 1988). *Why* and *how* questions assess and promote comprehension during reading, at least for the ideas probed and used to answer the questions, and are likely to help the reader in understanding since they require integration of ideas.

Another method for the study of on-line understanding is to ask a reader to narrate a series of events depicted in pictures. This method allows one to study comprehension by nonreaders or prereaders as well as readers. For example, we (Trabasso & Nickels, 1992; Trabasso & Rodkin, 1994; Trabasso & Stein, 1994; Trabasso et al., 1992) analyzed the narrations generated by 3-, 4-, 5-, and 9-year-old children in response to a 24-page picture book. Knowledge of goals and plans of action used to understand narrative discourse are also used to understand pictorial events that tell a story. A causal analysis using Trabasso and colleagues (1989) and Warren, Nicholas, and Trabasso (1979) revealed that 3-year-olds described and identified isolated events, 4-year-olds focused on describing actions relevant to a plan, and 5-year-olds explained these actions with purposes and described their causal outcomes. Thus, by age 5, children communicated their use of planning knowledge in interpreting the actions of protagonists through on-line narration.

A third method for revealing understanding during reading is to ask the reader or listener to tell about her understanding as she reads or hears a unit of discourse. Suppose, then, that the reader reads one sentence at a time and after reading each sentence, tells someone else how she understands it. This method is called "thinking aloud." Thinking aloud was originated by Newell and Simon (1972) and Ericsson and Simon (1993) as a method of studying problem solving. Ericsson (1988) and Pressley and Afflerbach (1995) summarize the work that uses think-aloud protocols to assess understanding.

Suh and Trabasso (1993) studied goal-based inferences that college students made when they read a story. Verbal protocols revealed goal-based explanations of goals, actions, outcomes, and reactions where they were predicted to occur by the causal network model of Trabasso and colleagues

(1989). The model and verbal protocol data, in turn, predicted where readers, during silent reading, would spontaneously use goal information in explanation. Readers answered true–false recognition questions involving goals faster after they read a story sentence whose content could be explained by a goal than after the same sentence in another story whose content could not be explained by the same goal. By the use of well-matched experimental and control stories, these differences in prediction were accomplished on sentences that were identical in content but required different bases of explanation across different story versions. The combination of the use of discourse analysis, verbal protocols, and on-line, "behavioral" methods constitutes what Magliano and Graesser (1991) have called a "three-pronged" approach. Together, these methods converge and validate the discourse model.

Trabasso and Suh (1993) validated what was discovered in think-aloud protocols against reading times per sentence, immediate recall, recall 2 days after reading, and coherence judgments of stories. Reading times were faster for those sentences where more direct explanations were made in the think-aloud protocols. Stories that allowed readers to retrieve goals and use them to explain events also are rated as more coherent (Magliano & Trabasso, 1994; Trabasso, Suh, & Payton, 1994).

Think-aloud protocols during reading reveal stable individual differences in the quality and quantity of mental operations carried out during comprehension. Trabasso, Suh, Payton, and Jain (1994) analyzed think-aloud data obtained on third-grade readers and found high correlations across different stories on the number of explanations. These differences also highly correlated with subsequent retention of the stories.

In sum, having a reader think aloud while trying to comprehend what he is reading yields a verbal protocol that enables us to reveal inference and memory operations necessary to comprehension. This method approximates a natural or normal form of communication between the reader and a teacher. What is done during reading as revealed by the think-aloud method is related to other measures of processing during and after reading. The quality of the protocols can be used to evaluate instructional interventions and how considerate or coherent are the texts.

## HOW THINK-ALOUD PROTOCOLS
## REVEAL INFERENCES AND THE EFFECTS
## OF A QUESTION INTERVENTION

We now report a study of thinking aloud during comprehension by 24 third-grade children. The study shows how and what the think-aloud method reveals about inferences and memory, how these processes affect retention of what is read, and how an intervention with *why* and *how* questions promotes changes in thinking during comprehension.

In the study, the children each read three stories in succession. The stories were written with the structure of the causal network shown in Figure 7.2. In each story, a protagonist wants something (to become a king, do something special for mother's birthday, or obtain a new bicycle), and this higher-order goal is introduced in the first episode. The protagonist tries and fails in the first episode (the brother becomes king, everything at a store is too expensive, or the mother refuses to buy a bicycle). In the second episode, the protagonist generates a subordinate goal that fits the plan of the original goal and succeeds (removes a rival, knits a sweater, or earns money). In the third episode, the protagonist carries out attempts and succeeds in attaining the original goal (becomes king, gives mother the sweater, or buys the bicycle). The stories were 14, 15, and 13 sentences long, respectively.

The children were instructed to understand each sentence in the context of the story and to tell the experimenter about their understanding after reading each sentence. During reading and thinking aloud about the second story, the experimenter intervened with five questions. In one condition, the children were asked *why* questions on two goals and on one action, and *how* questions on two outcomes; in a second condition, they were asked *what* questions on each of the same five statements. The *why* and *how* questions tap causal understanding, whereas the *what* questions tap associative understanding. Since answering causal questions promotes integrative understanding, the children who answered those questions should explain and predict more in thinking aloud about the third story, which followed the questioning, than they did in the first story, relative to those children who answered associative, *what* questions.

After reading all three stories, the children recalled, in order, the first and third stories. If explaining and predicting events led to integration of story information into a functional memory representation, those children who explained and/or predicted more during thinking aloud also should remember more of what they read.

## THE INFERENCES OF TWO VERY DIFFERENT READERS

Two very different readers are compared on their verbal protocols for purposes of illustrating think-aloud procedures. One child (Reader 1) interprets and integrates sentences by a variety of inferences; the other (Reader 2) focuses her processing mainly on the sentence itself. Tables 7.1 and 7.2 show the think-aloud protocols of these readers.

Each table contains the sentence read, the clauses thought aloud, and

**TABLE 7.1.** Example think-aloud protocol, Reader 1, John Story, first 7 sentences.

| STORY SENTENCES | CLAUSES | INFERENCES |
|---|---|---|
| 1. John was the second son of a king in a country. | c1. He was a boy | Association |
| | c2. and he was like the son of the king in a country | Paraphrase |
| 2. John wanted to be king. | c1. He wanted to become king | Paraphrase |
| 3. John worked hard to make his father happy. | c1. He worked real hard | Paraphrase |
| | c2. because his father was king | Explanation |
| | c3. and he wanted to be the king | Explanation |
| | c4. when he grew up | Association |
| 4. But his father gave the throne to the first son, William, instead of John. | c1. Maybe since he was the first son | Explanation |
| | c2. he gave it to William instead of John | Paraphrase |
| | c3. maybe he was more important or something | Explanation |
| 5. John could not accept his father's decision. | c1. He wanted to be the king | Explanation |
| | c2. and his older brother was now king | Explanation |
| 6. John did not like William. | c1. Maybe they fight a lot | Explanation |
| | c2. because they're kids | Explanation |
| 7. John decided to poison William. | c1. He wanted to be the king | Explanation |
| | c2. and he didn't like him | Explanation |
| | c3. so he didn't want him to be king | Explanation |
| | c4. so he poisoned him | Prediction |
| | c5. he gave him stuff | Prediction |
| | c6. to make him die | Explanation |

the kinds of inferences made. In classifying thoughts, we distinguished between paraphrases, explanations, association, and predictions. A *paraphrase* is a translation of a sentence into new wording that preserves the meaning of the original sentence. Paraphrases often are near repeats of what was read, but often, as shown in Table 7.2, they alter the wording and modify the sentence by key word changes or additions. An *association* is the adding of new information to the situation by activating relevant world knowledge. An *explanation* is a reason, purpose, cause, or condition for something that happened. A *prediction* is a causal consequence or a future happening. Predictions are often purposes expressed as future outcomes.

Reader 1 interprets and integrates sentences by explanations and predictions. This reader also associates to and occasionally paraphrases a sentence. However, the majority of inferences by Reader 1 are explanatory in

**TABLE 7.2.** Example think-aloud protocol, Reader 2, John Story, first 7 sentences.

| STORY SENTENCES | CLAUSES | INFERENCES |
|---|---|---|
| 1. John was the second son of a king in a country. | c1. He was the second one born from the king | Paraphrase |
| 2. John wanted to be the king. | c1. He wanted to be in charge | Explanation |
| 3. John worked hard to make his father happy. | c1. He did a lot of stuff for the king | Paraphrase |
| 4. But his father gave the throne to the first son, William, instead of John | c1. He didn't let John be the next king | Paraphrase |
| 5. John could not accept his father's decision. | c1. He couldn't figure out why the king didn't pick him | Explanation |
| 6. John did not like William. | c1. He didn't like his brother | Paraphrase |
| 7. John decided to poison William. | c1. He decided to kill him with poison | Paraphrase |

nature. Note also that Reader 1 carries over or retrieves information in order to explain, associate, or predict. In contrast, Reader 2 mainly paraphrases sentences.

To show the relations among inference and memory processes of these two readers, networks of their thoughts were created. Figures 7.3 and 7.4 show the networks that were derived for the first seven sentences of the John King story for Readers 1 and 2, respectively.

Reader 1 in Figure 7.3 paraphrased the first four sentences. This reader made associations to sentences 1 and 3. However, explanations were made at sentences 2, 3, 4, 5, 6, and 7. In order to make explanations at sentences 3, 5, and 7, information was retrieved from sentences 1, 2, and 5, respectively. Likewise, information from sentences 4 and 6 was carried over and used to explain sentences 5 and 7, respectively. A pair of predictions was generated at sentence 7. In contrast, Figure 7.4 shows that Reader 2 paraphrased sentences 1, 3, 4, 6, and 7. Only two explanations were offered, at sentences 2 and 5, and one association was made to sentence 4. Information from sentence 4 was the only carryover made, and this was used to explain sentence 5.

These protocols illustrate extreme possibilities that actually occurred. The vast majority of the third-grade readers fell in between these two. In the data that are reported next, evidence is given in support of this assertion. The findings that are reported are on frequencies of different inferences and memory operations, sources of information used to make the inferences, and the relationships between inferences made and memory for the text. Comparisons are made between adult, skilled readers, and third-grade readers during comprehension.

## GROUP FINDINGS ON INFERENCES AND MEMORY PROCESSES

In this section, we compare the third-grade readers' performance with that of adult, college students on inferences and memory processes revealed in the think-aloud protocols.

*Inferences.* Table 7.3 summarizes the average number and proportion of clauses that were inferences and paraphrases. Third-grade performance is compared with that of four college students on the same two stories (data taken from Trabasso & Magliano, 1994).

The children averaged 27.56 thoughts (clauses) per story, or 1.84 thoughts per sentence. Of the average number of clauses per story, 19.27 were inferences and 8.29 were paraphrases. The differences among the three kinds of inferences and paraphrases were statistically significant ($F = 7.45$, $p < .01$). The third-graders' modal thought was to explain. Their explana-

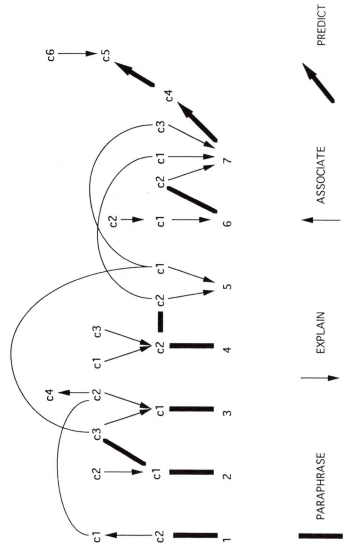

**FIGURE 7.3.** Think-aloud network for Reader 2: First 7 sentences of the King John Story.

**TABLE 7.3.** Comparison of third grade readers' and college students' think-aloud protocols on inferences and paraphrases made to each sentence.

| Reader | Explain | Associate | Predict | Paraphrase |
|---|---|---|---|---|
| Third grade average number | 9.12 | 5.50 | 4.65 | 8.29 |
| Proportion of clauses | .32 | .21 | .17 | .30 |
| College students average number | 21.38** | 4.50 | 4.00 | 7.13 |
| Proportion of clauses | .58** | .12** | .11* | .19** |

$^*p < .05$   $^{**}p < 01$

**FIGURE 7.4.** Relationship between explanatory and predictive inferences during comprehension and memory for stories.

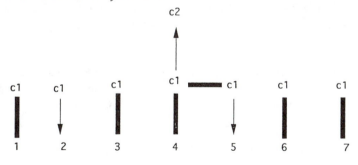

tions averaged 9.12 clauses per story, significantly more than the 4.65 paraphrases (t(23) = 3.04) or 5.50 associations (t(23) = 2.91). In comparison with the college students, the younger readers' distributions were similar in shape. However, the third graders made proportionately fewer explanations (t(23) = −9.06) and more associations (t(23) = 4.89), predictions (t(23) = 2.19, p < .05), and paraphrases (t(23) = 4.36) than their older counterparts.

On balance, understanding by young and more experienced, older readers is explanation-based rather than expectation-driven. Both groups made more explanations than predictions. Integrative inferences were more frequent than associative inferences. The developmental differences in the number of explanations may depend on having greater knowledge and expertise with respect to inferring and using goals and plans to understand actions and outcomes (Trabasso et al., 1992). Readers who are more expert, in general, engage in more explanation than those who are less expert (Chi, Bassok, Lewis, Reimann, & Glaser, 1989; Chi, de Leeuw, Chiu, & LaVancher, 1994).

***Memory operations and sources of information for inferences.*** Three sources of information are available to readers during comprehension: activation of world knowledge relevant to explaining, associating, or predicting; carrying over or retrieving prior activations or thoughts; or carrying over or retrieving sentence information from the prior text (Trabasso & Magliano, 1994).

The findings on information sources and memory operations are summarized in Table 7.4. The third-grade readers averaged 12.44 new activations per story, and retrieved or carried over 0.96 old activations and 5.92

**TABLE 7.4.** Information sources and memory operations during comprehension.

| Readers | Activation | | Prior text | Memory Carry overs | Operations Retrievals |
|---|---|---|---|---|---|
| | New | Prior | | | |
| Third graders | | | | | |
| average number | 12.44 | 0.96 | 6.04 | 3.94 | 2.85 |
| Proportion | .63 | .05 | .33 | .58 | .42 |
| College students | | | | | |
| average number | 17.63 | 2.00 | 10.50 | 7.75 | 4.63 |
| Proportion | .60 | .06 | .33 | .63 | .37 |

text sources per story $(F(2,69) = 56.50, p < .01)$ in trying to understand what they read. Individual comparisons indicated that new activations occurred more than text as sources for inferences and that both of these sources occurred more than the use of prior thoughts in understanding new sentences (all $p < .01$). In comparison with the college students, the younger readers had more new activations $(t(23) = 2.40, p < .05)$ and used fewer prior thoughts or old activations $(t(23) = 2.87, p < .01)$. They did not differ on the proportion of times they used the text as a source for an inference. Since associations depend on new activations, the use of sources reflects the grade differences in inferences reported in the prior section.

Table 7.4 also reports data on information carried over from the previous sentence or from more distant points in the text. The college students performed both memory operations more often than did the third graders $(p < .01)$. In terms of comparisons between the two operations, the two groups resembled one another in that they carried over information from the prior sentence at a higher rate than they retrieved it from sentences two or more prior to the current one. These data indicate that processing of text depends to a large extent on what information is readily accessible from working memory. Thoughts or text from the immediately prior sentence are more available than those from sentences two or more back in the text. However, Magliano and Trabasso (1994) showed that readers maintain higher-order goal information in working memory by continuing to carry over goal information and using it to explain or predict actions or outcomes. By maintaining information in working memory, it is possible to integrate text at greater distances without retrieving it from the long-term memory representation, as assumed by a number of models of discourse comprehension (e.g., Fletcher & Bloom, 1988; Kintsch & van Dijk, 1978; McKoon & Ratcliff, 1992).

*Relationship between inferences during comprehension and retention of what was read.* Explanations and predictions should lead to better retention of what was read. Integration of prior text with the current sentence occurs when prior text is retrieved. Future text is integrated with the current sentence when predictions from it are later substantiated by the content of the text. We examined, via multiple regression for each individual, the relation between the number of explanations and predictions and the average number of sentences recalled per story. The correlation between these inferences and memory was $r = +.58$ (df $= 23, p < .01$), indicating that recall increased as did the number of integrative inferences. To depict the relationship more clearly, we divided the third-grade readers into three groups according to the total number of explanations and predictions

**FIGURE 7.5.** Mean number of explanations and predictions (lowest, middle, and upper third groups).

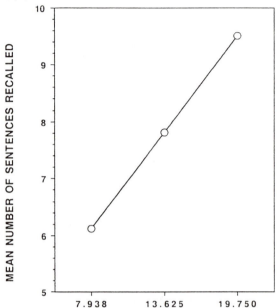

MEAN NUMBER OF EXPLANATIONS AND PREDICTIONS
(Lowest, Middle, & Upper Third Groups)

made. Then, we found the mean number of sentences recalled per story for each of the three groups. The relationship between recall and whether a third grader was in the lower, middle, or upper third of the grade in terms of explanations and predictions is shown in Figure 7.5.

The relationship depicted in Figure 7.5 is strikingly linear. As the average number of explanations and predictions increases per group, there is a corresponding, linear increase in the amount recalled. Those readers who integrate text during comprehension by explaining and predicting learn and retain more information later. Not only is understanding largely explanation-based, but those who understand better also remember better. Chi and colleagues (1989) found that students who self-explained frequently in thinking aloud during the study of physics passages also retained knowledge of problems and solutions better than those who self-explained less often.

### THE QUESTION-INTERVENTION PHASE

As already noted, the third-grade readers read three stories, and during their reading of the second story, we intervened and asked half the children *why* questions (e.g., Why did John decide to poison William?) or *what* questions (e.g., What did John decide to do to William?). A *why* question requires that the child carry over or retrieve prior text or thoughts to explain John's decision to poison William (e.g., He did not like William; William became king; John wanted to be king), whereas a *what* question requires only that information within the sentence be given (e.g., poison him). For the group asked *why* questions, we also asked *how* questions on outcomes (e.g., How did John become king?). To answer this kind of question, the reader has to reconstruct a sequence of prior text events (goals, actions, or outcomes) or thoughts as answers (e.g., John wanted to become king and he did not like him so he poisoned his brother who was the king and impressed his father with his skill).

Given the contrasting requirements of the *why/how* versus the *what* questions, we expected different effects on subsequent comprehension processes during reading. In particular, we anticipated that the reader's strategies for processing the text would change. *Why/how* questions should increase explanations and reduce other inferences. *What* questions should increase paraphrasing since answering *what* questions and paraphrasing both reflect within-sentence understanding.

**Question effects on inferences.** Table 7.5 summarizes the findings on the question effects on inferences and paraphrases. The questions occurred during the reading of the second story so that their effects could occur in understanding the third story. The effects were assessed by the difference in proportions between the third and first stories. Table 7.5 shows the overall gain or loss from the *why* versus *what* question intervention.

TABLE 7.5. Question intervention effects: Differences in proportion of inferences or paraphrase between the third and first stories.

|  | Explain | Associate | Predict | Paraphrase |
|---|---|---|---|---|
| Why difference | +.11 | -.09 | -.05 | +.04 |
| What difference | -.01 | -.06 | -.03 | +.09 |
| Net why question gain/loss | +.12 | -.03 | -.02 | -.05 |

The data in Table 7.5 show a 12% net gain in explanations as a result of *why* versus *what* questioning (t(22) = 1.92, 1-tailed p < .05). There are small but consistent decreases in associations and predictions for the *why* question group and larger increases in paraphrasing or focusing on the sentence itself in the *what* question group. Taken together, the 10% net decrease in associations, predictions, and paraphrases for the *why* versus the *what* questions is also significant (t(22) = 1.85, 1-tailed p < .05).

***Question effects on information sources used and memory operations.*** With respect to the use of newly activated knowledge versus prior thoughts or text, we expected that *why* questions might reduce the reliance on one's world knowledge and increase the use of prior thoughts or text to explain the current sentence. *Why* questions require looking backward in time for reasons or causes. *What* questions focus attention on the current sentence and new, associative activations of knowledge. With respect to memory strategies, *why* questioning might promote retrieval of earlier information in order to explain the current sentence. Causes and reasons for goals, actions, outcomes, and emotions lie most often in sentences at a distance from the current one; this is especially true for higher-order goal information.

Table 7.6 provides the comparison data on *why* and *what* questions for gains or losses between stories three and one and for the *why* over the *what* questioning on information sources and memory strategies. Table 7.6 shows that readers who were asked *why* (and *how*) questions tended to increase their use of prior text and did not change in their use of prior thoughts. Their use of world knowledge to make inferences while trying to

**TABLE 7.6.** Question effects: Differences in proportions of information sources used and memory operations.

|  | Activation | | Prior | | |
|  | New | Prior | text | Carry over | Retrieval |
| --- | --- | --- | --- | --- | --- |
| Why difference | -.09 | .00 | +.09 | -.11 | +.11 |
| What difference | .00 | -.04 | .00 | +.04 | +.04 |
| Net why question gain/loss | -.09 | +.04 | +.09 | -.07 | +.07 |

understand a sentence decreased, therefore, to the same degree. *Why* questions tended to promote retrieval at the expense of carrying over information more than did *what* questions. While these effects were in the expected direction, they did not reach levels of statistical significance.

The think-aloud method revealed that *why* questions promoted better integrative understanding than did *what* questions. Readers were more likely to explain sentences following the reading of a story that featured *why* and *how* questions. They were less likely to focus on the sentence they were reading and devote more of their efforts to the integration of sentence information through explanation. Further, readers who had a *why* and *how* question intervention were more likely to pay attention to and use information from the text and rely less on world knowledge. Finally, readers who had *why* and *how* questioning as an intervention tended to retrieve prior text and use it to explain the current sentence more than did readers whose attention was focused on within-sentence constituents promoted by *what* questioning.

## WHAT CAN WE DO TO ASSESS
## AND PROMOTE COMPREHENSION?

In this section we discuss instructional implications of the think-aloud method. In our discussion, we consider the method itself and point out how it is similar to that used in reciprocal teaching; we also examine the use of questions in other group reading situations.

### USE OF THE THINK-ALOUD METHOD

The think-aloud method focused the reader's attention on a sentence and asked the reader to understand it in the context of the story. A sentence with one main predicate (equivalent to a clause) contains the information necessary to refer to a state, an event, or an activity. Clauses are thus sufficient to specify conditions and causes. This information is necessary in the circumstances of the story to integrate it with information from other clauses. Once a reader is able to read words and relate them into a meaningful clause, she is in a position to generate inferences that link these interpretations into higher-order, mental representations of the text. The basic processes of determining what the sentence refers to and how its referent is related to other sentences, constitute, for us, basic understanding. From this basic sentence understanding, one can move on to interpretive frameworks involving evaluation and generalization. Our study showed that third graders were quite accomplished at interpreting and integrating narrative texts.

The think-aloud method can be adapted to classroom contexts with either individual readers or with a group of readers. The method could serve as a means to both assess and promote comprehension. The reader or readers could be asked to tell the teacher what they understand when they read a segment of text. This segment could be a word, a phrase, a sentence, or even a paragraph. The choice of the size of the unit for understanding may depend on the goals of the teacher or on the form of the text. Whatever the unit, the think-aloud method allows one to focus on what and how the reader understands it. In groups, readers could take turns, either by volunteering or by being asked to interpret different segments. The teacher should interact with the readers by offering her own interpretations as to how she understands the text. The teacher could pose *why* and *how* questions, answer them, provide explanations, set up expectations or predictions, and associate to the text by adding relevant information that supports explanation or prediction. The readers should be encouraged to perform the same processes. The teacher and the readers should strive for coherence by relating what is being understood to higher-order goals and purposes, including those of the author and the readers. In thinking aloud, the teacher herself becomes a model for how to understand the text and how to think aloud and communicate one's understanding to others. In this way, understanding may be seen as a social, constructive process.

The think-aloud protocols reveal the inference strategies and memory processes that readers use in trying to understand the text and how they communicate their understanding. What the reader communicates about understanding via this method tells us whether the reader is focused on individual words or phrases, sentences, or integration across sentences. The verbal protocol of the reader can thus be used both as a diagnostic tool and as a basis for assisting the reader on different levels of understanding.

We have found that texts vary in the quantity and quality of the inferences that readers make (Trabasso, Suh, & Payton, 1994) so that a reader may be having difficulty because a particular text is problematic and not because the reader is a poor reader. It is necessary and desirable to assess a reader across several texts or passages in order to establish how that reader consistently understands a variety of texts. It is also necessary to assess a particular text across a number of different readers in order to establish how considerate and how coherent the text is. Difficult texts are inconsiderate in that they do not provide the definition or other explicit information necessary for making inferences. It is important not to confuse text difficulty with a reader's ability to understand texts.

The think-aloud method can promote understanding. Loxterman, Beck, and McKeown (in press) found that thinking aloud during reading leads to qualitatively better recall of what was read. Readers who thought aloud during reading were more likely to include elaborative inferences in their recall than were those who read silently. One reason why thinking aloud may promote comprehension is that it requires more focused attention, deeper processing, and communication of ideas regarding the text. Silent readers are not as likely to be as motivated or aroused to attend to and read the text as deeply as readers who are required to communicate what they understand. The deeper processing would come about through the making of explanatory and predictive inferences that connect ideas, and through the richer elaboration of the reader's model of the text through associations.

A second reason that thinking aloud might promote comprehension is that it involves monitoring as well as comprehending. For example, Chi and colleagues (1989) had subjects think aloud during the solving of physics word problems. They found that the problem solvers engaged in self-explanation of the problems but that they also communicated when they were and were not understanding a section of a problem. Monitoring and communication of self-understanding also are likely to be promoted by the think-aloud method. Monitoring and communication of self-understanding also would aid the teacher in knowing whether and where understanding succeeds or fails and would enable the teacher to intervene by providing supporting information, clarification, examples, and so on, or to pose questions.

The think-aloud method may underlie the success of some well-known interventions with poor readers. For example, in a widely cited study by Palincsar and Brown (1984), the teacher first communicated overtly her understanding of a text and then allowed the student to communicate how she understood another passage. The teacher posed and answered questions, stated expectations about what was going to happen, drew implications or causal consequences, made generalizations, and stated evaluations. Comprehension monitoring also was communicated during understanding. The teacher made inferences identified by our analysis, particularly where *why* and *how* questions were posed and answered, where predictions were made and confirmed or not confirmed against the text, where explanations occurred, and where relevant information was added as associations to what was being read. Palincsar and Brown (1984) may have succeeded because they taught poor readers how to understand and what procedures to use in understanding.

## USE OF QUESTIONS

Efficacy of explanation and prediction in understanding also can be assessed and promoted by the use of *why* and *how* questions about what is being read. Trabasso and colleagues (1988) argued that the contradictory findings on the effects of questioning on comprehension (Anderson & Biddle, 1975) could have resulted from (1) asking questions after or before rather than during reading, (2) the kinds of questions asked, and (3) what was probed by questioning. Our argument is that one has to ask *why* and *how* questions on key constituents of the text (e.g., goals, actions, or outcomes). The answers to these questions should serve to relate prior text and ideas to the current sentence or to anticipate future ideas and text.

The present study showed that *why* questions facilitated better understanding. Asking readers to explain why something occurred increased explanatory and retrieval processes as well as the use of prior thoughts and text during the understanding of subsequent sentences of a story. Since explanatory processes facilitate problem solving (Chi et al., 1989) and retention (Chi et al., 1994; Trabasso & Suh, 1993), it would seem that explanatory questions also could be used to both assess and promote understanding. Systematic and extended use of explanatory questioning of understanding (King, 1989, 1991; Liu, 1985; Nix, 1985) promotes comprehension. However, the gains reported are small and often result only from very intense and focused questioning.

Questioning alone is one-sided. Embedding the questions in the context of a communicative setting concerning understanding what is read (McKeown, Beck, & Sandora, Chapter 5, this volume) may be more effective. Beck and her colleagues (Beck, McKeown, Worthy, Sandora, & Kucan, in press) have a comprehension program for groups of readers that uses questions to engage the readers in a conversation with the teacher. Asking the reader to "question the author," as Beck and her colleagues do, removes the onus of the reader's comprehending an object — the text — and shifts the focus to attempting to understand a communication by a fallible author. In our reading of their verbal protocols, there is considerable explanation-based understanding. The teacher asks for purposes or reasons *why* something is done. For example, "Did they mean they have some kinds of deer that they use for meat and [different kinds] that they use for milk?" asks the readers to distinguish between different kinds of deer on the basis of their functions or purposes. "How can we give them [the Japanese] our money?" asks for plans of action to accomplish the goal of exchanging our money for foreign goods.

McKeown, Beck, and Sandora (Chapter 5, this volume) appear to have found a very effective classroom procedure for assessing and fostering comprehension. The discussion that results in an effort to find meaning is a kind of shared thinking aloud. The Questioning the Author method has much to recommend it for its social and communicative aspects, for its flexibility in questioning, and for its range of applicability. The teacher and readers model by communication what they understand the author or writer to mean. The teacher uses questions to direct comprehension and foster communication. Individual differences in readers can be taken into account by the kind of questions posed, the support and answers provided by the teacher, and the assistance of other readers.

ACKNOWLEDGMENT. This research was supported by a grant from the Spencer Foundation to T. Trabasso and by a National Research Service Award from the National Institute of Deafness and Other Communications Disorders (Fellowship # 1 F32 DC00158-01) to J. Magliano. The authors would like to thank Rachna Jain for her assistance in the collection of the data and Fraeda Friedman for her assistance in the analysis of the data.

## REFERENCES

Anderson, R. C., & Biddle, W. B. (1975). On asking people questions about what they are reading. In G. H. Bower (Ed.), *The psychology of learning and motivation* (Vol. 9, pp. 90–132). New York: Academic Press.

Beck, I. L., McKeown, M. G., Worthy, J., Sandora, C. A., & Kucan, L. (in press). Questioning the Author: A year-long classroom implementation to engage students with text. *The Elementary School Journal*.

Chi, M. T. H., Bassok, M., Lewis, M. W., Reimann, P., & Glaser, R. (1989). Self-explanations: How students study and use examples in learning to solve problems. *Cognitive Science, 13*, 145–182.

Chi, M. T. H., de Leeuw, N., Chiu, M., & LaVancher, C. (1994). Eliciting self-explanations improves understanding. *Cognitive Science, 18*, 439–477.

Ericsson, K. A. (1988). Concurrent verbal reports on text comprehension: A review. *Text, 8*, 295–335.

Ericsson, K. A., & Simon, H. A. (1993). *Protocol analysis: Verbal reports as data.* Cambridge, MA: MIT Press.

Fletcher, C. R., & Bloom, C. P. (1988). Causal reasoning in the comprehension of simple narrative texts. *Journal of Memory and Language, 27*, 235–244.

Graesser, A. C. (1981). *Prose comprehension beyond the word.* New York: Springer-Verlag.

Graesser, A. C., & Black, J. B. (Eds.). (1985). *The psychology of questions.* Hillsdale, NJ: Erlbaum.

Graesser, A. C., & Clark, L. F. (1985). *Structures and procedures of implicit knowledge.* Norwood, NJ: Ablex.

Graesser, A. C., Singer, M. S., & Trabasso, T. (1994). Constructing inferences during narrative text comprehension. *Psychological Review, 101*, 371–395.

King, A. (1989). Effects of self-questioning training on college students' comprehension of lectures. *Contemporary Educational Psychology, 14*, 1–16.

King, A. (1991). Effects of training in strategic questioning on children's problem-solving performance. *Journal of Educational Psychology, 83*, 307–317.

Kintsch, W., & van Dijk, T. A. (1978). Toward a model of text comprehension and production. *Psychological Review, 85*, 363–394.

Lehnert, W. G. (1978). *The process of question answering*. Hillsdale, NJ: Erlbaum.

Liu, L. G. (1985). Using causal questions to assess and promote children's understanding and memory for narratives that vary in causal structure. Unpublished doctoral dissertation, University of Chicago.

Loxterman, J. A., Beck, I. L., & McKeown, M. G. (in press). The effects of thinking aloud during reading on students' comprehension of more or less coherent text. *Reading Research Quarterly*.

Magliano, J. P., & Graesser, A. C. (1991). A three-pronged method for studying inference generation in literary text. *Poetics, 20*, 193–232.

Magliano, J. P., & Trabasso, T. (1994, November). *Local and global coherence in text understanding*. Paper presented at the 35th annual meeting of the Psychonomic Society, St. Louis.

Mandler, J. M., & Johnson, N. J. (1977). Remembrance of things parsed: Story structure and recall. *Cognitive Psychology, 9*, 111–151.

McKoon, G., & Ratcliff, R. (1992). Inference during reading. *Psychological Review, 99*, 440–446.

Newell, A., & Simon, H. A. (1972). *Human problem solving*. Englewood Cliffs, NJ: Prentice-Hall.

Nezworski, T., Stein, N. L., & Trabasso, T. (1982). Story structure versus content in children's recall. *Journal of Verbal Learning and Verbal Behavior, 21*, 196–206.

Nix, D. (1985). Notes on the efficacy of questioning. In A. C. Graesser & J. B. Black (Eds.), *The psychology of questions* (pp. 297–333). Hillsdale, NJ: Erlbaum.

Omanson, R. C. (1982). The relation between centrality and story category variation. *Journal of Verbal Learning and Verbal Behavior, 21*, 326–337.

Palincsar, A. S., & Brown, A. L. (1984). Reciprocal teaching of comprehension-fostering and comprehension-monitoring activities. *Cognition and Instruction, 1*, 117–175.

Pressley, M., & Afflerbach, P. (1995). *Verbal protocols of reading: The nature of constructively responsive reading*. Hillsdale, NJ: Erlbaum.

Stein, N. L., & Glenn, C. (1979). An analysis of story comprehension in elementary school children. In R. O. Freedle (Ed.), *New directions in discourse processing: Vol. 2. Advances in discourse processes* (pp. 53–120). Norwood, NJ: Ablex.

Stein, N. L., Trabasso, T., & Liwag, M. (1994). The Rashamon phenomenon: Personal frames and future-oriented appraisals in memory for emotional events. In M. M. Haith, J. Benson, B. Pennington, & R. Roberts (Eds.), *The development of future oriented processes* (pp. 409–435). Chicago: University of Chicago Press.

Suh, S., & Trabasso, T. (1993). Inferences during on-line processing: Converging evidence from discourse analysis, talk-aloud protocols, and recognition priming. *Journal of Memory and Language, 32*, 279-301.

Trabasso, T. (1993). The power of the narrative. In J. Osborn (Ed.), *Reading, language and literacy* (pp. 187-200). Hillsdale, NJ: Erlbaum.

Trabasso, T., & Magliano, P. A. (1994). Understanding emotional understanding. In N. Frijda (Ed.), *Proceedings of International Society for Study of Emotion* (pp. 78-82). Storrs, CT: ISRE Publications.

Trabasso, T., & Nickels, M. (1992). The development of goal plans of action in the narration of picture stories. *Discourse Processes, 15*, 249-275.

Trabasso, T., & Rodkin, P. C. (1994). Knowledge of goal/plans: A conceptual basis for narrating *Frog, where are you?*. In R. A. Berman & D. I. Slobin (Eds.), *Different ways of relating events in narrative: A cross-linguistic study* (pp. 85-106). Hillsdale, NJ: Erlbaum.

Trabasso, T., Secco, T., & van den Broek, P. (1984). Causal cohesion and story coherence. In H. Mandl, N. L. Stein, & T. Trabasso (Eds.), *Learning and comprehension of text* (pp. 83-111). Hillsdale, NJ: Erlbaum.

Trabasso, T., & Sperry, L. L. (1985). Causal relatedness and importance of story events. *Journal of Memory and Language, 24*, 595-611.

Trabasso, T., & Stein, N. L. (1994). Using goal/plan knowledge to merge the past with the present and the future in narrating events on-line. In M. M. Haith, J. B. Benson, R. J. Roberts Jr., & B. F. Pennington (Eds.), *The development of future oriented processes* (pp. 323-349). Chicago: University of Chicago Press.

Trabasso, T., Stein, N. L., & Johnson, L. R. (1981). Children's knowledge of events: A causal analysis of story structure. In G. Bower (Ed.), *Learning and motivation* (Vol. 15, pp. 237-281). New York: Academic Press.

Trabasso, T., Stein, N. L., Rodkin, P. C., Munger, G. P., & Baughn, C. (1992). Knowledge of goals and plans in the on-line narration of events. *Cognitive Development, 7*, 133-170.

Trabasso, T., & Suh, S. (1993). Understanding text: Achieving explanatory coherence through on-line inferences and mental operations in working memory. *Discourse Processes, 16*, 3-34.

Trabasso, T., Suh, S., & Payton, P. (1994). Explanatory coherence in communication about narrative understanding of events. In M. A. Gernsbacher & T. Givon (Eds.), *Text coherence as a mental entity* (pp. 189-214). Amsterdam: John Benjamins.

Trabasso, T., Suh, S., Payton, P., & Jain, R. (1994). Explanatory inferences and other strategies during comprehension and their effect on recall. In R. Lorch & E. O'Brien (Eds.), *Sources of coherence in text comprehension* (pp. 219-239). Hillsdale, NJ: Erlbaum.

Trabasso, T., & van den Broek, P. (1985). Causal thinking and the representation of narrative events. *Journal of Memory and Language, 24*, 612-630.

Trabasso, T., van den Broek, P., & Liu, L. (1988). A model for generating questions that assess and promote comprehension. *Question Exchange, 2*, 25-38.

Trabasso, T., van den Broek, P., & Suh, S. (1989). Logical necessity and transitivity of causal relations in stories. *Discourse Processes, 12*, 1-25.

van den Broek, P. W. (1988). The effect of causal relations and goal failure position on the importance of story statements. *Journal of Memory and Language*, *27*, 1–22.

Warren, W. H., Nicholas, D. W., & Trabasso, T. (1979). Event chains and inferences in understanding narratives. In R. O. Freedle (Ed.), *New directions in discourse processing: Vol. 2. Advances in discourse process* (pp. 25–52). Norwood, NJ: Ablex.

RESPONSE

# On Becoming Literate:
# The Many Sources
# of Success and Failure in Reading

## PAUL VAN DEN BROEK
*University of Minnesota*

Few areas of instruction have been investigated in as much detail as reading. The reasons for this are obvious. To be successful in modern society, it is virtually imperative that one be literate. Forms need to be filled out, information for everyday life is presented via print, and, perhaps most important, the vast majority of schooling takes place in a manner that depends heavily on students' ability to make sense of texts. Furthermore, for better or for worse, written materials have a profound effect on the socialization of individuals into our culture. For reasons such as these, reading has taken a prominent place in our educational systems and in research on those systems.

The chapters by Joseph Torgesen and Steven Hecht and by Tom Trabasso and Joseph Magliano represent two examples of this area of research. Torgesen and Hecht investigate the role that phonological processes — the processes by which individuals distinguish the sounds of the various phonemes and recognize the correspondences between orthographic symbols (such as letters) and sounds — play in successful reading. They show that students who have difficulty with these processes are likely to experience reading problems in future years. Indeed, phonological processing difficulties are the major source of failures to read in one large subgroup of students with reading disabilities. Through a combination of basic research, literature review, and systematic comparison of various instructional techniques, these authors provide a convincing argument that, at least for these readers, phonological processes are crucial and frequently are the source of failures to become fluent readers.

Trabasso and Magliano investigate a very different aspect of reading—how readers extract meaning from what they read. They show that successful comprehension of a text depends on the reader's ability to connect different parts of the text by means of inferences. Through careful analyses of the structure of texts and of the ways in which readers make inferences, Trabasso and Magliano provide us with a unique insight into the delicate interaction between a reader's prior knowledge and reading skills, properties of the texts, and comprehension. Furthermore, they demonstrate that these processes *during* reading have a direct and profound bearing on the ability to remember what was read. Good readers routinely engage in extensive inferential processes, and these processes not only allow them to understand but also to remember what they read.

At first glance, these chapters represent very different views of the reading process. Torgesen and Hecht concentrate on the development of basic processes in reading, that is, learning how to translate individual letters into individual sounds and how to combine sounds into words; Trabasso and Magliano focus on what one might describe as the end stages of successful reading, that is, the ability to place what one reads in the context of what one knows and, therefore, the construction of meaning. Furthermore, Trabasso and Magliano focus on relatively advanced readers who experience no particular problems in reading, whereas Torgesen and Hecht focus on beginning readers with reading disabilities. Despite these obvious differences, the two studies share many features and are complementary in important respects. Indeed, together they present a rather complete and detailed picture of the immensely complex process that we call reading.

In the following commentary, I first highlight some of the features of the "big picture" that I think are particularly important yet often neglected by advocates and policy makers in the area of reading. In the second section, I briefly explore some implications for educational practice. I conclude with some remarks on how we study reading and reading instruction.

## READING AND COMPREHENSION: INTERWOVEN PATHS OF DEVELOPMENT

Phonological skills and comprehension can be thought of as the beginning and ending points, respectively, of the development of reading skills. Phonological skills described by Torgesen and Hecht represent the first, hesitant steps of the reader on the path toward literacy. The child already is familiar with the sounds of his language and with the meaning of words but now has to recognize how "nonsense" symbols on paper or screen somehow translate into the very same sounds and hence represent meaning. Once this skill has been mastered, words can be identified and, eventually, combined into entire sentences. Subsequent to this point in the learning process, the comprehension processes described by Trabasso and Magliano form the bulk of development toward literacy. The beginning reader recognizes the meaningful relations between adjacent sentences and, eventually, between groups of sentences or entire texts. In this fashion, the reader gradually comes to fully appreciate the richness of texts and literature, finding correspondences between her own real-life experiences and what is presented in texts.

It is tempting to think of this development as linear, that is, with each step depending on the successful completion of the previous step. Indeed, most textbooks on literacy acquisition depict the process in this fashion. Such a depiction of the development of literacy, however, is too simplistic. There are two major reasons for this. First, at any point during reading, we rely on both phonological and comprehension processes, regardless of whether we are beginning or advanced readers. The emphasis at a particular point during reading may be on one or the other of these processes, but rarely, if ever, do they take place in isolation from each other. Second, when a child is first exposed to written language, he draws on (usually extensive) prior knowledge of the language in its oral form, both of sounds and of meaning. Let me briefly elaborate on these two reasons.

As Torgesen and Hecht point out, the development of phonological skills benefits from, indeed is dependent on, a child's understanding of the context. A meaningful context helps the child acquire phonological skills in several ways. First, it enhances the child's motivation and pleasure derived from learning to read. Second, the presence of the context teaches the child that the phonological processes are only one component of a much larger process rather than an end in and of themselves. Third, and most important, the meaningful context *directly* influences the acquisition of phonological skills. It gives the child feedback about her phonological awareness (i.e., it tells the child whether the way in which she has translated the written symbols into sounds and meaning makes sense), and it provides crucial *scaffolding*: The meaningful context allows the child to make educated guesses about the sounds of letters or words that she does not recognize.

The interdependence between phonological skills and comprehension also holds in the opposite direction. As Trabasso and Magliano state, the ability to comprehend a text always depends on the ability to identify the meaning of words and individual sentences. Unless a minimum of words is identified, comprehension processes have nothing to work with and hence are due to fail. Furthermore, if comprehension fails, the reader can fall back on his word decoding skills to make sense of the text. This aspect of the interdependence is perhaps most easily grasped in the context of second language reading (e.g., Horiba, 1993; Horiba, van den Broek, & Fletcher, 1993). When confronted with a moderately difficult text, second language readers engage in *both* higher-level comprehension activities and lower-level phonological processes more often than do native readers. Thus, on the one hand they fall back on their phonological decoding skills to try to recognize or decompose unknown words, while on the other hand they rely heavily on their comprehension processes to try to "fill in" missing information. There is extensive evidence that similar processes occur in first language readers (cf. Adams & Bruck, 1995; Perfetti & Zhang, Chapter 3, this volume).

The depiction of the acquisition of literacy as a linear path from phonological processes to comprehension is simplistic in yet another way. As Trabasso and Magliano point out, a child's comprehension skills have begun to develop long before the child is able to read, even at the most basic level. There is ample evidence (van den Broek, Bauer, & Bourg, 1996) that the development of comprehension skills begins in early infancy and has reached considerable levels of sophistication by the time the child is in the preschool years. Moreover, the correspondence between these preschool (perhaps more appropriately, "extra-school") comprehension skills and the skills used during reading comprehension is overwhelming. Thus, the child does not come to her first reading experiences as a "tabula rasa," a blank slate, that perhaps is eager to learn how to read but has few skills to go on. [1]

The picture of reading development that emerges is one of the simultaneous and interwoven development of many different skills. As one skill (e.g., phonological awareness) develops, it draws heavily on accomplishments with respect to other skills (e.g., comprehension); in turn, the latter skills benefit from the development of the former. Moreover, many skills, such as comprehension, are bound to undergo strong development outside of the domain of reading. In all, the attainment of literacy consists of the coming together of many skills at the same time. Individual readers, even those with similar "overall" reading ability, differ in their strengths and weaknesses in these skills. As a result, they rely on the different skills to various degrees. Furthermore, for some readers continued improvement in reading depends on the further development of one skill, whereas for others it depends on the development of another.

## INDIVIDUAL DIFFERENCES IN READING:
## IMPLICATIONS FOR INSTRUCTION

The view that reading consists of the simultaneous application of many different skills has important implications for our understanding of the successes and failures that readers experience as well as for the kinds of educational programs that we should implement. The reason for this is that in reading, as in all cognitive activities, there are many roads that lead to Rome: There are many paths to successful reading and hence many paths to successful reading instruction. On the one hand, failures to read may result from deficiencies in any of the subskills of literacy. On the other hand, readers with strong skills in one facet of reading are bound to be able to compensate for possible weaknesses with respect to other skills. We already have seen, for example, how second language readers use their comprehension and inferential skills to compensate for a lack of vocabulary and word identification skills. Thus, it is true that readers not only can fail to accomplish literacy for many different reasons, but also can succeed for different reasons.

Individual differences in reading skills are nicely illustrated in the two chapters. Individual differences in comprehension is the central topic of the chapter by Trabasso and Magliano. They demonstrate how individual differences at one level, that is, inference making during reading, directly affects performance at another level, that is, the ability to remember the text. Torgesen and Hecht note that they observed striking individual differences not only in the skill levels of individual children but also in the learning patterns for these skills. Although they did not directly explore individual differences in their chapter, their detailed description of the components of basic reading skills lays the foundation for future study of individual differences in phonological skills.

An analogy may help illustrate the importance of individual differences. Consider a successful basketball team. All the players on the team may be considered excellent basketball players, yet they each derive the label "excellent" from different skills. One player may have excellent dribbling skills but, relatively speaking, poor passing skills. Another player may be a great shooter but may be too short to be an effective rebounder. Like the basketball players, readers can become "excellent" by developing different skills. Some have great vocabulary-access skills and can read difficult texts without problems. Others have great ability to commit what they read to memory and to remember and apply it after long periods of time. A third group may have great intratextual inferential skills and may be able to see connections between different parts of the text that remain obscure to most other readers. As a final example, some readers may have great ability to integrate what they read with their world knowledge and personal experience. Thus, "excellence" can be attained in different ways.

The analogy illustrates several other points. First, although the basketball players derive their excellence from different sources, they all have minimal achievement in each skill. They must possess minimal ball-handling skills, awareness of the other players, and so on. Even tall players must have at least some dribbling skills, and short players must be able to rebound to some extent. Likewise, excellent readers must possess at least minimal achievement in each reading skill. For example, although comprehension skills can partially compensate for a lack in word identification skills, and vice versa, this compensation cannot be complete. We *all* need some achievement in all skills, such as decoding and comprehension, to be able to understand what we read. Second, achievement of excellence in one area may interfere with excellence in another. For example, as a basketball player develops superb individual skills, she may become less of a team player. This applies even more strongly to reading, where skills actually may be inversely related. For example, people who have great skills integrating what they read with their prior knowledge are less likely to have complete and accurate memory for surface features of the text, such as the exact words used (van Dijk & Kintsch, 1983). Finally, occasionally a player joins the team who deserves the label "excellent" in virtually every aspect of the game. Likewise, some readers develop superb skills in every aspect of reading. Expecting all players or readers to reach those levels, however, sets students and instructors alike up for failure. Not every excellent basketball player needs to be a Michael Jordan, nor does every successful reader need to be a literary critic.

An understanding of the complex interactions in literacy has important implications for educational practice. Perhaps the most important implication is that "one-fits-all" instructional programs are doomed to fail in practice. To return to our basketball analogy, it would be silly to spend precious workout time training a 5'2" player in rebounding skills or a 7-foot center in dribbling skills. Educational researchers and policy makers often seem to propose just such a one-fits-all instructional program. In the area of reading, for example, the debate between proponents of phonics and those of whole language pits two one-fits-all programs against each other. Both common sense and the results of research, such as the studies presented in this volume, show the fruitlessness of such a debate between extremes. Sadly, of course, students with different needs and different strengths and weaknesses are the victims of such polarized debates. On the bright side, as Torgesen and Hecht note, most teachers have more common sense and adopt hybrid models of instruction on their own.

In the context of the current discussion this means, for example, that there will be beginning students who have sufficient comprehension skills to be immersed in written language without extensive training in decoding skills and who, via the application of their comprehension skills, will be able to become fluent and literate readers. Other beginning readers, however, may benefit from explicit training in some component skills. In our basketball analogy, some beginning players — perhaps those that have experience with other similar sports — simply can be given a ball and put on a basketball court, whereas others would benefit from some basic exercises in dribbling and shooting skills. In the end, though, all players and readers need to have acquired minimal levels of proficiency in all component skills. [2]

## THE SCIENTIFIC STUDY OF READING
## AND EDUCATIONAL PRACTICE

The research presented in these two chapters provides important insights into literacy and its many components. It illustrates that a firm understanding of what literacy is, is a crucial step toward the development of instructional techniques. As we have seen, such an understanding brings to the foreground the enormous individual differences that exist among readers, even within a particular skill level. It also provides insights into the remediation of problems. For example, Trabasso and Magliano show that individual ability to remember a text may be a direct result of differences in the inferential processes in which readers engage. In these cases, training in comprehension monitoring and inference making during reading will be more beneficial than direct training and instruction in memory skills. Similarly, Torgesen and Hecht demonstrate that failure to sound out words in many cases is related to a child's underdeveloped awareness of phonological distinctions. Here, too, instruction and practice in the component skill is more likely to be successful than training in the composite skill. These examples illustrate how an understanding of the reading process can help us implement effective reading programs. Teachers as well as researchers should be exposed in their training to what we know about the reading process. They, as well as the aspiring readers whom they teach, deserve it.

As studies such as these illuminate the complexity of reading, it becomes clear that one-fits-all instructional techniques have reached the end of their effectiveness. Beginning readers are individuals with enormously varying constellations of skills and weaknesses. Educational programs should reflect this richness and variety rather than attempt to mold every child into the same instructional straightjacket. Within the practical confines of a classroom situation, the opportunity for individualizing instruction are, of course, limited. This does not dictate, however, that instruction be completely individualized but rather that the program be flexible enough to allow individuals to work on different skills as they need them. Thus, this commentary can be read as an urgent plea to give teachers the training, flexibility, and authority to adjust their curricular programs to fit their students' needs. It is only then that our beginning readers can travel one of the many roads to Rome and attain their destination, literacy.

ACKNOWLEDGMENT. I would like to thank Chris Espin, Michael Graves, and Chris Larson for their comments on an earlier draft of this chapter.

## REFERENCES

Adams, M. J., & Bruck, M. (1995). Resolving the "great debate." *American Educator*, *19*, 7, 10–20.

Horiba, Y. (1993). The role of causal reasoning and language competence in narrative comprehension. *Studies in Second Language Acquisition*, *15*, 49–81.

Horiba, Y., van den Broek, P., & Fletcher, C. R. (1993). Second language readers' memory for narrative texts: Evidence for structure-preserving top-down processing. *Language Learning*, *43*, 345–372.

van Dijk, T. A., & Kintsch, W. (1983). *Strategies of discourse comprehension*. New York: Academic Press.

van den Broek, P., Bauer, P., & Bourg, T. (Eds.). (1996). *Developmental spans in event comprehension: Bridging fictional and actual events*. Hillsdale, NJ: Erlbaum.

## NOTES

1. Indeed, many children may develop sufficient decoding skills even outside of formal education so that they need little or no explicit instruction in such skills in school. This has tempted researchers to draw the erroneous conclusion that these children do not use or need such skills.

2. The determination of exactly what are the "minimal levels of proficiency" for the various component skills is problematic. Tests of skills such as comprehension and decoding tell us only where students stand *relative to each other*, not in terms of absolute absence or presence of the skill. Yet, arguments (e.g., the debate over phonics and whole language instruction) often seem to reduce exactly to such absolute statements: whether decoding skills are *necessary* or "merely" very useful for literacy, whether comprehension skills can be *sufficient* for successful reading or always require other, more basic skills. For both logical and practical reasons, issues about the "extremes" of successful reading may never be resolved. Moreover, focus on these theoretical issues, although interesting, has little relevance for the vast majority of students, who fall in between these extremes. It is safe to assume that most, if not all, students need minimal proficiency in all component skills.

# PART IV

# TEACHER DEVELOPMENT AND CLASSROOM ASSESSMENT

CHAPTER 8

# Improving the Literacy Achievement of Low-Income Students of Diverse Backgrounds

KATHRYN H. AU
CLAIRE L. ASAM
*University of Hawaii*

What can be done in American schools to bring low-income students of diverse backgrounds to high levels of literacy? The term low-income students of diverse backgrounds is used here to refer to students of African American, Asian American, Hispanic American, and Native American backgrounds who are from low-income families and come to school speaking a home language other than standard English. These students may be contrasted with students of mainstream backgrounds in terms of their ethnicity, social class, and primary language. The gap between the literacy achievement of these two groups of students has long been documented (Coleman et al., 1966). Furthermore, demographic studies indicate that a steadily increasing number of low-income students of diverse backgrounds will be entering the schools well into the next century (Pallas, Natriello, & McDill, 1989).

A major influence shaping American education today is the standards movement (Pearson, 1993), which is being watched carefully by educators concerned about the literacy achievement of disadvantaged students of diverse backgrounds. Some fear that the standards movement will have a detrimental effect on the learning opportunities of this group of students. For example, the standards movement might lead to a valuing only of

English language development, thus stifling programs that encourage students to read and write in their first language (Garcia, 1993).

Proponents of the standards movement suggest that students of diverse backgrounds can benefit from national discussions that will make standards for literacy achievement public and accessible to all groups (Pearson, 1993). They argue that this situation would be preferable to the present one, in which standards exist but are kept implicit, understood by those from mainstream backgrounds but not by others. In addition, in the movement toward whole language and other holistic approaches to literacy instruction, teachers may lack a clear sense of the goals they should have for students' learning. Broad standards, consistent with holistic approaches, might assist teachers in directing instruction toward major outcomes.

Issues of standards and holistic curricula figured very prominently in recent work at the Kamehameha Elementary Education Program (KEEP), as we explored the question of how best to address the literacy achievement gap of young Native Hawaiian students in low-income communities (for reports of earlier work, see Tharp & Gallimore, 1988; Tharp et al., 1984). In the elementary grades, these students as a group typically score in the lowest quartile on standardized tests of reading achievement. As a long-term research and development effort, in operation from 1971 to 1994, KEEP sought to bring about change in student achievement by helping public school teachers improve their effectiveness in literacy instruction.

KEEP's work was central to our professional lives for more than 20 years. We were hired as educational specialists at KEEP shortly after graduation from college. We spent our first years working in a laboratory school with one class each at kindergarten through third grade. We taught in the classroom for about half the day and spent the rest of the time either coaching other teachers or working with researchers. Most of our students lived in public housing projects and were from families receiving welfare. During our years in the classroom, we came to realize that these students had the intellectual ability to succeed in school but learned best with forms of instruction that departed from typical school patterns (Au & Mason, 1983; Jordan, 1985).

Our teaching experiences, even as rank beginners, were extraordinarily public. From the observation deck of the laboratory school, staff members and visitors could watch us teach at any time. We grew accustomed to being videotaped, studying our own teaching, and discussing our successes and failures with others. The KEEP research staff taught us the approaches to data collection and analysis used in their fields, which included psychology, anthropology, and linguistics. Our experiences ranged from coding behavior in 30-second intervals to conducting fieldwork with families in public housing projects.

After working as educational specialists, we moved within KEEP in somewhat different career directions. Kathy focused on curriculum development and classroom-based research. Claire worked as a consultant, helping teachers to become more expert in language arts instruction, then directed efforts to disseminate KEEP's work to 10 public schools.

## A BRIEF HISTORY OF KEEP

In this section we look at the work at KEEP, with a focus on its most recent changes. We begin with a discussion of our theoretical perspective, move to a discussion of the initial program and the need for changes, then describe KEEP's efforts to develop a more effective approach, requiring changes in three components: curriculum, assessment, and teacher development. We next provide the context for changes in these components by outlining events that occurred over a 5-year period. We conclude with practical implications and suggestions for further research.

### THEORETICAL PERSPECTIVE: SOCIAL CONSTRUCTIVISM

We approached the three components of curriculum, assessment, and teacher development from the perspective of constructivism, in particular social constructivism (see Schwandt, 1994). The central concern of constructivism is lived experience, or the world as it is understood by social actors. Social constructivism is based on the principle that both social and cognitive structures originate and are situated in interactions among people (Mehan, 1981). Social constructivists argue that reality is created through processes of social exchange, and they are interested in the collective generation of meaning among people.

The theorist who has had the greatest influence on literacy researchers working from a social constructivist perspective is, of course, Vygotsky (Hiebert, 1991). Vygotsky saw the focus of psychology as the study of consciousness or mind, and he wanted to discover how higher or "artificial" mental functions — such as literacy — developed from the "natural" psychological functions that emerged through maturation (Rosa & Montero, 1990). Vygotsky's view of consciousness included two subcomponents, intellect and affect, which he regarded as inseparable (Wertsch, 1985). In keeping with social constructivism, we too believed that cognitive and affective factors were equally important to development in students' literacy learning and in teachers' becoming experts in language arts instruction.

Vygotsky took a holistic approach to learning and insisted on the study of higher mental functions in all their complexity (Moll, 1990; Wertsch,

1985). He rejected a reductionist approach, the idea that higher mental functions result from the accumulation of primitive psychological mechanisms (Moll, 1990). In our view, the social constructivist perspective implies that learners need to engage in authentic literacy activities, not activities contrived for practice. A closely related position is taken by advocates of whole language (Goodman, 1986), who suggest that school literacy activities should involve the full processes of reading and writing rather than the practice of skills in isolation. Similarly, we believed that teacher development activities should revolve around teachers' ongoing instructional experiences in the classroom.

Vygotsky proposed that the internalization of higher mental functions, such as literacy, involved a movement from performance assisted by others to performance controlled by the individual. The concept of the *zone of proximal development* is central to his views of the social origin of higher mental functions. This zone is the "difference between the child's actual level of development and the level of performance that he achieves in collaboration with the adult" (Vygotsky, 1987, p. 209). According to his theory, a child's learning is mediated by interactions with adults or knowledgeable peers. A teacher's learning is similarly mediated by interactions with knowledgeable others. For teachers, learning can take place through scaffolding provided by other educators and through involvement in a system of support for professional development.

## The Initial Program, Expansion, and the Need for Change

From 1972 to 1978, KEEP staff members worked on developing an effective reading program in the laboratory school. In 1978, when the laboratory school program had begun to show good results, dissemination efforts to two public schools began. Over the next decade, the program expanded steadily. By 1988, KEEP was serving 137 teachers and 2,896 students in grades K–6 in nine public schools on three islands.

Standardized achievement test scores were monitored each year, and over time it became apparent that the promising results obtained with first- and second-grade students did not hold past third grade. By sixth grade, the majority of students scored in stanines 1, 2, and 3; and virtually no students received scores in stanines 7, 8, and 9. In the fall of 1988, a report critical of KEEP's results was issued by the Northwest Regional Laboratory, under a contract with the Hawaii State Department of Education. As a result, policy makers at KEEP's home institution, the Kamehameha schools, asked that changes in the program be made as quickly as possible. We began planning for a new curriculum and related assessment system in the spring of 1989, with implementation scheduled for the fall. As will be seen, bringing about changes in classrooms to reflect the new curriculum and assessment system required considerable time, and high levels of program implementation occurred only after changes were made in the model of teacher development.

## Changes in Curriculum: 1989

In this section, we discuss the first component to be changed, the curriculum. We developed a new curriculum consistent with a social constructivist perspective on literacy, teaching, and learning.

*Before.* The KEEP curriculum in place from 1978 to 1988, called the Kamehameha Reading Objectives System (KROS), drew on behavioral and early cognitive views rather than notions of learning and literacy stemming from social constructivism. KROS resembled other skills-oriented curricula in focusing on the cognitive strategies and skills used by effective readers. However, it differed from conventional curricula of its time in emphasizing reading comprehension, rather than word identification, as the basis for beginning reading (Au et al., 1986; Crowell, 1981).

*After.* Given the social constructivist perspective, we wanted the whole literacy curriculum to be broader in scope than KROS. We thought it should emphasize writing as well as reading, since both appear to be of equal importance in children's literacy development, and since learning to write can have positive effects on learning to read (Shanahan, 1990). The KROS curriculum paid little attention to students' will or motivation to use their reading skills independently. In the whole literacy curriculum, we decided to highlight the affective as well as cognitive dimensions of students' literacy development.

The whole literacy curriculum addressed six aspects of literacy:

1. ownership
2. reading comprehension
3. writing process
4. language and vocabulary knowledge
5. word reading strategies and spelling
6. voluntary reading

The first aspect of the curriculum, ownership, was also the overarching goal of the curriculum. Ownership has to do with students valuing their own ability to read and write. Students who have ownership of literacy have a positive attitude toward reading and writing and routinely use reading and writing in their everyday lives.

The next aspect of the curriculum is reading comprehension. In the whole literacy curriculum, reading comprehension was seen to involve a dynamic interaction among the reader, the text, and the situation or social context in which reading takes place (Wixson, Peters, Weber, & Roeber, 1987). Similarly, use of the term writing process for the third aspect of the curriculum conveyed that writing was seen as dynamic and nonlinear, including such activities as planning, drafting, revising, editing, and publishing (Graves, 1983).

The fourth aspect of the curriculum, word reading strategies and spelling, drew on Clay's (1985) notion that effective word identification requires the simultaneous use of information from different cue systems. Children must learn to take a problem-solving approach, cross-checking their responses with information available from meaning (i.e., passage and sentence context), structural, and visual cues.

Language and vocabulary knowledge, the fifth aspect of the curriculum, involves the ability to understand and use appropriate terms and structures in both spoken and printed English. It includes the ability to learn the meanings of new words. The whole literacy curriculum followed an approach to vocabulary consistent with the knowledge hypothesis (Mezynski, 1983), the idea that vocabulary represents a person's knowledge of particular topics as opposed to dictionary-style definitions.

In voluntary reading, the final aspect of the curriculum, students select the materials they wish to read for either information or pleasure. Ideally, students also choose the times when they will read (Spiegel, 1981). While the terms recreational or independent reading refer to similar concepts, voluntary reading is perhaps better for capturing the idea of students being motivated to read on their own.

In short, the whole literacy curriculum placed writing at the same level of importance as reading and gave equal attention to the affective and cognitive dimensions of literacy, in keeping with a social constructivist perspective.

In most classrooms, instruction in the whole literacy curriculum occurred in two blocks of time called the writers' workshop and the readers' workshop. The writers' workshop typically began with a minilesson and teacher and student sharing, followed by a period when students could write on their own (Calkins, with Harwayne, 1991; Graves, 1983). Teacher and peer conferences occurred during this time. Near the end of the workshop, the teacher generally gathered the students together for the author's chair (Graves & Hansen, 1983), a time when one or two students read aloud their drafts or published books to the class.

The organization of the readers' workshop varied more than that of the writers' workshop, due primarily to the teacher's decision about when to schedule sustained silent reading and teacher read-alouds. The workshop often began with the teacher reading aloud or conducting a minilesson. Then, the teacher met with students in small groups to discuss works of literature. Teachers used different approaches to grouping. In the primary grades, students were grouped by ability about half the time, and by interest (for example, in reading a particular book or in doing research on a particular topic) the rest of the time. In the upper grades, students were usually grouped by interest. Small-group discussions generally began with students sharing their writing in response to literature. When not meeting with the teacher, students read independently or with a partner, wrote in their literature response logs, and worked on individual and small-group projects. (For further information about the writers' and readers' workshops, see Au, Blake, Carroll, Oshiro, & Scheu, 1993.)

A feature that remained unchanged in KEEP's shift to a whole literacy curriculum was cultural responsiveness in instruction. Culturally responsive instruction allows students to achieve academic goals through means consistent with the values and standards for behavior of the home culture (Au, 1993b). For example, many Hawaiian families attach great value to the well-being of the extended family or *'ohana*. The ability to work with others for the good of the family is judged more important than a person's individual achievements. In contrast, schools typically place greater value on individual achievement. Three specific aspects of culturally responsive instruction played a prominent part in both KROS and the whole literacy curriculum: peer teaching–learning interactions (Jordan, 1985), a style of classroom management described as "a smile with teeth" (D'Amato, 1988), and the talk story style of discussion (Au & Kawakami, 1985). (For more information about culturally responsive instruction, see Au & Kawakami, 1994.)

## CHANGES IN ASSESSMENT: 1989

Along with curriculum changes, we found it necessary to make changes in our approach to assessment. We moved from a criterion-referenced system to a portfolio system anchored to grade-level benchmarks.

*Before.* In the earlier KROS curriculum, students' learning had been assessed through multiple-choice, criterion-referenced tests consistent with the principles of mastery learning (Bloom, 1976), and the effects of the program had been evaluated through standardized tests. With the change to the whole literacy curriculum, the need for new forms of assessment became obvious.

*After.* We knew that evaluation of the whole literacy curriculum would require methods of assessment and evaluation that took a holistic view of the reading and writing processes, rather than the narrower, skills-oriented view reflected in standardized tests. The whole literacy curriculum involved students in activities that called for the actual use of reading and writing (e.g., reading a work of literature, composing a personal narrative) rather than the practice of skills.

We looked for the answer in some form of portfolio assessment. Portfolio assessment can serve different purposes, such as documenting students' progress over a period of time or showcasing their best work (e.g., Wolf, LeMahieu, & Eresh, 1992). Because we were under considerable pressure to demonstrate the effectiveness of the whole literacy curriculum, we designed the KEEP portfolio assessment system to address issues of program evaluation. To fulfill this purpose, our portfolio assessment system was anchored to standards, which we termed grade-level benchmarks. Thus, we undertook on a small scale the task of evaluating portfolios with respect to standards. This process eventually may be carried out on a grand scale in the United States, if assessment moves in the direction described by Pearson (1993), with districts and states electing to use portfolios anchored to national standards.

The KEEP benchmarks described the desired achievements of the hypothetical average student at the end of each grade level. The sources for the benchmarks were (1) the language arts curriculum guide issued by the Hawaii State Department of Education, (2) the reading objectives of the National Assessment of Educational Progress (1989), (3) a well-known standardized test series used in the state's testing program for elementary schools, and (4) recently published basal reading, language arts, and literature programs. In areas not traditionally evaluated, such as ownership and voluntary reading, we developed benchmarks based on the available research.

We took care to state the benchmarks in terms that reflected the philosophy of the whole literacy curriculum, so our benchmarks did not look like outcomes in a skills-oriented approach. Still, we wanted the benchmarks to be specific enough to provide guidance to teachers. In the area of writing (ownership of writing and the writing process), we developed 10 benchmarks for kindergarten, rising to 38 by sixth grade, with comparable numbers in the area of reading (ownership of reading, reading comprehension, language and vocabulary knowledge, word reading strategies, and voluntary reading).

For example, benchmarks for ownership of writing at the third-grade level included the following:

- Shows interest in others' writing
- Writes outside of school

Third-grade benchmarks for the writing process included:

- Selects own topics for writing
- Tries to make writing interesting for the reader
- Writes in two formats (e.g., stories, plays, poetry)

Among the reading comprehension benchmarks at third grade were the following:

- Shares written responses to literature in a small group
- Comprehends and writes about theme/author's message
- Writes a summary that includes story elements

As these sample benchmarks indicate, we believed process to be important. However, we also were concerned about product. Thus, we included a benchmark indicating that the holistic quality of students' writing samples had to be judged at grade level with respect to an anchor piece. Similarly, to be rated at grade level in reading comprehension, students' instructional reading level (as judged from the difficulty of works read and discussed during small-group instruction) had to reflect grade-level performance (e.g., a reading level of $3^2$ [third grade, second semester] for the end of third grade).

Students' performance in the six aspects of literacy could be measured against the benchmarks, and their performance rated as above, at, or below grade level. This made it possible to aggregate data across classrooms and report program results in terms of the number of students above, at, or below grade level for each aspect of literacy. (For a full discussion of the portfolio assessment system, see Au, 1994; Au, Blake, Carroll, Oshiro, & Scheu, 1993.)

Although its primary purpose was program evaluation, KEEP's portfolio assessment system also gave teachers detailed information about students' progress and so could foster improved instruction in all aspects of literacy. In addition, the system allowed students to become aware of the expectations for their grade level, to set their own goals, and to monitor their own progress.

## CHANGES IN TEACHER DEVELOPMENT: 1989

The final component requiring change was that of teacher development. In this area we moved from an expert–novice model to a collaborative, problem-solving approach.

*Before.* KEEP's initial teacher development efforts were based on the triadic model developed for the treatment of clients by clinical psychologists (Tharp & Wetzel, 1969). In the triadic model, the clinician does not bring about change by working directly with the client but instead utilizes natural relationships, working through a person or persons influential in the client's life. For example, if the client is a child, the clinician works with the child's parents in order to effect change in the behavior of the child. Following this model, KEEP did not provide direct services to students but sought to improve students' literacy learning by working with classroom teachers. Through the development of the teacher's expertise, student learning and achievement would be facilitated. This model was economical (compared with a direct services model that would affect only 25 students) because a KEEP staff member working with eight public school teachers might bring about improved achievement in a group of 160 or more students.

Once a school elected to become involved with KEEP, teachers volunteered to participate in the program. Each volunteer was then assigned to a KEEP consultant, who usually worked with eight to 10 teachers. The consultants were experienced teachers who had completed a one-year course of study to become proficient both in the KEEP curriculum and in approaches for furthering teacher development.

The work of the consultants involved primarily the following activities, conducted on a one-to-one basis with teachers: observation of students and teachers in classrooms, data collection, data analysis, and individual meetings with teachers to discuss observations.

One feature of this clinical approach was that, as in most traditional teacher education approaches, the consultants spent more time providing information and less time working with teachers on collaborative problem solving. This approach to dissemination proved effective in enabling most teachers to implement the majority of features considered essential to the KROS curriculum (Au & Blake, 1984). Yet, although the teacher–consultant relationship was generally a positive and supportive one, it did not tend to foster feelings of equality or to promote teachers' sense of responsibility for their own professional development (Giuli, 1985).

A second feature of the clinical approach was that it led consultants to devote the greatest amount of time to teachers with the lowest levels of expertise. Most of the KEEP schools experienced high levels of teacher turnover. The rate could be as high as 33% in a given school and averaged 20% a year across all KEEP schools. There was a constant influx of new teachers, often recent college graduates sorely in need of help with the basics of classroom organization and management. Consultants worked effectively with these new teachers, who seemed readily to accept a more directive form of assistance. Consultants seemed less sure about how to structure experiences to work effectively with veteran teachers and tended to feel their services would be of little benefit to these teachers.

*After.* We decided to try a new model of teacher development, after the old model proved ineffective in helping teachers to achieve high levels of expertise in the whole literacy curriculum. In the new model, we asked consultants to focus on the teachers most capable of achieving high levels of implementation, rather than on the teachers most in need of assistance. Consultants engaged teachers in goal setting and supported them in reaching their goals. Rather than giving answers, consultants sought to involve teachers in collaborative problem solving related to the whole literacy curriculum. Further details of the new model of teacher development are provided below, as we turn to a chronology that shows the relationships among the three components of change — curriculum, assessment, and teacher development — over time.

## THE STRUGGLE FOR CHANGE AND ITS EFFECTS: 1989-1994

The chronology of changes during KEEP's efforts to implement the whole literacy curriculum can be divided into distinct phases: (1) an effort to bring about a change in philosophy, (2) a failed large-scale implementation effort, and (3) a successful small-scale effort termed the demonstration classroom project.

### YEAR 1: WRESTLING WITH THE CHANGE IN PHILOSOPHY

As mentioned earlier, under pressure to institute a new and more effective program, KEEP staff members worked throughout the spring of 1989 to develop the new, whole literacy curriculum and portfolio assessment system. The goal was to begin implementation of the new program the following fall. This tight timeline did not permit an adequate degree of collaboration with KEEP staff working in the schools and with cooperating public school teachers.

Disagreements soon surfaced on many levels. Consultants and teachers alike wrestled with the paradigm shift to new ways of thinking about teaching, learning, and literacy. Many teachers felt they had experienced success with the previous KROS curriculum and were reluctant to change. Consultants did not feel prepared to facilitate change since they, too, had a stake in the previous curriculum and had not had adequate time to learn about and become confident in their knowledge of the new, whole literacy curriculum. Teachers experienced difficulty conducting a readers' workshop or a writers' workshop, and consultants were uncertain about how to assist them. Because they were struggling with so many issues of classroom organization and instruction, consultants and teachers did not attempt to implement portfolio assessment during Year 1.

Somewhat surprisingly, the grade-level benchmarks provoked relatively little discussion. Because of their experience with KROS, the teachers were accustomed to behavioral objectives and criterion-referenced testing and did not object to the outcomes represented by the benchmarks. In general, they judged the benchmarks to be at appropriate levels of difficulty for the various grades. However, many teachers did not think it possible for the majority of their students to achieve at the level indicated by the benchmarks. The issue of teacher expectations is an important one and will receive further discussion below.

During Year 1, we gave no thought to changing the model of teacher development, and consultants continued to work with teachers following the clinical model. However, consultants quickly discovered that their lack of familiarity with the whole literacy curriculum made it difficult to continue in the role of answer givers. Unfortunately, during Years 1, 2, and 3, our response was to provide consultants with workshops to strengthen their knowledge of the whole literacy curriculum, rather than to change the model of teacher development.

## YEARS 2 AND 3: ATTEMPTS TO IMPLEMENT A WHOLE LITERACY CURRICULUM

During these 2 years, teachers and consultants became comfortable with the new curriculum philosophy and settled down to working out the details of conducting effective writers' workshops and readers' workshops. Gradually, teachers and consultants began to understand how the workshops would look at different grade levels. Students appeared productively engaged during both the readers' and writers' workshops, learning to take the initiative in reading books of their own choosing and writing on topics of their own choosing. Teachers and consultants consistently commented on the students' positive attitudes toward reading and writing.

During Year 2, consultants managed to collect portfolio assessment data for the first time. Many consultants did not ask teachers to become involved because they felt teachers faced an already overwhelming task in conducting the readers' and writers' workshops. Figure 8.1 shows the results for grade 3, which are representative of the results obtained at all grades. As the figure shows, portfolio assessment results for Year 2 were decidedly mixed (for details, see Au, 1994). Students showed promise in three aspects of literacy: ownership, voluntary reading, and word reading strategies (the

FIGURE 8.1. Year 2, grade 3 results.

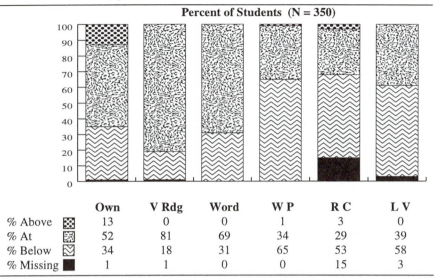

| | | Own | V Rdg | Word | W P | R C | L V |
|---|---|---|---|---|---|---|---|
| % Above | | 13 | 0 | 0 | 1 | 3 | 0 |
| % At | | 52 | 81 | 69 | 34 | 29 | 39 |
| % Below | | 34 | 18 | 31 | 65 | 53 | 58 |
| % Missing | | 1 | 1 | 0 | 0 | 15 | 3 |

three bars on the left of the graph). Half the students or more were rated at or above grade level in these aspects of literacy. However, approximately two-thirds of the students were rated below grade level on the other three aspects of literacy: the writing process, reading comprehension, and language and vocabulary knowledge (the three bars on the right). Apparently, the change to the whole literacy curriculum had encouraged students to develop positive attitudes toward literacy and to do more independent reading. Also, perhaps because the volume of reading increased, they became more skillful in word reading strategies. However, they did not make substantial gains in the more intellectually demanding aspects of literacy, including composing their own texts and interpreting the texts of others.

We attributed the poor results obtained in Year 2 to a lack of experience with the whole literacy curriculum, on our part as well as that of the teachers. We believed that Year 3 would yield improved results, as we and the teachers developed a better understanding of classroom practices in the whole literacy curriculum. Teachers' involvement with portfolio assessment increased during Year 3, although consultants continued to bear the bulk of responsibility for data collection.

Other KEEP staff members and the teachers were certain that Year 3 would bring improved results in student achievement. Unfortunately, the results for Year 3 were virtually identical to those for Year 2, with roughly two-thirds of the students continuing to perform below the grade-level benchmarks for the writing process, reading comprehension, and language and vocabulary knowledge. The situation clearly called for change.

## YEARS 4 AND 5: THE DEMONSTRATION CLASSROOM PROJECT

The poor results obtained in Years 2 and 3 led to our decision to revamp KEEP's model of teacher development. The changes were centered on what we termed the demonstration classroom project. The goal during Year 4 became that of demonstrating that the whole literacy curriculum, when fully implemented, could make a difference in students' achievement as measured by the portfolio assessment system. Our assumption was that the whole literacy curriculum had not yet received a fair test, due to spotty implementation. If the curriculum failed this test, we were prepared to go back to the drawing board.

*New implementation strategy.* For the previous 3 years, the consultants had tried to achieve across-the-board implementation of the whole literacy curriculum, working with all teachers, including those with little or no experience in the profession. For Year 4, we decided instead to adopt a strategy described by Peters and Waterman (1982) as that of "small wins," building on the expertise of the small group of people most likely to be successful. Instead of trying to achieve across-the-board implementation of the whole literacy curriculum, which had resulted in mediocre levels of implementation in all classrooms, we aimed for full implementation of either the readers' workshop or the writers' workshop in just a handful of classrooms. During a visit to KEEP, Jan Turbill and Brian Cambourne from the University of Wollongong, educators experienced in assisting teachers in the transition to whole language, described the process to us succinctly: "Go with the goers." That became our motto.

At the beginning of Year 4, we asked each consultant to select the one teacher, from those assigned to her, who was most likely to achieve full implementation of the whole literacy curriculum that year. As noted above, we further narrowed the focus of teacher development by asking consultants to work with their teachers on either the writers' workshop or the readers' workshop, because we had come to believe that the task of learning to manage both at once, along with portfolio assessment, was too complex. We presented this strategy to consultants as a process of rebuilding the program at their schools, starting with just one teacher.

We saw the strategy of focusing on these teachers, whom we called demonstration teachers, as having several possible advantages. First, we needed to give the curriculum a fair test, and these were the teachers who could help us do so. We planned to monitor closely the student achievement results obtained in their classrooms. Second, in collaboration with the consultants, these teachers could work out many of the details of the readers' and writers' workshops. The demonstration teacher and the consultant could then share this information with other teachers. We hoped the demonstration teachers eventually would lead networks of teachers, all working toward full implementation of the whole literacy curriculum. Finally, following Peters and Waterman, we felt it important to prove that success was possible. If the demonstration teachers succeeded, their example would be an inspiration to other teachers.

Most consultants disagreed with this strategy, which was diametrically opposed to the previous approach of providing help primarily to the least experienced teachers. Consultants worried about an elitist system in which services were provided only to a select group. Our argument was that teachers who appeared able to achieve the greatest gains in students' learning, through full implementation of the curriculum, should be supported in doing so. Other teachers would receive this degree of support when they, too, were ready to contribute at the same level. Consultants were asked to explain this logic to the teachers.

At this point we had to arrive at a clear definition of what constituted full implementation of the two workshops, so that the consultants and demonstration teachers would know what to aim for. We developed two classroom implementation checklists, one for the readers' workshop and one for the writers' workshop, each with nearly 70 items. The checklists were developed on the basis of classroom observations and feedback from consultants. We did not want the checklists to be overly prescriptive, which would not have been in keeping with the spirit of the whole literacy curriculum. Therefore, we tried to write the items on the checklists to describe the "what" in four areas: classroom organization, the teacher's participation, students' opportunities for learning, and assessment. However, we did not specify the "how," so each item could then be accomplished in the way the teacher saw fit. For example, one item concerned the teacher sharing her own writing with students. Some teachers read to students from their notebooks, others showed students their literacy portfolios, and others copied their poetry on charts for the students to read.

*Demonstration teachers.* Eleven consultants worked with one demonstration teacher each. One worked with two teachers, who had decided that they wanted to participate in the project together. The 13 teachers had varied amounts of teaching experience, ranging from 2 to 27 years, with a mean of 11.9 years. Their involvement with KEEP also varied, ranging from 1 to 14 years, with a mean of 5.3 years. The group included teachers in grades K–5.

Eleven of the 13 teachers elected to focus on the writers' workshop, 2 on the readers' workshop. We encouraged a focus on the writers' workshop, primarily because we believed it offered the better chance for full implementation. Some of the demonstration teachers had nearly 10 years of experience with the process approach to writing and an excellent understanding of how to conduct a writers' workshop. The writing folders in place in most classrooms formed a ready basis for portfolio assessment. Most teachers, as well as KEEP staff members, had far less experience with literature-based instruction and the readers' workshop.

***Project procedures.*** Project coordinators supervised data collection for the demonstration classrooms at each school. We asked the teachers to select six target students, representing high, middle, and low levels of achievement in the class. Each month, portfolio assessment data for these students were reviewed by the teacher, consultant, and project coordinator. Each teacher also was observed once a month by the consultant and project coordinator for the entire writers' or readers' workshop. Half the time was spent observing the teacher's instruction, while the other half was spent observing the target students. On the basis of their observations, the consultant and project coordinator completed the classroom implementation checklist. These results were then shared with the teacher, who decided on her goals for the coming month. Consultants assisted teachers in meeting these goals, for example, by providing model lessons or by brainstorming with the teacher about ways to make the benchmarks visible to students. Both the consultant and project coordinator wrote up their observations, and copies were given to the teacher.

## YEAR 4 IMPLEMENTATION RESULTS

Because 11 of the 13 Year 4 demonstration teachers decided to focus on the writers' workshop, we will highlight those results. Out of a possible 68 items on the implementation checklist, the 11 Year 4 demonstration teachers in the writers' workshop began the year by implementing a mean of 43 items, or 63%. By the end of the year, they had implemented a mean of 63 items, or 92%. We were satisfied with these results, because we judged a level of 85% or higher to constitute sound implementation of the curriculum.

An item analysis indicated that the teachers started the project with a good understanding of most aspects of the writers' workshop, with two exceptions: portfolio assessment and the teacher as writer (for a discussion of the teacher as writer, see Calkins, 1994; Graves, 1990). We were particularly concerned about the teachers' ability to implement portfolio assessment, which we believed critical to guiding students to meet the grade-level benchmarks. At the start of the year, the teachers had implemented a mean of only six items, or 43%, of the 14 items related to portfolio assessment. By the end of the year, they had implemented a mean of 13 items, or 93%. We believed that the key to improved student achievement was the teachers' commitment to portfolio assessment, which focused their attention and the attention of students on the grade-level benchmarks (for a complete discussion, see Au, 1993a). In most classrooms, the grade-level benchmarks were prominently displayed for all to see, and older students monitored their own progress in meeting various benchmarks.

In Year 4, we gave greater attention than before to students' progress toward the benchmarks. At the end of the first semester of the previous year, we had asked consultants to make predictions about student achievement, and these predictions proved to be highly inflated. In Year 4, we asked not just for predictions about student achievement but for a full report from each consultant on how the teacher's implementation had changed since the start of the school year and how the students had progressed toward the grade-level benchmarks. In January and again in May, each consultant presented her report to an audience of her fellow consultants and other KEEP staff members. The sharing of these reports enabled consultants to learn from one another and to receive feedback on their work. Additionally, the January reports indicated that the achievement of students was lower than we had anticipated. This information led to an increased focus on the benchmarks between February and May.

During Year 4, we also instituted an audit of the portfolio results (see Asam et al., 1993). We asked the consultants to make certain that each student's rating on each benchmark was supported by evidence (e.g., anecdotal records and interviews for ownership, running records for word reading strategies, and drafts and published pieces for the writing process). The need for evidence to support each benchmark rating imposed a tremendous burden on the teachers and consultants, due to the large number of benchmarks. In some instances, teachers taught students to identify and tag evidence for achievement of the various benchmarks. In addition to allowing us to vouch for the accuracy of the portfolio assessment results, the audit and the need to provide evidence for achievement had the effect of further heightening awareness of the benchmarks on the part of the consultants, teachers, and students.

*Student achievement.* Student achievement results for Year 4 showed a dramatic turnabout. There was measurable improvement when the results were compared with those achieved by students during the previous year. In the 11 writers' workshop classrooms, with a total of 234 students, 9% were judged to be above grade level, 59% at grade level, and 32% below grade level in the writing process. While about two-thirds of the students had been rated below grade level during the previous 2 years, about two-thirds were now rated at or above grade level.

Figure 8.2 shows the results for Years 3 and 4 obtained by the seven Year 4 demonstration teachers for whom results also were available in Year 3. The pair of bars on the left show the results for ownership of writing, while the pair on the right show the results for the writing process. These results suggest that improvements were indeed related to differences in the teacher's implementation of the curriculum, because these same teachers had not achieved comparable results the year before. (For a full report of results, refer to Asam et al., 1993.)

### CONTINUING THE PROJECT IN YEAR 5

Our goal during Year 5 was to double the number of teachers and students in the demonstration classroom project. We exceeded our goal somewhat, as consultants recruited a total of 29 demonstration teachers who completed work in the project during Year 5. Twenty teachers were in the project for the first time (to be called Year 5 demonstration teachers), and nine teachers were returning for a second year (Year 4 demonstration teachers). The backgrounds of the Year 4 and Year 5 demonstration teachers did not differ

**FIGURE 8.2.** Results for Year 4 demonstration teachers during Years 3 and 4.

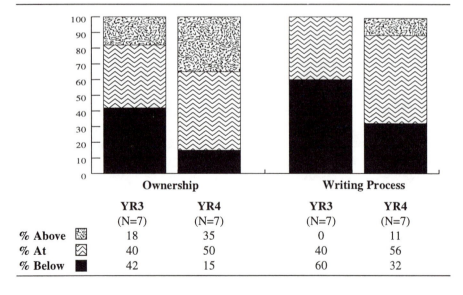

|  |  | Ownership | | Writing Process | |
|---|---|---|---|---|---|
|  |  | YR3 | YR4 | YR3 | YR4 |
|  |  | (N=7) | (N=7) | (N=7) | (N=7) |
| % Above | 🔲 | 18 | 35 | 0 | 11 |
| % At | 🔲 | 40 | 50 | 40 | 56 |
| % Below | ■ | 42 | 15 | 60 | 32 |

significantly. The two groups combined had a mean of 13 years of teaching experience, with a range of 1 to 28 years, and they had been associated with KEEP for a mean of 6 years, with a range of 1 to 15 years.

The observation and consultation procedures used with the Year 5 demonstration teachers were the same as those of the previous year. The Year 4 demonstration teachers were observed formally once a quarter, rather than once a month. Because 26 of the 29 teachers (18 Year 5 teachers and eight Year 4 teachers) elected to focus on the writers' workshop, we will again highlight these results.

During Year 5, the Year 4 demonstration teachers showed increased ownership of the project. With the addition of the Year 5 teachers, the Year 4 teachers quickly assumed leadership roles, sharing their knowledge and experience. Consultants facilitated this sharing through the establishment of demonstration teacher networks. The Year 4 teachers reported being much more comfortable with the project, in large part, we believe, because they understood the benchmarks and the portfolio assessment system and knew how to pace their teaching and assessment over the course of the year (Oshiro, 1994). As the year progressed, their reliance on the consultants decreased, while their independence increased.

Implementation results for the Year 4 and Year 5 demonstration teachers combined indicate that the teachers started the year by implementing a mean of 37 items, or 51%, finishing with a mean of 66 items, or 93%. Overall, these results are very similar to those obtained the previous year. The Year 5 demonstration teachers started the year at a considerably lower level, implementing a mean of 30 items, or 42%, versus 50 items, or 71%, for the second-year project teachers. By the end of the year, the Year 5 demonstration teachers had improved to a mean of 64 items, or 90%, a level approaching that of the 69 items, or 97%, achieved by Year 4 demonstration teachers.

The overall results for the spring of 1994 replicated those of the previous year. Of the 547 students in the writers' workshop classes, 7% were rated above grade level, 59% at grade level, and 34% below grade level, with the students of Year 4 demonstration teachers performing just slightly better than those of Year 5 demonstration teachers.

Figure 8.3 compares the Year 5 results obtained by Year 5 demonstration teachers for whom Year 3 results also were available. (Year 3 results were available because during Year 3, portfolio assessment data were collected from all KEEP teachers. No Year 4 results were available for these classrooms, because during that year portfolio data were collected only for the demonstration classrooms.) Like their counterparts the year before, these teachers succeeded in helping a much higher proportion of students

**FIGURE 8.3.** Results for Year 5 demonstration teachers during Years 3 and 5.

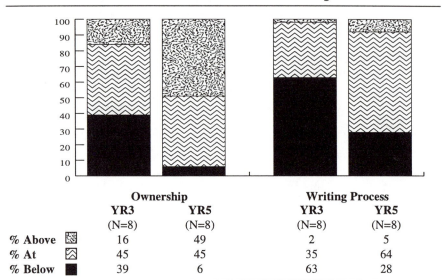

| | | Ownership | | Writing Process | |
|---|---|---|---|---|---|
| | | **YR3** | **YR5** | **YR3** | **YR5** |
| | | (N=8) | (N=8) | (N=8) | (N=8) |
| % **Above** | | 16 | 49 | 2 | 5 |
| % **At** | | 45 | 45 | 35 | 64 |
| % **Below** | | 39 | 6 | 63 | 28 |

reach levels of achievement at or above grade level in both ownership and the writing process. We took heart in having replicated the positive pattern of results seen the year before.

## OUR CONCLUSIONS AND SUGGESTIONS
## FOR FUTURE RESEARCH

Thus far in the chapter, we have described the three components of change and situated them within the chronology of the last 5 years of KEEP's work. Through these experiences, we became convinced of the value of holistic curricula for improving the literacy achievement of low-income students of diverse backgrounds, such as the Native Hawaiian students in the KEEP classrooms. In this section, we reflect on what we have learned and possible implications for researchers and educators concerned with improving the school literacy learning of low-income students of diverse backgrounds.

First, we see a need for researchers to conduct detailed investigations of what students are learning in holistic curricula in other settings. This is no small feat, as it necessitates the development and implementation of suitable forms of assessment, such as portfolios, that will be sensitive to the kinds of learning that such curricula emphasize. We judge standardized tests to be inadequate for this purpose, because they are not designed to assess ownership of literacy, personal responses to literature, writing on self-selected topics, or other major outcomes generally associated with holistic curricula.

As might be expected, holistic curricula do not provide a ready-made solution to issues of students' literacy achievement. We found that results were easier to obtain in some areas than others. Teachers experienced immediate success in strengthening students' ownership, voluntary reading, and word reading strategies. Positive affect may have formed the basis for learning, but improvements in the writing process, reading comprehension, and language and vocabulary knowledge did not follow naturally. Concerted instructional efforts by the teachers, plus a focus on grade-level benchmarks, were required before gains were made in aspects of literacy demanding higher-level thinking.

Second, we believe that there is a great need for research on the process by which teachers and administrators in schools, individually and collectively, make the change from behaviorist, skills-oriented curricula to social constructivist, holistic curricula. Because holistic curricula pose such a challenge to educators, the spread of these curricula may well depend on the small wins strategy or "going with the goers." We learned that we needed to narrow the focus of our efforts with teachers—to just a few teachers, who concentrated on only one of the workshops. We believe that a fruitful and needed area of research lies in the strategies used by school districts to support teachers' transitions to holistic curricula.

We gained some hints about one way in which the change process might proceed. We found that teachers needed considerable time and support to make the transition from a skills-oriented approach (see Routman, 1991). We learned that teachers needed to make changes in classroom organization and instruction first, before they were ready, willing, and able to attend to benchmarks and portfolio assessment.

As we gained more experience with the whole literacy curriculum, we came to see that *holistic* did not have to be synonymous with *vague*. The classroom implementation checklists proved an important tool in assisting teachers to become expert instructors in the readers' and writers' workshops. The checklists helped to communicate what had become our shared vision of the workshops. They also allowed teachers to chart the course of their own development within the context of the whole literacy curriculum. If the goal is to bring holistic curricula within the reach of the majority of teachers, it may well be necessary for educators and researchers to think in terms of tools like the checklists we developed. The checklists changed somewhat from the first year to the second, and, in general, such checklists should probably be in a continuous process of revision.

Third, we see a great need for research on the role of standards (Pearson, 1993) and alternative forms of assessment in improving students' literacy achievement. At the outset, neither the teachers nor the consultants saw portfolio assessment or the benchmarks as particularly useful. We attributed much of their initial resistance to the top-down manner in which these elements were imposed. But even when the demonstration teachers made the commitment to implement portfolio assessment, they still struggled with it. Although difficult to implement, the portfolio assessment system, particularly a focus on the benchmarks, proved to be the key to improving students' achievement. Once teachers started planning to help their students meet the benchmarks, they experienced a high degree of success. The benchmarks contributed to a raising of teacher expectations.

We agree with the approach of having just a few broad standards for language arts at the state and national levels. Having just a few standards will allow the new vision of the language arts to be understood by educators and the public. But we believe that standards must be converted into something like grade-level benchmarks before they can be expected to affect instruction. The demonstration teachers in grades K–5 benefited from knowing the benchmarks for their particular grade levels.

We believe that benchmarks or standards can play a part in improving the literacy achievement of students of diverse backgrounds. However, it should be clear from our experience at KEEP that simply instituting standards will not do the job. Standards must be accompanied by a process that supports teacher development. Furthermore, it appears that this process works well when it follows a small wins strategy, focusing on the teachers most likely to be successful. An across-the-board strategy, attempting to bring all teachers along at the same time, may well fail.

In our experience, an across-the-board strategy amounted to no more than dabbling with a holistic approach. It simply did not work. The whole literacy curriculum did not lead to changes in students' literacy achievement until teachers reached high levels of implementation, including attending to the benchmarks and portfolio assessment. At lower levels of implementation, achievement results remained unchanged. We can easily imagine situations in other school systems where a holistic approach will appear ineffective because it is not being fully implemented.

In conclusion, it appears that the three components of change (curriculum, assessment, and teacher development) must work together in combination, if the literacy achievement of low-income students of diverse backgrounds is to be improved. Holistic curricula appear promising, when features of classroom implementation can be described and these curricula can be fully implemented. Portfolio assessment appears promising, when coupled with the use of grade-level benchmarks. Most important, the success of changes in both curriculum and assessment appears to be facilitated by high levels of support for "goers," the teachers with the best chance of achieving high levels of implementation and serving as an inspiration for others.

## REFERENCES

Asam, C., Au, K., Blake, K., Carroll, J., Jacobsen, H., Kunitake, M., & Scheu, J. (1993). In J. Carroll (Ed.), *The demonstration classroom project: Report of year 1.* Kamehameha Elementary Education Program, Honolulu.

Au, K. H. (1993a, December). *Implementing a portfolio assessment system: Relationships to students' literacy learning.* Paper presented at the annual meeting of the National Reading Conference, Charleston, SC.

Au, K. H. (1993b). *Literacy instruction in multicultural settings.* Fort Worth, TX: Harcourt Brace Jovanovich.

Au, K. H. (1994). Portfolio assessment: Experiences at the Kamehameha Elementary Education Program. In S. W. Valencia, E. H. Hiebert, & P. P. Afflerbach (Eds.), *Authentic reading assessment: Practices and possibilities* (pp. 103–126). Newark, DE: International Reading Association.

Au, K., & Blake, K. (1984). *Implementation of the KEEP reading program, 1982–83: Results and methodological issues* (Tech. Rep. No. 112). Honolulu: Kamehameha Schools, Center for Development of Early Education.

Au, K., Blake, K., Carroll, J., Oshiro, M., & Scheu, J. (1993). *Literacy curriculum guide.* Honolulu: Kamehameha Schools, Center for Development of Early Education.

Au, K. H., Crowell, D. C., Jordan, C., Sloat, K. C. M., Speidel, G. E., Klein, T. W., & Tharp, R. G. (1986). Development and implementation of the KEEP reading program. In J. Orasanu (Ed.), *Reading comprehension: From research to practice* (pp. 235–252). Hillsdale, NJ: Erlbaum.

Au, K. H., & Kawakami, A. J. (1985). Research currents: Talk story and learning to read. *Language Arts, 62*(4), 406–411.

Au, K. H., & Kawakami, A. J. (1994). Cultural congruence in instruction. In E. R. Hollins, J. E. King, & W. C. Hayman (Eds.), *Teaching diverse populations: Formulating a knowledge base* (pp. 5–23). Albany: State University of New York Press.

Au, K. H., & Mason, J. M. (1983). Cultural congruence in classroom participation structures: Achieving a balance of rights. *Discourse Processes, 6* (2), 145–167.

Bloom, B. S. (1976). *Human characteristics and school learning.* New York: McGraw-Hill.

Calkins, L. (1994). *The art of teaching writing* (2nd ed.). Portsmouth, NH: Heinemann.

Calkins, L. M., with Harwayne, S. (1991). *Living between the lines.* Portsmouth, NH: Heinemann.

Clay, M. M. (1985). *The early detection of reading difficulties* (3rd ed.). Auckland: Heinemann.

Coleman, J. S., Campbell, E. Q., Hobson, C. J., McPartland, J., Mood, A. M., Weinfeld, F. D., & York, R. L. (1966). *Equality of educational opportunity.* Washington, DC: Office of Education, U.S. Department of Health, Education and Welfare.

Crowell, D. C. (1981). *Kamehameha Reading Objective System.* Honolulu: Kamehameha Schools, Center for Development of Early Education.

D'Amato, J. (1988). "Acting": Hawaiian children's resistance to teachers. *Elementary School Journal, 88*(5), 529–544.

Garcia, G. (1993). Linguistic diversity and national standards. *Focus on Diversity, 3*(1), 1–2.

Giuli, C. (1985). *Responsive consulting: Test of a model* (Tech. Rep. No. 131). Honolulu: Kamehameha Schools, Center for Development of Early Education.

Goodman, K. (1986). *What's whole in whole language?* Portsmouth, NH: Heinemann.

Graves, D. (1983). *Writing: Teachers and children at work.* Exeter, NH: Heinemann.

Graves, D. (1990). *Discover your own literacy.* Portsmouth, NH: Heinemann.

Graves, D., & Hansen, J. (1983). The author's chair. *Language Arts, 60*(2), 176–183.

Hiebert, E. H. (Ed.). (1991). *Literacy for a diverse society: Perspectives, practices, and policies.* New York: Teachers College Press.

Jordan, C. (1985). Translating culture: From ethnographic information to educational program. *Anthropology and Education Quarterly, 16*, 105–123.

Mehan, H. (1981). Social constructivism in psychology and sociology. *The Quarterly Newsletter of the Laboratory of Comparative Human Cognition, 3*(4), 71–77.

Mezynski, K. (1983). Issues concerning the acquisition of knowledge: Effects of vocabulary training on reading comprehension. *Review of Educational Research, 53*, 253–279.

Moll, L. C. (1990). Introduction. In L. C. Moll (Ed.), *Vygotsky and education: Instructional implications and applications of sociohistorical psychology* (pp. 1–27). Cambridge: Cambridge University Press.

National Assessment of Educational Progress. (1989). *Reading objectives, 1990 assessment* (No. 21-R-10). Princeton, NJ: Educational Testing Service.

Oshiro, G. (1994). *Experiences of first and second year teachers in the KEEP demonstration classroom project: Spring 1994.* Unpublished manuscript, Kamehameha Schools Bishop Estate, Early Education Division, Evaluation Department, Honolulu.

Pallas, A. M., Natriello, G., & McDill, E. L. (1989). Changing nature of the disadvantaged population: Current dimensions and future trends. *Educational Researcher, 18*(5), 16–22.

Pearson, P. D. (1993). Standards for the English language arts: A policy perspective. *JRB: A Journal of Literacy, 25*(4), 457–475.

Peters, T. J., & Waterman, R. H., Jr. (1982). *In search of excellence: Lessons from America's best-run companies.* New York: Warner Books.

Rosa, A., & Montero, I. (1990). The historical context of Vygotsky's work: A sociohistorical approach. In L. C. Moll (Ed.), *Vygotsky and education: Instructional implications and applications of sociohistorical psychology* (pp. 59–88). Cambridge: Cambridge University Press.

Routman, R. (1991). *Invitations: Changing as teachers and learners K–12.* Portsmouth, NH: Heinemann.

Schwandt, T. A. (1994). Constructivist, interpretivist approaches to human inquiry. In N. K. Denzin & Y. S. Lincoln (Eds.), *Handbook of qualitative research* (pp. 118–137). Thousand Oaks, CA: Sage.

Shanahan, T. (Ed.). (1990). *Reading and writing together: New perspectives for the classroom.* Norwood, MA: Christopher-Gordon.

Spiegel, D. L. (1981). *Reading for pleasure: Guidelines.* Newark, DE: International Reading Association.

Tharp, R. G., & Gallimore, R. (1988). *Rousing minds to life: Teaching, learning and schooling in social context.* Cambridge: Cambridge University Press.

Tharp, R. G., Jordan, C., Speidel, G. E., Au, K. H., Klein, T. W., Calkins, R. P., Sloat, K. C. M., & Gallimore, R. (1984). Product and process in applied developmental research: Education and the children of a minority. In M. E. Lamb, A. L. Brown, & B. Rogoff (Eds.), *Advances in developmental psychology* (Vol. III, pp. 91–141). Hillsdale, NJ: Erlbaum.

Tharp, R. G., & Wetzel, R. J. (1969). *Behavior modification in the natural environment.* New York: Academic Press.

Tikunoff, W. J., Ward, B. A., & Van Broekhuizen, L. D. (1993). *KEEP evaluation study: Year 3 report.* Los Alamitos, CA: Southwest Regional Laboratory.

Vygotsky, L. S. (1987). Thinking and speech. In R. W. Rieber & A. S. Carton (Eds.), *The collected works of L. S. Vygotsky: Vol. 1. Problems of general psychology* (pp. 37–285). New York: Plenum.

Wertsch, J. V. (1985). *Vygotsky and the social formation of mind.* Cambridge, MA: Harvard University Press.

Wixson, K. K., Peters, C. W., Weber, E. M., & Roeber, E. D. (1987). New directions in statewide reading assessment. *The Reading Teacher, 40*(8), 749–754.

Wolf, D. P., LeMahieu, P. G., & Eresh, J. (1992). Good measure: Assessment as a tool for educational reform. *Educational Leadership, 49*(8), 8–13.

CHAPTER 9

# Assessing Critical Literacy: Tools and Techniques

## ROBERT CALFEE
*Stanford University*

*Examinations are formidable even to the best prepared, for the greatest fool may ask more than the wisest man can answer.*

Charles Caleb Colton, *Lacon*, 1830

In 1943, when I was in fourth grade, Friday mornings meant tests. Mrs. Aiken administered exams in reading, writing, spelling, and math (I don't remember science and history). The tests covered materials we had studied earlier in the week. Monday morning she returned the papers with grades and commentary. The right answer was important, but so was "showing your work," neatness, and (I suspect) several other criteria known only to Mrs. Aiken. On Monday night, parents asked how their students did on the test. A tightly linked, locally controlled scenario — the teacher decided what to teach and how to test it; students knew what to study and how to perform; parents handled praise and penalty. Some readers may remember those days. Things have changed since the 1940s, and I will now sketch this history from my perspective.

## MY LIFE AS A TEST MAKER

Table 9.1 summarizes significant shifts in curriculum, instruction, and assessment, with special attention to the latter. In the 1950s, achievement

TABLE 9.1. Summary of historical trends in curriculum, instruction, and assessment, showing for assessment the source of authority, typical activities and scheduling, evaluation standards, and methods of reporting for various audiences.

| Key Phrase | Autonomous Teacher (Pre 1950s) | Standardized Tests (1950-1965) | Curriculum Tests (1965-1985) | Authentic Assessment (1990s) |
|---|---|---|---|---|
| **Curriculum** | | | | |
| | Classical academics | Behavioral objectives | Curriculum objectives | Cognitive and communicative skills |
| **Instruction** | | | | |
| | Teacher direction | Textbook direction | Textbook direction | Teacher as facilitator |
| | Student recitation | Individual recitation and worksheets | Individual recitation and worksheets | Student learning is active, social, reflective |
| **Assessment** | | | | |
| Authority | Individual teacher determines when and how to assess | External mandates for when and how to test | External mandates for management by instructional objectives | Teachers as professional community decide when and how to assess for various purposes |
| | | Textbook end-of-unit tests | | |
| Activity/ Timing | Written answers, "Show your work" | Multiple-choice and fill-in-the-blank | External mandates for management by instructional objectives | Group and individual projects |
| | Weekly progress tests, end-of-semester finals for grades | End-of-unit for progress and remediation | | Working and showcase portfolios |
| | | End-of-year for public accountability | | Continuous assessment, end-of-semester and end-of-year projects |
| Evaluation Standards | Decided by individual teacher; grading on the curve | Objective scoring | Multiple-choice, continuous progress against criterion-referenced standards | Review by student and teacher against locally established and moderated rubrics |
| | | Norm-referenced and criterion-referenced standards | | |
| Reporting/ Audience | Test scores available immediately from teacher to students and parents | End-of-unit scores used by teachers for group decisions and quarter grades | Weekly scores for students | Evaluation a continuing dialogue between student and teacher |
| | | Standardized tests for yearly accountability | Quarterly reports to parents | Quarterly evaluation for parents |
| | | | Standardized tests for yearly accountability | Yearly evaluation for accountability |

testing took a new turn. School administrators relied increasingly on standardized tests for public accountability. These tests differed greatly from teacher-based methods: multiple-choice rather than open-ended, externally mandated rather than locally developed, technically reliable, yearly rather than weekly administration, and feedback measured in months rather than days. This format came to serve not only for accountability, but also for placement in special classes and program evaluation. Standardized test scores became the primary indicator for public debate about schooling; for instance, the Reagan administration relied on tests in 1983 to inform us that we were "a Nation at Risk."

These tests certainly had their critics — raising questions about validity (do the tests measure what they claim to measure?), bias (minorities do more poorly than majorities), and external control (one size seldom fits all). Nonetheless, the tests were cheap and simple indicators of productivity and performance. Today, they remain the dominate source of information about student achievement in the core curriculum areas — reading, writing, and arithmetic.

In the 1960s, when I began my professional life, researchers were exploring the use of standardized tests for instructional decision making. Curriculum-embedded tests, end-of-unit tests, and computer-based assessments became the object of considerable research and development efforts. At the University of Wisconsin, Richard Venezky and I joined this effort. Our first studies examined the validity of reading readiness tests for assessing the perceptual and cognitive skills of young children (Calfee & Venezky, 1969). We found that, while these instruments predicted reading achievement in the later elementary grades, the predictions reflected differences in children's entering experiences (children from homes that taught them about letters, words, and books did better on the tests) and instructional experiences (children from such homes were more likely to learn phonics and read more challenging books). This work led me to explore the development of "clean tests," instruments that depended less on prior experience, that scaffolded young test-takers to ensure that they understood the task, and that aimed toward optimal performance (Calfee, Chapman, & Venezky, 1972). An early finding from these explorations was the identification of phonemic awareness as an important predictor of success in learning to read.

At about this same time, I became interested in alternatives to multiple-choice tests of reading achievement, and developed the Interactive Reading Assessment System (IRAS). Modeled on the informal reading inventory, this system provided researchers and practitioners with an instrument for independent assessment of the componential skills in reading: decoding and spelling, vocabulary abilities, and comprehension of narrative and expository texts (Calfee, 1977). Research based on IRAS led me to conclude that, counter to Davis's (1968) assertion that reading achievement was a single entity, the components listed above were separable in the early years of schooling. As a student moves through the grades, however, failure to develop skill in decoding and spelling leaves some children behind others in various facets of literacy; access to the print code becomes increasingly critical for access to text.

In the mid-1980s, partly in response to innovations in curriculum and instruction, alternative assessment emerged with dramatic speed and vigor. The movement goes under several labels: *authentic assessment*, *performance tests*, and *portfolios*. All of these techniques have certain features in common, which distinguish this movement from previous scenarios (Calfee & Perfumo, in press). These developments parallel a paradigm shift in our conception of education. Elsewhere (Calfee, 1995) I have laid out three features of this change.

- The shift from cognitive to behavioral views of learning and thinking
- The shift from factory-model to information-age models of schooling
- The shift from externally mandated testing to internally guided assessment

Guy Bond, who was honored in the conference that prompted this book, would appreciate these tensions, because his professional life spanned the decades that foreshadowed current events. His early work was grounded in the pragmatics of behavioral psychology. Basic literacy skills sufficed for most citizens. When he and Bob Dykstra conducted the First Grade Studies (Bond & Dykstra, 1967), standardized tests were the established technology for gauging reading achievement. More than a quarter-century later, cognitive psychology prevails as theory (although with less effect on practice), assembly-line jobs have disappeared, and authentic assessment is all the rage. Bond's generation confronted tough issues—the Depression, fascism, nuclear bombs—but believed that they could prevail. Today—especially when it comes to the well-being of children—we seem much less certain.

However, I remain an optimist. The good news is that we have created new visions of the potential inherent in the literate use of language, and we have discovered trustworthy techniques for ensuring that virtually every child realizes this potential. The bad news is largely political: Do the nation, our citizens, and the teaching profession have the will to pursue this vision? I think the answer must be yes, because it's the only right answer.

How well can today's students read and write? How well should they read and write? What should we teach as reading and writing? How should we teach it? As we move through the 1990s toward the end of the century, my work has centered around these questions. In the remainder of this chapter, I first describe critical literacy, a conception of literacy that I think fits the challenges confronting tomorrow's graduates. After that, I describe a framework for assessment of critical literacy and two attempts to set up statewide assessments of critical literacy. Then, in the longest section of the chapter, I describe the development of a program to assist teachers in classroom assessment of students' growth in critical literacy.

## CRITICAL LITERACY

As literate persons, we all know something about reading, writing, and literacy. In fact, though, our understandings vary widely. Some view reading and writing as low-level skills. Stage theory (Chall, 1983) puts this position most plainly: Students learn to read, and then they read to learn. Reading comes first, and then writing can begin. Instruction starts with phonics, goes to fluent oral reading, then moves to comprehension. The basal reader provides the foundation; teachers need only follow the manual. Achievement is gauged by behavioral measures: standardized tests, reading rate, and the like. Assessment is externally mandated; average scores tell the tale.

A contrasting position appears in the whole language movement (Goodman, Goodman, & Hood, 1989), which portrays reading as a natural process. Immerse young children in good literature, and they will become good readers. Reading is still the focus, but students also are encouraged early on to write their personal experiences and thoughts; literacy and language development are an organic whole. The teacher's role is to care, to encourage, to "kid-watch." Achievement is gauged by teacher judgment of student performance. Narratives of individual student learning provide the foundation for negotiating assessment among teacher, student, and parent.

The "great literacy debate" sketched above has a long history, which I will not recapitulate here. For present purposes, the essential point is that decisions about assessment practices depend on how we define literacy. In my work, I have created the concept of *critical literacy*, by which I mean the capacity to use language as a tool for thinking and communicating (Calfee, 1994). From this perspective, literacy is not a matter of medium (speech vs. print) but manner (natural vs. formal usage). The literacy curriculum balances meaning and skill, literature and exposition, and teacher-

and student-centered activities. The perspective is developmental rather than stage-wise. Kindergartners can compose oral reports before they have figured out the English spelling system; first graders can enjoy and analyze complex stories that they cannot yet read aloud. Learning to decode and spell are important parts of the curriculum, not as barriers to be surmounted before "getting to the good stuff," but as texts in their own right.

Instruction for critical literacy builds on cognitive principles; effective learning is active, social, and reflective. The teacher's role is to facilitate student learning in a setting where desired literacy outcomes are explicit (e.g., character and plot are important concepts for comprehending and composing stories), but where the acquisition of these outcomes takes place in a project-based context. Students spend the entire school day becoming literate in the use of language, but activities are embedded in "real" explorations in the domains of literature, science, social studies, and even mathematics — reading and writing taught not as separate topics, but integrated into everything that happens in the classroom.

## A FRAMEWORK FOR ASSESSMENT
## OF CRITICAL LITERACY

At the outset, let me suggest that curriculum, instruction, and assessment that promote critical literacy depend on the professional judgment of classroom teachers; I cannot imagine "packaging" these concepts and practices. Moreover, professional judgments are inherently reflective; professionals can explain and justify their decisions and actions to other professionals and to their clients.

What principles should guide teachers' reflections about literacy assessment? Colleagues and I have wrestled with this question for the past few years as part of a project on writing portfolios with the Center for the Study of Writing at the University of California, Berkeley. The enormous outpouring of information about portfolios has overwhelmed researchers, practitioners, and policy makers. To guide our thinking in the project, we developed the following framework for teacher-based assessment. These five components — purpose, design, collection and analysis of evidence, interpretation and evaluation, and reporting — have a parallel interpretation as stages in an applied research model (cf. Hiebert & Calfee, 1992).

*Purpose.* What objectives and goals serve various assessment activities? What audiences do they address? For what reasons and in what ways are they initiated? What "problems" are informed by the assessment? For assessment of critical literacy, a clearly explicated developmental curriculum design is essential. The ultimate purposes of the assessment are to guide instructional decisions, to give students feedback about their progress, to inform parents of students' accomplishments, and to ensure the broader public that the schools are doing an adequate job of educating children.

*Design.* What is the plan of action for obtaining information? Suppose the aim is to determine students' skills in analyzing narratives. What stories might best serve this purpose for various students? Several methods can be employed to tap students' abilities in this domain: written summaries, class discussion, responses to specific questions, self-assessment. Which methods are most appropriate for the situation? This element of the framework is a placeholder for validity and reliability. A sound design generates information about the consistency of the evidence for specific outcomes. The challenge here is to create a design that is coherently structured but flexible. With a few exceptions (e.g., Herman, Aschbacher, & Winters, 1992), my reading and experience have turned up a twofold message for teachers: (1) portfolios are highly individualistic and serve teachers and students in diverse and largely idiosyncratic ways for gauging student progress, and (2) the assembling of a wide array of student artifacts is the essence of portfolio assessment. "There is no 'right' way to implement portfolios, each classroom will reflect a unique approach . . . and each child's collection of documents will differ" (Tierney, Carter, & Desai, 1991, p. vii). The underlying philosophy is the taking back of assessment from standardized testing programs and the return of authority to the classroom teacher. Less frequent is discussion of purposes that relate explicitly to curriculum and instructional objectives. The result, all too often, is the absence of any clearly articulated design.

*Collection and analysis of evidence.* What evidence should be collected? What should the teacher do with the information? Design becomes critical in answering these questions, as does a broad conception of "evidence." Many events that inform the development of critical literacy occur not in the artifacts (student papers), but in the social events that surround these activities. Observations and conversations are therefore essential sources of data. When a curriculum of critical literacy is fully implemented, data about student achievement permeate the entire classroom. Practical questions arise around the balance of ongoing observation and explicit performance, long-term and short-term assessments, individual and teamwork activities, and data about behavior, understanding, and motivation. As the teacher assembles the evidence, issues of consistency and validity come again to the fore.

*Interpretation and evaluation.* Viewing assessment as applied research emphasizes the critical role of making sense of evidence as analyzed, and of clarity about the "bottom line." What do the data mean? What do they say about the adequacy of student growth and achievement? Also, what do they say about the instructional program? Externally mandated assessments answer such questions by fiat; teachers are told how to view the data and how to assign scores. But as teachers assume greater responsibility for assessment, they must move beyond prescriptions. Interpretation is a dynamic activity. If a student's summary of *Charlotte's Web* neglects the conflict between Charlotte and Wilbur at the beginning of the story, this can mean that he (1) does not comprehend the conflict, (2) understands it but does not know how to describe it, or (3) understands it but does not realize the importance of telling about it. Each interpretation calls not for a judgment of "failed," but for further "experimentation." Application of standards depends on the purpose and placement of the assessment during the school year. For a third grader at the beginning of the school year, the bottom line is a call for instruction; for a sixth grader in June, the bottom line may be a grade.

*Reporting.* Much of the assessment information gathered during the school year serves as a basis for ongoing dialogue between teacher and students. Parents need to know how their children are doing. If teacher-based assessment is to inform public accountability, the evidence must take a form appropriate to this need. How can the classroom teacher effectively transform the data to suit these different audiences? And beyond these client groups, how can the evidence be effectively employed as teachers reflect on their instruction both individually and as members of a professional community? Reporting in the new approach occurs at at least three levels. *Student and teacher* engage in an ongoing discussion of growth and quality, based on actual performance and a common understanding of the rubrics. Quarterly *parent–teacher conferences* (or parent–teacher–student conferences in which students report and reflect, as described by Stiggins, 1994) are the occasion for a summative report. Tied to reporting is grading, often a problem for alternative assessment advocates. If one believes that each student can excel (or not excel) in a variety of ways, then what is the meaning of a grade? On the other hand, in a competitive society like ours, parents often want to know, "How well is my kid doing?" Finally, a number of districts and states are turning to alternative assessment methods as a basis for *public accountability*. The "public" is the audience for these reports; practically speaking, the public wants numbers, averages, "hard data," and "bottom lines." The challenge is to transform soft data collected under nonstandardized conditions into trustworthy and interpretable indicators.

In my recent work, this framework has been used to illuminate a variety of current practices, programs, and problems. For example, in a national survey of nominated portfolio assessment projects, I used the framework to examine classroom practices in writing assessment (Calfee & Perfumo, in press). It also has guided my thinking in the work described in the following sections. In the next section, I discuss some observations stemming from my involvement with California and Kentucky in reviews of statewide programs for alternative assessment of reading and writing. Following that, I describe my current efforts to assist teachers in classroom assessment of students' growth in critical literacy.

## MANDATING ASSESSMENT OF CRITICAL LITERACY: TWO STATE STUDIES

In the early 1990s, I became tangentially involved with efforts by California and Kentucky to develop alternative strategies for assessing student literacy at the state level. (I should note that educational programs in both of these states are in considerable flux and that the following accounts are already out of date. California did away with all statewide assessment in 1994, and Kentucky continues to revise and refine its program based on input from consultants and practitioners.) The aim here is to show how the framework can inform these efforts — both laudatory, in my judgment — to bring statewide assessment more in line with statewide efforts to reform curriculum and instruction.

In Kentucky, students in grades 4, 8, and 12 assemble literacy portfolios for statewide assessment. The design includes a table of contents, a personally selected "best piece" with a reflective letter about the reasons for the choice, a personal narrative, and one or more fictional and expository compositions. The purpose of the portfolio is laid out in documents for teachers, students, and parents. For example, the *Guidebook for Kentucky Parents* explains that "the selections in the Kentucky Writing Portfolio reflect an emphasis on writing for a variety of purposes. At the heart of the experience is a variety of higher level thinking skills students must exercise" (Kentucky State Department of Education, 1994, p. 13). The portfolio is assembled during the school year, and teachers are free to scaffold the students' preparation as they think appropriate. The *Guidebook* describes the rubrics (four categories from novice to distinguished) and the criteria (purpose/audience, idea development, organization, language, sentences, and conventions). Each district decides who is to evaluate the portfolios. In some districts, classroom teachers grade their own students. Other districts arrange for multiple readings by teams of teachers. A Teacher's Handbook provides extensive information about the concept of a writing portfolio, including descriptions of the process approach to writing, holistic scoring techniques, and extensive "benchmark" examples for each of the four rubrics. Each portfolio receives a single holistic score based on the state guidelines. The effort behind this initiative is rather incredible: Kentucky sees authentic assessment as a core element in statewide educational reform.

The California Learning Assessment System (CLAS) took a different approach to alternative assessment (CLAS was vetoed by Governor Wilson in 1994). This on-demand assessment was administered to the vast majority of students in grades 4, 8, and 10; students with learning disabilities and those not proficient in English were excluded. (It is perhaps worth noting that California experimented with a portfolio design, but it never became part of the statewide system.) The CLAS reading–writing assessment comprised three segments of 30–50 minutes each. In the first segment, students read an extended passage, jotting comments in the right margin; they then answered several open-ended questions about the excerpt. Some questions called for text-based responses, others for personal reactions. The second segment was a group task; teams of four students discussed the selection and planned a writing assignment on a topic related to the selection. In the third segment, individual students drew on their discussion notes to compose papers. The teachers' role was limited to administering the assessment, passing out the materials, and reading the standardized instructions. Teachers were prohibited from providing any information or assistance. After the tasks were completed, the school shipped the materials to Sacramento for scoring. Each test booklet received two scores, one for reading (the first segment) and the other for writing (the third segment). The group work did not count.

The contrasts between assessment policy and practice in these two states are substantial. The Kentucky portfolios are assembled over weeks or even months based on general directions about what to collect and how to collect it; CLAS was an on-demand assessment administered during three sessions based on standardized instructions. Kentucky teachers can play an essential instructional role in assisting students with their portfolios; California teachers were prohibited from providing instructional support during the assessment, although they could prepare students beforehand for the exercise. Virtually every Kentucky teacher in the target grades is directly involved in evaluating performance of students in the school or district; CLAS scoring was done by paid volunteers who scored the exercises anonymously. Kentucky provides extensive staff development for teachers in the target grades; California concentrated staff development on the scorers. Information about the outcomes for individual students is almost instantly available to Kentucky teachers; in California, results were not known for months, and then only for schools (the governor vetoed CLAS partly because the Department of Education did not provide scores for individual students).

The framework illuminates these two case studies in a variety of ways. At one level, for instance, the purposes appear quite similar. In both states, the assessments parallel curriculum objectives in state frameworks that portray literacy as a constructive and collaborative activity. CLAS clearly integrated reading and writing, while the Kentucky portfolio emphasizes writing but does not exclude a link to reading. Both state assessments downplay the mechanics and conventions of reading and writing, and stress instead the importance of audience, voice, organization, and other high-level features of literacy. However, curriculum is not linked directly to assessment, so assessment easily can become a separate activity.

The designs differ substantially between the two states. Kentucky calls for a richer array of genre, with substantial leeway for student (and teacher) choice. The Kentucky portfolio requires students to reflect on at least one composition. California actually included a variety of genre in various forms of CLAS, but each student was assessed on a single form, so that contrasts between genre were not easily evaluated. In Kentucky, although teachers can assist students with their portfolios, guidance in how to provide this assistance has been relatively scattershot. CLAS spelled out the process for data collection in complete detail, denying students any assistance. In California, teachers might prepare students for the exercise, but districts differed substantially in how they disseminated information about the test. During the 1993 administration, I found some teachers preparing their classes in early January, while others did not learn about the assessment from district administrators until March. The result of these design decisions is that student differences in both Kentucky and California partly reflect differences in instructional opportunity. Since Kentucky reports scores for individual students, the way is open for student differences to reflect teacher/class and district effects.

Both states specify how student performance is to be analyzed and reported. Analysis depends on prespecified rubrics in both states. Reporting in California mirrored practices typical of standardized testing programs; the state issued the results for schools (and the media) months after the testing. Reporting in Kentucky is more complex — a combination of local assimilation of the information along with state monitoring and distribution. California's process is routinized and centrally controlled; in Kentucky, local variations are more typical.

These two case studies also illustrate the importance of contextual variables. For instance, both states are attempting to use assessment to influence curriculum and instruction. In neither state is this effort accompanied by an equally substantial investment in professional development to directly influence what is taught and how it is taught. The result, I suspect, is that most teachers try to enhance test performance (both assessments are "high stakes") but without fundamental changes in current conceptions of curriculum and instruction. Schools and districts that are forward-looking and have the resources will be in tune with the intended reforms, but most will have to rely on a quick fix.

A second contextual point: In Kentucky, the teacher plays a much more central role than in California, but in both states only selected grades and, hence, selected teachers are on the firing line. If the concept of a professional community is to take root, then both states need to find a way to hold the entire school responsible for student achievement. Finally, neither program relates the mandated assessment to the rest of the literacy program: staff development, textbook selection and use, teacher evaluation, and so on. The assessment is an add-on, one more thing to do. Surveys suggest that teachers in both states are supportive of these new approaches to assessment of student achievement; the mandates actually provide attractive models! The problem lies in bridging the gap between long-standing practice and the innovation intended by the mandate.

Let me turn back to the purpose of the assessments. As noted earlier, both assessment programs aim to reform classroom instruction in reading and writing. In California, this purpose depends on a "push" policy. By establishing high standards of achievement, publicizing the scores of schools and districts, and recognizing schools that do well and castigating those that do poorly, CLAS aimed to press schools and districts toward higher achievements. In the past, CLAS scores were reported at the school level, but the legislature and the governor have insisted that the state testing program provide scores for individual students. This emphasis on reporting individual scores reflects a belief that the state can pressure students to respond to state mandates. In Kentucky, the purpose appears more in line with a "pull" policy. The portfolios, one part of a comprehensive assessment system, serve as models to districts, schools, teachers, and students. The assessments have high-stakes consequences, to be sure. Kentucky schools can be rewarded or punished based on their assessment outcomes. However, they are in a better position than California schools to understand and influence the outcomes. The state offers external incentives, but the local agencies can create their own incentives. Teachers, and for that matter students, can determine the design, the analysis, and even the reporting of assessment information. Realizing the potential of this strategy is likely to require additional statewide support for districts, schools, and teachers, but the framework suggests that the potential is there.

In both states, however, separation of curriculum and assessment promotes a "test preparation" model. I have seen some Kentucky portfolios that clearly seem driven by the concept of critical literacy; evidence of opportunity to learn appears in dates (work stretching from the winter into the spring) and progressions (successive drafts beginning with a teacher-provided brainstorming sheet and moving through teacher-annotated drafts to a polished final paper complete with student comments on the process). However, such examples are exceptions; all too frequently, the evidence suggests that teachers directly prepare students for the test.

## BUILDING A PROGRAM TO ASSESS CRITICAL LITERACY

This section describes my current efforts to assist teachers and schools in thinking about local strategies to assess efforts to implement curriculum and instruction consistent with the concept of critical literacy. The goals of these efforts differ in many ways from the statewide activities described above, but an underlying theme in my work has been the goal of closing the gap between externally mandated and internally based assessment. I will explore this question in more detail in the concluding section of the chapter — I have a dream about a time when this chasm will be bridged by methods grounded in informed teacher judgments. Here, I will focus on five questions designed to guide a school faculty in thinking about a school-based program for assessing student literacy: *what to assess*, *how to design assessment*, *how to assess*, *what to make of it*, and *how to tell about it*. In exploring these questions, I have in mind the elementary and middle grades, where each teacher spends most of the day with a class of 25–35 students.

As the broad context for this section, I return to Mrs. Aiken, who in her time was professionally responsible for making informed judgments about instruction *and* for public accountability. To be sure, she did not have to contend with national standards, and the public was the local community. Parents respected her, students stood in awe of her, the principal supported her, and these were the people who mattered. Of course, the 1930s context was one in which most students did *not* graduate from high school, did *not* need the highest levels of literacy, and were *not* ensured equity. On the other hand, my recollection is that Mrs. Aiken tried to motivate many students to complete their education, and that she held high standards for reading and writing. The 1930s were not perfect, but there are lessons to learn from this era.

In particular, we can learn that teachers are capable of judging student achievement. Can we trust teachers to perform this professional function? The response to this question, in my judgment, is that we can and we must.

But as long as significant assessments are remotely controlled by individuals far removed from the classroom, the potential of teachers to perform as professionals is undermined. Let me now describe how I approach a school faculty with a plan of action for informed teacher-based assessment.

## WHAT TO ASSESS

An essential first step in setting the purpose of an assessment is clarity about the target. In working with a school faculty, I emphasize that assessment depends on agreement about curriculum and instruction—what to teach and how to teach it. I have described elsewhere (Calfee & Patrick, 1995) the elements of a developmental approach to critical literacy, an integrated language arts curriculum with four components: narrative, exposition, concept and vocabulary development, and decoding and spelling. These components cover comprehension and composition, both spoken and written, from kindergarten through high school and beyond.

The narrative strand illustrates the concept of a developmental curriculum. The essential ingredients of a story are *character*, *plot*, *setting*, and *theme*. These elements apply to fairy tales and high school novels, to soap operas and classics, to reading and writing. Figure 9.1 shows the narrative continuum constructed by a local school for the developmental progression from kindergarten through the late elementary grades. The figure lays out a design for what to teach—and what to assess—across this entire span. The continuum applies broadly to all stories, without prescribing selections for each grade level. All four story elements are covered at every grade level in developmental fashion. Kindergartners handle plot as beginning–middle–end, while fifth graders are accountable for episodic analysis. The aim is not "mastery of objectives," but progress toward more sophisticated understandings and explanations, progress shared by all grade levels and hence all members of the school faculty. Without a shared conception of the curriculum, a common purpose is impossible.

Another dimension of "what" distinguishes between learning and accomplishment. The student who enters third grade unable to analyze stories but who talks knowledgeably about character and plot at the end of the school year has progressed—she has learned a lot. In the primary years of schooling, learning is the primary goal, and so this student's growth should be reported, even if she has not attained the level expected of the typical third grader. When a student reaches the late elementary grades, however, assessment should focus on accomplishment, on the capacity to carry out designated tasks at a high level of quality. It is then that standards become important—not simply a minimal awareness of the concepts of character

FIGURE 9.1. The narrative continuum constructed by a local school.

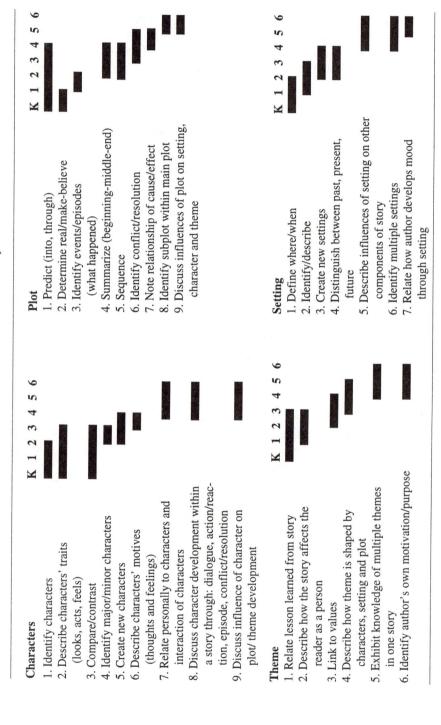

**Characters**

K 1 2 3 4 5 6

1. Identify characters
2. Describe characters' traits (looks, acts, feels)
3. Compare/contrast
4. Identify major/minor characters
5. Create new characters
6. Describe characters' motives (thoughts and feelings)
7. Relate personally to characters and interaction of characters
8. Discuss character development within a story through: dialogue, action/reaction, episode, conflict/resolution
9. Discuss influence of character on plot/ theme development

**Theme**

K 1 2 3 4 5 6

1. Relate lesson learned from story
2. Describe how the story affects the reader as a person
3. Link to values
4. Describe how theme is shaped by characters, setting and plot
5. Exhibit knowledge of multiple themes in one story
6. Identify author's own motivation/purpose

**Plot**

K 1 2 3 4 5 6

1. Predict (into, through)
2. Determine real/make-believe
3. Identify events/episodes (what happened)
4. Summarize (beginning-middle-end)
5. Sequence
6. Identify conflict/resolution
7. Note relationship of cause/effect
8. Identify subplot within main plot
9. Discuss influences of plot on setting, character and theme

**Setting**

K 1 2 3 4 5 6

1. Define where/when
2. Identify/describe
3. Create new settings
4. Distinguish between past, present, future
5. Describe influences of setting on other components of story
6. Identify multiple settings
7. Relate how author develops mood through setting

and plot, but a demonstrated capacity to use these concepts to comprehend and compose stories. Most rubrics for literacy assessment commingle learning and accomplishment, leading to confusion.

The final facet of "what" centers around the deeper aspects of literacy. Genuine understanding is seldom mirrored in performance immediately after learning, but shows up later on transfer tasks. The history of research on transfer is a mixed bag. Sometimes learners can apply what they have learned only to similar situations. School is not much like real life, which is rather discouraging for transfer. Salomon and Perkins (1989), however, have reviewed research showing that transfer is possible; students can learn strategies that apply to a broad range of situations. The key to transfer is the capacity to reflect — to think about thinking and learning.

Reflection takes time and support. Students are told to write a "reflective letter" for their portfolios. This is a tough assignment! The student has to review his material, think about the strengths and weaknesses, and compose a document pulling together these thoughts. Preparing the portfolio is relatively straightforward — the student assembles a collection of accomplishments. The reflective letter demonstrates transfer — an analysis of the accomplishments that goes beyond superficial comments. "I should have written a longer story." "I will check my spelling and punctuation." Some students employ alternative routes, to be sure. They discover that if they copy the back-cover summary of a chapter book, the teacher may think that they genuinely understand the thematic issues of the narrative. They are not reflective and cannot go much beyond copying. Other students may be able to tell a good story and may even understand how they approach this task, but are hard-pressed to explain (in writing) what they can do.

It is undoubtedly easier for teachers to support reflective learning when they have time to reflect themselves. But teachers lead a busy life, with little time for consultation and thoughtfulness. The question is not capability. My work with teachers convinces me that, when they are attuned to careful examination of student work, they have the talent (if not always the time) to go to the heart of authentic learning and authentic assessment. Such inquiries cannot be mandated, nor can they be "shrinkwrapped" into preprocessed procedures. They depend on teachers working together as colleagues, so that they can delve more deeply into their understanding of comprehension and composition.

The collecting of internal information might seem especially challenging in the assessment of reading. Conventional wisdom holds that writing is more easily assessed because a concrete product is available, while reading depends on asking questions — an uncertain and time-consuming process. I think that this analysis misses the point. For writing, the "product" is but one indicator of underlying cognitions. Preliminary drafts offer important evidence, but more is needed to get at students' thinking. For reading, a student's comprehension of a story may be a personal matter, but the teacher can ask for commentary, for reactions, for written responses. CLAS, by connecting reading and writing assessment, offers a model that is significant mainly because writing-from-reading has been neglected for so long. Today's students are seldom asked to connect what they read with what they write or to search out text-based resources as a foundation for written assignments.

## HOW TO DESIGN ASSESSMENT

As clarity about "what" is achieved, several practical chores come into view. When the teacher assumes genuine responsibility for assessment, several facets must be considered in the ongoing design of assessment. The first and perhaps most important — often taken for granted — is time. Existing programs tend to treat the year as a loaf of salami, one slice the same as another, one day the same as the next, interrupted on occasion by special events (e.g., spring testing). Assuming that a school can design the program, one question for the faculty to decide is what assessment activities to conduct at different times during the year. A differentiated school year seems sensible. The first week or two is a time for setting the stage, for learning about the students — their abilities, interests, strengths, and limits — not through formal testing but through observation and conversations with students. After that comes what I call "teaching for testing," short lessons around simple materials, designed to discover what students can do with instructional support. The teacher reads students a short, familiar story, then poses questions about analysis. The class develops a fantasy about "Our Favorite Summer." Which students contribute ideas? What words and ideas come to the fore? What does the class know about framing a story? October through December offers engaging opportunities for teacher-guided instruction in areas needing development and reinforcement, assessment in the background. The holidays can be used to teach students strategies and skills for composing stories and reports in situations that interest them. January is a time to reassess skills and knowledge over the winter break, and then on to thematic projects, where performance is the foundation for assessment. When May rolls around, the assessment agenda turns from formative to summative evaluation, especially in the later grades.

The point behind this design is the importance of an explicit assessment plan shared by the entire faculty. Time is one dimension; other significant decisions include variation in tasks and materials. With regard to the task dimension, a student unable on his own to explain how he approaches writing may make reasonable choices given a set of alternatives — "Do you start with the first sentence, or think about the end of the paper, or work on the middle?" Stepping back and considering one's own writing is a tough job. "Why did you pick 'the middle?'" may lead to a shrug and "I don't know." Again, offering alternatives may tap understandings buried in the student's mind. Explaining oneself is not a natural act, and requires support, practice, and reinforcement.

Materials matter. Reading assessment often depends on passages graded by readability — familiar words and short sentences. If the assessment goal is to check the student's oral reading fluency, then readability is important. If the goal is to determine comprehension skill, then interest is important. Students may discuss complex and lengthy texts with knowledge and enthusiasm if they can connect with them. Assessing interest requires a classroom library with a wide variety of books, and a teacher attentive to students' choices during free reading.

An assessment design builds around the creation of an array of possibilities for comprehension and composition, some relatively easy and engaging, others more difficult and challenging. As the year moves along, the challenge is to discover the conditions under which children show success and those where they struggle. These patterns can guide instruction and inform assessments of student achievement. I think that the most important assessment task is to search for conditions where students can succeed.

## How to Assess

Numerous books describe assessment methods, and I will not review this area in any detail. Stiggins (1994) is new and quite comprehensive, linking traditional examination techniques with newer assessment practices. While methods are part of the "how," equally important is the frame of mind, the "why" that guides the teacher's behavior. Standardized methods can easily be performed mindlessly. For assessing critical literacy, the appropriate mind-set leads to a process of applied research, where methods are selected to satisfy the teacher's curiosity, to check on hypotheses, and to raise questions. Reading–writing portfolios can be as mindless as multiple-choice tests if not guided by an inquiring disposition, and a multiple-choice strategy can be a thoughtful exercise. The focus in most methods approaches is on student activities — reading, writing, exam performance, portfolios, and so on. Equally important but generally neglected are the teacher's observations, which are especially appropriate in the early years of schooling. "Kidwatching" can be a disciplined form of inquiry, especially when linked to other sources of evidence. "Talking-with-kids" is equally important for assessment; it can take place during group discussions, in casual conversations, or through more structured interviews. As Cazden (1988) and others have noted, classroom discourse is poorly suited to genuine assessment, and therefore assessment-oriented discourse strategies are an important arena for both conceptual and practical developments. In my work with school faculties, assessment is integrated with discussions of curriculum and instruction appropriate for the development of critical literacy; thus, discussions about authentic discourse cover both instruction and assessment practices. Teacher talk still tends to dominate classroom practice, however, and I have found that creating discourse patterns that inform students' understandings and reflections is a tough nut to crack.

The choice of methods raises the issue of standardization. Some outcomes call for dynamic assessment, with free-form variation in tasks, materials, support, and so on. Other purposes require consistency in the examining conditions. The reality is that students need to learn to deal with sit-down-and-take-out-the-number-2-pencil tests, because these are part of the real world. They need to be able to handle the demands of a structured interview for the same reason. At the same time, the world outside of school usually entails situations of the sort celebrated by advocates of portfolios and performance tasks: Time and resources are available, the premium is on group collaboration, the project is done in stages from problem framing through initial draft to final product, evaluation covers the entire process from beginning to end, and the bottom line is a complex qualitative judgment. For teachers accustomed to standardized assessments, it can be eye-opening to see what students can do when supported by a range of assessment methods and instruction that helps them apply skills and knowledge.

## WHAT TO MAKE OF THE DATA

Several years ago, I visited a classroom where students had assembled portfolios during the school year. The teacher led me to a three-drawer file cabinet holding the collections and asked, "What do you think I should do with these?" A curriculum of critical literacy calls for assessment based on a rich array of student productions, but even the richest data are mute until interpreted. For standardized tests, practitioners can rely on a century-long psychometric tradition in transforming test performance into quantitative indices and for evaluating the trustworthiness of these indices.

When we turn to alternative assessments, the technology for making sense of the data is still in the early stages of development. Left on their own, teachers are disinclined to convert qualitative information into quantitative measures; they are uneasy about numbers, grades, and even rubrics. Their preference is a written narrative; however, large class sizes and limited time often defeat this approach. Most often, interpretation occurs on the fly during teacher–parent conferences, when a teacher "talks through" the student's work. In working with a school faculty, I find that developmental curriculum charts like the one in Figure 9.1 provide a foundation for quantifying growth, but uneasiness with scores, numbers, and grades remains.

The resolution of this problem, in my judgment, comes through opportunities for teachers to connect with one another around the task of interpreting assessment data. Surveys show that teachers who attend professional development sessions for judging portfolios and other authentic assessments testify without exception to the value of the experience. U. S. teachers have relatively few professional opportunities for serious exchange of ideas about development and learning. In England, by contrast, each school annually reviews its policy on the development of language and literacy, and teachers routinely assemble for "moderation" sessions designed to ensure consistency in their evaluation of student learning and performance. To the degree that externally mandated assessments like those in Kentucky and California offer similar opportunities to U. S. teachers, they are initiating a dialogue with important lasting consequences. Missing from this scenario, unfortunately, is the impetus for equally serious discussions at the local school level. Richert (1993) describes the value of discussions centering around student work samples and teachers' written commentaries, but such experiences are all too infrequent.

## How to Tell the Story

As noted above, one way to report the results from qualitative assessment is through a narrative. This strategy works well for some purposes at the local level. Although parents may demand a "grade," they also are interested in the story. They are less interested in averages and standard deviations than in how their child is doing. But how can teachers reach audiences other than parents? Students and parents — even principals — may be satisfied with grades and stories. But school boards, state superintendents, legislators, and the public want statistics, graphs, and trend lines.

Classroom teachers face a dilemma at this point. Numeric summaries are a pale image of their realities and certainly are not trustworthy guides for educational decision making. However, if teachers do not report their judgments in a format that is accessible to the broader public, then someone else will handle public accountability. I urge teachers to take the bull by the horns and enter the public policy arena. Likewise, policy makers need to learn to deal with data that are "soft" but close to the realities and with the potential to illuminate issues most in need of action. Teachers are the key, in my judgment.

## QUO VADIS?

In this concluding section, I look toward the future by describing a strategy for building a system for reporting student achievements grounded in teacher judgment, illustrating the strategy by policy initiatives in California. The public forum for Mrs. Aiken comprised parents, colleagues, the immediate neighborhood, and occasionally the broader community. Today's teachers deal with these audiences, but also with the local media, school boards, state and national reviews, and virtually any gadfly who appears on the scene. Small wonder that teachers tend to retreat to their classrooms, students, and parents. Their "reports" seldom if ever surface in the national dialogues. To be sure, the Gallup polls for Phi Delta Kappa (Calfee & Patrick, 1995) show that parents think that their local schools are doing pretty well (a grade of B+), but that the nation's schools are in trouble (a grade of C). One of my aspirations for the next few years is to design a system in which teacher judgments of student achievement come to the forefront of discussions about public schooling. In these discussions, issues of reliability, validity, opportunity to learn, challenging curriculum goals, national standards—the beefy issues—will be grounded not only in public policy but in the voices of practice. Such is my dream: the teacher's voice predominating not just in parent–teacher conferences but in school "report cards," school board reviews, and statewide assessments.

California demonstrates the practical possibilities for such a system, and also illustrates the pitfalls. I described CLAS earlier in this chapter, a standardized literacy assessment incorporating many features of a curriculum of critical literacy: response to reading, collaborative student planning, and process writing. In addition, a School Report Card (SRC) is prepared for every California school, summarizing programs and progress. (One might imagine that CLAS results would be featured in the SRC, except that CLAS no longer exists.) Finally, every 3 years each California school must conduct a Program Quality Review (PQR), a detailed self-study of curriculum and instructional programs, along with patterns of student achievement.

Unfortunately, these programs are not connected to one another. CLAS, unlike Kentucky's portfolio program, was centralized, and relatively few teachers played any role in conducting or evaluating student performance. Teachers did not receive timely feedback about the assessment. Only if they chose to volunteer as scorers did they participate in professional activities around the CLAS concept. The SRC is a bureaucratic activity, with 13 categories defined by legislative fiat; for example, class size, per capita library books, quality of school instruction, and leadership. Districts prepare the reports, and local schools have little investment in the process.

The PQR, in contrast, is taken seriously by school faculties, who spend enormous time and energy in reviewing programs and defining problems. They review curriculum and instruction, prepare analyses of student achievement, and develop plans for school improvement. Unfortunately, these efforts are linked to neither CLAS nor SRC, and receive little or no attention by either local boards or the State Department of Education. In short, the pieces are in place to create a coherent assessment of curriculum, instruction, and school organization, but they are not linked.

And so my dream—to build on existing theory, practice, and policy to develop models in which assessment and evaluation provide leverage for local school improvement and for public accountability. This dream begins with the school as the locus of reform, a theme that has pervaded discussions of school improvement since the 1960s. For teacher-based assessment to become a worthwhile endeavor, it needs to build on genuine purposes and authentic audiences.

A second element in my dream is establishing the centrality of curriculum as the foundation for developmental assessment. School restructuring in recent years has emphasized administrative and organizational issues. The chief business of schooling is learning, and attainment of a course of study provides direction for that business. We rely today on textbooks, which provide some guidance, but a curriculum of critical literacy depends on reflective teachers whose cognitive "image" of the course of study provides the guidance.

Finally, assessment requires a more secure technology. I have suggested elsewhere the concept of the teacher logbook (Calfee & Perfumo, in press). Unlike standardized systems, where the teacher's role is that of bookkeeper, the logbook documents professional judgment. It assumes a teacher with a clear conception of a developmental curriculum in which a few core domains lead students toward expertise in reading and writing. It assumes a teacher with a clear conception of assessment as applied research. It assumes genuine purposes and audiences for assessment.

A truncated version of the logbook is shown in Figure 9.2. As can be seen, it has three sections. The middle section, an anecdotal record, contains the teacher's activities as a "kid-watcher," as a naturalist of student learning. Practically speaking, this section is a journal in which the teacher records evidence of student learning in the form of brief notes. These jottings may refer to portfolio entries, to on-the-fly observations, or to formal examinations. They are to be synoptic; teachers are busy. They are driven by hypotheses and questions centered around the curriculum. Early in the school year, the aim is to create a portrait of the class as a whole, along with comments about students who depart from the general picture. As the year progresses, the notes move from starting points to records of growth.

**FIGURE 9.2.** Truncated version of the teacher logbook.

THE TEACHER LOGBOOK

**Section I: Student Summary**
Fall Entry Level

| Student | Reading/Writing/Language | | | | Math... |
|---------|--------|----------|-------|--------|------|
| | Vocab | Narrative | Expos | Skills | |
| Able, J. | | | | | |
| . . . | | | | | |
| Zeno, K. | | | | | |

**Section II: Journal Notes**
Week of _____

```
┌─────────────────────────────────────────────┐
│                                               │
│                                               │
└─────────────────────────────────────────────┘
```

**Section III: Curriculum Plan/ Record**
Plans for Fall Qtr

| | | |
|---|---|---|
| Sept: | Activities | Vocab Narr Expos Skills |
| | Update | |
| Dec: | Activities | Vocab Narr Expos Skills |
| | Update | |

The initial section of the logbook is the place where the teacher records her quarterly reckoning of individual students' developmental level in the core areas of the literacy curriculum. In early October, for instance, the teacher estimates the entry level for each student. The numbers in this summary are based on curriculum charts like that shown in Figure 9.1. The evidence to support the numbers comes from the journal notes and from artifacts and observations tied to those notes. In January, the teacher completes a second summary, this time reflecting student progress since the beginning of the year. A final summary comes in May and serves as the basis for a report to the principal and perhaps to the school board.

At the back of the logbook, a third section connects curriculum planning and adaptations to assessments of class and student performance. The teacher may discover in the fall that the class is ahead of schedule in the narrative domain, and so may decide to shift his emphasis to expository reports. Plans for thematic projects can be adapted to reflect needs, interests, and opportunities. The conventional curriculum is insulated from current events; if an earthquake rocks the San Francisco Bay Area, perhaps it makes sense to delay further study of *Velveteen Rabbit* or the causes of the

Civil War, and turn the class toward the stories in the local newspapers and the topic of plate tectonics.

The logbook concept supports teacher assessment and decision making in two respects. First, it supplies a coherent structure for these tasks, a structure that links all teachers in a school while offering leeway for individual style. Much like the medical chart used by doctors, the "slots" call for action but do not dictate the responses. Second, it is a framework for documenting the teacher's professional activities and reflections. It is a genuine "running record," a foundation for professional dialogue and for accountability to clients.

Finally, the logbook provides a potential for bridging internal and external accountability. At one level, it serves teachers in making instructional decisions and in reporting on student progress to parents and colleagues. The linkage to a developmental curriculum also provides a rubric for describing growth. The challenge here is to policy makers: to give attention to standards of growth as well as accomplishment. Today's discussions of national standards center around what students should be able to do when they leave various levels of schooling; these are standards of accomplishment. Missing from these discussions is any consideration of patterns of progress—how to assess students' movement toward those accomplishments. As noted above, the result is that only teachers at the critical grades bear the burden of standards. In a "learning" school, all teachers will be connected to this task.

I think that technological support akin to the logbook is fundamental to further progress in teacher-based assessment, but it is not sufficient. As numerous observers have noted, sustained school-wide opportunities for professional development are essential for the attainment of concepts like critical literacy, process writing, and authentic assessment. Policy makers and central authorities may mandate standards and issue regulations, but the local school remains the locus of fundamental change. State and national leaders can establish frameworks and support innovations—indeed, these are their responsibilities. But the type of education needed for tomorrow's children cannot be dictated.

Assessment is a critical ingredient in reforming education. The challenge is to create assessment practices and policies grounded in the local school as a community of inquiry, an old idea whose time finally may have come (Calfee, 1992). Authentic assessment of critical literacy in the elementary and middle grades is of central importance for promoting genuine change in the quality of education. This task cannot rest on the shoulders of fourth- and eighth-grade teachers, but must become a school-wide responsibility. It cannot depend on a single exam or artifact, but requires ongoing compilation and interpretation of data. Finally, it cannot be judged by strangers; the classroom teacher is best positioned to render an assessment of student accomplishments. Some may worry that we cannot rely on teachers for this task, but to achieve the educational outcomes needed for the next generation, we have no choice but to depend on teachers for this task. I am optimistic that they can accomplish the job with the ideas and tools now available. My goal for the future is to work with schools and teachers toward that end.

## REFERENCES

Bond, G., & Dykstra, R. (1967). The cooperative research program in first-grade reading instruction. *Reading Research Quarterly, 2,* 5–141.

Calfee, R. C. (1977). Assessment of independent reading skills: Basic research and practical applications. In A. S. Reber & D. L. Scarborough (Eds.), *Toward a psychology of reading* (pp. 289–323). Hillsdale, NJ: Erlbaum.

Calfee, R. C. (1992). The inquiring school: Literacy for the year 2000. In C. Collins & J. N. Mangieri (Eds.), *Teaching thinking: An agenda for the twenty-first century* (pp. 147–166). Hillsdale, NJ: Erlbaum.

Calfee, R. C. (1994). Critical literacy: Reading and writing for a new millennium. In N. J. Ellsworth, C. N. Hedley, & A. N. Baratta (Eds.), *Literacy: A redefinition* (pp. 19–38). Hillsdale, NJ: Erlbaum.

Calfee, R. C. (1995). Implications of cognitive psychology for authentic assessment and instruction. In T. Oakland & R. Hambleton (Eds.), *Test use with children and youth* (pp. 25–48). Boston: Kluwer Academic.

Calfee, R. C., Chapman, R., & Venezky, R. L. (1972). How a child needs to think to learn to read. In L. Gregg (Ed.), *Cognition in learning and memory* (pp. 139–182). New York: Wiley.

Calfee, R. C., & Patrick, C. P. (1995). *Teach our children well.* Stanford, CA: Stanford Portable.

Calfee, R. C., & Perfumo, P. (Eds.). (in press). *Writing portfolios: Policy and practice.* Hillsdale, NJ: Erlbaum.

Calfee, R. C., & Venezky, R. L. (1969). Component skills in beginning reading. In K. S. Goodman & J. T. Fleming (Eds.), *Psycholinguistics and the teaching of reading.* Newark, DE: International Reading Association.

Cazden, C. (1988). *Classroom discourse: The language of teaching and learning.* Portsmouth, NH: Heineman.

Chall, J. S. (1983). *Stages of reading development.* New York: McGraw-Hill.

Davis, F. B. (1968). Research in comprehension in reading. *Reading Research Quarterly, 3,* 499–545.

Goodman, K. S., Goodman, Y. M., & Hood, W. J. (1989). *The whole language evaluation book.* Portsmouth, NH: Heinemann.

Herman, J. L., Aschbacher, P. R., & Winters, L. (1992). *A practical guide to alternative assessment.* Alexandria, VA: Association for Supervision and Curriculum Development.

Hiebert, E. H., & Calfee, R. C. (1992). Assessment of literacy: From standardized tests to performances and portfolios. In A. E. Farstrup & S. J. Samuels (Eds.), *What research says about reading instruction* (pp. 70–100). Newark, DE: International Reading Association.

Kentucky State Department of Education. (1994). *Guidebook for Kentucky parents*. Frankfurt: Author.

Richert, A. E. (1993). Teaching teachers to reflect. *Journal of Curriculum Studies*, *22*, 509–527.

Salomon, G., & Perkins, D. N. (1989). Rocky roads to transfer: Rethinking a neglected phenomenon. *Educational Psychologist*, *24*, 113–142.

Stiggins, R. J. (1994). *Student-centered classroom assessment*. New York: Merrill.

Tierney R. J., Carter, M. A., & Desai, L. E. (1991). *Portfolio assessment in the reading-writing classroom*. Norwood, MA: Christopher-Gordon.

# Improving Literacy Instruction and Assessment for All Children

## SUSAN M. WATTS

*University of Minnesota*

An assumption underlying Kathryn Au and Claire Asam's chapter is that our goal in the field of literacy education is to provide *all* children with literacy instruction that affords them access to the joys of reading and writing as well as the power of reading and writing for academic, political, and economic success. In other words, we must begin to include children who, for one reason or another, have been excluded from the literacy club. Robert Calfee would argue that in order to provide these opportunities, we must engage children in *critical literacy* and design assessment accordingly.

In their chapter, Au and Asam discuss changes in curriculum, instruction, assessment, and teacher development that led to increased literacy achievement among Native Hawaiian children. The situation described by Au and Asam is a familiar one. Based on the results of standardized tests over a period of years, it was determined that most children in the Kamehameha Elementary Education Program (KEEP) were leaving sixth grade reading below grade level, even after promising beginnings in first and second grade. As a result, KEEP policy makers requested a change that would raise student achievement.

The "before" and "after" approach taken in this chapter sheds light on the complexities embedded in large-scale, programmatic change when the mandate for change comes from the outside. Au and Asam's description of the nuts and bolts of effecting change in practices of instruction, assessment, and teacher development illuminates questions and issues inherent in such change, while simultaneously adding to the knowledge base on ways to improve literacy levels for students who often are marginalized by the experience of schooling.

In his chapter, Calfee provides a framework and related guiding questions for the assessment of critical literacy. This framework provides a clear and concise plan for developing and implementing teacher-based assessment in schools. His critique of two state-mandated assessments of critical literacy provides further insight into the challenges that must be overcome if we are truly to bring together external and internal assessment. Although Calfee's framework is designed to contribute toward closing the gap between externally mandated assessment and internally based assessment, the efforts of California and Kentucky clearly illustrate the tension between external and internal factors in assessment. It is clear from Calfee's chapter that closing this gap will require more than a reform of assessment; it will require rethinking assumptions and redesigning practice in the areas of curriculum, teaching, and teacher development.

Although Au and Asam, and Calfee focus on different topics in their chapters, they share some common ground, raise some common questions, and point to some common directions for continued work. I am particularly struck by the degree to which both chapters point to the importance of explicitness, collaboration, and the teacher as the hub of change. For me, the chapters are complementary and useful to read in tandem.

The remainder of my response will focus on key points raised in the two chapters as they relate to curriculum and instruction, assessment, and teacher development.

## CURRICULUM AND INSTRUCTION

Both Calfee and Au and Asam call for a curriculum based on a developmental rather than a stage-wise model of reading, although with different primary goals in mind. Calfee believes such a model fosters critical literacy; Au and Asam believe such a model maximizes literacy achievement among low-income students of diverse backgrounds. The authors differ when it comes to the actual components of such a curriculum. The KEEP curriculum is composed of both cognitive and affective dimensions of literacy acquisition, whereas Calfee's proposed curriculum focuses solely on the cognitive. I wonder how Calfee views the role of affect in the development of critical readers and writers. Others might wonder whether KEEP's dual focus on the cognitive and the affective will inhibit the development of critical literacy.

The initial KEEP curriculum — skills-oriented and based on behavioral notions of learning — did not lead to long-term literacy growth. As a result, a whole literacy curriculum focusing on ownership, reading comprehension, the writing process, language and vocabulary knowledge, word reading strategies and spelling, and voluntary reading was put into effect. This curricular change is significant because it contradicts long-held notions about how best to teach children who are "at risk" of experiencing difficulty with learning to read. However, it is in line with Walmsley and Allington's (1995) assertion that movement from a skills-based approach to a holistic approach with defined dimensions of literacy is necessary to meet the needs of at-risk students. It is also in line with current understandings of how to facilitate literacy development among linguistically diverse learners (Farnan, Flood, & Lapp, 1994; Heath & Mangiola, 1991; Peregoy & Boyle, 1993).

KEEP's whole literacy curriculum is not a linear array of sequenced skills but rather a collection of six dimensions of literacy. It was assumed that aspects of literacy such as ownership, voluntary reading, and reading comprehension could (and should) be addressed simultaneously with aspects such as word reading strategies, as opposed to being addressed only *after* certain other "basic" skills had been acquired.

In addition to changes in curriculum, teachers were expected to change their instructional practices by using workshop approaches to reading and writing. Au and Asam's description of teachers' and consultants' struggles in implementing these workshops is informative. As has been documented elsewhere, the process of moving to holistic literacy instruction is slow, even for those who embrace the idea. What happened in the KEEP program parallels my own experiences with teachers, in that it was easier for them to use writers' workshop than to use readers' workshop and so they began with writers' workshop. In a period of 5 years, teachers had come a good distance, but still only part of the way, in a journey toward more holistic methods of instruction.

With this in mind, it is not surprising that long-term results showed student growth in writing but not in reading. Not only were teachers resistant to the readers' workshop, but they were not at all encouraged to implement it at the beginning. Au and Asam believe that the results in writing achievement suggest that reading would be similarly improved if the readers' workshop was implemented. I agree with the authors, but since the KEEP program is no longer in operation, there will be no opportunity to empirically test their belief.

Finally, Au and Asam briefly address the importance of culturally responsive pedagogy in both the initial and the revised KEEP curricula. Although Au and others have discussed this in detail elsewhere (see, for example, Au & Kawakami, 1994; Delpit, 1988; Nieto, 1996; Shade & New, 1993; Villegas, 1991), I must underscore its importance in ensuring that

"The First R" is, in fact, accessible to *all* children. Culturally responsive pedagogy must move beyond its current status as a hot topic of discussion to the status of a regular dimension of practice.

The challenge here is not small, especially since the demography of the school-age population in major cities is changing rapidly, while the demography of the populations of classroom teachers and faculty in colleges of education remains relatively constant (Garcia & Pugh, 1992). The call for culturally responsive pedagogy carries with it serious implications for those of us in teacher education and staff development, including the necessity to explore the effects of culturally responsive pedagogy at the level of individual schools and individual classrooms. Au and Asam found that teachers needed to know, explicitly, what the new whole literacy curriculum "looked like" before they were able to implement it. Similarly, discussions of culturally responsive instruction need examples and pictures of "what it looks like."

## ASSESSMENT

Au and Asam discuss assessment within the context of improving the literacy achievement of students in the KEEP program. Specifically, they describe an approach to portfolio assessment designed to gauge program effectiveness and work in concert with changes in curriculum. Theirs is a concrete, close-up example of one assessment as it was devised and carried out in one literacy program. Calfee discusses assessment on a broader scale. His framework for teacher assessment of critical literacy is meant to structure and guide the kinds of decisions made by the many teachers and administrators who are in the process of transforming assessment practices. Elements of such decision making are evidenced in recent assessment projects in Arizona (Garcia & Verville, 1994), Maryland (Kapinus, Collier, & Kruglanski, 1994), and Rhode Island (Snider, Lima, & DeVito, 1994).

Four aspects of Calfee's framework are particularly noteworthy. First, assessment is a problem-solving process; it is driven by questions and hypotheses. It seems that in order to foster literacy development for *all* children, the questions asked must be student- and curriculum-centered; they must focus on students' strengths, needs, and interests relative to the literacy curriculum. In reality, these are only some of the questions asked. In reality, the questions asked reflect the orientation and interests of those who have the power to ask them.

Relating Wixson, Valencia, and Lipson's (1994) discussion of issues surrounding external and internal assessment to Calfee's considerations suggests at least two options for merging them. One is for those who represent different interests to start to ask the same questions — that is, we must all (teachers, parents, principals, school board members, legislators, and others) become interested primarily in the same thing. Another is to devise assessments that are capable of answering multiple questions simultaneously. Calfee seems to lean toward the latter option, and yet if assessment is truly question-driven, one wonders whether that is a true possibility.

Another important feature of Calfee's framework is that assessment is tied to instruction; they are two sides of the same coin. We assess what we teach, and the results of our assessments can influence what and how we teach. In addition, the act of engaging in certain types of assessment can itself directly change instructional practices. Although the Kentucky model did not tie the results of portfolio assessment to instruction as closely as it could have, the implementation of the assessment, in and of itself, influenced instruction. The creation of portfolios became part of the instructional day.

Third, assessment is ongoing. I appreciate Calfee's argument that we need to move away from the "salami model" of the school year. By capitalizing on the cumulative aspect of time, the link between assessment and instruction can be strengthened. Further, by viewing assessment as ongoing, there is a tendency to reject assessments targeted only at certain grade levels.

Finally, assessment must be explicit. Teachers must know what they are looking for and when they have found it. And they must be able to explain and defend their evaluations. How will teachers know what they are looking for? How will they know when they have found it? How will they defend their evaluations? In the KEEP program, this meant tying portfolio assessment to benchmarks, or standards, that manifested themselves in explicit statements. Teachers knew and defended their knowledge based on an external model; they were told from outside. My sense is that this occurred primarily because the changes required of teachers were substantial, and the timeline for change was short. Thus, the portfolio approach was modified. However, in other cases this occurs because of how portfolio assessment is defined in a given context.

As illustrated by Stowell and Tierney (1995), there are many ways in which portfolio assessment manifests itself, and some are more top-down than others. Many argue that when portfolio assessment is implemented from a top-down perspective, it is not true portfolio assessment. Yet, KEEP benchmarks did raise teacher expectations, facilitate teacher use of the portfolio system, and facilitate the quantitative aggregation of data for determining program effectiveness — the primary purpose for which it was designed.

Both the KEEP example and Calfee's description of the innovative state-wide assessment practices developed in California and Kentucky are helpful in highlighting the challenges involved in making real changes in assessment. Although the California system involved an on-the-spot test and the Kentucky system employed literacy portfolios, both suffered from some of the same problems. By highlighting three critical pitfalls of each system, Calfee is able to argue the importance of extensive staff development, total school responsibility for student progress (rather than responsibility of particular grade-level teachers), and school-wide connections between assessment and the literacy program.

In both Calfee's and Au and Asam's discussions of assessment, consideration of the role of the students in assessment was noticeably absent. Although Calfee acknowledges that students will need time to practice "reflecting" and "explaining themselves," there is no discussion of how to prepare them to do that. Similarly, Au and Asam did not address student preparation for portfolio assessment, even though student surveys were used to assess ownership, reading logs were used to assess voluntary reading, and written samples were used to assess most everything else. We must take time to educate students — as well as parents and the public — if we are to be successful in reaching a variety of audiences with new assessment techniques.

The backdrop for all of Calfee's recommendations is a new definition of accountability, one in which external and internal views of assessment are balanced. As he sees it, assessment should produce both qualitative and quantitative information about student achievement. By producing both qualitative and quantitative information, Calfee argues, we can meet the needs of various audiences for assessment, including the student, the parent, and the public. This may be true, but if teachers continue to tailor their stories to current public conceptions of how they should be told, then how will the public ever come to value the teacher's story and his way of telling it? The question here is one of pragmatics. How do we educate the public to understand and accept stories that are not told with numbers?

## TEACHER DEVELOPMENT

Teacher development is a strong theme in both chapters. How do teachers move from one curriculum and instruction approach to another? How do teachers move from one assessment approach to another? How can teachers be supported as they strive to make substantive changes in their practice? As Calfee notes, schools have long operated under a factory model, and it is only recently that we have been seeing a transformation to the informa-tion-age model. The factory model has applied to teachers as well as students.

Au and Asam note that early efforts to engage teachers in change were unsuccessful in large part because the KEEP consultants attempted to give information *to* teachers rather than engaging in problem solving *with* teachers. It was not until teachers became integrally involved in their *own* change processes that they actually were able to effect change. I believe that those of us interested in helping teachers to change must ourselves change. We must spend less time providing teachers with ideas and more time working with them in constructing ideas — engaging them in the planning, the implementation, and the evaluation of their own change efforts. In Au and Asam's words, teachers must feel responsible for "their own professional development." They cannot feel this responsibility unless they have it.

Professional development was apparent at all levels of the KEEP program. Teachers were supported in their work with students, and consultants were supported in their work with teachers. Building such support into the program reflects an assumption that there *would* be questions and there *would* be confusion, not only for teachers but also for consultants. As the model for teacher development changed, so too did the model for consultant development. Consultants needed clear objectives for working with teachers, just as teachers needed clear objectives for working with students.

Both Au and Asam and Calfee give us some new ways to think about inservice teacher education and staff development. Clearly, we need to design ways of dealing with professional development that move beyond single staff development days and toward the integration of staff development into the day-to-day running of schools. Teachers need to be engaged in professional discussion groups on a regular basis. Teacher development must be ongoing and built into the daily operations of schools, and successful teacher development efforts should be documented and disseminated. Nistler and Shepperson (1993–94), for example, describe one approach to long-term collaborative problem solving between university faculty and elementary school teachers.

This is more than an issue of how to empower — that is, give power to — teachers. This is also an issue of how to encourage teachers to accept that power. As Seda (1994) notes, change can threaten whatever sense of expertise and effectiveness a teacher currently possesses, and assessment is one area where teachers often feel limited in expertise at the beginning. Teachers may rely on their own judgments for the planning of daily instruction, but they often defer to standardized tests when it comes to assessing the overall effectiveness of their programs (Klenk & Palincsar, 1994). The implications for teacher development are vast and multilayered. They have to do with providing teachers with avenues for finding their own expertise and then legitimating that knowledge by deferring to their judgments instead of supplanting it with other sources of information.

Collaboration seems to be a key to teacher development. Whether through cross-checking teacher summary judgments as a means of establishing validity in assessment — as described by Calfee — or, as in the KEEP program, working together to clarify the portfolio assessment process, collaboration seems to me to be *vital* to supporting the teacher as the hub of change in curriculum, instruction, and assessment. Perhaps the ultimate question is one of power and responsibility: Are those who currently hold the power willing to give it? Are teachers willing to accept it?

## REFERENCES

Au, K. H., & Kawakami, A. J. (1994). Cultural congruence in instruction. In E. R. Hollins, J. E. King, & W. C. Hayman (Eds.), *Teaching diverse populations: Formulating a knowledge base* (pp. 5–23). Albany: State University of New York Press.

Delpit, L. (1988). The silenced dialogue: Power and pedagogy in educating other people's children. *Harvard Educational Review, 58,* 280–298.

Farnan, N., Flood, J., & Lapp, D. (1994). Comprehending through reading and writing: Six research-based instructional strategies. In K. Urbschat-Spangenberg & R. Pritchard (Eds.), *Kids come in all languages: Reading instruction for ESL students* (pp. 135–157). Newark, DE: International Reading Association.

Garcia, J., & Pugh, S. L. (1992). Multicultural education in teacher preparation programs. *Phi Delta Kappan, 72,* 213–219.

Garcia, M., & Verville, K. (1994). Redesigning teaching and learning: The Arizona Student Assessment Program. In S. W. Valencia, E. H. Hiebert, & P. F. Afflerbach (Eds.), *Authentic reading assessment: Practices and possibilities* (pp. 228–246). Newark, DE: International Reading Association.

Heath, S. B., & Mangiola, L. (1991). *Children of promise: Literate activity in linguistically and culturally diverse classrooms.* Washington, DC: National Education Association.

Kapinus, B., Collier, G. V., & Kruglanski, H. (1994). The Maryland school performance assessment program: A new view of assessment. In S. W. Valencia, E. H. Hiebert, & P. F. Afflerbach (Eds.), *Authentic reading assessment: Practices and possibilities* (pp. 255–276). Newark, DE: International Reading Association.

Klenk, L., & Palincsar, A. S. (1994, December). *Dynamic classroom observations: Assessing the interaction of individual learner characteristics and classroom literacy instruction for young children referred to special education.* Paper presented at the annual meeting of the National Reading Conference, San Diego, CA.

Nieto, S. (1996). *Affirming diversity: The sociopolitical context of multicultural education* (2nd ed.). New York: Longman.

Nistler, R., & Shepperson, G. M. (1993–94). Negotiating change: Teachers and university professors working together. *Journal of Reading Education, 19*(2), 29–45.

Peregoy, S. F., & Boyle, O. W. (1993). *Reading, writing, and learning in ESL: A resource book for K–8 teachers.* New York: Longman.

Seda, I. (1994). Commentary on "Portfolio Assessment: Experiences at the Kamehameha Elementary Education Program." In S. W. Valencia, E. H. Hiebert, & P. F. Afflerbach (Eds.), *Authentic reading assessment: Practices and possibilities* (pp. 127–133). Newark, DE: International Reading Association.

Shade, B. J., & New, C. A. (1993). Cultural influences on learning: Teaching implications. In J. A. Banks & C. A. Banks (Eds.), *Multicultural education: Issues and perspectives* (2nd ed., pp. 317–331). Needham Heights, MA: Allyn & Bacon.

Snider, M. A., Lima, S. S., & DeVito, P. J. (1994). Rhode Island's literacy portfolio assessment project. In S. W. Valencia, E. H. Hiebert, & P. F. Afflerbach (Eds.), *Authentic reading assessment: Practices and possibilities* (pp. 71–88). Newark, DE: International Reading Association.

Stowell, L. P., & Tierney, R. J. (1995). Portfolios in the classroom: What happens when teachers and students negotiate assessment? In R. L. Allington & S. A. Walmsley (Eds.), *No quick fix: Rethinking literacy programs in America's elementary schools* (pp. 78–94). New York: Teachers College Press.

Villegas, A. M. (1991). *Culturally responsive pedagogy for the 1990s and beyond.* Princeton, NJ: Educational Testing Service.

Walmsley, S. A., & Allington, R. L. (1995). Redefining and reforming instructional support programs for at-risk students. In R. L. Allington & S. A. Walmsley (Eds.), *No quick fix: Rethinking literacy programs in America's elementary schools* (pp. 19–44). New York: Teachers College Press.

Wixson, K. K., Valencia, S. W., & Lipson, M. Y. (1994). Issues in literacy assessment: Facing the realities of internal and external assessment. *Journal of Reading Behavior, 26*, 315–337.

CONCLUSION

# Reclaiming the Center

## P. DAVID PEARSON
*Michigan State University*

Since the mid-1980s, we have witnessed, if not the demise, the considerable erosion of largely curriculum-centered views of the language arts curriculum. Such views have dominated our work, as Robert Calfee (Chapter 9, this volume) has indicated, since World War II. Concomitantly, we have witnessed the ascendency of highly constructivist, child-centered views, usually traveling under the label whole language, but often adopting the label of one of its intellectual cousins — literature-based reading, process writing, or whole literacy. In writing, we have emphasized the writing process and focused on celebrating the individual generation of ideas rather than the formal features of the message and the convincing character of the arguments presented. In this new approach, conventional features such as grammatical appropriateness, spelling, and punctuation have assumed a background role, or no role at all, in the curriculum.

In reading, the enabling features of instruction — phonics skills, word analysis strategies, vocabulary knowledge, and explicit comprehension strategies — have been de-emphasized in favor of reader response to literature. This has led to a curricular approach in which we rely on highly idiosyncratic personal responses to the reading of high-quality literary texts as the primary vehicle for developing reading skill (even if, as has been observed in some well-meaning, literature-based programs, the teacher has to read *to* students). The presumption, as near as I can tell, is that through meaningful encounters with the great ideas of good literature, all those skills that we used to regard as prerequisite to independence in reading will emerge and develop quite naturally, without arduous effort on the part of teachers, thus allowing students to read new texts on their own.

The purpose of my contribution, which was first presented at the end of a conference in which we were treated to many good ideas about improving the quality of literacy instruction, is to conduct a cost–benefit analysis of recent changes in curricular perspective. I want to ask whether the progress that we have made in embracing child-centered principles of literacy learning and teaching have come at a cost that is too dear to pay. I also want to ask whether we need to reconsider the efficacy of these principles; to ask whether we have, as professional educators, acted selfishly in embracing what could be construed as a politically correct approach (one that permitted us to stand on the shoulders of figures of the stature of Comenius and Dewey) in siding for individuality, inquiry, authenticity, and empowerment. Furthermore, I want to know whether the cost of our actions may be that some children are not doing as well in our schools as they ought to.

In asking these difficult, and in some circles unpopular, questions, I do not want to be construed as taking sides against children, or motherhood or the supreme deity, for that matter. I merely want us to take stock of where we have traveled in the past several years, to evaluate what we have gained and what we have lost, and to ask ourselves whether we should consider trying to regain some of those losses.

After I have described this curricular journey in some detail, making sure to provide my reading of the underlying principles and impact of this movement, I will conclude with a set of design principles for building the next generation of reading curriculum. As those who have read most of this book or who attended the Bond Conference will recognize, nearly all of the design principles that I will present have been introduced by one or another of the other participants in the conference and contributors to this volume.

The year 1994 marked the thirtieth year of my career as a professional educator. During those years, I have witnessed all kinds of movements and fads and panaceas—the whole-word versus phonics debate in the 1960s, open education, mastery learning, outcomes-based education, learning styles, neurological impress, and the cognitive revolution, to name but a few of the more memorable ones. We in reading seem to have a knack for inventing new panaceas, one after another after another. But I have really never witnessed anything like the whole language movement. I have never seen anything spread so rapidly as it has spread. It bears a strong similarity to, I think, earlier incarnations of the child-centered movement—the open school movement and progressive education—but it is quite different in some ways. It seems to have more of the details worked out, more of an infrastructure to it. The infrastructure keeps the movement alive and well because it helps its advocates and implementors deal with unanswered questions and unsolved problems.

The flavor of the movement is captured in its vocabulary. Just listen to any talk or read any article, and the key vocabulary literally jumps off the page at you. Advocates describe their own tasks and texts as *functional, natural, genuine,* and *authentic*; they describe tasks and texts arising from the conventional wisdom (which seems to be any basal reader program, accompanied, of course, by the obligatory standardized test) as *dysfunctional, unnatural, ingenuine, unauthentic,* and *contrived.*

In the new way, readers read to *construct* their own interpretation of texts written by *authors* whose genuine intent was to *communicate* with an audience for purposes of entertainment, information, or persuasion. In the conventional wisdom, by contrast, readers read to *regurgitate* unrelated facts from texts written by *hack writers* whose purpose in writing them was to *force* students to practice unnecessary and fragmented reading skills in order to complete consumable workbooks. In the new way, teachers work with students, the real curricular informants, in a *collaborative* milieu in order to plan and revise integrated curricular events that facilitate growth in each individual's emerging repertoire of literacy tools. Teachers become aware of student progress by *kid-watching* — observing growth in students' repertoire of language activity while they complete authentic literacy tasks. In the conventional wisdom, publishers and administrators control the game and call the shots; they *mandate* materials and activities to teachers, who, in turn, foist them on students. The whole enterprise is monitored with a panoply of *piecemeal assessments* of both student performance (usually *tests*) and teacher behavior (usually *prescribed checklists* of teacher actions known to be associated with effective teaching).

As the rhetoric strongly suggests, there definitely appears to be an Us and Them in this curricular debate.

## UNDERLYING CONCEPTS

The principles that undergird the infrastructure of the whole language movement come from three arenas of discourse — the *philosophical,* the *political,* and the *curricular.* The movement is much more than a way of teaching reading and writing. It has a particular position on epistemology — how we come to know what we know. Compared with the conventional wisdom, the whole language movement makes very different assumptions about who is in charge of schools and learning and teaching. The whole language movement's intensely integrationist view of curriculum, if taken seriously, will influence everything taught in schools, not just reading and writing.

As I just noted, the whole language movement has the potential to influence virtually all aspects of the curriculum. However, there are two key curricular concepts in the movement — integration and authenticity.

*Integration.* Integration is important in at least three senses.

1. The curriculum is integrated in the sense that it seeks to preserve the wholeness or integrity of literacy events; no literacy act is mercilessly and unnecessarily decomposed into subskills. It is undoubtedly this sense of integration that has spawned the *whole* in the whole language label (which, as Yetta Goodman pointed out in 1989, has its roots in the introduction to Comenius's *Pictus Orbis*).

2. The curriculum is integrated in the sense that artificial boundaries are not set up between any of the four language functions — reading, writing, speaking, and listening. All are regarded as supportive facets of the same underlying cognitive and linguistic phenomenon of human communication. Growth in one supports growth in all.

3. The curriculum is integrated in the sense that the literacy curriculum is not viewed as separate from social studies, science, literature, art, music, or mathematics curricula. In the spirit of the integrated day curriculum of the British infant school tradition and, even earlier, the project approach of Kilpatrick so often associated with Dewey's concept of progressive education (Cremin, 1961), whole language thrives on the principle that literacy tasks should never be ends unto themselves; instead, they should be means to other ends, such as learning, enjoyment, persuasion, and communication.

*Authenticity.* Authenticity is the second key curricular attribute of the movement. It is very much related to the second sense of integration; that is, when students pursue language activities out of genuine communicative intent, those activities will be authentic. Conventional programs got us into trouble because they were either getting kids ready for the real thing — this thing called reading — or because they provided us with simulations, mere shadows, of the real thing.

The *readiness* perspective, for example, suggests that real reading and writing are tough sledding, so educators must try to make life easier for their novice students. The best way to reduce complexity is to decompose reading and writing into simpler component subskills, each of which can be mastered in sequence, in order to get students ready for the real thing. As a result, according to the whole language critique, students are always getting ready to do real reading and writing ("Just hang in there, guys, as soon as we get these sounds down, we'll be able to read real stories on our own.") rather than doing real reading and writing in the first place. Advocates of the movement, therefore, support real reading and writing from the very outset of schooling. So important is reading and writing right from the start that a new vocabulary term, *emergent literacy,* was coined to distinguish these activities from the more conventional readiness stage in our conventional materials. Another term, *invented spelling,* was coined to capture the constructive intent of the work of the youngest and most emergent of writers in constructing texts.

According to the movement, simulations, to take another example, are even more subtle and insidious than the readiness perspective. Worksheets on which students mark vowels or correct errors in grammar or spelling are so clearly simulations that their inauthenticity is transparent and easy to detect. What about an activity in which each first grader writes an invitation to the principal to visit the class to hear stories written by the children? Or what about grade 2 literature groups in which all of the students are reading a real book instead of one of those fake books perpetrated by basal publishers? Do those represent genuine, authentic literacy acts?

Some advocates of the whole language movement would say "yes," but others would argue "no." Some would call these activities simulations of real reading and writing. In the invitation task, the students know perfectly well that only one invitation is necessary to accomplish the communicative goal. In the literature group task, the teacher controls the content and perhaps even the way the book gets discussed. According to the purist perspective, greater authenticity would accrue to a writing activity in which each student invited someone different (provided each wanted to invite someone) or to literature groups in which children got together on their own to discuss the different books that each had read.

As near as I can tell, the criterion for authenticity is a "real-world" criterion; that is, a school task is regarded as authentic to the degree that it represents the kind of task a literate individual would exercise of her own free will (unfettered by an authority figure in the process of doing school). The curricular goal seems to be to eliminate the gap between school literacy tasks and real-world literacy tasks.

## THE PHILOSOPHICAL PERSPECTIVE

Advocates of the movement accept, at a minimum, a constructivist view of knowledge and comprehension. There is no meaning in a text; there is no meaning for a text until a reader constructs it for himself, and no two readers will construct identical meanings for a given text. Since meaning does not reside in the text, all comprehension is, by its very nature, a form of interpretation. Furthermore, since each reader must construct her own meaning, there can be no such thing as an authoritative interpretation. Each interpretation is, in this sense, every bit as valid as any other interpretation. What makes communication possible is shared, not identical, interpretations: We see things in common, but in our own idiosyncratic ways.

This epistemological perspective carries important curricular and political implications. First, when it comes to comprehension, we are all—students, teachers, administrators, authors, critics—equals. A teacher's job is to understand, rather than correct, a student's interpretation because, as language users, understanding is our job in all communicative contexts. Second, an active interpretive community is necessary to support comprehension. What keeps us from idiosyncratic hallucination is that community with whom we negotiate meaning and share knowledge. Our personal meaning for a text can be whatever we want it to be, but when that meaning enters the arena of social discourse, a different set of rules apply; other community members demand rules of evidence and argument, and they want to know why and how we came to hold our personal meanings.

## THE POLITICAL PERSPECTIVE

For those in the whole language movement, the primary political question to ask about school curricula is, *Who's in charge?* For all too long, advocates of the movement tell us, *we* (those of us who are teachers and students and live in classrooms) have given up our birthright; we have ceded the power to decide what will be learned and how it will be learned to *them* (administrators, curriculum directors, curriculum committees, school boards, professors, publishers, basal authors, and state or national standards committees). It is time, they tell us, to empower teachers and students; it is time for curriculum and standards to be returned to the communities of teachers and students who must live with and give life to them. It is no accident that the whole language movement has made its greatest curricular inroads in an era in which site-based management has reached its acme. A motto for whole language curriculum might be this: *All decisions should be made as close as possible to the situation in which they will be implemented.*

If curriculum is returned to teachers and students, so too must assessment be. Were this to occur, then only "situated" (i.e., arising from the situation) assessment, the kind that teachers and students would develop to suit their own curriculum, would count. Standardized tests and basal reading tests would serve no purpose in the curriculum, for neither would provide any information about real reading. Furthermore, the goal of every teacher assessment, even when it is situated, would be to promote student self-assessment, as Calfee (Chapter 9, this volume) has suggested in his characterization of curriculum. This focus on sharing authority with students and promoting student independence underscores the child-centered character of the movement.

So there it is — my characterization of the whole language movement — a grass-roots curriculum reform movement based on constructivist epistemological principles and committed to privileging in our schools all we know about how literacy functions in authentic situations. In fact, to eliminate the differences between literacy in schooling and literacy in life (at least, the good life) might be construed as a goal of the whole language movement.

## IMPACT OF RECENT CURRICULAR CHANGES

I do not want to give the impression that the acceptance of this reform perspective is universal. To the contrary, there is considerable resistance to whole language and literature-based reading throughout the country. In California, one could almost characterize it as a backlash. California's plummet to the bottom of the 1992 NAEP distribution (Mullis, Campbell, & Farstrup, 1993), coupled with an extreme reaction to constructivist underpinnings of its curriculum and assessment initiatives by the radical religious right, has seriously damaged the efficacy of the literature-driven California Framework of the late 1980s (California State Department of Education, 1987). In many places throughout the country, whole language has never really gained a foothold. Furthermore, the reaction of the religious right, when it learns that we have assessments in which there is more than one right answer or in which we re-embrace values, will be loud and clear.

These qualifications notwithstanding, I do believe that this reform perspective has, in a very real sense, become the conventional wisdom and a kind of professional ideal to which we all respond.

There is a great deal of evidence to support this assertion. Most dramatic, I think, have been the changes in basal readers in the past decade. Vocabulary control is virtually gone in basals, even in the early readers that first graders receive. The practice of writing stories to fit into a sequence is dead; only trade books are used. Stories and chapters are no longer adapted to fit a particular level of difficulty, and they are excerpted much less frequently than in the 1980s. Workbooks have been replaced by journals (to be honest, some still look like workbooks), and there is precious little opportunity for students to practice skills in independent learning situations. Skills that a decade ago were proudly foregrounded now often are relegated to appendix-like status. In the thumb test of today's basals, it is hard to find them.

The rhetoric of professional articles has changed substantially, too. A decade ago, even 5 years ago, articles were written with the presumption of a different conventional wisdom — a world filled with skills, contrived readers, and workbooks. Now, they are written with the presumption that the reform movement, while not fully ensconced in America's schools, is well on its way to implementation. The arguments in today's articles are less about first principles of whole language and more about fine tuning one's teaching repertoire. The meetings of the Whole Language Umbrella are larger than most large state conventions and regional conferences of the International Reading Association. Whole language is no longer a collection of guerilla sorties into the land of skills; it has, I believe, become the conventional wisdom, in rhetoric if not in reality.

In the process of ascendency, the movement has celebrated and privileged several important principles of literacy learning: authenticity of text and task, curricular integration, student and teacher empowerment, the primacy of constructing meaning, and a recontextualization of learning within a community context. In my view, all these have been positive developments — ones that all members of the profession, quite irrespective of their philosophical dispositions, can celebrate.

Still, the controversy between whole language and the conventional wisdom has been likened to a war — a holy war. As in all wars, holy and otherwise, there have been some casualties. I already mentioned two — the loss of vocabulary control and the hiding of skills. The replacement of carefully controlled basal stories with authentic texts written by regular authors even at the earliest levels has meant that some beginning readers are forced to stumble over word after word they don't know. The relegation of skills to the appendix has meant that we have all but accepted the premise that skills are better *caught* in the act of reading and writing genuine texts for authentic purposes than *taught* directly and explicitly by teachers. The argument is the same for phonics, grammar, text conventions, and structural elements. These entities may be worthy of learning, but they are unworthy of teaching.

We are presented with a serious conundrum as a profession. Our earlier skill instruction, with decontextualized lessons and practice on "textoids" in workbook pages, surely deserved the disdain accorded to it. However, I am not convinced that a complete retreat from any and all skill instruction is the answer. The data presented by Elfrieda Hiebert (Chapter 2, this volume) suggest that many children do not catch the alphabetic principle by sheer immersion in print or by listening to others read aloud.

A third casualty has been strategy instruction. This loss has been particularly difficult for those of us who spent the better part of the early 1980s convincing those who control the tools of instruction that the thoughtful teaching of flexible strategies for making and monitoring meaning ought to replace the direct teaching of skills that were taught as though they were immutable laws. However, the strategy lessons that filled our basals in the mid- to late 1980s — direct advice from teachers about how to summarize what one has read, how to use text structure to infer relations among ideas, how to distinguish fact from opinion, how to determine the central thread of a story, how to use context to infer word meanings, and how to make and evaluate the accuracy of predictions — are virtually nonexistent in the basals of the early 1990s.

Again, there is no bias in whole language or literature-based reading against the learning and use of a whole range of cognitive strategies. There is, as with phonics and grammar, a serious question about whether direct, explicit instruction in how to use them will really help. Again, the advice is to let them emerge from attempts to solve real reading problems and puzzles, the kind students encounter in genuine encounters with authentic text. Again, there is reason for disdain of what we did in the 1980s, but the answer may not be complete rejection. Later I will argue that Margaret McKeown and her colleagues' work (Chapter 5, this volume) provides us with an alternative to all or nothing.

A fourth casualty of these holy wars has been the emphasis on structure that we had just gained, as a matter of fact, in roughly the same time frame and from roughly the same source (cognitive psychology) as strategy instruction. This has been a rejection not only of the tradition of formal grammars identified with traditional English classes. The rejection of structure extends to just about any systematic analysis of the infrastructure of just about any structural account of just about any linguistic phenomenon. So story grammars, rhetorical structures, and intersentential relations are as suspect as formal grammar or rules for usage.

As with skills, reformers do not claim that students should not learn these structural tools; they simply claim that, like skills, these tools are best inferred from reading and writing authentic texts in the process of making meaning. The advocates are comfortable in adopting Frank Smith's (1983) admonition to encourage children to read like a writer (meaning to read the text with a kind of critical eye toward understanding the tools and tricks of the trade that the author uses to make his points and achieve his effects on readers), but they would likely reject a systematic set of lessons designed to teach and assess children's control of story grammar elements (such as plot, characterization, style, mood, or theme) or some system for dealing with basic patterns of expository text. In Calfee's analysis (Chapter 9, this volume), we see an alternative to both the formulaic approach of the early 1980s and the "discovery" approach of the new reforms. He suggests that dealing with these structural elements as they emanate from stories that a group is currently reading can provide some guidance and useful tools for students and teachers.

A fifth casualty is reading in the content areas. In general, content area texts — expository texts in general — are not privileged in our new world of literature-based reading. This is ironic, because when I ask teachers about their most serious concerns in literacy instruction, they invariably say — and this is especially true if they teach fourth grade or higher — "Well, if you think my kids have trouble with stories, you should come and see what we do with our social studies and science class. That's where the real trouble begins." Our colleagues at the middle school and high school level have worked diligently over the past 3 decades to convince their colleagues that content area reading instruction, study skills, and attention to text structure are important. It appears to have been destroyed with one stroke of the literary pen.

The cost here has been very dear. If you look in middle school and high school classrooms to examine the role of expository text, you are virtually forced to conclude that it has none. Occasionally teachers assign expository texts for homework, but when students come to class the next day, clearly having avoided the assignment, teachers provide them with an oral version of what they would have gotten out of the text if they had bothered to read it. Most high school teachers have quite literally given up on the textbook for the communication of any important content. While understandable, this approach is, of course, ultimately counterproductive. There comes a time in the lives of students — either when they go to college or enter the world of work — when others expect them to read and understand informational text.

## A PLAN FOR RECLAIMING THE CENTER

As I began thinking about my presentation for the Bond Conference almost a year before the conference took place, I decided to use this forum as an opportunity to think about how we might reach some consensus, as a profession of reading teachers, about instructional goals and strategies. I have grown weary of the holy instructional wars that have characterized the past 15 years of rhetoric about practice. I have grown even wearier of the lack of civility in our scholarly debates, as evidenced in the professional literature (for example, the Fall 1994 issue of *Reading Research Quarterly*). That desire for consensus and civility provided the motivation for the title of this chapter, "Reclaiming the Center." What I propose is a set of core principles for building a curriculum that will encompass the goals of most of us in the profession.

The sources of my proposed common core are myriad. I readily and happily admit that many of the elements in my core are completely consistent with the whole language movement, and one could draw the inference that they come directly from whole language. However, they are also consistent with much of the work that was rejected in the wake of whole language's ascendency. More to the point of this volume, they are also consistent with the work of McKeown and her colleagues (Chapter 5, this volume) on Questioning the Author and with that of Tom Trabasso and Joseph Magliano (Chapter 7, this volume) on constructing meaning from text. They are consistent with Hiebert's (Chapter 2, this volume) admonitions about the shortcomings of literature-based reading, especially for students who depend on schools for their literacy learning. They are also consistent with Richard Allington and his colleagues' (Chapter 4, this volume) warnings about the dangers of creating a second-class curriculum for children of poverty, and they could be inferred from the underlying instructional model in Robert Calfee's (Chapter 9) critical-literacy program. They are even consistent with Chuck Perfetti and Sulan Zhang's (Chapter 3) and Joe Torgesen and Steve Hecht's (Chapter 6) comments about the centrality of the alphabetic principle of English writing. But more than any other source, they could easily have been derived from the KEEP program that Kathy Au and Claire Asam (Chapter 8, this volume) described.

Let me end with my candidate core—my list of the characteristics of effective instruction and thoughtful teachers. However, before I provide my overarching list, let me single out two linguistic principles that, while not unique to early reading, are so salient in early reading that I feel compelled to single them out for special consideration. To my mind, the early reader must learn two key principles in order to be successful.

## Two Linguistic Principles

First, students must understand that oral and written language, while surely not identical, emanate from the common wellspring of language that resides deep in our being. As Perfetti made explicit and others have implied, once they discover this principle, they can bring to the task of reading and writing all that they have spent the better part of their lives learning. Nothing could be more unfair than to provide texts and instruction that deny students access to this wellspring of inner oral language.

Second, students must embrace the alphabetic principle. They must discover the cipher, as Phil Gough (1972) calls it. For once they have learned that great secret — that English writing represents sounds — two entire whole worlds are opened to them: first, that wellspring of inner oral language; and second, through that language, a seemingly unending world of books.

Recognition of the importance of these two principles provides several implications for teaching phonics in our schools:

1. Begin the development of phonics knowledge on a strong base of phonemic awareness and alphabet recognition. The cipher will make no sense unless both the oral language and written language units (the sounds as well as the letters, the phonemes as well as the graphemes) are accessible to children. In this regard, the suggestions of Barbara Taylor (this volume) for game-like activities and Hiebert (Chapter 2, this volume) for word study are helpful and appropriate.

2. Teach phonics as one more tool in a kit students need for rendering texts sensible. The best models I know of are those provided by Reading Recovery (Clay, 1979), Taylor (this volume), and Hiebert (Chapter 2, this volume). The point is to help students learn that phonics — along with contextual analysis, structural analysis, and attention to meaning — can help them decipher unknown words and bring meaning to otherwise confusing text.

3. Regard phonics as a means to an end rather than an end unto itself. An examination of what we were doing with mastery learning and basal reading programs a decade ago — with a huge emphasis on the assessment of phonics — supports the accusation that we had made phonics an outcome rather than a means to an end. The danger in regarding phonics as an outcome is that we deceive ourselves into believing that we have actually accomplished something of value by having taught the system. I would argue strongly that the value is realized only when students can use phonics to make and monitor meaning. A first step toward achieving this functional status would be to eliminate assessments that regard phonics as an outcome rather than as a resource for making meaning.

4. Get phonics off workbook pages and into real reading and writing. The ability to circle letters or pictures on workbook pages is not the point of phonics instruction. To the contrary, the point is being able to use it to decipher real words that stand in the way of constructing meaning. Reading Recovery, with its emphasis on teaching phonics on the fly (teach a little lesson that actually helps with a particular word the student cannot decode) is exemplary on this point. Also, patterned books, in which students get an opportunity to read lots of rhyming words or words with the same initial sound, provide awareness and practice in a real reading context.

Having emphasized these two vital linguistic principles—the importance of building on students' oral language and the importance of doing phonics right—I turn now to my core list of characteristics of effective instruction and thoughtful teachers.

## PRINCIPLES FOR BUILDING A NEW LITERACY CURRICULUM

*Thoughtful teachers look for authenticity in all aspects of instruction.* In the past decade, we have provided students with texts that are more authentic than those found in many basals (and, by the way, in many earlier trade books); and to a greater extent than previously possible, we are asking students to read and write for real reasons (the kind real people in the real world have) rather than for the fake reasons we give them in school. To put it succinctly, school is often all too school-like. These lessons of authenticity from the whole language movement should be embraced and embraceable by all teachers of reading. One only wonders why we had to have someone come along and point out that our materials and methods were so unauthentic; then again, in education we seem to need to be reminded often that "the emperor has no clothes!"

Authenticity is about contexts as well as about texts and tasks. The comments of McKeown and her colleagues (Chapter 5, this volume) and of Trabasso and Magliano (Chapter 7, this volume) provide us with some hints about what was wrong with our 1980s instruction for comprehension strategies and structural elements of text. We made the same miscalculation for them as we did for phonics—viewing them as ends unto themselves. By making them legitimate goals in their own right, we abstracted them from real texts, real problems, and real situations. I think that the work both of McKeown and her colleagues and of Trabasso and Magliano suggests a common observation and a paradox that we should embrace. The observation is that what goes under the name of skill, strategy, or structure instruction is much more accessible, interesting, and sensible when it is embedded within a real problem, a real text, or a real body of content. The paradox is—and this has been the real discovery for me and for others who pushed the earlier, more abstract approach to such instruction—that the best way to help students develop highly transferable, context-free literacy tools is to teach these tools as if they were entirely context-bound. In other words, if we want students to become better at determining the central story thread or evaluating the efficacy of an argument, then don't give them an abstract routine; give them real stories to talk about and real disputes to settle.

*Thoughtful teachers base their curriculum on positive and optimistic views of student potential.* Another attribute of thoughtful teachers for which we can thank the whole language movement is a different, more generous, and, I would argue, more accurate set of assumptions about what students know and can do when they show up at school. We can assume that students are in classes to succeed, not fail; to learn how to be independent rather than to rely on us for every bit of knowledge they will gain. We can assume that there is a level at which every student comes to us already literate. That is the point of the emergent literacy perspective. Even the 3-year-old who recognizes that *if an arch is in sight, a hamburger is not far away* has learned the basic principle of signs — that our world is filled with things that "stand for" other things. If we assume that young children are already literate, we are more likely to engage them in tasks in which they can demonstrate their literacy and use those successes as bridges to even more challenging literacy activities.

This, by the way, is exactly the point that I tried to make 16 years ago in *Teaching Reading Comprehension* (Pearson & Johnson, 1978) — that a teacher's job is always to bridge from the known to the new. There really is no other choice. Children are who they are. They know what they know. They bring what they bring. Our job is not to wish that students knew more or knew differently. Our job is to turn students' knowledge and the diversity of knowledge we encounter into a curricular strength rather than an instructional inconvenience. We can do that only if we hold high expectations for all students, convey great respect for the knowledge and culture they bring to the classroom, and offer lots of support in helping them achieve those expectations.

***Thoughtful teachers demonstrate and model literate behavior at every opportunity.*** Teachers can and should share the agonies and ecstasies of their own literacy development, letting children in on their own trade secrets about how to approach the range of literacy tasks we provide in our curricula. As long as we remember that the purpose of demonstration is to help students do it on their own rather than to do it for them, I think we can be genuinely helpful. I also would suggest that if we are serious about this modeling, sometimes when we watch a teacher demonstrating how to solve a particular literacy puzzle, it will look a whole lot like what we used to call direct or explicit instruction. That does not bother me because it is not skill instruction that I object to but rather the rigid, formulaic, and decontextualized kind of instruction that has stripped skill learning from real contexts of reading and writing.

***Thoughtful teachers scaffold the learning environment to help students cope with complexity.*** Scaffolding to me is our only hope of helping students cope with the complexity of learning to read, especially if we reject — as I think we must — the principle of decomposition. It is better to provide extensive scaffolding to help students complete authentic, and perhaps quite difficult, tasks than it is to decompose the task into components and thereby decontextualize it to a point where students can no longer see any purpose to it. As Michael and Bonnie Graves (1994) richly illustrate, scaffolding allows us, as teachers, to intervene in an environment and provide the cuing, questioning, coaching, corroboration, and plain old information needed to allow students to complete a task before they are able to complete it independently and while they gradually gain control of it.

*Thoughtful teachers place a premium on student control.* Any program that, or any teacher who, reserves all rights of curriculum planning and all rights of assessment and evaluation fails to comprehend the importance of real engagement and true empowerment. While teachers must be the curriculum leaders in classrooms, students need opportunities to assume responsibility for their own literacy development by participating in curriculum decision making and self-assessment. Otherwise, how will they ever decide whether they have understood or communicated well when they are on their own?

*Thoughtful teachers build and respect community.* We must, I believe, help students learn to be active members of literacy communities — communities that provide scaffolding when the going gets tough, communities filled with real live peers with whom to exchange oral and written communications that render our activities authentic, and communities that celebrate and honor our individual and collective accomplishments. The principle of community must come into play in another sense, also. The literacy that is spawned in our schools, if it is to survive and receive full nurture, must be extended into the communities in which children live. Conversely, those communities, and the language and traditions that define them, must extend into the schools; otherwise our rhetoric about respect for cultural traditions will be empty and our children will be marginalized by insensitive curricula.

*Thoughtful teachers are always looking for connections.* These other principles really devolve into a single principle, and it is Ernest Boyer's (Chapter 1, this volume) notion of connectedness. Everything we do with our students in our classrooms must be connected to the rest of their lives in every conceivable way: to other curricula; to everyday life; to oral and written texts; to students' families and their cultures; to their work; to their leisure; to the core of their existence. Disconnectedness is at the heart of many of our social and most of our educational problems. Indeed, I would say all of them. Helping children reconnect and building curricula worth connecting to — those are the most important professional challenges we face.

There you have it. My search for a common core on which to build thoughtful curricula, on which to base thoughtful instruction, on which to build consensus and civility, from which to transcend ideology so that we can focus our energy on children's literacy rather than political correctness. Better to be helpful than correct. Better to be involved than right.

## REFERENCES

California State Department of Education. (1987). *English-language arts framework*. Sacramento: Author.

Clay, M. M. (1979). *The early detection of reading difficulties.* Auckland: Heinemann.

Cremin, L. A. (1961). *The transformation of the school: Progressivism in American education, 1876–1957.* New York: Knopf.

Goodman, Y. (1989). Roots of the whole-language movement. *Elementary School Journal, 90,* 113–127.

Gough, P. B. (1972). One second of reading. In J. F. Kavanagh & I. G. Mattingly (Eds.), *Language by ear and eye.* Cambridge, MA: MIT Press.

Graves, M. F., & Graves, B. B. (1994). *Scaffolding reading experiences: Designs for student success.* Norwood, MA: Christopher-Gordon.

Mullis, I. V. S., Campbell, J. R., & Farstrup, A. E. (1993). *NAEP 1992 reading report card for the nation and the states.* Washington, DC: U.S. Department of Education.

Pearson, P. D., & Johnson, D. D. (1978). *Teaching reading comprehension.* New York: Holt, Rinehart and Winston.

*Reading Research Quarterly.* (1994, Fall). *29*(4).

Smith, F. (1983). Reading like a writer. *Language Arts, 60,* 558–567.

# About the Contributors

**Richard Allington** is Professor of Education in the Department of Reading at the State University of New York at Albany. Dr. Allington received his PhD in Elementary and Special Education from Michigan State University in 1973 and his BA and MA from Western Michigan University. Dr. Allington's research focuses on the literacy experiences of less-skilled readers and special education students. He currently directs a project studying the use of literature-based curricula in schools serving large numbers of poor children. His recent books include *Classrooms That Work* (1995, with Patricia Cunningham) and *No Quick Fix: Rethinking Reading Programs in American Elementary Schools* (1995, with Sean Walmsley), and he has authored more than 100 journal articles and 14 children's books. Dr. Allington received the Albert J. Harris Award from the International Reading Association for his work contributing to the understanding of reading disabilities, and he is currently Vice President of the National Reading Conference and on the Board of Directors of the International Reading Association.

**Claire L. Asam** is currently a doctoral candidate in Educational Administration at the College of Education at the University of Hawaii. Additionally, Ms. Asam serves as a curriculum developer and administrator at the Kamehameha Schools in Hawaii. She received her MA in Education from the University of Hawaii and her BA in Child Development from Connecticut College. Her research interests focus on teacher change, educational innovation, and the school achievement of Native Hawaiian children.

**Kathryn H. Au** is Associate Professor in the College of Education at the University of Hawaii. Prior to joining the University, she was an educational psychologist at the Kamehameha Schools in Honolulu, Hawaii. Dr. Au received her PhD in Educational Psychology from the University of Illinois in 1980, her MA in Psychology from the University of Hawaii, and her BA in History from Brown University. Her research interest is in the school literacy learning of children of diverse cultural and linguistic background, and her recent studies have centered on whole literacy learning and portfolio assessment. She is the author of *Literacy Instruction in Multicultural Settings* (1993) and more than 40 journals and book chapters on the topic. She serves or has served on the editorial review boards of the *Reading*

*Research Quarterly*, the *Review of Educational Research, JRB: A Journal of Literacy*, and *The Reading Teacher*; and she has served as a Vice President of the American Educational Research Association and a Board Member of the National Reading Conference.

**Kim Baker** is currently a doctoral student in Reading at the University at Albany, the State University of New York. She received her MA in Elementary Education: Reading at The University at Albany, and her BA in Elementary Education at Washington University. For 5 years she has been a research assistant with The National Research Center on Literature, Teaching and Learning, examining literature-based instruction with at-risk students. A former elementary teacher, her research interests include enhancing the effectiveness of the literacy instruction offered special education and remedial students and studying the factors that influence teacher change.

**Isabel L. Beck** is Professor of Education and a senior scientist at the Learning Research and Development Center at the University of Pittsburgh. Dr. Beck received her PhD in Education from the University of Pittsburgh in 1973; her BA and MA are also from the University of Pittsburgh. Dr. Beck's research focuses on dimensions that affect students' comprehension of text. Building on the cognitive science based research on text understanding, she has investigated such issues as requisite background knowledge, text coherence and structure, the acquisition of vocabulary knowledge, and the development of tactics for enhancing students' abilities to learn from difficult texts. She has authored over 60 journal articles and book chapters and made numerous presentations at national meetings, school districts, and universities. In 1988 she received the Oscar S. Causey award for outstanding reading research from the National Reading Conference; in 1995 she was inducted into the International Reading Association's Hall of Fame; and she is presently the Co-Editor of *Cognition and Instruction*.

**Ernest L. Boyer** was the President of The Carnegie Foundation for the Advancement of Teaching. Dr. Boyer received his PhD in Speech Pathology and Audiology from the University of Southern California, his MA in Speech Pathology and Audiology from the University of Southern California, and his BA in History from Greenville College in Greenville, Illinois. Prior to his appointment at the Carnegie Foundation, he served as United States Commissioner of Education (under President Carter) and as Chancellor of the State University of New York. As President of The Carnegie Foundation, he helped shape the national education debate and has authored a number of influential books, including *High School: A Report on Secondary Education* (1983); *College: The Undergraduate Experience* (1987); and *Ready to Learn: A Mandate for the Nation* (1991). Dr. Boyer was named by three presidents — Nixon, Ford, and Carter — to national commissions. He was also a Senior Fellow at the Woodrow Wilson School at Princeton University, a Visiting Fellow at Cambridge University, a Distinguished Fulbright Scholar in India and Chile, and an education columnist for *The London Times*. In 1990, Dr. Boyer was named Educator of the Year by *U.S. News & World Report*. Dr. Boyer died in December, 1995. In acknowledging his death, President Clinton called him "a distinguished scholar and educator whose work will help students well into the next century."

**Robert Calfee** is Professor of the Committee on Language, Literacy and Culture and the Committee on Psychological Studies in the School of Education at Stanford University. Dr. Calfee received his PhD in Psychology from the University of California at Los Angeles in 1965; he also received his MA and BA in Psychology from UCLA. His research focuses on school as a literate environment, and his recent research activities include developing classroom reading programs that promote critical literacy, creating designs for effective textbooks, and investigating methods of alternative assessment. His recent books include *Teach Our Children Well* (1995, with Cynthia Patrick), *Today's Textbooks, Tomorrow's Minds* (in press, with Marilyn Chambliss), and the *Handbook of Educational Psychology* (in press, edited with David Berliner); and he is the author of over 200 journal articles and book chapters on topics in education and psychology. He has been a Fellow at the Center for Advanced Study in the Behavioral Sciences, has served as the Editor of the *Journal of Educational Psychology*, and is currently the Founding Editor of *Educational Assessment*.

**Michael F. Graves** is Professor in the Department of Curriculum and Instruction at the University of Minnesota. He received his PhD in Education from Stanford University in 1971 and his MA and BA in English from California State College at Long Beach. His research interests include vocabulary development, comprehension development, and effective instruction. His recent books include *Scaffolding Reading Experiences: Designs for Student Success* (1994, with Bonnie Graves), *Essentials of Classroom Teaching: Elementary Reading Methods* (1994, with Susan Watts and Bonnie Graves), and *Reading and Learning in Content Areas* (1994, with Randall Ryder); and he has published monographs for the International Reading Association and the National Council of Teachers of English, as well as over 80 journal articles and book chapters. Dr. Graves serves or has served on the editorial review boards of *Reading Research Quarterly, Journal of Reading Behavior*, and *Journal of Reading*. He is the former editor of *Journal of Reading Behavior*, the former associate editor of *Research in the Teaching of English*, and the coauthor of *Quest*, a reading program for fourth to eighth grade students.

**Sherry Guice** is an Assistant Professor of Education in the Department of Reading at the University at Albany, the State University of New York. She received her EdD in Language Education from the University of Georgia in 1991, her MEd in Middle School Education from Mercer University in Atlanta, and her BS in Middle School Education from the University of Georgia. Dr. Guice's research focuses on children's responses to literature and on teaching and learning in literature-based classrooms. She has published articles in the *Journal of Reading Behavior, Teaching and Teacher Education*, and the *NRC Yearbook*.

**Steven A. Hecht** is a graduate student in the Cognitive and Behavioral Science Program at Florida State University. He received his MA in Psychology from Florida State University in 1994 and his BA in Psychology from the University of South Florida. He is currently working on a qualifying paper using structural equation models to examine the influence of individual differences in phonological abilities on the growth of math skills in young children. His research interests include individual differences in growth of word reading and math skills in young children as well as information processing models of language comprehension processes.

**Elfrieda H. Hiebert** is Professor of Education at the University of Michigan. She received her PhD in Educational Psychology from the University of Wisconsin at Madison in 1979, her MA in Education from the University of Illinois–Urbana/Champaign, and her BA in History from Fresno Pacific College. Dr. Hiebert's research focuses on how literacy learning for children can be enhanced through instruction and alternative forms of assessment. Her research has been published in such journals as the *American Educational Research Journal, Reading Research Quarterly*, and *Journal of Educational Psychology*; and her books include *Becoming a Nation of Readers* (1995, with Richard Anderson, Judith Scott, and Ian Wilkinson). *Getting Reading Right from the Start: Effective Early Literacy Interventions* (1994, with Barbara Taylor), and *Authentic Reading Assessment: Practices and Possibilities* (1994, with Sheila Valencia and Peter Afflerbach). Dr. Hiebert has been the recipient of a Spencer Fellowship from the National Academy of Education, has written the Research Direction column for *Language Arts*, and served as the 1994 program chair for the Division on Instruction and Learning of the American Educational Research Association.

**Shouming Li** is a research associate in the Department of Special Education at the University of Maryland at College Park. He received his PhD in Reading from the State University of New York at Albany in 1994, his MA in TESOL from Beijing Normal University in China, and his BA in English Language and Literature from Beijing Normal University. His research focuses on comprehension difficulties and strategies of inexperienced readers.

**Joseph P. Magliano** is currently a postdoctoral fellow in the Psychology Department at the University of Chicago. He received his PhD in Cognitive Psychology from Memphis State University in 1992, his MS in Cognitive Psychology from Memphis State University, and his BA in Psychology from the University of Dayton. His doctoral thesis, which was published in 1993, investigated the time course in which inferences are generated during text comprehension. The focus of his current research is on the question of how people understand events as they experience them over time. In addressing this question, he has studied how people understand narratives conveyed in written discourse and in film. He is specifically interested in how readers and viewers construct coherent representations for a story. Dr. Magliano has published several research articles and book chapters on this topic.

**Margaret G. McKeown** is a research scientist at the Learning Research and Development Center at the University of Pittsburgh. Dr. McKeown received her PhD in Education from the University of Pittsburgh in 1983, her MS in Education from Cornell University, and her BS in Education from Skidmore College. Dr. McKeown's research involves applying cognitive theory and research to instructional design and teacher professional development in social studies, reading comprehension, and vocabulary. Her work has examined textbooks and students' understanding of them, the process of students' learning words from context and dictionary definitions, and has recently led to the development of an instructional approach to help students engage with what they read. She is the co-editor of *The Nature of Vocabulary Acquisition* (1987, with Mary Curtis) and she has authored over 40 journal articles and book chapters. Dr. McKeown received the Outstanding Dissertation Award from the International Reading Association, and she was awarded a Spencer Fellowship from the National Acad-

emy of Education for a research project on developing dictionary definitions for young learners.

**Nancy Michelson** is Assistant Professor of Education at Salisbury
State University in Salisbury, Maryland. She received her PhD in Reading
from the State University of New York at Albany, as well as her MA and
BA. Dr. Michaelson is a former high school and middle school English and
remedial reading teacher, and she worked for 4 years as a research assistant
for the National Research Center for Literature Teaching and Learning at
SUNY. She is particularly interested in teacher professional development
across the career span.

**P. David Pearson** is the John A. Hannah Professor of Education in
the School of Education at Michigan State University. Dr. Pearson received
his PhD in Education from the University of Minnesota in 1969 and his BA
in History from the University of California at Berkeley. His research focuses on reading instruction and reading assessment policies and practices.
His books include *Teaching Reading Comprehension* (1978, with D. Johnson), *Teaching Reading Vocabulary* (1978/1984, with D. Johnson), and the
*Handbook of Reading Research* (1984/1991, edited with R. Barr, M.
Kamil, and P. Mosenthal); and he has published more than 150 journal
articles and book chapters on various aspects of reading. He has served as
co-editor of *Reading Research Quarterly*, as Dean of the College of Educa-
tion at the University of Illinois, and as President of both the National
Reading Conference and the National Conference on Research in English.
In 1989, he received the Oscar Causey Award from the National Reading
Conference, and in 1990 he received the William S. Gray Citation of Merit
from the International Reading Association.

**Charles A. Perfetti** is Professor of Psychology and Linguistics (and
Chair of Psychology) and a Senior Scientist at the Learning Research and
Development Center at the University of Pittsburgh. Dr. Perfetti received
his PhD in Psychology from the University of Michigan in 1967 and his BS
in Psychology from the University of Illinois. Dr. Perfetti's research focuses
on reading and language processes of both children and adults and has
included cognitive and psycholinguistic analysis of reading skill and investigation of text-based learning and reasoning. His books include *Reading
Ability* (1985); *Learning and Reasoning from Texts: Studies of Learning
History* (1995, with M. A. Britt and M. Georgi), and three co-edited books
on reading; and he has authored more than 80 journal articles and book
chapters on research in reading and language. Dr. Perfetti has been a visiting scholar at the Max Planck Institute for Psycholinguistics and a Fellow

at The Netherlands Institute for Advanced Studies, and he is currently a Fellow of the American Psychological Association and the American Psychological Society.

**S. Jay Samuels** is a Professor in the Department of Educational Psychology at the University of Minnesota. Dr. Samuels received his EdD in Educational Psychology from the University of California at Los Angeles in 1965, his MA and BA in Elementary Education from Queens College in New York City. His research focuses on reading processes and learning from text. His books include *What Research Has To Say About Reading Instruction* (1992, edited with Alan Farstrup), *Changing School Reading Programs: Principles and Case Studies* (1988, edited with P. David Pearson), and *Comprehending Oral and Written Language* (1987, edited with Rosalind Horowitz); and he is the author of over 150 journal articles and book chapters on topics in reading education. He has served as the co-editor of *Reading Research Quarterly*, has received the Oscar Causey Award from the National Reading Conference, and has received the William S. Gray Citation of Merit and been appointed to the Reading Hall of Fame by the International Reading Association.

**Cheryl A. Sandora** is currently Assistant Professor of Education at Bethany College in Bethany, West Virginia. She completed her PhD in English Education in 1995, her MEd in 1987, and her BA in 1981, all at the University of Pittsburgh. Her research focus is on enhancing the abilities of teachers of English, particularly in the areas of literature discussion and writing. She has authored several journal articles and a book chapter, and has presented papers at several national meetings.

**Barbara M. Taylor** is a Professor and Chair of the Department of Curriculum and Instruction at the University of Minnesota. Dr. Taylor received her EdD from Virginia Polytechnic University in 1978, her MEd as a Reading Specialist from Georgia State University, and her BA in English from Tufts University. Dr. Taylor's current research involves working with first- and second-grade teachers to develop early reading intervention programs to be used with groups of children and working with fourth-grade teachers to develop supplemental reading programs for struggling older readers. Dr. Taylor's books include *Reading Difficulties: Instruction and Assessment* (1995, with Larry Harris, David Pearson, and Georgia Garcia) and *Getting Reading Right From the Start: Effective Early Literacy Interventions* (1994, edited with Elfrieda Hiebert); and she has published over 35 articles and book chapters on reading and reading instruction. Dr. Taylor is the former associate editor of the *Journal of Reading Behavior* and one of the principal developers of *Early Success*, an early intervention program for first- and second-grade students who are experiencing difficulties in reading.

**Joseph K. Torgesen** is Professor and Director of the Center for the Study of Reading and Reading Disabilities at Florida State University. Dr. Torgesen received his PhD in Developmental and Clinical Psychology from the University of Michigan in 1976, his MA in Psychology from the University of Michigan, and his BA in Psychology from Brigham Young University. Dr. Torgesen's research interests include memory functioning in children with learning disabilities, computer-assisted instruction in basic reading skills, and phonological language disabilities in children. His publications include *Cognitive and Behavioral Characteristics of Learning Disabled Children* (1990), *Phonological Awareness Training for Reading* (1993, with B. Bryant), and over 100 research chapters and articles. Dr. Torgesen is a member of the Professional Advisory Board for the National Adult Literacy and Learning Disabilities Center, currently serves on the Research Committee for the Division of Learning Disabilities of the Council for Exceptional Children, and is a recent recipient of a 5-year grant from the National Institutes of Health to study the prevention and remediation of reading disabilities in young children.

**Tom Trabasso** is the Irving B. Harris Professor of Psychology at the University of Chicago. Dr. Trabasso received his PhD in General Experimental Psychology from Michigan State University in 1961, his MA is in Quantitative Psychology and Mathematical Statistics from Michigan State University, and his BA is in Psychology from Union College. Dr. Trabasso's research focuses on narratives and how their content is reflected in our use of theories of intentional action and causation. His six books include *Attention in Learning: Theory and Research* (1968, with G. H. Bower) and *Psychological and Biological Approaches to Emotion* (1990, with N. L. Stein and B. Leventhal), and he has authored more than 100 journal articles and book chapters on cognitive processes in thinking, reasoning, memory, and language comprehension. Dr. Trabasso has been a visiting scholar at the Center for the Study of Reading at the University of Illinois and a fellow at the Center for Advanced Study in the Behavioral Sciences in Palo Alto, and he is currently an associate editor of *Discourse Processes*.

**Paul van den Broek** is Professor in the Departments of Educational Psychology, Child Development, and Psychology and the Director of the Center for Research in Learning, Perception and Cognition at the University of Minnesota. He received his PhD in Educational Psychology from the University of Chicago in 1985. He also holds doctoral degrees in Experimental Psychology and in Developmental Psychology from the University of Leiden in the Netherlands. His research interests are in reading and reading comprehension in adults and children, applications of psychology to educational settings, and the development and instruction of memory and reasoning skills. His books include *Developmental Spans in Event Comprehension and Representation: Bridging Fictional and Actual Events* (in press, edited with P. Bauer and T. Bourg) and *The Study of Cognition: Conceptual and Methodological Issues* (1992, edited with H. Pick and D. Knill); and he is the author of over 40 journal articles and book chapters. Dr. van den Broek has received distinguished teaching awards at both the University of Minnesota and the University of Kentucky.

**Susan M. Watts** is an Assistant Professor in the Department of Curriculum and Instruction at the University of Minnesota. Dr. Watts received her PhD in Reading Education from the State University of New York at Buffalo in 1991, her MA in Reading Education from the State University of New York at Buffalo, and her BA in Exceptional and Elementary Education from State University College at Buffalo. Dr. Watts' research interests include meeting the needs of diverse student populations in urban schools, meeting the needs of students experiencing difficulty in reading in the intermediate grades, and vocabulary development. She is the author of *Essentials of Classroom Teaching: Elementary Reading* (1994, with Michael Graves and Bonnie Graves) and of book chapters and journal articles dealing with reading instruction. Dr. Watts has served as President of the Twin Cities Area Reading Council and as Program Chair for the Minnesota Reading Association Convention.

**Sulan Zhang** is currently a research scientist with Monterey Technologies in the San Francisco area and a PhD Candidate in Cognitive Psychology at the University of Pittsburgh. She holds MS degrees in both Cognitive Psychology and Computer Information Science from the University of Pittsburgh, as well as an MS in Cognitive Psychology from Beijing Normal University in China. Her research has included work in natural language processing, human-computer interface design, and human factors analysis. She is the author of 11 publications in English, and in 1994 she received the Tim Post Memorial Award for outstanding research in cognitive psychology.

# Index

Ability grouping, and literature-based instruction, 88
Adams, M. J., 21, 63, 64, 138, 192
Affective factors, x, xiv
Afflerbach, P., 74, 77, 168
Agee, James, 5
Alegria, J., 42
Alejandro, Ann, 5
Alexander, A., 143
Allington, Richard L., xv, 17, 19, 64, 67, 73–96, 74, 77, 78, 80, 81, 83, 85, 87, 92, 93, 120, 125, 128–129, 252, 269
Alphabetic principle
  lexical representations and, 51
  nature of, 41–42
  in reading, 121, 138, 139–141, 143–144, 269–270
Alphabet-spelling method, 121
Alvermann, D. E., 105
American Council on Education, xii
American Library Association, 83
Amon, R. J., 80
Analytical Reading Inventory (ARI), 28
Andersen, H., 143
Anderson, L. M., 81
Anderson, R. C., 21, 22, 31, 184
Arizona, assessment project in, 253
Asam, Claire L., xvii, xviii, 115, 153, 199–223, 215, 216, 250–253, 255–256, 269
Aschbacher, P. R., 230
Assessment methods, xvi–xvii
  in Arizona, 253
  building a program of, 236–243
  in California, 232–236, 243–245, 255
  for critical literacy, 229–243, 254
  in Hawaii, 205–207, 209, 210, 214–215, 217, 253–255
  historical trends in, 225
  in KEEP program, 205–207, 209, 210, 214–215, 217, 253–255
  in Kentucky, 232–236, 243, 254, 255
  in literature-based instruction, 28–30, 77–78

  and narrative continuum, 237–239
  and parent–teacher conferences, 231
  for phonologically based reading disabilities, 150–152
  portfolio. See Portfolio assessment system
  and public accountability, 231
  reading, 241
  in Rhode Island, 253
  standardized tests, 151, 226, 227, 242
  teacher logbooks, 245–247
Assisted performance, 115
Assisted reading, 18–20
At-lexical phonology, 48
At-risk students
  literacy achievement of, 199–221
  literature-based instruction for, 73–93, 128–129
Attention deficit disorder (ADD), 147
Atwell, N., 24
Au, Kathryn H., x, xvii, xviii, 115, 153, 199–223, 200, 203, 205, 207, 208, 210, 215, 216, 250–253, 252, 255–256, 269
Auditory Discrimination in Depth program, 143, 148–149, 154
Authentic assessment. See Portfolio assessment system
Authenticity, in whole language approach, 262–263
Automaticity, 33

Baddeley, A. D., 135
Baker, Kim, 73–96, 74, 78, 83
Baldwin, L. E., 33
Bally, H., 136
Barker, T. A., 141
Baron, J., 45
Basal anthologies, in literature-based instruction, 75–76, 78, 79, 81
Basic literacy skills, xiv, 227
Basic School, The (Boyer), 4
Bassok, M., 176, 178, 183, 184
Battle, J., 32, 75
Bauer, P., 192

Baughn, C., 162, 168, 176
Baumann, J., 28
*Bay Psalm Book, The*, 121
Beck, Isabel L., x, 39, 42, 97–119, 98, 99, 100, 101, 104, 126, 182, 184
Behaviorism
  and reading, 123–124
  switch to social constructivist approach, 219
Bell, L., 39, 42, 50
*Ben and Me* (Lawson), 110–111
Benchmark School, 25
Bentin, S., 50
Bentley, J. L., 32
Berent, I., 49
Bern, H., 98
Bertelson, P., 42
Besner, D., 50
Biddle, W. B., 184
Binet, Alfred, 123
Birman, B. F., 80
Black, J. B., 98, 167
Blake, K., 205, 207, 208, 215, 216
Bloom, B. S., 205
Bloom, C. P., 177
Blumenfeld, P. C., 115
Bond, Guy L., x, 1, 4, 8, 15, 16, 21, 31, 68, 227
Book Club project, 32
Books, in literature-based instruction, 78, 79, 81, 82–84
Borden, S. L., 142
Boudberg, P. A., 44
Bourg, T., 192
Boyd, F. B., 32
Boyer, Ernest L., xiv, 1–12, 4, 9, 273
Boyle, O. W., 252
Bradley, L., 42
Bressman, B., 42
Bridge, Connie A., 20
Britt, M. A., 38
Bronk, G., 75, 79
Brown, A. L., 115, 143, 183
Brown, I. S., 141–142
Brown, R. G., 91
Bruck, M., 192
Bruer, John T., xii–xiii
Bryant, P. E., 42
Buchanan, James, 112–113
Burgess, S., 137
Burnett, R., 115

Caldwell, J., 28
Calfee, Robert C., xi, xvii–xviii, 21, 22, 224–249, 250, 251, 253–257, 259, 265, 267–268, 269
California
  assessment of critical literacy in, 232–236, 243–245, 255
  California Learning Assessment System (CLAS), 233–236, 240, 244–245
  impact of curriculum changes in, 265
  Program Quality Review (PQR), 244
  School Report Card (SRC), 244, 245
California State Department of Education, 265
Calkins, L. M., 204, 214
Calkins, R. P., 200
Cambourne, Brian, 212
Campbell, E. Q., 199
Campbell, J. R., xi, xii, 15, 31, 66, 67, 75, 265
Canney, G., 75, 79
Carnegie Foundation for the Advancement of Teaching, 4, 7
Carpenter, P. A., 98
Carroll, J., 205, 207, 215, 216
Carter, M. A., 230
Cary, L., 42
Cattell, James, 122–123
Catto, S. L., 17–18, 21, 30, 33, 144
Causal analysis, 164, 165, 168
Cazden, C., 105, 114–115, 242
Chall, Jeanne S., 21, 33, 123–124, 228
Chapman, R., 226
Chapter I programs, 15, 24, 66
Chen, M. J., 54
Chen, Y., 49
Chi, M. T. H., 176, 178, 183, 184
Chiesi, H. L., 98
Chinese, xiv–xv
  reading, 45–49, 53–56
  writing system, 43–45, 51–53, 62–65
Chiu, M., 176, 184
Chomsky, C., 19–20, 33
Chomsky, Noam, 124
Clapp, G., 2
Clark, D. B., 141, 143
Clark, L. F., 167, 168
Clarke, L. S., 20–21
Clay, Marie M., 21, 144, 204, 270
Cleary, Beverly, 109
Clinton, Bill, 86–87

Coaching, 115
Cobb, P., 115
Cochran, C., 115
Cognitive psychology, and reading, 124–125, 127, 267
Cohen, A. L., 135
Cohen, D. K., 89, 115
Coleman, J. S., 199
Collaborative programs, university–school, 32–33
Collier, G. V., 253
Colt, J. M., 17–18, 21, 30, 33, 76, 144
Coltheart, M., 50
Colton, A. M., 115
Colton, Charles Caleb, 224
Comenius, 260, 262
Commerce Department, U.S., xii
Compensatory literacy programs, xiv
Comprehension, xvi–xvii, 39, 160–185, 190–192
    after reading, 166–167
    and goal-based inferences, 168–169, 173–178
    and memory operations, 176–178
    and narrative text analysis, 161–165
    and question intervention, 170, 178–181, 183–185
    during reading, 168–169
    and think-aloud protocols, 168–178, 181–183
    in whole literacy curriculum, 204
Comprehensive literature programs, 82
Context sensitivity, x, 58
Cooley, W., 80, 81, 85
Cooter, R. B., 74
Cremin, L. A., 262
Critical literacy, xvii–xviii, 228–248, 250–251
    assessment of, 229–243, 254
    concept of, 228–229
    instruction for, 229
    and new literacy curriculum, 271–274
Crowell, D. C., 203
Cullinan, Bernice E., 3
Cullinan, D., 141
Cunningham, P. M., 21, 22, 64, 93
Curriculum, xviii
    developmental versus stage model of, 251–253
    historical trends in, 225
    impact of recent changes in, 265–268

for literature-based instruction. See Literature-based instruction
    new literacy, 271–274
    and whole language approach, 262–265
    whole literacy. See Whole literacy curriculum
Curriculum-embedded tests, 226

Dahl, K., 77
Dahl, P. R., 19
D'Amato, J., 205
Davidson, K. C., 147
Davis, C., 143
Davis, F. B., 227
DeCastell, S., 102
Decoding, x, 38–39, 65, 124, 125, 139
DeFord, D. E., 30
DeFrancis, J., 44–45
Dejerine, Joseph, 122
Delaney, S., 50
de Leeuw, N., 176, 184
Delpit, L., 252
Denckla, Martha B., 136
Desai, L. E., 230
DeVito, P. J., 253
Dewey, John, 260, 262
Dickens Charles, 8
Dillon, D. R., 105
Discourse, xv–xvi
    assessment-oriented, 241–242
    and Questioning the Author, 101–117, 125–128
Diversity of students
    and Kamehameha Elementary Education Program (KEEP), 218–221
    and literacy achievement, 199–221
    and literature-based instruction, 90–91
Donahue, P., 67
Donaldson, S. A., 138, 142
Donlan, Dan, 127
Dowhower, S. S., 19
Downer, M. A., 21, 22, 25
Duffy, G. G., 115
Duffy, T. M., 115
Durkin, Dolores D., 20, 124, 128
Dykstra, Robert, 15, 21, 227
Dyslexia. See Phonologically based reading disabilities

Echoic reading, 18–20
Effective schools, 93

Ehri, L. C., 39, 145, 155
Elementary schools
  literature-based instruction in, 23–30, 78–85
  Questioning the Authors in, 103–117
  think-aloud protocols for, 170–181
Embedded phonics (EP), 146–150
Emergent literacy, 263
Englert, C. S., 23
Epstein, M. H., 141
Eresh, J., 206
Ericsson, K. A., 168
Evans, W., 5
Explanation, 172
Eye movements, 122

Farest, C., 32
Farnan, N., 252
Farstrup, A. E., xi, xii, 15, 31, 66, 75, 265
Feingold, I., 141
Felton, R. H., 141–142, 147
Ferrand, L., 50
Fielding, L. F., 74, 76, 77
First Grade Studies, 227
Fisher, Charles W., 17, 20, 76
Flesch, Rudolph, 123–124
Fletcher, C. R., 177, 192
Fletcher, J. M., 147
Flood, J., 252
Flores, D'Arcais, G. B., 52
Flowers, L., 147
Fourth grade, and Questioning the Author, 103–117
Fraatz, J. M. B., 88
Fractor, J. S., 75, 84
Francis, D. J., 147
Frankiewicz, R. G., 141
Frederiksen, J. R., 98
Frost, J., 155
Frost, R., 50
Frye, B., 80
Funkhouser, J. E., 80

Gage, Nate, xviii–xix
Gallimore, R., 115, 200
Gallup polls, 244
Garcia, G. E., 23, 200
Garcia, G. N., 80
Garcia, J., 253
Garcia, M., 253

Gardner, John W., 11
Gaskins, I. W., 21, 22
Gelb, I. J., 41
Giddings, L. R., 74
Gillingham, Anna, 141
Gittelman, R., 141
Giuli, C., 208
Glaser, R., 176, 178, 183, 184
Glazer, Susan, 125
Gleitman, L. R., 41
Glenn, C., 166, 167
Goal-based inferences, 168–169, 173–178
Goatley, V. J., 32
Goldenberg, C., 32
Goodlad, John L., ix, x, 105
Goodman, Kenneth S., 17, 124–125, 202, 228
Goodman, Yetta M., 228, 262
Gordon, C., 98
Gore, Al, 86–87
Gough, Phil B., 39, 140, 270
Graesser, A. C., 161, 167, 168, 169
Grainger, J., 50
Grammar, 7
Grapheme-phoneme correspondences, 138, 141, 144, 155, 269–271
Graves, Bonnie B., 78, 273
Graves, D., 204, 214
Graves, Michael F., ix–xix, 78, 273
Greenstein, J., 135
Gromoll, E. W., 98, 100
Guice, Sherry, 73–96, 74, 78, 83
*Guidebook for Kentucky Parents* (Kentucky State Department of Education), 232–233
Guided writing, 64–65
Gury, E. C., 17–18, 21, 30, 33, 144

Haertel, G. D., 133
Hagen, E. P., 146
Hagerty, P., 29
Hansen, J., 98, 204
Hardwick, N., 138, 142
Harwayne, S., 204
Haugen, D., 115
Hawaii
  Kamehameha Reading Objectives System (KROS), 203, 205, 208
  KEEP program in, xvii, 200–221, 250, 251–255
Heath, S. B., 252

Hecht, Steven A., xvi, 133–159, 137, 189–
    191, 193–194, 269
Heilman, P. C., 143
Henry, M. K., 21, 22–23, 33
*Henry and Mudge in the Sparkle Days* (Ry-
    lant and Stevenson), 26
Herman, J. L., 230
Herman, P. A., 20
Herriman, M. L., 42
Hiebert, Elfrieda H., x, xiv, 15–36, 17–18,
    20, 21, 23, 29, 30, 31, 32, 33, 65–68, 74,
    76, 144, 201, 229, 266, 269, 270
Higgins, L., 115
Hill, C., 115
Hillinger, M. L., 39
Hindman, S., 141
History, 97–117
    and Questioning the Author, 98, 101–106,
    125–128
Hobson, C. J., 199
Hoffman, J. V., 32, 75
Homophones, 45, 48
Hood, W. J., 228
Horiba, Y., 192
Houck, G., 134, 135
Huck, C. S., 82, 91
Huey, Edmund B., 39, 121
Hughes, C., 39, 42
Hulme, C., 138
Hung, D. L., 49

Independent writing, 65
Instruction
    for critical literacy, 229
    historical trends in, 225
Integrative approach, xi, 262
Interactive approach, x, 226–227
Interactive Reading Assessment System
    (IRAS), 226–227
International Reading Association, 125, 266
Intervention programs, x
    for reading disabilities, 138–145, 152–
    155
Invented spelling, 65, 263
Iversen, S., 144

Jackson-Keller Elementary School (San An-
    tonio), 3
Jacobs, V. A., 33
Jacobsen, H., 215, 216
Jain, R., 169

Javal, Emile, 122
Jenkins, L., 66
Jiminez, R. T., 23
Johns, M. S., 138, 142
Johnson, D. D., 272
Johnson, L. R., 162
Johnson, N. J., 166
Johnston, P. A., 17, 74, 77, 83
Jones, K., 135
Jordan, C., 200, 203, 205
Jorm, A. F., 139
*Journal of Adolescent and Adult Literacy*, xi
*Journal of Reading Behavior*, 16
Juel, C., 20, 21, 29, 32, 63
Jung, R. K., 80
Just, M. A., 98

Kamehameha Elementary Education Pro-
    gram (KEEP), xvii, 200–221, 250
    assessment in, 205–207, 209, 210, 214–215,
    217, 253–255
    chronology of changes in, 209–218
    diversity of students in, 218–221
    initial program, 202–203
    social constructivism in, 201–202, 203
    student achievement in, 215–216
    teacher development in, 207–209, 212–214,
    217, 256
    whole literacy curriculum, 203–205, 206,
    209, 210–212, 213–214, 218–219, 251–
    253
Kamehameha Reading Objectives System
    (KROS), 203, 205, 208
Kapinus, B., 31, 253
Katz, L., 50
Kauffman, James M., 153
Kawakami, A. J., 205, 252
Kawakami, M., 52
Keller, Helen, 6–7
Kentucky, assessment of critical literacy in,
    232–236, 243, 254, 255
Kentucky State Department of Education,
    232–233
King, A., 184
Kintsch, W., 177, 194
Klein, T. W., 200, 203
Klenk, L., 256
Knapp, M. S., 80
Knowledge hypothesis, 204
Kozol, J., 92
Krajcik, J. S., 115

Kruglanski, H., 253
Kucan, L., 104, 184
Kunitake, M., 215, 216

Labbo, L., 32
LaBerge, D., 19, 121
*Lacon* (Colton), 224
Langer, J. A., 67, 92
Language, origins of use of, 2–3
Language development, reading and, 2–4
*Language Instinct, The* (Pinker), 1
Language to Literacy project, 32
Lapp, D., 252
LaSalle, R. A., 21
Lau, L. L., 54
Laughon, P., 137
LaVancher, C., 176, 184
Lawson R., 110
*Learning to Read* (Chall), 123–124
Lederman, Leon, 10
Lee, S-Y., 54
Lehnert, W. G., 167
LeMahieu, P. G., 206
Leong, C. K., 53
Leslie, L., 28
Levin, H. M., 92
Lewis, M. W., 176, 178, 183, 184
Lexical representations, 51–53
Li, Shouming, 73–96, 78
Liberman, A. M., 136
Liberman, Isabelle Y., 39, 136
Libraries
    classroom, 83–84
    school, 83
Lima, S. S., 253
Lindamood, C. H., 143, 148
Lindamood, Patricia C., 143, 148, 153
Lipson, M. Y., 253
Literacy
    and diversity of students, 199–221
    as holistic concept, 9
    language of the arts in, 10
    symbol systems and, 3, 10–11
    understanding and, 9
Literature-based instruction, xi, xv–xvi, 8,
    16–30, 65–68, 73–93, 128–129, 259
    applications of, 75–85
    assessment practices in, 28–30, 77–78
    for at-risk students, 73–93, 128–129

basal anthologies in, 75–76, 78, 79, 81
books in, 78, 79, 81, 82–84
and collegial support for teachers, 77–78,
    89, 93
and diversity of students, 90–91
in elementary schools, 23–30, 78–85
and institutional constraints, 86–87
literature review on, 16–23
remedial programs, 17, 22–23, 65–68
repeated (echoic, assisted) reading in, 18–
    20, 121
skills-oriented instruction versus, 17, 73,
    76, 81
small groups in, 25–27
standardization and, 87–89
and teacher change, 86–87, 92–93
and teacher knowledge of children's litera-
    ture, 84–85
in third grade, 23–30
time allocation for, 79–82, 87
whole language approach to. *See* Whole
    language approach
Word Walls in, 25
Liu, L. G., 167, 168, 184
Liwag, M., 162
Lobel, Arnold, 26
Logography, 43, 44
Lovett, M. W., 138, 142
Loxterman, J. A., 101, 182
Lukatela, G., 50
Luke, A., 102
Luke, C., 102
Lundberg, I., 42, 143, 155
Lyon, G. R., 142
Lyons, C., 30

Magliano, Joseph P., xvi–xvii, 98, 160–188,
    168, 169, 177, 189, 190–193, 195, 269,
    271
Magliano, P. A., 166, 173, 176
Mandler, J. M., 166
Mangiola, L., 252
Manis, F. R., 139
Mann, Horace, 121
Mann, V. A., 42
Martinez, M., 75, 84
Maruyama, G., 80
Marx, R. W., 115
Mason, J. M., 200
Mazzeo, J., xii

McCaffrey, M., 115
McCarthey, S., 20
McClelland, J. L., 51
McCutchen, D., 39, 49
McDaniel, Kristy, 3
McDill, E. L., 199
McGill-Franzen, A. M., 67, 74, 80, 92
McGuffey readers, 122
McKeown, Margaret G., x, xv, 97–119, 120,
     125–129, 182, 184, 267, 269, 271
McKoon, G., 177
McLaughlin, M. W., 115
McMahon, S. I., 32
McPartland, J., 199
Medo, M., 21, 32
Mehan, H., 201
Mehlenbacher, B., 115
Memory
   and comprehension, 176–178
   and reading disabilities, 134–135, 136
Memory codes, and reading disabilities, 135
Mervar, K., 74, 76
Metacognition, x, xiv, 21–23, 33
Mezynski, K., 204
Michaelson, N., 74, 83
Michelson, Nancy, 73–96, 78
Miller, P., 129
Modeling
   of literate behavior, 272
   and Questioning the Author, 102, 115
   reading process and, 3, 18–20, 25, 32
Moe, A. J., 28
Moll, L. C., 201–202
Montero, I., 201
Mood, A. M., 199
Moore, M. T., 80
Morais, J., 42
Morgan, Ronald, 26
Morphemes, reading process and, 21–23
Morphology, 43–44
Morris, R., 136
Morrison, D. R., 80
Morrison, F. J., 138
Morrow, L. M., 74
Motivation, 5
Mullis, I. V. S., xi, xii, 15, 31, 66, 67, 75,
     265
Munger, G. P., 162, 168, 176
Murray, B. A., 155
Myers, P., 32

National Assessment of Educational Prog-
     ress (NAEP), xi–xii, 66, 67, 75, 206, 265
National Center for Educational Statistics
     (NCES), xii, 80
National Institute of Child Health and Hu-
     man Development, 136, 145–152
National Institute of Mental Health
     (NIMH), 155
Natriello, G., 199
Naylor, C., 147
Neesdale, A. R., 42
Neuman, S., 67
New, C. A., 252
Newell, A., 168
New England Primer, The, 121–122
New Zealand Department of Education, 5
Nezworski, T., 166, 167
Nicholas, D. W., 168
Nickels, M., 162, 168
Nieto, S., 252
Nistler, R., 256
Nix, D., 184
Noel, R. R., 50
Nolte, H., 127
Nuba-Scheffler, Hannah, 3

O'Brien, D. G., 105
Ogden, S., 141
Oliver Twist (Dickens), 8
Olson, D. R., 102
Olson, R. K., 138
Omanson, R. C., 167
One-on-one instruction, 152
   in Reading Recovery program, 29–30, 66–
     67, 144, 153, 270
Orland, M. E., 80
Orthography, in word reading acquisition,
     139–141
Orton, Samual, 141
Oshiro, G., 217
Oshiro, M., 205, 207

Paap, K. R., 50
Pace, G., 77
Palincsar, A. S., 115, 143, 183, 256
Pallas, A. M., 199
Paraphrasing, 172
Pardo, L. S., 32
Parent–teacher conferences, 231
Passage Comprehension test, 151

Patrick, C. P., 237, 244
Payton, P., 169, 182
Pearson, P. David, x, xiv, xviii, 23, 73, 98, 199, 200, 206, 220, 259–274
Peng, D. L., 49
Peregoy, S. F., 252
Perfetti, Charles A., x, xiv, xv, 37–61, 38, 39, 40, 42, 44, 45, 46, 47, 48, 49, 50, 51, 54, 62–65, 68, 98, 192, 269
Performance tests. See Portfolio assessment system
Perfumo, P., 227, 232, 245
Perkins, D. N., 239
Perkins, David, xii
Persky, H., 67
Peters, C. W., 204
Peters, T. J., 212, 213
Peterson, O., 155
Phillips, G. N., xii
Phonemes, 41, 42, 63–64
Phonics, 5–7, 270–271
Phonological awareness training plus synthetic phonics (PASP), 146–151
Phonologically based reading disabilities, xvi, 22–23, 133–155, 189–190
    initial discoveries of, 134–136
    intervention research on, 138–145, 152–155
    longitudinal study of, 137–138
    nature of, 134–138
    preventive instruction for, 145–152
    theory of, 138
Phonology, 39, 42, 45–50, 55–56, 57, 191
Pinker, Steven, 1, 41
Pinnell, G. S., 30, 144
Pin Yin instruction, 54–56
Place, A. W., 30
Place Called School, A (Goodlad), ix
Polanyi, Michael, 9
Pollatsek, A., 139
Portes, P., 135
Portfolio assessment system, xiv, 228–248
    audit of, 215
    benchmarks in, 206–207, 210, 214–215, 219, 220
    and critical literacy, 229–243
    in KEEP program, 206–207, 209, 210, 214–215, 217, 254–255
Poverty, xii
    Chapter I programs, 15, 24, 66
    literature-based curricula and, 73–93, 128–129

Prawat, R. S., 115
Prediction, 172
Press, Frank, 9
Pressley, M., 168
Prior knowledge, x
Process writing, 259
Professional conversation groups, 89, 93
Program Quality Review (PQR), 244
Project READ, 22, 33
Psycholinguistics, 37–38
Psychology
    behaviorism, 123–124, 219
    cognitive psychology, 124–125, 127, 267
    and reading, 122–125
Psychosemantics, 38
Public accountability, 231
Pugh, S. L., 253
Purcell, L., 143
Purcell-Gates, V., 77
Putnam, L. R., 3, 9

Qualitative Reading Inventory (QRI), 28
Questioning the Author, xvi, 98, 101–117, 125–128, 184–185, 269
    categories of student responses in, 108–114
    classroom application of, 103–104
    discourse and, 101–117, 125–128
    Engagement Queries in, 103
    modeling, 102, 115
    outcomes of, 104–106
    principles of, 102
    proportion of student/teacher talk in, 105–106, 107
    student-initiated comments in, 106, 107
    teacher involvement in, 103–104, 107, 114–116
    and teaching for understanding, 115
Question intervention, 178–181
    comprehension and, 170, 178–181, 183–185
    effects on inferences, 179–180
    effects on information sources, 180–181
    instructional implications of, 183–185
    what questions in, 170, 179–181, 182, 183
    why and how questions in, 170, 179–181, 182, 183

Rack, J. P., 138
Ralph S. Mouse (Cleary), 109–110
Ransby, M. J., 138, 142
Raphael, T. E., 32
Rashotte, C. A., 135, 137, 146

Ratcliff, R., 177
Ravitch, D., 92
Rayner, K., 139
Read, C., 20
Read-along procedure, 19
Reader's workshop, 24
Readiness perspective, 3, 262–263
Reading
    alphabetical principle in, 138, 139–141,
        143–144, 269–270
    of Chinese, 45–49, 53–56
    comprehension of. *See* Comprehension
    decoding, x, 38–39, 65, 124, 125, 139
    and early language development, 2–4
    enabling features of instruction in, 259–
        260
    individual differences in, 193–195
    and learning disabled students, xvi, 22–23,
        133–155, 189–190
    meaning in, 7
    metacognition in, x, xiv, 21–23, 33
    modeling of, 3, 18–20, 25, 32
    phonics and, 5–7, 270–271
    remedial instruction in, 15–16, 17, 22–23,
        24, 65–68, 140
    and teacher expectations for students, xiv,
        4, 5, 8, 31, 32, 63
    and teaching styles, 5–7, 8
    voluntary, 204
    writing and, 7, 8, 20–21
*Reading Ability* (Perfetti), 39
Reading aloud
    in literature-based instruction, 18–20, 25,
        32, 81
    modeling and, 3, 18–20, 25, 32
    repeated reading of text, 18–20, 121
*Reading Difficulties* (Bond and Tinker), x,
    4, 16, 68
Reading disabilities, xvi, 22–23, 133–155,
    189–190
    intervention research on, 138–145, 152–
        155
    nature of, 134–138
    preventive instruction for, 145–152
Reading readiness tests, 3
Reading Recovery program, 29–30, 66–67,
    144, 153, 270
Reading research
    in historical context, 120–125
    on intervention for phonologically based
        reading disabilities, 138–145

*Reading Research Quarterly* (journal), 16, 268
*Reading Teacher, The* (journal), xi
Redundancy principle, 51, 54
Reese, C. M., xii
Regular classroom support group (RCS),
    146, 147, 150
Reimann, P., 176, 178, 183, 184
Reisner, E. R., 80
Reitsma, P., 139
Remedial instruction, 15–16, 17, 22–23, 24,
    65–68, 140
Repeated reading of text, 18–20, 121
Resnick, Lauren, xii
Reutzel, D. R., 74
Rhode Island, assessment project in, 253
Rice, Joseph, 123
Richardson, V., 115
Richert, A. E., 243
Rimes, 22
Rodkin, P. C., 162, 168, 176
Roeber, E. D., 204
Roehler, L. R., 115
Rosa, A., 201
Rose, Elaine, 153
Roser, N. L., 32, 75
Routman, R., 219
Rozin, P., 41, 42
Rudel, R., 136
Rumelhart, D. E., 51
Russell, T., 115
Rylant, Cynthia, 26

Saito, H., 52
Salomon, G., 239
Samuels, S. Jay, x, xvi, 19, 120–130, 121
Sandburg, Carl, 11
Sandora, Cheryl A., 97–119, 104, 184
Sattler, J. M., 146
Scaffolding, 115, 191, 272–273
Scanlon, D. M., 42
Scharer, P. L., 74, 77, 89
Schema-theoretic model of reading, x
Scheu, J., 205, 207, 215, 216
School Report Card (SRC), 244, 245
Schwandt, T. A., 201
Scott, J. A., 31
Secco, T., 98, 161, 163–165
Seda, I., 256
Seidenberg, M. S., 49
Self-teaching model, of word reading acquisi-
    tion, 139–141

Semantic effects, 45–46
Sexton, M. A., 135
Shade, B. J., 252
Shanahan, T., 203
Shanklin, N., 77
Shankweiler, D., 39, 136
Share, David L., 138, 139, 140
Sheiman, D., 3
Shepperson, G. M., 256
Short-term memory, and reading disabilities, 134–135, 136
Sidlin, Murry, 10
Silver Burdett, 100
Silver Burdett Ginn Reading Placement Inventory, 28
Simmons, K., 137
Simon, H. A., 168
Simon, Theodore, 123
Sinatra, G. M., 101
Singer, Harry, 127
Singer, M. S., 161
Skinner, B. F., 124
Sloane, S., 115
Sloat, K. C. M., 200, 203
Small-group discussions, 25–27, 205
Smith, Frank, 45, 125, 267
Smith, S., 115
Snider, M. A., 253
Snowling, M. J., 138
Social constructivism, x
   described, 201
   in KEEP program, 201–202, 203
   switch from behaviorism, 219
Soloway, E., 115
Solsken, J. W., 77
Sparks-Langer, G. M., 115
Specificity principle, 51, 54
Speidel, G. E., 200, 203
Sperry, L., 166
Spiegel, D. L., 204
Spilich, G. J., 98
Spillane, J. P., 89
Spreen, O., 133
Stage theory, 228
Stahl, S. A., 129, 155
Stanchfield, Jo, 9
Standardization, and literature-based instruction, 87–89
Standardized tests, 151, 226, 227, 242
Standards movement, 199–200
Stanford-Binet test, 146

Stanovich, K. E., 63, 138, 139, 140, 141
Stein, N. L., 162, 166, 167, 168, 176
Stephens, Diane L., 6
Stevenson, H. W., 54
Stevenson, S., 26
Stewart, S., 23
Stiggins, R. J., 231, 241
Stillman, Bessie, 141
Stimulated Onset Asynchrony (SOA), 47
Stowell, L. P., 254
Strait, J., 21, 32
Strawson, C., 45
Strickland, Dorothy, 6, 75, 79
Stuebing, K. K., 147
Suh, S., 162, 167, 168–169, 182, 184
Sulzby, E., 21
Sweden, 42
Syllables, reading process and, 21–23
Symbol systems, 3, 10–11
   writing systems, 40–45
Syntax, 7
Synthetic phonics approach, 142

Tachistoscope, 122–123
Taft, M., 42
Talbert, J. E., 115
Taylor, Barbara M., x, xv, 15, 21, 32, 62–69, 80, 270
Teacher as writer, 214–215
Teacher change, and literature-based instruction, 86–87, 92–93
Teacher development, xviii, 255–257
   in demonstration classroom project, 212–214, 217–218
   in KEEP program, 207–209, 212–214, 217, 256
Teachers
   change by, 86–87, 92–93
   collegial support for, 77–78, 89, 93
   expectations for students, xiv, 4, 5, 8, 31, 32, 63
   institutional constraints on, 86–87
   knowledge of children's literature, 84–85
   and literature-based instruction, 77–78, 84–85
   logbooks of, 245–247
   and new literacy curriculum, 271–274
   professional conversation groups for, 77–78, 89, 93
   and Questioning the Author, 103–104, 105, 107, 114–116

*Teacher's Word Book, The* (Thorndike), 123
Teaching for testing, 240
Teaching for understanding, 115
*Teaching Reading Comprehension* (Pearson and Johnson), 272
Teaching styles, reading and, 5-7, 8
Teale, W., 75, 84
Text analysis
  history textbook, 98-101
  narrative text, 161-165
Textbooks
  analysis of student use of, 98-101
  basal anthologies, 75-76, 78, 79, 81
  depth-of-processing approach to, 98, 101-117, 125-128
  history, 97-117
  Questioning the Author, xvi, 98, 101-117, 125-128, 184-185, 269
Tharp, R. G., 115, 200, 203, 208
Think-aloud protocols, 168-178
  for adult readers, 173-178
  illustrated, 170-173
  instructional implications of, 181-183
  and question intervention, 170
  for third grade readers, 170-181
Third grade
  literature-based instruction in, 23-30
  think-aloud protocols for, 170-181
Thomas, Lewis, 2
Thompson, N. M., 147
Thorndike, Edward L., 123
Thorndike, R. L., 146
Thoughtful schools, 91-92
Tierney, R. J., 230, 254
Time allocation, in literature-based instruction, 79-82, 87
Tinker, Miles A., x, 16, 31, 68
Torgesen, Joseph K., x, xvi, 133-159, 134, 135, 136, 137, 138, 141, 143, 146, 189-191, 193-194, 269
Torneus, M., 42
Trabasso, Tom, x, xvi-xvii, 98, 160-188, 189, 190-193, 195, 269, 271
Tracking, and literature-based instruction, 88
Triadic model of teacher development, 208-209
Tunmer, W. E., 42, 144
Turbill, Jan, 212
Turnbull, B. J., 80

Turner, S. D., 141
Turvey, M. T., 50
Tzeng, O. J. L., 49

Understanding. *See* Comprehension
U.S. Office of Education (USOE), 15-16
Universal Phonological Principle (UPP), 49-51
University-school programs, 32-33

Valencia, S. W., 253
van den Broek, Paul W., x, xvii, 98, 161, 162, 163-169, 184, 189-196, 192
van Dijk, T. A., 177, 194
Van Doren, Mark, 8
Van Orden, G. C., 50
Vaughn, S., 153
Vellutino, F. R., 42
Venezky, Richard L., 226
Verville, K., 253
Villegas, A. M., 252
Voeller, K. S., 143
Voluntary reading, 204
Voss, J. F., 98
Vygotsky, L. S., 201-202

Wagner, E. B., 8
Wagner, R. K., 136, 137, 141, 146
Walberg, H. J., 133
Wallace, D., 115
Walmsley, S. A., 74, 75, 76-77, 79, 92, 252
Walp, T. P., 74, 76-77
Walsh, M. A., 140
Wang, M. C., 133
Wang, W. S-Y., 49
Warren, W. H., 168
Warren-Chaplin, P.M., 142
Waterman, R. H., Jr., 212, 213
Waters, M. D., 135
Watkins, K., 3
Watts, Susan, M., x, xviii, 250-258
Weber, E. M., 204
Webster, Noah, 122
Weinfeld, F. D., 199
Weiss, K., 75, 79
Weisskopf, Victor, 9, 10
Wertsch, J. V., 201-202
West, R. F., 140, 141
Wetzel, R. J., 208
*What Schools Are For* (Goodlad), ix

Whole language approach, xi, xviii, 17–18, 124–125, 150, 202, 228
curricular perspective on, 262–265
philosophical perspective on, 263–264
political perspective on, 264–265
principles of, 261–265
Whole literacy curriculum
implementation of, 210–212, 213
in KEEP program, 203–205, 206, 209, 210–212, 213–214, 218–219, 251–253
readers' workshop in, 204–205, 209–210, 214
writers' workshop in, 204–205, 210, 214
Whole-word method, 121, 123–124, 142, 145
*Why Johnny Can't Read* (Flesch), 123
Wilkinson, I. A. G., 31
Williams, J. P., 142–143
Williams, P. L., xii
Wilson, Pete, 233
Winters, L., 230
Wixson, K. K., 204, 253
Wolf, D. P., 206
Wolf, Marianne, 136
Wood, F., 147
Wood, T. W., 115
Woodman, D. A., 32
Woodruff, M., 75, 84

Woods, M. J., 28
Word Attack test, 150
Word Identification test, 151
Word-level skills, 38–39
Word manipulation, 64
Word reading acquisition, self-teaching model for, 139–141
Word Walls, 25
Worthy, J., 104, 184
Writing systems, 40–45, 56–58, 62–65
alphabetic, 41–42, 51, 62–65
Chinese, 43–45, 51–53, 62–65
reading and, 7, 8, 20–21
in whole literacy curriculum, 204

Yopp, R., 127
York, R. L., 199
Young, Y., 49
Yung, J. F., 54

Zarillo, J., 74
Zhang, C. F., 55
Zhang, Sulan, xiv, xv, 37–61, 62–65, 68, 192, 269
Zhou, Y. G., 44
Zigmond, N., 80, 81, 85
Zone of proximal development (Vygotsky), 202